39

$ 3⁰⁰
Fic

The
Book of
Irish
Weirdness

The Book of Irish Weirdness

A Treasury of Classic Tales of the Supernatural, Spooky and Strange

Published 1997 by Sterling Publishing Company, Inc.
387 Park Avenue South, New York, N.Y. 10016
This collection, originally published in the United States by the Quality Paperback Book
Club and © 1995 by Book-of-the-Month Club, Inc., is based on *Irish Wonders* (first
published in 1888 by the Riverside Press, Cambridge) and on *Celtic Tales of Terror,
Famous Irish Ghost Stories,* and *The Leprechaun Book,* all © 1994 by Sterling
Publishing Company, Inc.
Distributed in Canada by Sterling Publishing
% Canadian Manda Group, One Atlantic Avenue, Suite 105
Toronto, Ontario, Canada M6K 3E7
Distributed in Great Britain and Europe by Cassell PLC
Wellington House, 125 Strand, London WC2R 0BB, England
Distributed in Australia by Capricorn Link (Australia) Pty Ltd.
P.O. Box 6651 Baulkham Hills, Business Centre, NSW 2153, Australia

10 9 8 7 6 5 4 3 2 1

Sterling ISBN 0-8069-9936-5

CONTENTS

The
Book of
Irish
Weirdness

Hertford O'Donnell's Warning
Charlotte Riddell

MANY A YEAR, before chloroform was thought of, there lived in an old rambling house, in Gerrard Street, Soho, a clever Irishman called Hertford O'Donnell.

After Hertford O'Donnell he was entitled to write, MRCS for he had studied hard to gain this distinction, and the older surgeons at Guy's (his hospital) considered him one of the most rising operators of the day.

Having said chloroform was unknown at the time this story opens, it will strike my readers that, if Hertford O'Donnell were a rising and successful operator in those days, of necessity he combined within himself a larger number of striking qualities than are by any means necessary to form a successful operator

1

in these.

There was more than mere hand skill, more than even thorough knowledge of his profession, then needful for the man, who, dealing with conscious subjects, essayed to rid them of some of the diseases to which flesh is heir. There was greater courage required in the manipulator of old than is altogether essential at present. Then, as now, a thorough mastery of his instruments, a steady hand, a keen eye, a quick dexterity were indispensable to a good operator; but, added to all these things, there formerly required a pulse which knew no quickening, a mental strength which never faltered, a ready power of adaptation in unexpected circumstances, fertility of resource in difficult cases, and a brave front under all emergencies.

If I refrain from adding that a hard as well as a courageous heart was an important item in the program, it is only out of deference to general opinion, which, among other strange delusions, clings to the belief that courage and hardness are antagonistic qualities.

Hertford O'Donnell, however, was hard as steel. He understood his work, and he did it thoroughly; but he cared no more for quivering nerves and shrinking muscles, for screams of agony, for faces white with pain, and teeth clenched in the extremity of anguish, than he did for the stony countenances of the dead, which so often in the dissecting room appalled younger and less experienced men.

He had no sentiment, and he had no sympathy. The human body was to him merely an ingenious piece of mechanism, which it was at once a pleasure and a profit to understand. Precisely as Brunel loved the Thames Tunnel, or any other singular engineering feat, so O'Donnell loved a patient on whom he had operated successfully, more especially if the ailment possessed by the patient were of a rare and difficult character.

And for this reason he was much liked by all who came under his hands, since patients are apt to mistake a surgeon's interest in their cases for interest in themselves; and it was gratifying to John Dicks, plasterer, and Timothy Regan, laborer, to be the happy possessors of remarkable diseases, which produced a cordial understanding between them and the handsome Irishman.

If he had been hard and cool at the moment of hacking them to pieces, that was all forgotten or remembered only as a virtue, when, after being discharged from hospital like soldiers who have served in a severe campaign, they met Mr. O'Donnell in the street, and were accosted by that rising individual just as though he considered himself nobody.

He had a royal memory, this stranger in a strange land, both for faces and cases; and like the rest of his countrymen, he never felt it beneath his dignity to talk cordially to corduroy and fustian.

In London, as at Calgillan, he never held back his tongue from speaking a cheery or a kindly word. His manners were pliable enough, if his heart were not; and the porters, and the patients, and the nurses, and the students at Guy's were all pleased to see Hertford O'Donnell.

Rain, hail, sunshine, it was all the same; there was a life and a brightness about the man which communicated itself to those with whom he came in contact. Let the mud in the Borough be a foot deep or the London fog as thick as peasoup, Mr. O'Donnell never lost his temper, never muttered a surly reply to the gatekeeper's salutation, but spoke out blithely and cheerfully to his pupils and his patients, to the sick and to the well, to those below and to those above him.

And yet, spite of all these good qualities, spite of his

handsome face, his fine figure, his easy address, and his unquestionable skill as an operator, the dons, who acknowledged his talent, shook their heads gravely when two or three of them in private and solemn conclave talked confidentially of their younger brother.

If there were many things in his favor, there were more in his disfavor. He was Irish—not merely by the accident of birth, which might have been forgiven, since a man cannot be held accountable for such caprices of Nature, but by every other accident and design which is objectionable to the orthodox and respectable and representative English mind.

In speech, appearance, manner, taste, modes of expression, habits of life, Hertford O'Donnell was Irish. To the core of his heart he loved the island which he declared he never meant to re-visit; and among the English he moved to all intents and purposes a foreigner, who was resolved, so said the great prophets at Guy's, to rush to destruction as fast as he could, and let no man hinder him.

"He means to go the whole length of his tether," observed one of the ancient wiseacres to another; which speech implied a conviction that Hertford O'Donnell, having sold himself to the Evil One, had determined to dive the full length of his rope into wickedness before being pulled to that shore where even wickedness is negative—where there are no mad carouses, no wild, sinful excitements, nothing but impotent wailing and gnashing of teeth.

A reckless, graceless, clever, wicked devil—going to his natural home as fast as in London anyone possibly speeds thither; this was the opinion his superiors held of the man who lived all alone with a housekeeper and her husband (who acted as butler) in his big house near Soho.

Gerrard Street—made famous by De Quincey—was not then

an utterly shady and forgotten locality; carriage-patients found their way to the rising young surgeon—some great personages thought it not beneath them to fee an individual whose consulting rooms were situated on what was even then considered the wrong side of Regent Street. He was making money, and he was spending it; he was over head and ears in debt—useless, vulgar debt—senselessly contracted, never bravely faced. He had lived at an awful pace ever since he came to London, a pace which only a man who hopes and expects to die young can ever travel.

Life was good, was it? Death, was he a child, or a woman, or a coward, to be afraid of that hereafter? God knew all about the trifle which had upset his coach, better than the dons at Guy's.

Hertford O'Donnell understood the world pretty thoroughly, and the ways thereof were to him as roads often traversed; therefore, when he said that at the Day of Judgment he felt certain he should come off as well as many of those who censured him, it may be assumed, that, although his views of post-mortem punishment were vague, unsatisfactory and infidel, still his information as to the peccadilloes of his neighbors was such as consoled himself.

And yet, living all alone in the old house near Soho Square, grave thoughts would intrude into the surgeon's mind—thoughts which were, so to say, italicized by peremptory letters, and still more peremptory visits from people who wanted money.

Although he had many acquaintances he had no single friend, and accordingly these thoughts were received and brooded over in solitude—in those hours when, after returning from dinner, or supper, or congenial carouse, he sat in his dreary rooms, smoking his pipe and considering means and ways, chances and certainties.

In good truth he had started in London with some vague idea that as his life in it would not be of long continuance, the pace at which he elected to travel could be of little consequence; but the years since his first entry into the Metropolis were now piled one on the top of another, his youth was behind him, his chances of longevity, spite of the way he had striven to injure his constitution, quite as good as ever. He had come to that period in existence, to that narrow strip of tableland, whence the ascent of youth and the descent of age are equally discernible—when, simply because he has lived for so many years, it strikes a man as possible he may have to live for just as many more, with the ability for hard work gone, with the boon companions scattered, with the capacity for enjoying convivial meetings a mere memory, with small means perhaps, with no bright hopes, with the pomp and the circumstance and the fairy carriages, and the glamor which youth flings over earthly objects, faded away like the pageant of yesterday, while the dreary ceremony of living has to be gone through today and tomorrow and the morrow after, as though the gay cavalcade and the martial music, and the glittering helmets and the prancing steeds were still accompanying the wayfarer to his journey's end.

Ah! my friends, there comes a moment when we must all leave the coach, with its four bright bays, its pleasant outside freight, its cheery company, its guard who blows the horn so merrily through villages and along lonely country roads.

Long before we reach that final stage, where the black business claims us for its own special property, we have to bid goodbye to all easy, thoughtless journeying, and betake ourselves, with what zest we may, to traversing the common of reality. There is no royal road across it that ever I heard of. From the king on his throne to the laborer who vaguely imagines what manner of being a king is, we have all to tramp across that desert at one period of our lives, at all events; and that period usually is when, as I have said, a man starts to find the hopes, and the strength, and the buoyancy of youth left behind, while years and years of life lie stretching out before him.

The coach he has traveled by drops him here. There is no appeal, there is no help; therefore, let him take off his hat and wish the new passengers good speed, without either envy or repining.

Behold, he has had his turn, and let whosoever will mount on the box-seat of life again, and tip the coachman and handle the ribbons—he shall take that pleasant journey no more, no more forever.

Even supposing a man's springtime to have been a cold and ungenial one, with bitter easterly winds and nipping frosts biting the buds and retarding the blossoms, still it was spring for all that—spring with the young green leaves sprouting forth, with the flowers unfolding tenderly, with the songs of the birds and the rush of waters, with the summer before and the autumn afar off, and winter remote as death and eternity, but when once the trees have donned their summer foliage, when the pure white blossoms have disappeared, and the gorgeous red and orange and purple blaze of many-colored flowers fills the gardens, then if there come a wet, dreary day, the idea of autumn and winter is not so difficult to realize. When once twelve o'clock is reached, the evening and night become facts, not possibilities; and it was of the afternoon, and the evening, and the night, Hertford O'Donnell sat thinking on the Christmas Eve, when I crave permission to introduce him to my readers.

A good-looking man ladies considered him. A tall, dark-complexioned, black-haired, straight-limbed, deeply divinely blue-eyed fellow, with a soft voice, with a pleasant brogue, who had ridden like a centaur over the loose stone walls in Connemara, who had danced all night at the Dublin balls, who had walked across the Bennebeola Mountains, gun in hand, day after day, without weariness, who had fished in every one of the hundred lakes you can behold from the top of that mountain near the Recess Hotel, who had led a mad, wild life in Trinity College, and a wilder, perhaps, while "studying for a doctor"— as the Irish phrase goes—in Edinburgh, and who, after the death of his eldest brother left him free to return to Calgillan, and pursue the usual utterly useless, utterly purposeless, utterly pleasant life of an Irish gentleman possessed of health, birth, and expectations, suddenly kicked over the paternal traces, bade adieu to Calgillan Castle and the blandishments of a certain beautiful Miss Clifden, beloved of his mother, and laid out to be his wife, walked down the avenue without even so much company as a gossoon to carry his carpet-bag, shook the dust from his feet at the lodge gates, and took his seat on the coach, never once looking back at Calgillan, where his favorite mare was standing in the stable, his greyhounds chasing one another round the home paddock, his gun at half-cock in his dressing-room and his fishing-tackle all in order and ready for use.

He had not kissed his mother, or asked for his father's blessing; he left Miss Clifden, arrayed in her brand-new riding-habit, without a word of affection or regret; he had spoken no syllable of farewell to any servant about the place; only when the old woman at the lodge bade him good morning and God-blessed his handsome face, he recommended her bitterly to look at it well for she would never see it more.

Twelve years and a half had passed since then, without either Miss Clifden or any other one of the Calgillan people having set eyes on Master Hertford's handsome face.

He had kept his vow to himself; he had not written home; he had not been indebted to mother or father for even a tenpenny-piece during the whole of that time; he had lived without friends; and he had lived without God—so far as God ever lets a man live without him.

One thing only he felt to be needful—money; money to keep him when the evil days of sickness, or age, or loss of practice came upon him. Though a spendthrift, he was not a simpleton; around him he saw men, who, having started with fairer prospects than his own, were, nevertheless, reduced to indigence; and he knew that what had happened to others might happen to himself.

An unlucky cut, slipping on a piece of orange-peel in the street, the merest accident imaginable, is sufficient to change opulence to beggary in the life's program of an individual, whose income depends on eye, on nerve, on hand; and, besides the consciousness of this fact, Hertford O'Donnell knew that beyond a certain point in his profession, progress was not easy.

It did not depend quite on the strength of his own bow and shield whether he counted his earnings by hundreds or thousands. Work may achieve competence; but mere work cannot, in a profession, at all events, compass fortune.

He looked around him, and he perceived that the majority of great men—great and wealthy—had been indebted for their elevation, more to the accident of birth, patronage, connection, or marriage, than to personal ability.

Personal ability, no doubt, they possessed; but then, little Jones, who lived in Frith Street, and who could barely keep himself and his wife and family, had ability, too, only he lacked the concomitants of success.

He wanted something or someone to puff him into notoriety—a brother at Court—a lord's leg to mend—a rich wife to give him prestige in Society; and in his absence of this something or someone, he had grown grey-haired and fainthearted while laboring for a world which utterly despises its most obsequious servants.

"Clatter along the streets with a pair of fine horses, snub the middle classes, and drive over the commonalty—that is the way to compass wealth and popularity in England," said Hertford O'Donnell, bitterly; and as the man desired wealth and popularity, he sat before his fire, with a foot on each hob, and a short pipe in his mouth, considering how he might best obtain the means to clatter along the streets in his carriage, and splash plebeians with mud from his wheels like the best.

In Dublin he could, by means of his name and connection, have done well; but then he was not in Dublin, neither did he want to be. The bitterest memories of his life were inseparable from the very name of the Green Island, and he had no desire to return to it.

Besides, in Dublin, heiresses are not quite so plentiful as in London; and an heiress, Hertford O'Donnell had decided, would do more for him than years of steady work.

A rich wife could clear him of debt, introduce him to fashionable practice, afford him that measure of social respectability which a medical bachelor invariably lacks, deliver him from the loneliness of Gerrard Street, and the domination of Mr. and Mrs. Coles.

To most men, deliberately bartering away their independence for money seems so prosaic a business that they strive to gloss it over even to themselves, and to assign every reason for their choice, save that which is really the influencing one.

Not so, however, with Hertford O'Donnell. He sat beside the fire scoffing over his proposed bargain—thinking of the lady's age, her money bags, her desirable house in town, her seat in the country, her snobbishness, her folly.

"It could be a fitting ending," he sneered, "and why I did not settle the matter tonight passes my comprehension. I am not a fool, to be frightened with old women's tales; and yet I must have turned white. I felt I did, and she asked me whether I were ill. And then to think of my being such an idiot as to ask her if she had heard anything like a cry, as though she would be likely to hear that, she with her poor parvenu blood, which I often imagine must have been mixed with some of her father's strong pickling vinegar. What a deuce could I have been dreaming about? I wonder what it really was." And Hertford O'Donnell pushed his hair back off his forehead, and took another draught from the too familiar tumbler, which was placed conveniently on the chimney-piece.

"After expressly making up my mind to propose, too!" he mentally continued. "Could it have been conscience—that myth, which somebody, who knew nothing about the matter, said, 'Makes cowards of us all'? I don't believe in conscience; and even if there be such a thing capable of being developed by sentiment and cultivation, why should it trouble me? I have no intention of wronging Miss Janice Price Ingot, not the least. Honestly and fairly I shall marry her; honestly and fairly I shall act by her. An old wife is not exactly an ornamental article of furniture in a man's house; and I do not know that the fact of her being well gilded makes her look any handsomer. But she shall have no cause for complaint; and I will go and dine with her tomorrow, and settle the matter."

Having arrived at which resolution, Mr. O'Donnell arose, kicked down the fire—burning hollow—with the heel of his boot, knocked the ashes out of his pipe, emptied his tumbler, and bethought him it was time to go to bed. He was not in the habit of taking his rest so early as a quarter to twelve o'clock; but he felt unusually weary—tired mentally and bodily—and lonely beyond all power of expression.

"The fair Janet would be better than this," he said, half aloud;

and then, with a start and a shiver, and a blanched face, he turned sharply round, while a low, sobbing, wailing cry echoed mournfully through the room. No form of words could give an idea of the sound. The plaintiveness of the Aeolian harp—that plaintiveness which so soon affects and lowers the highest spirits—would have seemed wildly gay in comparison with the sadness of the cry which seemed floating in the air. As the summer wind comes and goes among the trees, so that mournful wail came and went—came and went. It came in a rush of sound, like a gradual crescendo managed by a skilful musician, and died away in a lingering note, so gently that the listener could scarcely tell the exact moment when it faded into utter silence.

I say faded, for it disappeared as the coastline disappears in the twilight, and there was total stillness in the apartment.

Then, for the first time, Hertford O'Donnell looked at his dog, and beholding the creature crouched into a corner beside the fireplace, called upon him to come out.

His voice sounded strange even to himself, and apparently the dog thought so too, for he made no effort to obey the summons.

"Come here, sir," his master repeated, and then the animal came crawling reluctantly forward with his hair on end, his eyes almost starting from his head, trembling violently, as the surgeon, who caressed him, felt.

"So you heard it, Brian?" he said to the dog. "And so your ears are sharper than Miss Ingot's, old fellow. It's a mighty queer thing to think of, being favored with a visit from a Banshee in Gerrard Street; and as the lady has traveled so far, I only wish I knew whether there is any sort of refreshment she would like to take after her long journey."

He spoke loudly, and with a certain mocking defiance, seeming to think the phantom he addressed would reply; but when he stopped at the end of his sentence, no sound came through the stillness. There was a dead silence in the room—a silence broken only by the falling of cinders on the hearth and the breathing of his dog.

"If my visitor would tell me," he proceeded, for whom this lamentation is being made, whether for myself, or for some member of my illustrious family, I should feel immensely obliged. It seems too much honor for a poor surgeon to have such attention paid him. Good Heavens! What is that?" he exclaimed, as a ring, loud and peremptory, woke all the echoes in the house, and brought his housekeeper, in a state of distressing dishabille, "out of her warm bed," as she subsequently stated, to the head of the staircase.

Across the hall Hertford O'Donnell strode, relieved at the prospect of speaking to any living being. He took no precaution of putting up the chain, but flung the door wide. A dozen burglars would have proved welcome in comparison with that ghostly intruder he had been interviewing; therefore, as has been said, he threw the door wide, admitting a rush of wet, cold air, which made poor Mrs. Coles' few remaining teeth chatter in her head.

"Who is there? What do you want?" asked the surgeon, seeing no person, and hearing no voice. "Who is there? Why the devil can't you speak?"

When even this polite exhortation failed to elicit an answer, he passed out into the night and looked up the street and down the street, to see nothing but the driving rain and the blinking lights.

"If this goes on much longer I shall soon think I must be either mad or drunk," he muttered, as he re-entered the house and locked and bolted the door once more.

"Lord's sake! What is the matter, sir?" asked Mrs. Coles,

from the upper flight, careful only to reveal the borders of her night-cap to Mr. O'Donnell's admiring gaze. "Is anybody killed? Have you to go out, sir?"

"It was only a runaway rig," he answered, trying to reassure himself with an explanation he did not in his heart believe.

"Runaway—I'd run away them!" murmured Mrs. Coles, as she retired to the conjugal couch, where Coles was, to quote her own expression, "snoring like a pig through it all."

Almost immediately afterwards she heard her master ascend the stairs and close his bedroom door.

"Madam will surely be too much of a gentlewoman to intrude here," thought the surgeon, scoffing even at his own fears; but when he lay down he did not put out his light, and made Brian leap up and crouch on the coverlet beside him.

The man was fairly frightened, and would have thought it no discredit to his manhood to acknowledge as much. He was not afraid of death, he was not afraid of trouble, he was not afraid of danger; but he was afraid of the Banshee; and as he lay with his hand on the dog's head, he recalled the many stories he had been told concerning this family retainer in the days of his youth.

He had not thought about her for years and years. Never before had he heard her voice himself. When his brother died she had not thought it necessary to travel up to Dublin and give him notice of the impending catastrophe. "If she had, I would have gone down to Calgillan, and perhaps saved his life,' considered the surgeon. "I wonder who this is for? If for me, that will settle my debts and my marriage. If I could be quite certain it was either of the old people, I would start tomorrow."

Then vaguely his mind wandered on to think of every Banshee story he had ever heard in his life. About the beautiful lady with the wreath of flowers, who sat on the rocks below Red

Castle, in the County Antrim, crying till one of the sons died for love of her; about the Round Chamber at Dunluce, which was swept clean by the Banshee every night; about the bed in a certain great house in Ireland, which was slept in constantly, although no human being ever passed in or out after dark; about that General Officer who, the night before Waterloo, said to a friend, "I have heard the Banshee, and shall not come off the field alive tomorrow; break the news gently to poor Carry"; and who, nevertheless, coming safe off the field, had subsequently news about poor Carry broken tenderly and pitifully to him; about the lad, who, aloft in the rigging, hearing through the night a sobbing and wailing coming over the waters, went down to the captain and told him he was afraid they were somehow out of their reckoning, just in time to save the ship, which, when morning broke, they found but for his warning would have been on the rocks. It was blowing great guns, and the sea was all in a fret and turmoil, and they could sometimes see in the trough of the waves, as down a valley, the cruel black reefs they had escaped.

On deck the captain stood speaking to the boy who had saved them, and asking how he knew of their danger; and when the lad told him, the captain laughed, and said her ladyship had been outwitted that time.

But the boy answered, with a grave shake of his head, that the warning was either for him or his, and that if he got safe to port there would be bad tidings waiting for him from home; whereupon the captain bade him go below, and get some brandy and lie down.

He got the brandy, and he lay down, but he never rose again; and when the storm abated—when a great calm succeeded to the previous tempest—there was a very solemn funeral at sea; and on their arrival at Liverpool the captain took a journey to

Ireland to tell a widowed mother how her only son died, and to bear his few effects to the poor desolate soul.

And Hertford O'Donnell thought again about his own father riding full-chase across country, and hearing, as he galloped by a clump of plantation, something like a sobbing and wailing. The hounds were in full cry, but he still felt, as he afterwards expressed it, that there was something among those trees he could not pass; and so he jumped off his horse, and hung the reins over the branch of a Scotch fir, and beat the cover well, but not a thing could he find in it.

Then, for the first time in his life, Miles O'Donnell turned his horse's head from the hunt, and, within a mile of Calgillan, met a man running to tell him his brother's gun had burst, and injured him mortally.

And he remembered the story also, of how Mary O'Donnell, his great aunt, being married to a young Englishman, heard the Banshee as she sat one evening waiting for his return; and of how she, thinking the bridge by which he often came home unsafe for horse and man, went out in a great panic, to meet and entreat him to go round by the main road for her sake. Sir Edward was riding along in the moonlight, making straight for the bridge, when he beheld a figure dressed all in white crossing it. Then there was a crash, and the figure disappeared.

The lady was rescued and brought back to the hall; but next morning there were two dead bodies within its walls—those of Lady Eyreton and her stillborn son.

Quicker than I write them, these memories chased one another through Hertford O'Donnell's brain; and there was one more terrible memory than any, which would recur to him, concerning an Irish nobleman who, seated alone in his great town house in London, heard the Banshee, and rushed out to get rid of the phantom, which wailed in his ear, nevertheless, as he strode down Piccadilly. And then the surgeon remembered how that nobleman went with a friend to the opera, feeling sure that there no Banshee, unless she had a box, could find admittance, until suddenly he heard her singing up among the highest part of the scenery, with a terrible mournfulness, and a pathos which made the prima donna's tenderest notes seem harsh by comparison.

As he came out, some quarrel arose between him and a famous fire-eater, against whom he stumbled; and the result was that the next afternoon there was a new Lord, for he was killed in a duel with Captain Bravo.

Memories like these are not the most enlivening possible; they are apt to make a man fanciful, and nervous, and wakeful; but as time ran on, Hertford O'Donnell fell asleep, with his candle still burning, and Brian's cold nose pressed against his hand.

He dreamt of his mother's family—the Hertfords of Artingbury, Yorkshire, far-off relatives of Lord Hertford—so far off that even Mrs. O'Donnell held no clue to the genealogical maze.

He thought he was at Artingbury, fishing; that it was a misty summer morning, and the fish rising beautifully. In his dreams he hooked one after another, and the boy who was with him threw them into the basket.

At last there was one more difficult to land than the others; and the boy, in his eagerness to watch the sport, drew nearer and nearer to the bnnk, while the fisher, intent on his prey, failed to notice his companion's danger.

Suddenly there was a cry, a splash, and the boy disappeared from sight.

Next instance he rose again, however, and then, for the first time, Hertford O'Donnell saw his face.

It was one he knew well.

In a moment he plunged into the water, and struck out for the lad. He had him by the hair, he was turning to bring him back to land, when the stream suddenly changed into a wide, wild, shoreless sea, where the billows were chasing one another with a mad demoniac mirth.

For a while O'Donnell kept the lad and himself afloat. They were swept under the waves, and came up again, only to see larger waves rushing towards them; but through all, the surgeon never loosened his hold, until a tremendous billow, engulfing them both, tore the boy from his grasp.

With the horror of his dream upon him he awoke to hear a voice quite distinctly:

"Go to the hospital—go at once!"

The surgeon started up in bed, rubbing his eyes, and looked around. The candle was flickering faintly in its socket. Brian, with his ears pricked forward, had raised his head at his master's sudden movement.

Everything was quiet, but still those words were ringing in his ear:

"Go to the hospital—go at once!"

The tremendous peal of the bell overnight, and this sentence, seemed to be simultaneous.

That he was wanted at Guy's—wanted imperatively—came to O'Donnell like an inspiration. Neither sense nor reason had anything to do with the conviction that roused him out of bed, and made him dress as speedily as possible, and grope his way down the staircase, Brian following.

He opened the front door, and passed out into the darkness. The rain was over, and the stars were shining as he pursued his way down Newport Market, and thence, winding in and out in a southeasterly direction, through Lincoln's Inn Fields and Old

Square to Chancery Lane, whence he proceeded to St Paul's.

Along the deserted streets he resolutely continued his walk. He did not know what he was going to Guy's for. Some instinct was urging him on, and he neither strove to combat nor control it. Only once did the thought of turning back cross his mind, and that was at the archway leading into Old Square. There he had paused for a moment, asking himself whether he were not gone stark, staring mad; but Guy's seemed preferable to the haunted house in Gerrard Street, and he walked resolutely on, determined to say, if any surprise were expressed at his appearance, that he had been sent for.

Sent for?—yea, truly; but by whom?

On through Cannon Street; on over London Bridge, where the lights flickered in the river, and the sullen splash of the water flowing beneath the arches, washing the stone piers, could be heard, now the human din was hushed and lulled to sleep. On, thinking of many things: of the days of his youth; of his dead brother; of his father's heavily encumbered estate; of the fortune his mother had vowed she would leave to some charity rather than to him, if he refused to marry according to her choice; of his wild life in London; of the terrible cry he had heard overnight—that unearthly wail which he could not drive from his memory even when he entered Guy's, and confronted the porter, who said:

"You have been sent for, sir; did you meet the messenger?"

Like one in a dream, Hertford O'Donnell heard him; like one in a dream, also, he asked what was the matter.

"Bad accident, sir; fire; fell off a balcony—unsafe—old building. Mother and child—a son; child with compound fracture of thigh."

This, the joint information of porter and house-surgeon, mingled together, and made a boom in Mr. O'Donnell's ears like the sound of the sea breaking on a shingly shore.

Only one sentence he understood properly—"Immediate amputation necessary." At this point he grew cool; he was the careful, cautious, successful surgeon, in a moment.

"The child you say?" he answered. "Let me see him."

The Guy's Hospital of today may be different to the Guy's Hertford O'Donnell knew so well. Railways have, I believe, swept away the old operating room; railways may have changed the position of the former accident ward, to reach which, in the days of which I am writing, the two surgeons had to pass a staircase leading to the upper stories.

On the lower step of this staircase, partially in shadow, Hertford O'Donnell beheld, as he came forward, an old woman seated.

An old woman with streaming grey hair, with attenuated arms, with head bowed forward, with scanty clothing, with bare feet; who never looked up at their approach, but sat unnoticing, shaking her head and wringing her hands in an extremity of despair.

"Who is that?" asked Mr. O'Donnell, almost involuntarily.

"Who is what?" demanded his companion.

"That—that woman," was the reply.

"What woman?"

"There—are you blind?—seated on the bottom step of the staircase. What is she doing?" persisted Mr. O'Donnell.

"There is no woman near us," his companion answered, looking at the rising surgeon very much as though he suspected him of seeing double.

"No woman!" scoffed Hertford. "Do you expect me to disbelieve the evidence of my own eyes?" and he walked up to the figure, meaning to touch it.

But as he assayed to do so, the woman seemed to rise in the

air and float away, with her arms stretched high up over her head, uttering such a wail of pain, and agony, and distress, as caused the Irishman's blood to curdle.

"My God! Did you hear that?" he said to his companion.

"What?" was the reply.

Then, although he knew the sound had fallen on deaf ears, he answered:

"The wail of the Banshee! Some of my people are doomed!"

"I trust not," answered the house-surgeon, who had an idea, nevertheless, that Hertford O'Donnell's Banshee lived in a whisky bottle, and would at some remote day make an end to the rising and clever operator.

With nerves utterly shaken, Mr. O'Donnell walked forward to the accident ward. There with his face shaded from the light, lay his patient—a young boy, with a compound fracture of the thigh.

In that ward, in the face of actual danger or pain capable of relief, the surgeon had never known faltering or fear; and now he carefully examined the injury, felt the pulse, inquired as to the treatment pursued, and ordered the sufferer to be carried to the operating room.

While he was looking out his instruments he heard the boy lying on the table murmur faintly:

"Tell her not to cry so—tell her not to cry."

"What is he talking about?" Hertford O'Donnell inquired.

"The nurse says he has been speaking about some woman crying ever since he came in—his mother, most likely," answered one of the attendants.

"He is delirious then?" observed the surgeon.

"No, sir," pleaded the boy, excitedly, "no; it is that woman—that woman with the grey hair. I saw her looking from the upper window before the balcony gave way. She has never left me since, and she won't be quiet, wringing her hands and crying."

"Can you see her now?" Hertford O'Donnell inquired, stepping to the side of the table. "Point out where she is."

Then the lad stretched forth a feeble finger in the direction of the door, where clearly, as he had seen her seated on the stairs, the surgeon saw a woman standing—a woman with grey hair and scanty clothing, and upstretched arms and bare feet.

"A word with you, sir," O'Donnell said to the house-surgeon, drawing him back from the table. "I cannot perform this operation: send for some other person. I am ill; I am incapable."

"But," pleaded the other, "there is no time to get anyone else. We sent for Mr. West, before we troubled you, but he was out of town, and all the rest of the surgeons live so far away. Mortification may set in at any moment and—."

"Do you think you require to teach me my business?" was the reply. "I know the boy's life hangs on a thread, and that is the very reason I cannot operate. I am not fit for it. I tell you I have seen tonight that which unnerves me utterly. My hand is not steady. Send for someone else without delay. Say I am ill—dead!—what you please. Heavens! There she is again, right over the boy! Do you hear her?" and Hertford O'Donnell fell fainting on the floor.

How long he lay in that death-like swoon I cannot say; but when he returned to consciousness, the principal physician of Guy's was standing beside him in the cold grey light of the Christmas morning.

"The boy?" murmured O'Donnell, faintly.

"Now, my dear fellow, keep yourself quiet," was the reply.

"The boy?" he repeated, irritably. "Who operated?"

"No one," Dr. Lanson answered. "It would have been useless cruelty. Mortification had set in and—"

Hertford O'Donnell turned his face to the wall, and his friend could not see it.

"Do not distress yourself," went on the physician, kindly. "Allington says he could not have survived the operation in any case. He was quite delirious from the first, raving about a woman with grey hair and—"

"I know," Hertford O'Donnell interrupted; "and the boy had a mother, they told me, or I dreamt it."

"Yes, she was bruised and shaken, but not seriously injured."

"Has she blue eyes and fair hair—fair hair all rippling and wavy? Is she white as a lily, with just a faint flush of color in her cheek? Is she young and trusting and innocent? No; I am wandering. She must be nearly thirty now. Go, for God's sake, and tell me if you can find a woman you could imagine having once been a girl such as I describe."

"Irish?" asked the doctor; and O'Donnell made a gesture of assent.

"It is she then," was the reply, "a woman with the face of an angel."

"A woman who should have been my wife," the surgeon answered; "whose child was my son."

"Lord help you!" ejaculated the doctor. Then Hertford O'Donnell raised himself from the sofa where they had laid him, and told his companion the story of his life—how there had been a bitter feud between his people and her people—how they were divided by old animosities and by difference of religion—how they had met by stealth, and exchanged rings and vows, all for naught—how his family had insulted hers, so that her father, wishful for her to marry a kinsman of his own, bore her off to a far-away land, and made her write him a letter of eternal farewell—how his own parents had kept all knowledge of the quarrel from him till she was utterly beyond his reach— how they had vowed to discard him unless he agreed to marry according to their wishes— how he left home, and came to London, and sought his fortune. All this Hertford O'Donnell repeated; and when he had finished, the bells were ringing for morning service— ringing loudly, ringing joyfully, "Peace on earth, goodwill towards men."

But there was little peace that morning for Hertford O'Donnell. He had to look on the face of his dead son, wherein he beheld, as though reflected, the face of the boy in his dream.

Afterwards, stealthily he followed his friend, and beheld, with her eyes closed, her cheeks pale and pinched, her hair thinner but still falling like a veil over her, the love of his youth, the only woman he had ever loved devotedly and unselfishly.

There is little space left here to tell of how the two met at last—of how the stone of the years seemed suddenly rolled away from the tomb of their past, and their youth arose and returned to them, even amid their tears.

She had been true to him, through persecution, through contumely, through kindness, which was more trying; through shame, and grief, and poverty, she had been loyal to the lover of her youth; and before the New Year dawned there came a letter from Calgillan, saying that the Banshee's wail had been heard there, and praying Hertford, if he were still alive, to let bygones be bygones, in consideration of the long years of estrangement—the anguish and remorse of his afflicted parents.

More than that. Hertford O'Donnell, if a reckless man, was honorable; and so, on the Christmas Day when he was to have proposed for Miss Ingot, he went to that lady, and told her how he had wooed and won, in the years of his youth, one who after many days was miraculously restored to him; and from the hour in which he took her into his confidence, he never thought her either vulgar or foolish, but rather he paid homage to the woman who, when she had heard the whole tale repeated, said, simply,

"Ask her to come to me till you can claim her—and God bless you both!"

Teig O'Kane and the Corpse

Douglas Hyde

THERE WAS ONCE a grown-up lad in the County Leitrim, and he was strong and lively, and the son of a rich farmer. His father had plenty of money, and he did not spare it on the son. Accordingly, when the boy grew up he liked sport better than work, and, as his father had no other children, he loved this one so much that he allowed him to do in everything just as it pleased himself. He was very extravagant, and he used to scatter the gold money as another person would scatter the white. He was seldom to be found at home, but if there was a fair, or a race, or a gathering within ten miles of him, you were dead certain to find him there. And he seldom spent a night in his father's house, but he used to be always out rambling, and, like Shawn Bwee long ago, there was

"grádh gach cailin i mbrollach a léine,"

"the love of every girl in the breast of his shirt," and it's many's the kiss he got and he gave, for he was very handsome, and there wasn't a girl in the country but would fall in love with him, only for him to fasten his two eyes on her, and it was for that someone made this *rann* on him—

> "Look at the rogue, it's for kisses he's rambling,
>> It isn't much wonder, for that was his way;
> He's like an old hedgehog, at night he'll be scrambling
>> From this place to that, but he'll sleep in the day."

At last he became very wild and unruly. He wasn't to be seen day or night in his father's house, but always rambling or going on his *kailee* (night visit) from place to place and from house to house, so that the old people used to shake their heads and say to one another, "It's easy seen what will happen to the land when the old man dies; his son will run through it in a year, and it won't stand him that long itself."

He used to be always gambling and card-playing and drinking, but his father never minded his bad habits, and never punished him. But it happened one day that the old man was told that the son had ruined the character of a girl in the neighborhood, and he was greatly angry, and he called the son to him, and said to him, quietly and sensibly—"Avic," says he, "you know I loved you greatly up to this, and I never stopped you from doing your choice thing whatever it was, and I kept plenty of money with you, and I always hoped to leave you the house and land, and all I had after myself would be gone; but I heard a story of you today that has disgusted me with you. I cannot tell you the grief that I felt when I heard such a thing of you, and I tell you now plainly that unless you marry that girl I'll leave house and land and everything to my brother's son. I never could leave it to anyone who would make so bad a use of it as you do yourself, deceiving women and coaxing girls. Settle with yourself now whether you'll marry that girl and get my land as a fortune with her, or refuse to marry her and give up all that was coming to you; and tell me in the morning which of the two things you have chosen."

"Och! *Domnoo Sheery!* father, you wouldn't say that to me, and I such a good son as I am. Who told you I wouldn't marry the girl?" says he.

But his father was gone, and the lad knew well enough that he would keep his word too; and he was greatly troubled in his mind, for as quiet and as kind as the father was, he never went back on a word that he had once said, and there wasn't another man in the country who was harder to bend than he was.

The boy did not know rightly what to do. He was in love with the girl indeed, and he hoped to marry her sometime or other, but he would much sooner have remained another while as he was, and follow on at his old tricks—drinking, sporting, and playing cards; and, along with that, he was angry that his father should order him to marry, and should threaten him if he did not do it.

"Isn't my father a great fool," says he to himself. "I was ready enough, and only too anxious, to marry Mary; and now since he threatened me, faith I've a great mind to let it go another while."

His mind was so much excited that he remained between two notions as to what he should do. He walked out into the night at last to cool his heated blood, and went on to the road. He lit a pipe, and as the night was fine he walked and walked on, until the quick pace made him begin to forget his trouble. The night was bright, and the moon half full. There was not a breath of wind blowing, and the air was calm and mild. He walked on for nearly three hours, when he suddenly remembered that it was late in the night, and time for him to turn. "Musha! I think I forgot myself," says he; "it must be near twelve o'clock now."

The word was hardly out of his mouth, when he heard the sound of many voices, and the trampling of feet on the road before him. "I don't know who can be out so late at night as this, and on such a lonely road," said he to himself.

He stood listening, and he heard the voices of many people talking, but he could not understand what they were saying. "Oh, wirra!" says he, "I'm afraid. It's not Irish or English they have; it can't be they're Frenchmen!" He went on a couple of yards further, and he saw well enough by the light of the moon a band of little people coming towards him, and they were carrying something big and heavy with them. "Oh, murder!" says he to himself, "sure it can't be that they're the good people that's in it!" Every *rib* of hair that was on his head stood up, and there fell a shaking on his bones, for he saw that they were coming to him fast.

He looked at them again, and perceived that there were about twenty little men in it, and there was not a man at all of them higher than about three feet or three feet and a half, and some of them were gray, and seemed very old. He looked again, but he could not make out what was the heavy thing they were carrying until they came up to him, and then they all stood round about him. They threw the heavy thing down on the road, and he saw on the spot that it was a dead body.

He became as cold as the Death, and there was not a drop of blood running in his veins when an old little gray *maneen* came up to him and said, "Isn't it lucky we met you, Teig O'Kane?"

Poor Teig could not bring out a word at all, nor open his lips, if he were to get the world for it, and so he gave no answer.

"Teig O'Kane," said the little gray man again, "isn't it timely you met us?"

Teig could not answer him.

"Teig O'Kane," says he, "the third time, isn't it lucky and

timely that we met you?"

But Teig remained silent, for he was afraid to return an answer, and his tongue was as if it was tied to the roof of his mouth.

The little gray man turned to his companions, and there was joy in his bright little eye. "And now," says he, "Teig O'Kane hasn't a word, we can do with him what we please. Teig, Teig,'" says he, "you're living a bad life, and we can make a slave of you now, and you cannot withstand us, for there's no use in trying to go against us. Lift that corpse."

Teig was so frightened that he was only able to utter the two words, "I won't"; for as frightened as he was he was obstinate and stiff, the same as ever.

"Teig O'Kane won't lift the corpse," said the little *maneen* with a wicked little laugh, for all the world like the breaking of a *lock* of dry *kippeens*, and with a little harsh voice like the striking of a cracked bell. "Teig O'Kane won't lift the corpse— make him lift it"; and before the word was out of his mouth they had all gathered round poor Teig, and they all talking and laughing through each other.

Teig tried to run from them, but they followed him, and a man of them stretched out his foot before him as he ran, so that Teig was thrown in a heap on the road. Then before he could rise up the fairies caught him, some by the hands and some by the feet, and they held him tight, in a way that he could not stir, with his face against the ground. Six or seven of them raised the body then, and pulled it over to him, and left it down on his back. The breast of the corpse was squeezed against Teig's back and shoulders, and the arms of the corpse were thrown around Teig's neck. Then they stood back from him a couple of yards, and let him get up. He rose, foaming at the mouth and cursing, and he shook himself, thinking to throw the corpse off his back. But his fear and his wonder were great when he found that the two arms had a tight hold round his own neck, and that the two legs were squeezing his hips firmly, and that, however strongly he tried, he could not throw it off, any more than a horse can throw off its saddle. He was terribly frightened then, and he thought he was lost. "Ochone! for ever," said he to himself, "it's the bad life I'm leading that has given the good people this power over me. I promise to God and Mary, Peter and Paul, Patrick and Bridget, that I'll mend my ways for as long as I have to live, if I come clear out of this danger—and I'll marry the girl."

The little gray man came up to him again, and said he to him, "Now, Teig*een*," says he, "you didn't lift the body when I told you to lift it, and see how you were made to lift it; perhaps when I tell you to bury it, you won't bury it until you're made to bury it!"

"Anything at all that I can do for your honor," said Teig, "I'll do it," for he was getting sense already, and if it had not been for the great fear that was on him, he never would have let that civil word slip out of his mouth.

The little man laughed a sort of laugh again. "You're getting quiet now, Teig," says he. "I'll go bail but you'll be quiet enough before I'm done with you. Listen to me now, Teig O'Kane, and if you don't obey me in all I'm telling you to do, you'll repent it. You must carry with you this corpse that is on your back to Teampoll-Démus, and you must bring it into the church with you, and make a grave for it in the very middle of the church, and you must raise up the flags and put them down again the very same way, and you must carry the clay out of the church and leave the place as it was when you came, so that no one could know that there had been anything changed. But that's not all. Maybe that the body won't be allowed to be buried in that church; perhaps some other man has the bed, and, if so, it's likely he won't share it with this one. If you don't get leave to bury it in Teampoll-Démus, you must carry it to Carrick-fhad-vic-Orus, and bury it in the churchyard there; and if you don't get it into that place, take it with you to Teampoll-Ronan; and if that churchyard is closed on you, take it to Imlogue-Fada; and if you're not able to bury it there, you've no more to do than to take it to Kill-Breedya, and you can bury it there without hindrance. I cannot tell you what one of those churches is the one where you will have leave to bury that corpse under the clay, but I know that it will be allowed you to bury him at some church or other of them. If you do this work rightly, we will be thankful to you, and you will have no cause to grieve; but if you are slow or lazy, believe me we shall take satisfaction of you."

When the gray little man had done speaking, his comrades laughed and clapped their hands together. "Glic! Glic! Hwee! Hwee!" they all cried; "go on, go on, you have eight hours before you till daybreak, and if you haven't this man buried before the sun rises, you're lost." They struck a fist and a foot behind on him, and drove him on in the road. He was obliged to walk, and to walk fast, for they gave him no rest.

He thought himself that there was not a wet path, or a dirty *boreen*, or a crooked contrary road in the whole county, that he had not walked that night. The night was at times very dark, and whenever there would come a cloud across the moon he could see nothing, and then he used often to fall. Sometimes he was hurt, and sometimes he escaped, but he was obliged always to rise on the moment and to hurry on. Sometimes the moon would break out clearly, and then he would look behind him and see the little people following at his back. And he heard them speaking amongst themselves, talking and crying out, and screaming like a flock of seagulls; and if he was to save his soul he never understood as much as one word of what they were saying.

He did not know how far he had walked, when at last one of them cried out to him, "Stop here!" He stood, and they all gathered round him.

"Do you see those withered trees over there?" says the old boy to him again. "Teampoll-Démus is among those trees, and you must go in there by yourself, for we cannot follow you or go with you. We must remain here. Go on boldly."

Teig looked from him, and he saw a high wall that was in places half broken down, and an old gray church on the inside of the wall, and about a dozen withered old trees scattered here and there round it. There was neither leaf nor twig on any of them, but their bare crooked branches were stretched out like the arms of an angry man when he threatens. He had no help for it, but was obliged to go forward. He was a couple of hundred yards from the church, but he walked on, and never looked behind him until he came to the gate of the churchyard. The old gate was thrown down, and he had no difficulty in entering. He turned then to see if any of the little people were following him, but there came a cloud over the moon, and the night became so dark that he could see nothing. He went into the churchyard, and he walked up the old grassy pathway leading to the church. When he reached the door, he found it locked. The door was large and strong, and he did not know what to do. At last he drew out his knife with difficulty, and stuck it in the wood to try if it were not rotten, but it was not.

"Now," said he to himself, "I have no more to do; the door is shut, and I can't open it."

Before the words were rightly shaped in his own mind, a voice in his ear said to him, "Search for the key on the top of the door, or on the wall."

He started. "Who is that speaking to me?" he cried, turning round; but he saw no one. The voice said in his ear again, "Search for the key on the top of the door, or on the wall."

"What's that?" said he, and the sweat running from his forehead; "who spoke to me?"

"It's I, the corpse, that spoke to you!" said the voice.

"Can you talk?" said Teig.

"Now and again," said the corpse.

Teig searched for the key, and he found it on the top of the wall. He was too much frightened to say any more, but he opened the door wide, and as quickly as he could, and he went in, with the corpse on his back. It was as dark as pitch inside, and poor Teig began to shake and tremble.

"Light the candle," said the corpse.

Teig put his hand in his pocket, as well as he was able, and drew out a flint and steel. He struck a spark out of it, and lit a burnt rag he had in his pocket. He blew it until it made a flame, and he looked round him. The church was very ancient, and part of the wall was broken down. The windows were blown in or cracked, and the timbers of the seats were rotten. There were six or seven old iron candlesticks left there still, and in one of these candlesticks Teig found the stump of an old candle, and he lit it. He was still looking round him in the strange and horrid place in which he found himself, when the cold corpse whispered in his ear, "Bury me now, bury me now; there is a spade and turn the ground." Teig looked from him, and he saw a spade lying beside the altar. He took it up, and he placed the blade under a flag that was in the middle of the aisle, and leaning all his weight on the handle of the spade, he raised it. When the first flag was raised it was not hard to raise the others near it, and he moved three or four of them out of their places. The clay that was under them was soft and easy to dig, but he had not thrown up more than three or four shovelfuls when he felt the iron touch something soft like flesh. He threw up three or four more shovelfuls from around it, and then he saw that it was another body that was buried in the same place.

"I am afraid I'll never be allowed to bury the two bodies in the same hole," said Teig, in his own mind. "You corpse, there on my back," says he, "will you be satisfied if I bury you down here?" But the corpse never answered him a word.

"That's a good sign," said Teig to himself. "Maybe he's getting quiet," and he thrust the spade down in the earth again. Perhaps he hurt the flesh of the other body, for the dead man that was buried there stood up in the grave, and shouted an awful shout. "Hoo! hoo!! hoo!!! Go! go!! go!!! or you're a dead, dead, dead man!" And then he fell back in the grave again. Teig said afterwards, that of all the wonderful things he saw that night, that was the most awful to him. His hair stood upright on his head like the bristles of a pig, the cold sweat ran off his face, and then came a tremor over all his bones, until he thought that he must fall.

But after a while he became bolder, when he saw that the second corpse remained lying quietly there, and he threw in the clay on it again, and he smoothed it overhead, and he laid down the flags carefully as they had been before. "It can't be that he'll rise up any more," said he.

He went down the aisle a little further, and drew near to the door, and began raising the flags again, looking for another bed for the corpse on his back. He took up three or four flags and put them aside, and then he dug the clay. He was not long digging until he laid bare an old woman without a thread upon her but her shirt. She was more lively than the first corpse, for he had scarcely taken any of the clay away from about her, when she sat up and began to cry, "Ho, you *bodach* (clown)!

Ha, you *bodach*! Where has he been that he got no bed?"

Poor Teig drew back, and when she found that she was getting no answer, she closed her eyes gently, lost her vigor, and fell back quietly and slowly under the clay. Teig did to her as he had done to the man—he threw the clay back on her, and left the flags down overhead.

He began digging again near the door, but before he had thrown up more than a couple of shovelfuls, he noticed a man's hand laid bare by the spade. "By my soul, I'll go no further, then," said he to himself; "what use is it for me?" And he threw the clay in again on it, and settled the flags as they had been before.

He left the church then, and his heart was heavy enough, but he shut the door and locked it, and left the key where he found it. He sat down on a tombstone that was near the door, and began thinking. He was in great doubt what he should do. He laid his face between his two hands, and cried for grief and fatigue, since he was dead certain at this time that he never would come home alive. He made another attempt to loosen the hands of the corpse that were squeezed round his neck, but they were as tight as if they were clamped; and the more he tried to loosen them, the tighter they squeezed him. He was going to sit down once more, when the cold, horrid lips of the dead man said to him, "Carrick-fhad-vic-Orus," and he remembered the command of the good people to bring the corpse with him to that place if he should be unable to bury it where he had been.

He rose up, and looked about him. "I don't know the way," he said.

As soon as he had uttered the word, the corpse stretched out suddenly its left hand that had been tightened round his neck, and kept it pointing out, showing him the road he ought to follow. Teig went in the direction that the fingers were stretched, and passed out of the churchyard. He found himself on an old rutty, stony road, and he stood still again, not knowing where to turn. The corpse stretched out its bony hand a second time, and pointed out to him another road—not the road by which he had come when approaching the old church. Teig followed that road, and whenever he came to a path or road meeting it, the corpse always stretched out its hand and pointed with its fingers, showing him the way he was to take.

Many was the crossroad he turned down, and many was the crooked *boreen* he walked, until he saw from him an old burying-ground at last, beside the road, but there was neither church nor chapel nor any other building in it. The corpse squeezed him tightly, and he stood. "Bury me, bury me in the burying-ground," said the voice.

Teig drew over towards the old burying-place, and he was not more than about twenty yards from it, when, raising his eyes, he saw hundreds and hundreds of ghosts—men, women, and children—sitting on the top of the wall round about, or standing on the inside of it, or running backwards and forwards, and pointing at him, while he could see their mouths opening and shutting as if they were speaking, though he heard no word, nor any sound amongst them at all.

He was afraid to go forward, so he stood where he was, and the moment he stood, all the ghosts became quiet, and ceased moving. Then Teig understood that it was trying to keep him from going in, that they were. He walked a couple of yards forwards, and immediately the whole crowd rushed together towards the spot to which he was moving, and they stood so thickly together that it seemed to him that he never could break through them, even though he had a mind to try. But he had no mind to try it. He went back broken and dispirited, and when he had gone a couple of hundred yards from the burying-ground, he stood again, for he did not know what way he was to go. He heard the voice of the corpse in his ear, saying "Teampoll-Ronan," and the skinny hand was stretched out again, pointing him out the road.

As tired as he was, he had to walk, and the road was neither short nor even. The night was darker than ever, and it was difficult to make his way. Many was the toss he got, and many a bruise they left on his body. At last he saw Teampoll-Ronan from him in the distance, standing in the middle of the burying-ground. He moved over towards it, and thought he was all right and safe, when he saw no ghosts nor anything else on the wall, and he thought he would never be hindered now from leaving his load off him at last. He moved over to the gate, but as he was passing in, he tripped on the threshold. Before he could recover himself, something that he could not see seized him by the neck, by the hands, and by the feet, and bruised him, and shook him, and choked him, until he was nearly dead; and at last he was lifted up, and carried more than a hundred yards from that place, and then thrown down in an old dyke, with the corpse still clinging to him.

He rose up, bruised and sore, but feared to go near the place again, for he had seen nothing the time he was thrown down and carried away.

"You corpse, up on my back?" said he, "shall I go over again to the churchyard?"—but the corpse never answered him. "That's a sign you don't wish me to try it again," said Teig.

He was now in great doubt as to what he ought to do, when the corpse spoke in his ear, and said, "Imlogue-Fada."

"Oh, murder!" said Teig, "must I bring you there? If you keep me long walking like this, I tell you I'll fall under you."

He went on, however, in the direction the corpse pointed out to him. He could not have told, himself, how long he had been going, when the dead man behind suddenly squeezed him, and said, "There!"

Teig looked from him, and he saw a little low wall, that was so broken down in places that it was no wall at all. It was in a great wide field, in from the road; and only for three or four great stones at the corners, that were more like rocks than stones, there was nothing to show that there was either graveyard or burying-ground there.

"Is this Imlogue-Fada? Shall I bury you here?" said Teig.

"Yes," said the voice.

"But I see no grave or gravestone, only this pile of stones," said Teig.

The corpse did not answer, but stretched out its long fleshless hand to show Teig the direction in which he was to go. Teig went on accordingly, but he was greatly terrified, for he remembered what had happened to him at the last place. He went on, "with his heart in his mouth," as he said himself afterwards; but when he came to within fifteen or twenty yards of the little low square wall, there broke out a flash of lightning, bright yellow and red, with blue streaks in it, and went round about the wall in one course, and it swept by as fast as the swallow in the clouds, and the longer Teig remained looking at it the faster it went, till at last it became like a bright ring of flame round the old graveyard, which no one could pass without being burnt by it. Teig never saw, from the time he was born, and never saw afterwards, so wonderful or so splendid a sight as that was. Round went the flame, white and yellow and blue sparks leaping out from it as it went, and although at first it had been no more than a thin, narrow line, it increased slowly until it was at last a great broad band, and it was continually getting broader and higher, and throwing out more brilliant sparks, till there was never a color on the ridge of the earth that was not to be seen in that fire; and lightning never shone and flame never flamed that was so shining and so bright as that.

Teig was amazed; he was half dead with fatigue, and he had no courage left to approach the wall. There fell a mist over his eyes, and there came a *soorawn* in his head, and he was obliged to sit down upon a great stone to recover himself. He could see nothing but the light, and he could hear nothing but the whirr of it as it shot round the paddock faster than a flash of lightning.

As he sat there on the stone, the voice whispered once more in his ear, "Kill-Breedya"; and the dead man squeezed him so tightly that he cried out. He rose again, sick, tired, and trembling, and went forward as he was directed. The wind was cold, and the road was bad, and the load upon his back was heavy, and the night was dark, and he himself was nearly worn out, and if he had had very much farther to go he must have fallen dead under his burden.

At last the corpse stretched out its hand, and said to him, "Bury me there."

"This is the last burying-place," said Teig in his own mind; "and the little gray man said I'd be allowed to bury him in some of them, so it must be this; it can't be but they'll let him in here."

The first faint streak of the ring of day was appearing in the east, and the clouds were beginning to catch fire, but it was darker than ever, for the moon was set, and there were no stars.

"Make haste, make haste!" said the corpse; and Teig hurried forward as well as he could to the graveyard, which was a little place on a bare hill, with only a few graves in it. He walked boldly in through the open gate, and nothing touched him, nor did he either hear or see anything. He came to the middle of the ground, and then stood up and looked round him for a spade or shovel to make a grave. As he was turning round and searching, he suddenly perceived what startled him greatly—a newly-dug grave right before him. He moved over to it, and looked down, and there at the bottom he saw a black coffin. He clambered down into the hole and lifted the lid, and found that (as he thought it would be) the coffin was empty. He had hardly mounted up out of the hole, and was standing on the brink, when the corpse, which had clung to him for more than eight hours, suddenly relaxed its hold of his neck, and loosened its shins from round his hips, and sank down with a plop into the open coffin.

Teig fell down on his two knees at the brink of the grave, and gave thanks to God. He made no delay then, but pressed down the coffin lid in its place, and threw in the clay over it with his two hands, and when the grave was filled up, he stamped and leaped on it with his feet, until it was firm and hard, and then he left the place.

The sun was fast rising as he finished his work, and the first thing he did was to return to the road, and look out for a house to rest himself in. He found an inn at last; and lay down upon a bed there, and slept till night. Then he rose up and ate a little, and fell asleep again till morning. When he awoke in the morning he hired a horse and rode home. He was more than twenty-six miles from home where he was, and he had come all that way with the dead body on his back in one night.

All the people at his own home thought that he must have left the country, and they rejoiced greatly when they saw him come back. Everyone began asking him where he had been, but he would not tell anyone except his father.

He was a changed man from that day. He never drank too much; he never lost his money over cards; and especially he would not take the world and be out late by himself of a dark night.

He was not a fortnight at home until he married Mary, the girl he had been in love with, and it's at their wedding the sport was, and it's he was the happy man from that day forward, and it's all I wish that we may be as happy as he was.

GLOSSARY—*Rann*, a stanza; *kailee (céilidhe)*, a visit in the evenings; *wirra (a mhuire)*, "Oh, Mary!" an exclamation like the French *dame; rib*, a single hair (in Irish, *ribe); a lock (glac)*, a bundle or wisp, or a little share of anything; *kippeen (cipín)*, a rod or twig; *boreen (bóithrín)*, a lane; *bodach*, a clown; *soorawn (suarán)*, vertigo. *Avic (a Mhic)* = my son, or rather, Oh, son. *Mic* is the vocative of *Mac*.

The Judge's House
Bram Stoker

WHEN THE TIME for his examination drew near Malcolm
Malcolmson made up his mind to go somewhere to read by
himself. He feared the attractions of the seaside, and also he
feared completely rural isolation, for of old he knew its charms,
and so he determined to find some unpretentious little town
where there would be nothing to distract him. He refrained from
asking suggestions from any of his friends, for he argued that
each would recommend some place of which he had knowledge,
and where he had already acquaintances. As Malcolmson
wished to avoid friends he had no wish to encumber himself
with the attention of friends' friends, and so he determined to
look out for a place for himself. He packed a portmanteau with
some clothes and all the books he required, and then took ticket
for the first name on the local time-table which he did not know.

When at the end of three hours' journey he alighted at Benchurch, he felt satisfied that he had so far obliterated his tracks as to be sure of having a peaceful opportunity of pursuing his studies. He went straight to the one inn which the sleepy little place contained, and put up for the night. Benchurch was a market town, and once in three weeks was crowded to excess, but for the remainder of the twenty-one days it was as attractive as a desert. Malcolmson looked around the day after his arrival to try to find quarters more isolated than even so quiet an inn as "The Good Traveller" afforded. There was only one place which took his fancy, and it certainly satisfied his wildest ideas regarding quiet; in fact, quiet was not the proper word to apply to it—desolation was the only term conveying any suitable idea of its isolation. It was an old rambling, heavy-built house of the Jacobean style, with heavy gables and windows, unusually small, and set higher than was customary in such houses, and was surrounded with a high brick wall massively built. Indeed, on examination, it looked more like a fortified house than an ordinary dwelling. But all these things pleased Malcolmson. "Here," he thought, "is the very spot I have been looking for, and if I can only get opportunity of using it I shall be happy." His joy was increased when he realized beyond doubt that it was not at present inhabited.

From the post-office he got the name of the agent, who was rarely surprised at the application to rent a part of the old house. Mr. Carnford, the local lawyer and agent, was a genial old gentleman, and frankly confessed his delight at anyone being willing to live in the house.

"To tell you the truth," said he, "I should be only too happy, on behalf of the owners, to let anyone have the house rent free for a term of years if only to accustom the people here to see it inhabited. It has been so long empty that some kind of absurd prejudice has grown up about it, and this can be best put down by its occupation—if only," he added with a sly glance at Malcolmson, "by a scholar like yourself, who wants its quiet for a time."

Malcolmson thought it needless to ask the agent about the "absurd prejudice"; he knew he would get more information, if he should require it, on that subject from other quarters. He paid his three months' rent, got a receipt, and the name of an old woman who would probably undertake to "do" for him, and came away with the keys in his pocket. He then went to the landlady of the inn, who was a cheerful and most kindly person, and asked her advice as to such stores and provisions as he would be likely to require. She threw up her hands in amazement when he told her where he was going to settle himself.

"Not in the Judge's House!" she said and grew pale as she spoke. He explained the locality of the house, saying that he did not know its name. When he had finished, she answered:

"Aye, sure enough—sure enough the very place. It is the Judge's House sure enough." He asked her to tell him about the place, why so called, and what there was against it. She told him that it was so called locally because it had been many years before—how long she could not say, as she was herself from another part of the country, but she thought it must have been a hundred years or more—the abode of a judge who was held in great terror on account of his harsh sentences and his hostility to prisoners at Assizes. As to what there was against the house itself she could not tell. She had often asked, but no one could inform her; but there was a general feeling that there was *something*, and for her own part she would not take all the money in Drinkwater's Bank and stay in the house an hour by herself. Then she apologized to Malcolmson for her disturbing talk.

"It is too bad of me, sir, and you—and a young gentleman, too—if you will pardon me saying it, going to live there all alone. If you were my boy—and you'll excuse me for saying it—you wouldn't sleep there a night, not if I had to go there myself and pull the big alarm bell that's on the roof!" The good creature was so manifestly in earnest, and was so kindly in her intentions, that Malcolmson, although amused, was touched. He told her kindly how much he appreciated her interest in him, and added:

"But, my dear Mrs. Witham, indeed you need not be concerned about me! A man who is reading for the Mathematical Tripos has too much to think of to be disturbed by any of these mysterious 'somethings,' and his work is of too exact and prosaic a kind to allow of his having any corner in his mind for mysteries of any kind. Harmonical Progression, Permutations and Combinations, and Elliptic Functions have sufficient mysteries for me!" Mrs. Witham kindly undertook to see after his commissions, and he went himself to look for the old woman who had been recommended to him. When he returned to the Judge's House with her, after an interval of a couple of hours, he found Mrs. Witham herself waiting with several men and boys carrying parcels, and an upholsterer's man with a bed in a cart, for she said, though tables and chairs might be all very well, a bed that hadn't been aired for mayhap fifty years was not proper for young bones to lie on. She was evidently curious to see the inside of the house; and though manifestly so afraid of the "somethings" that at the slightest sound she clutched on to Malcolmson, whom she never left for a moment, went over the whole place.

After his examination of the house, Malcolmson decided to take up his abode in the great dining-room, which was big enough to serve for all his requirements; and Mrs. Witham, with the aid of the charwoman, Mrs. Dempster, proceeded to arrange matters. When the hampers were brought in and unpacked, Malcolmson saw that with much kind forethought she had sent from her own kitchen sufficient provisions to last for a few days. Before going she expressed all sorts of kind wishes; and at the door turned and said:

"And perhaps, sir, as the room is big and drafty it might be well to have one of those big screens put round your bed at night—though, truth to tell, I would die myself if I were to be so shut in with all kinds of—of 'things' that put their heads round the sides, or over the top, and look on me!" The image which she had called up was too much for her nerves, and she fled incontinently.

Mrs. Dempster sniffed in a superior manner as the landlady disappeared, and remarked that for her own part she wasn't afraid of all the bogies in the kingdom.

"I'll tell you what it is, sir," she said; "bogies is all kinds and sorts of things—except bogies! Rats and mice, and beetles; and creaky doors, and loose slates, and broken panes, and stiff drawer handles, that stay out when you pull them and then fall down in the middle of the night. Look at the wainscot of the room! It is old—hundreds of years old! Do you think there's no rats and beetles there! And do you imagine, sir, that you won't see none of them! Rats is bogies, I tell you, and bogies is rats; and don't you get to think anything else!"

"Mrs. Dempster," said Malcolmson gravely, making her a polite bow, "you know more than a Senior Wrangler! And let me say, that, as a mark of esteem for your indubitable soundness of head and heart, I shall, when I go, give you possession of this house, and let you stay here by yourself for the last two months of my tenancy, for four weeks will serve my purpose."

"Thank you kindly, sir!" she answered, "but I couldn't sleep away from home a night. I am in Greenhow's Charity, and if I slept a night away from my rooms I should lose all I have got to live on. The rules is very strict; and there's too many watching for a vacancy for me to run any risks in the matter. Only for that, sir, I'd gladly come here and attend on you altogether during your stay."

"My good woman," said Malcolmson hastily, "I have come here on purpose to obtain solitude; and believe me that I am grateful to the late Greenhow for having so organized his admirable charity—whatever it is—that I am perforce denied the opportunity of suffering from such a form of temptation! Saint Anthony himself could not be more rigid on the point!"

The old woman laughed harshly. "Ah, you young gentlemen," she said, "you don't fear for naught; and belike you'll get all the solitude you want here." She set to work with her cleaning; and by nightfall, when Malcolmson returned from his walk—he always had one of his books to study as he walked—he found the room swept and tidied, a fire burning in the old hearth, the lamp lit, and the table spread for supper with Mrs.Witham's excellent fare. "This is comfort, indeed," he said, as he rubbed his hands.

When he had finished his supper, and lifted the tray to the other end of the great oak dining-table, he got out his books again, put fresh wood on the fire, trimmed his lamp, and set himself down to a spell of real hard work. He went on without pause till about eleven o'clock, when he knocked off for a bit to fix his fire and lamp and to make himself a cup of tea. He had always been a tea-drinker, and during his college life had sat late at work and had taken tea late. The rest was a great luxury to him, and he enjoyed it with a sense of delicious, voluptuous ease. The renewed fire leaped and sparkled, and threw quaint shadows through the great old room; and as he sipped his hot tea he reveled in the sense of isolation from his kind. Then it was that he began to notice for the first time what a noise the rats were making.

"Surely," he thought, "they cannot have been at it all the time I was reading. Had they been, I must have noticed it!" Presently, when the noise increased, he satisfied himself that it was really new. It was evident that at first the rats had been frightened at the presence of a stranger, and the light of fire and lamp; but that as the time went on they had grown bolder and were now disporting themselves as was their wont.

How busy they were! and hark to the strange noises! Up and down behind the old wainscot, over the ceiling and under the floor they raced, and gnawed, and scratched! Malcolmson smiled to himself as he recalled to mind the saying of Mrs. Dempster, "Bogies is rats, and rats is bogies!" The tea began to have its effect of intellectual and nervous stimulus, he saw with joy another long spell of work to be done before the night was past, and in the sense of security which it gave him, he allowed himself the luxury of a good look round the room. He took his lamp in one hand, and went all around, wondering that so quaint and beautiful an old house had been so long neglected. The carving of the oak on the panels of the wainscot was fine, and on and round the doors and windows it was beautiful and of rare merit There were some old pictures on the walls, but they were coated so thick with dust and dirt that he could not distinguish any detail of them, though he held his lamp as high as he could over his head. Here and there as he went round he saw some crack or hole blocked for a moment by the face of a rat with its bright eyes glittering in the light, but in an instant it was gone, and a squeak and a scamper followed. The thing that most struck him, however, was the rope of the great alarm bell on the roof, which hung down in a corner of the room on the right-hand side of the fireplace. He pulled up close to the hearth a great high-backed carved oak chair, and sat down to his last cup of tea. When this was done he made up the fire, and went back to his work, sitting at the corner of the table, having the fire to his left. For a little while the rats disturbed him somewhat with their perpetual scampering, but he got accustomed to the noise as one does to the ticking of a clock or to the roar of moving water; and he became so immersed in his work that everything in the world, except the problem which he was trying to solve, passed away from him.

He suddenly looked up, his problem was still unsolved, and there was in the air that sense of the hour before the dawn, which is so dread to doubtful life. The noise of the rats had ceased. Indeed it seemed to him that it must have ceased but lately and that it was the sudden cessation which had disturbed him. The fire had fallen low, but still it threw out a deep red glow. As he looked he started in spite of his *sang froid*.

There on the great high-backed carved oak chair by the right side of the fireplace sat an enormous rat, steadily glaring at him with baleful eyes. He made a motion to it as though to hunt it away, but it did not stir. Then he made the motion of throwing something. Still it did not stir, but showed its great white teeth angrily, and its cruel eyes shone in the lamplight with an added vindictiveness.

Malcolmson felt amazed, and seizing the poker from the hearth ran at it to kill it. Before, however, he could strike it, the rat, with a squeak that sounded like the concentration of hate, jumped upon the floor, and, running up the rope of the alarm bell, disappeared in the darkness beyond the range of the green-shaded lamp. Instantly, strange to say, the noisy scampering of the rats in the wainscot began again.

By this time Malcolmson's mind was quite off the problem;

and as a shrill cock-crow outside told him of the approach of morning, he went to bed and to sleep.

He slept so sound that he was not even waked by Mrs. Dempster coming in to make up his room. It was only when she had tidied up the place and got his breakfast ready and tapped on the screen which closed in his bed that he woke. He was a little tired still after his night's hard work, but a strong cup of tea soon freshened him up and, taking his book, he went out for his morning walk, bringing with him a few sandwiches lest he should not care to return till dinner time. He found a quiet walk between high elms some way outside the town, and here he spent the greater part of the day studying his Laplace. On his return he looked in to see Mrs. Witham and to thank her for her kindness. When she saw him coming through the diamond-paned bay window of her sanctum, she came out to meet him and asked him in. She looked at him searchingly and shook her head as she said:

"You must not overdo it, sir. You are paler this morning than you should be. Too late hours and too hard work on the brain isn't good for any man! But tell me, sir, how did you pass the night? Well, I hope? But, my heart! sir, I was glad when Mrs. Dempster told me this morning that you were all right and sleeping sound when she went in."

"Oh, I was all right," he answered smiling; "the 'somethings' didn't worry me, as yet. Only the rats; and they had a circus, I tell you, all over the place. There was one wicked looking old devil that sat up on my own chair by the fire and wouldn't go till I took the poker to him, and then he ran up the rope of the alarm bell and got to somewhere up the wall or the ceiling—I couldn't see where, it was so dark."

"Mercy on us," said Mrs. Witham, "an old devil, and sitting on a chair by the fireside! Take care, sir! take care! There's many a true word spoken in jest."

"How do you mean? 'Pon my word I don't understand."

"An old devil! The old devil, perhaps. There! sir, you needn't laugh," for Malcolmson had broken into a hearty peal. "You young folks thinks it easy to laugh at things that makes older ones shudder. Never mind, sir! never mind. Please God, you'll laugh all the time. It's what I wish you myself !" and the good lady beamed all over in sympathy with his enjoyment, her fears gone for a moment.

"Oh, forgive me!" said Malcolmson presently. "Don't think me rude; but the idea was too much for me—that the old devil himself was on the chair last night!" And at the thought he laughed again. Then he went home to dinner.

This evening the scampering of the rats began earlier; indeed it had been going on before his arrival, and only ceased whilst his presence by its freshness disturbed them. After dinner he sat by the fire for a while and had a smoke; and then, having cleared his table, began to work as before. Tonight the rats disturbed him more than they had done on the previous night. How they scampered up and down and under and over! How they squeaked, and scratched, and gnawed! How they, getting bolder by degrees, came to the mouths of their holes and to the chinks and cracks and crannies in the wainscoting till their eyes shone like tiny lamps as the firelight rose and fell. But to him, now doubtless accustomed to them, their eyes were not wicked; only their playfulness touched him. Sometimes the boldest of them made sallies out on the floor or along the mouldings of the wainscot. Now and again as they disturbed him Malcolmson made a sound to frighten them, smiting the table with his hand or giving a fierce "Hsh, hsh," so that they fled straightway to their holes.

And so the early part of the night wore on; and despite the

noise Malcolmson got more and more immersed in his work.

All at once he stopped, as on the previous night, being overcome by a sudden sense of silence. There was not the faintest sound of gnaw, or scratch, or squeak. The silence was as of the grave. He remembered the odd occurrence of the previous night, and instinctively he looked at the chair standing close by the fireside. And then a very odd sensation thnlled through him.

There, on the great old high-backed carved oak chair beside the fireplace sat the same enormous rat, steadily glaring at him with baleful eyes.

Instinctively he took the nearest thing to his hand, a book of logarithms, and flung it at it. The book was badly aimed and the rat did not stir, so again the poker performance of the previous night was repeated; and again the rat, being closely pursued, fled up the rope of the alarm bell. Strangely too, the departure of this rat was instantly followed by the renewal of the noise made by the general rat community On this occasion, as on the previous one, Malcolmson could not see at what part of the room the rat disappeared, for the green shade of his lamp left the upper part of the room in darkness, and the fire had burned low.

On looking at his watch he found it was close on midnight and, not sorry for the *divertissement*, he made up his fire and made himself his nightly pot of tea. He had got through a good spell of work, and thought himself entitled to a cigarette; and so he sat on the great carved oak chair before the fire and enjoyed it. Whilst smoking he began to think that he would like to know where the rat disappeared to, for he had certain ideas for the morrow not entirely disconnected with a rat-trap. Accordingly he lit another lamp and placed it so that it would shine well into the right-hand corner of the wall by the fireplace. Then he got all the books he had with him, and placed them handy to throw

at the vermin. Finally he lifted the rope of the alarm bell and
placed the end of it on the table, fixing the extreme end under
the lamp. As he handled it he could not help noticing how
pliable it was, especially for so strong a rope, and one not in
use. "You could hang a man with it," he thought to himself.
When his preparations were made he looked around, and said
complacently:

"There now, my friend, I think we shall learn something of
you this time!" He began his work again, and though as before
somewhat disturbed at first by the noise of the rats, soon lost
himself in his propositions and problems.

Again he was called to his immediate surroundings suddenly.
This time it might not have been the sudden silence only which
took his attention; there was a slight movement of the rope, and
the lamp moved. Without stirring, he looked to see if his pile of
books was within range, and then cast his eye along the rope. As
he looked he saw the great rat drop from the rope on the oak
armchair and sit there glaring at him. He raised a book in his
right hand, and taking careful aim, flung it at the rat. The latter,
with a quick movement, sprang aside and dodged the missile.
He then took another book, and a third, and flung them one after
another at the rat, but each time unsuccessfully. At last, as he
stood with a book poised in his hand to throw, the rat squeaked
and seemed afraid. This made Malcolmson more than ever
eager to strike, and the book flew and struck the rat a
resounding blow. It gave a terrified squeak, and turning on his
pursuer a look of terrible malevolence, ran up the chair-back
and made a great jump to the rope of the alarm bell and ran up it
like lightning. The lamp rocked under the sudden strain, but it
was a heavy one and did not topple over. Malcolmson kept his
eyes on the rat, and saw it by the light of the second lamp leap
to a moulding of the wainscot and disappear through a hole in

one of the great pictures which hung on the wall, obscured and invisible through its coating of dirt and dust.

"I shall look up my friend's habitation in the morning," said the student, as he went over to collect his books. "The third picture from the fireplace; I shall not forget." He picked up the books one by one, commenting on them as he lifted them. *Conic Sections* he does not mind, nor *Cycloidal Oscillations*, nor the *Principia*, nor *Quaternions*, nor *Thermodynamics*. Now for the book that fetched him!" Malcolmson took it up and looked at it. As he did so he started, and a sudden pallor overspread his face. He looked round uneasily and shivered slightly, as he murmured to himself:

"The Bible my mother gave me! What an odd coincidence." He sat down to work again, and the rats in the wainscot renewed their gambols. They did not disturb him, however; somehow their presence gave him a sense of companionship. But he could not attend to his work, and after striving to master the subject on which he was engaged, gave it up in despair, and went to bed as the first streak of dawn stole in through the eastern window.

He slept heavily but uneasily, and dreamed much; and when Mrs. Dempster woke him late in the morning he seemed ill at ease, and for a few minutes did not seem to realize exactly where he was. His first request rather surprised the servant.

"Mrs. Dempster, when I am out today I wish you would get the steps and dust or wash those pictures—specially that one the third from the fireplace—I want to see what they are."

Late in the afternoon Malcolmson worked at his books in the shaded walk, and the cheerfulness of the previous day came back to him as the day wore on, and he found that his reading was progressing well. He had worked out to a satisfactory conclusion all the problems which had as yet baffled him, and it was in a state of jubilation that he paid a visit to Mrs. Witham at

"The Good Traveller." He found a stranger in the cozy sitting-room with the landlady, who was introduced to him as Dr. Thornhill. She was not quite at ease, and this, combined with the doctor's plunging at once into a series of questions, made Malcolmson come to the conclusion that his presence was not an accident, so without preliminary he said:

"Dr. Thornhill, I shall with pleasure answer you any question you may choose to ask me if you will answer me one question first."

The doctor seemed surprised, but he smiled and answered at once, "Done! What is it?"

"Did Mrs. Witham ask you to come here and see me and advise me?"

Dr. Thornhill for a moment was taken aback, and Mrs. Witham got fiery red and turned away; but the doctor was a frank and ready man, and he answered at once and openly:

"She did, but she didn't intend you to know it. I suppose it was my clumsy haste that made you suspect. She told me that she did not like the idea of your being in that house all by yourself, and that she thought you took too much strong tea. In fact, she wants me to advise you if possible to give up the tea and the very late hours. I was a keen student in my time, so I suppose I may take the liberty of a college man, and without offense, advise you not quite as a stranger."

Malcolmson with a bright smile held out his hand. "Shake! as they say in America," he said. "I must thank you for your kindness and Mrs. Witham too, and your kindness deserves a return on my part. I promise to take no more strong tea —no tea at all till you let me—and I shall go to bed tonight at one o'clock at latest. Will that do?"

"Capital," said the doctor. "Now tell us all that you noticed in the old house," and so Malcolmson then and there told in minute detail all that had happened in the last two nights. He was interrupted every now and then by some exclamation from Mrs. Witham, till finally when he told of the episode of the Bible the landlady's pent-up emotions found vent in a shriek; and it was not till a stiff glass of brandy and water had been administered that she grew composed again. Dr. Thornhill listened with a face of growing gravity, and when the narrative was complete and Mrs. Witham had been restored, he asked:

"The rat always went up the rope of the alarm bell?"

"I suppose you know," said the Doctor after a pause, "what the rope is?"

"It is," said the Doctor slowly, "the very rope which the hangman used for all the victims of the Judge's judicial rancor!" Here he was interrupted by another scream from Mrs. Witham, and steps had to be taken for her recovery. Malcolmson having looked at his watch, and found that it was close to his dinner hour, had gone home before her complete recovery.

When Mrs. Witham was herself again she almost assailed the Doctor with angry questions as to what he meant by putting such horrible ideas into the poor young man's mind. "He has quite enough there already to upset him," she added. Dr. Thornhill replied:

"My dear madam, I had a distinct purpose in it! I wanted to draw his attention to the bell rope, and to fix it there. It may be that he is in a highly overwrought state, and has been studying too much, although I am bound to say that he seems as sound and healthy a young man, mentally and bodily, as ever I saw— but then the rats—and that suggestion of the devil." The doctor shook his head and went on. "I would have offered to go and stay the first night with him but that I felt sure it would have been a cause of offense He may get in the night some strange fright or hallucination and if he does I want him to pull that rope. All alone as he is, it will give us warning, and we may reach him in time to be of service. I shall be sitting up pretty late tonight and shall keep my ears open. Do not be alarmed if Benchurch gets a surprise before morning."

"Oh, Doctor, what do you mean? What do you mean?"

"I mean this; that possibly—nay, more probably—we shall hear the great alarm bell from the Judge's House tonight," and the Doctor made about as effective an exit as could be thought of.

When Malcolmson arrived home he found that it was a little after his usual time, and Mrs. Dempster had gone away—the rules of Greenhow's Charity were not to be neglected. He was glad to see that the place was bright and tidy with a cheerful fire and a well-trimmed lamp. The evening was colder than might have been expected in April, and a heavy wind was blowing with such rapidly-increasing strength that there was every promise of a storm during the night. For a few minutes after his entrance the noise of the rats ceased; but so soon as they became accustomed to his presence they began again. He was glad to hear them, for he felt once more the feeling of companionship in their noise, and his mind ran back to the strange fact that they only ceased to manifest themselves when that other—the great rat with the baleful eyes—came upon the scene. The reading-lamp only was lit and its green shade kept the ceiling and the upper part of the room in darkness, so that the cheerful light from the hearth spreading over the floor and shining on the white cloth laid over the end of the table was warm and cheery. Malcolmson sat down to his dinner with a good appetite and a buoyant spirit. After his dinner and a cigarette he sat steadily down to work, determined not to let anything disturb him, for he remembered his promise to the Doctor, and made up his mind to make the best of the time at his disposal.

For an hour or so he worked all right, and then his thoughts began to wander from his books. The actual circumstances around him, the calls on his physical attention, and his nervous susceptibility were not to be denied. By this time the wind had become a gale, and the gale a storm. The old house, solid though it was, seemed to shake to its foundations, and the storm roared and raged through its many chimneys and its queer old gables, producing strange, unearthly sounds in the empty rooms and corridors. Even the great alarm bell on the roof must have felt the force of the wind, for the rope rose and fell slightly, as though the bell were moved a little from time to time, and the limber rope fell on the oak floor with a hard and hollow sound.

As Malcolmson listened to it he bethought himself of the Doctor's words, "It is the rope which the hangman used for the victims of the Judge's judicial rancor," and he went over to the corner of the fireplace and took it in his hand to look at it. There seemed a sort of deadly interest in it, and as he stood there he lost himself for a moment in speculation as to who these victims were, and the grim wish of the Judge to have such a ghastly relic ever under his eyes. As he stood there the swaying of the bell on the roof still lifted the rope now and again; but presently there came a new sensation—a sort of tremor in the rope, as though something was moving along it.

Looking up instinctively Malcolmson saw the great rat coming slowly down towards him, glaring at him steadily. He dropped the rope and started back with a muttered curse, and the rat turning ran up the rope again and disappeared, and at the same instant Malcolmson became conscious that the noise of the rats, which had ceased for a while, began again.

All this set him thinking, and it occurred to him that he had not investigated the lair of the rat or looked at the pictures, as he had intended. He lit the other lamp without the shade, and, holding it up, went and stood opposite the third picture from the fireplace on the right-hand side where he had seen the rat disappear on the previous night.

At the first glance he started back so suddenly that he almost dropped the lamp, and a deadly pallor overspread his face. His knees shook, and heavy drops of sweat came on his forehead, and he trembled like an aspen. But he was young and plucky, and pulled himself together, and after the pause of a few seconds stepped forward again, raised the lamp, and examined the picture which had been dusted and washed, and now stood out clearly.

It was of a judge dressed in his robes of scarlet and ermine. His face was strong and merciless, evil, crafty, and vindictive, with a sensual mouth, hooked nose of ruddy color, and shaped like the beak of a bird of prey. The rest of the face was of a cadaverous color. The eyes were of peculiar bnlliance and with a terribly malignant expression. As he looked at them, Malcolmson grew cold, for he saw there the very counterpart of the eyes of the great rat. The lamp almost fell from his hand, he saw the rat with its baleful eyes peering out through the hole in the corner of the picture, and noted the sudden cessation of the noise of the other rats. However, he pulled himself together, and went on with his examination of the picture.

The Judge was seated in a great high-backed carved oak chair, on the right-hand side of a great stone fireplace where, in the corner, a rope hung down from the ceiling, its end lying coiled on the floor. With a feeling of something like horror, Malcolmson recognized the scene of the room as it stood, and gazed around him in an awestruck manner as though he expected to find some strange presence behind him. Then he looked over to the corner of the fireplace—and with a loud cry he let the lamp fall from his hand.

There, in the Judge's armchair, with the rope hanging behind, sat the rat with the Judge's baleful eyes, now intensified and with a fiendish leer. Save for the howling of the storm without there was silence.

The fallen lamp recalled Malcolmson to himself. Fortunately it was of metal, and so the oil was not spilt. However, the practical need of attending to it settled at once his nervous apprehensions. When he had turned it out, he wiped his brow and thought for a moment.

"This will not do," he said to himself. "If I go on like this I shall become a crazy fool. This must stop! I promised the Doctor I would not take tea. Faith, he was pretty right! My nerves must have been getting into a queer state. Funny I did not notice it. I never felt better in my life. However, it is all right now, and I shall not be such a fool again."

Then he mixed himself a good stiff glass of brandy and water and resolutely sat down to his work.

It was nearly an hour later when he looked up from his book, disturbed by the sudden stillness. Without, the wind howled and roared louder than ever, and the rain drove in sheets against the windows, beating like hail on the glass; but within there was no sound whatever save the echo of the wind as it roared in the great chimney, and now and then a hiss as a few raindrops found their way down the chimney in a lull of the storm. The fire had fallen low and had ceased to flame, though it threw out a red glow. Malcolmson listened attentively, and presently heard a thin, squeaking noise, very faint. It came from the corner of the room where the rope hung down, and he thought it was the creaking of the rope on the floor as the swaying of the bell raised and lowered it. Looking up, however, he saw in the dim light the great rat clinging to the rope and gnawing it. The rope was already nearly gnawed through—he could see the lighter color where the strands were laid bare. As he looked the job was completed, and the severed end of the rope fell clattering on the oaken floor, whilst for an instant the great rat remained like a knob or tassel at the end of the rope, which now began to sway to and fro. Malcolmson felt for a moment another pang of terror as he thought that now the possibility of calling the outer world to his assistance was cut off, but an intense anger took its place, and seizing the book he was reading he hurled it at the rat. The blow was well aimed, but before the missile could reach him the rat dropped off and struck the floor with a soft thud. Malcolmson instantly rushed over towards him, but it darted away and disappeared in the darkness of the shadows of the room. Malcolmson felt that his work was over for the night, and determined then and there to vary the monotony of the proceedings by a hunt for the rat, and took off the green shade of the lamp so as to insure a wider spreading light. As he did so the gloom of the upper part of the room was relieved, and in the new flood of light, great by comparison with the previous darkness, the pictures on the wall stood out boldly. From where he stood, Malcolmson saw right opposite to him the third picture on the wall from the right of the fireplace. He rubbed his eyes in surprise, and then a great fear began to come upon him.

In the center of the picture was a great irregular patch of brown canvas, as fresh as when it was stretched on the frame. The background was as before, with chair and chimney-corner and rope, but the figure of the Judge had disappeared.

Malcolmson, almost in a chill of horror, turned slowly round, and then he began to shake and tremble like a man in a palsy. His strength seemed to have left him, and he was incapable of action or movement, hardly even of thought. He could only see and hear.

There, on the great high-backed carved oak chair sat the

Judge in his robes of scarlet and ermine, with his baleful eyes glaring vindictively, and a smile of triumph on the resolute, cruel mouth, as he lifted with his hands a *black cap*. Malcolmson felt as if the blood was running from his heart, as one does in moments of prolonged suspense. There was a ringing in his ears. Without, he could hear the roar and howl of the tempest, and through it, swept on the storm, came the striking of midnight by the great chimes in the marketplace. He stood for a space of time that seemed to him endless stlll as a statue, and with wide-open, horror-struck eyes, breathless. As the clock struck, so the smile of triumph on the Judge's face intensified, and at the last stroke of midnight he placed the black cap on his head.

Slowly and deliberately the Judge rose from his chair and picked up the piece of the rope of the alarm bell which lay on the floor, drew it through his hands as if he enjoyed its touch, and then deliberately began to knot one end of it, fashioning it into a noose. This he tightened and tested with his foot, pulling hard at it till he was satisfied and then making a running noose of it, which he held in his hand. Then he began to move along the table on the opposite side to Malcolmson keeping his eyes on him until he had passed him, when with a quick movement he stood in front of the door. Malcolmson then began to feel that he was trapped, and tried to think of what he should do. There was some fascination in the Judge's eyes, which he never took off him, and he had, perforce, to look. He saw the Judge approach—still keeping between him and the door—and raise the noose and throw it towards him as if to entangle him. With a great effort he made a quick movement to one side, and saw the rope fall beside him, and heard it strike the oaken floor. Again the Judge raised the noose and tried to ensnare him, ever keeping his baleful eyes fixed on him, and each time by a mighty effort the student just managed to evade it. So this went on for many times, the Judge seeming never discouraged nor discomposed at failure, but playing as a cat does with a mouse. At last in despair, which had reached its climax, Malcolmson cast a quick glance round him. The lamp seemed to have blazed up, and there was a fairly good light in the room. At the many rat-holes and in the chinks and crannies of the wainscot he saw the rats' eyes; and this aspect, that was purely physical, gave him a gleam of comfort. He looked around and saw that the rope of the great alarm bell was laden with rats. Every inch of it was covered with them, and more and more were pouring through the small circular hole in the ceiling whence it emerged, so that with their weight the bell was beginning to sway.

Hark! it had swayed till the clapper had touched the bell. The sound was but a tiny one, but the bell was only beginning to sway, and it would increase.

At the sound the Judge, who had been keeping his eyes fixed on Malcolmson, looked up, and a scowl of diabolical anger overspread his face. His eyes fairly glowed like hot coals, and he stamped his foot with a sound that seemed to make the house shake. A dreadful peal of thunder broke overhead as he raised the rope again, whilst the rats kept running up and down the rope as though working against time. This time, instead of throwing it, he drew close to his victim, and held open the noose as he approached. As he came closer there seemed something paralyzing in his very presence, and Malcolmson stood rigid as a corpse. He felt the Judge's icy fingers touch his throat as he adjusted the rope. The noose tightened—tightened. Then the Judge, taking the rigid form of the student in his arms, carried him over and placed him standing in the oak chair, and stepping up beside him, put his hand up and caught the end of the swaying rope of the alarm bell. As he raised his hand the rats fled squeaking, and disappeared through the hole in the ceiling. Taking the end of the noose which was round Malcolmson's neck, he tied it to the hanging-bell rope, and then descending pulled away the chair.

* * *

WHEN THE ALARM bell of the Judge's House began to sound, a crowd soon assembled. Lights and torches of various kinds appeared, and soon a silent crowd was hurrying to the spot. They knocked loudly at the door, but there was no reply. Then they burst in the door, and poured into the great dining room, the Doctor at the head.

There at the end of the rope of the great alarm bell hung the body of the student, and on the face of the Judge in the picture was a malignant smile.

About the Fairies

D.R. McAnally, Jr.

THE ORIENTAL LUXURIANCE of the Irish mythology is nowhere more conspicuously displayed than when dealing with the history, habits, characteristics, and pranks of the "good people." According to the most reliable of the rural "fairy-men," a race now nearly extinct, the fairies were once angels, so numerous as to have formed a large heaven. When Satan sinned and drew throngs of the heavenly host with him into open rebellion, a large number of the less warlike spirits stood aloof from the contest that followed, fearing the consequences, and not caring to take sides till the issue of the conflict was determined. Upon the defeat and expulsion of the rebellious angels, those who had remained neutral were punished by banishment from heaven, but their offence being only one of omission, they were not consigned to the pit with Satan and his followers, but were sent to earth where they still remain, not without hope that on the last day they may be pardoned and readmitted to Paradise. They are thus on their good behaviour, but having power to do infinite harm, they are much feared, and spoken of either in a whisper or aloud, as the "good people."

Unlike Leprechawns, who are not considered fit associates for reputable fairies, the good people are not solitary, but quite sociable, and always live in large societies, the members of which pursue the coöperative plan of labor and enjoyment, owning all their property, the kind and amount of which are somewhat indefinite, in common, and uniting their efforts to accomplish any desired object, whether of work or play. They travel in large bands, and although their parties are never seen in the daytime, there is little difficulty in ascertaining their line of march, for, "sure they make the terriblest little cloud o' dust iver raised, an' not a bit o' wind in it at all," so that a fairy migration is sometimes the talk of the county. "Though, be nacher, they 're not the length av yer finger, they can make thimselves the bigness av a tower when it plazes thim, an' av that ugliness that ye 'd faint wid the looks o' thim, as knowin' they can shtrike ye dead on the shpot or change ye into a dog, or a pig, or a unicorn, or anny other dirthy baste they plaze."

As a matter of fact, however, the fairies are by no means so numerous at present as they were formerly, a recent historian remarking that the National Schools and societies of Father Mathew are rapidly driving the fairies out of the country, for "they hate larnin' an' wisdom an' are lovers av nacher entirely."

In a few remote districts, where the schools are not yet well established, the good people are still found, and their doings are narrated with a childlike faith in the power of these first inhabitants of Ireland, for it seems to be agreed that they were in the country long before the coming either of the Irishman or of his Sassenagh oppressor.

The bodies of the fairies are not composed of flesh and bones, but of an ethereal substance, the nature of which is not determined. "Ye can see thimselves as plain as the nose on yer face, an' can see through thim like it was a mist." They have the power of vanishing from human sight when they please, and the fact that the air is sometimes full of them inspires the respect entertained for them by the peasantry. Sometimes they are heard without being seen, and when they travel through the air, as they often do, are known by a humming noise similar to that made by a swarm of bees. Whether or not they have wings is uncertain. Barney Murphy, of Kerry, thought they had; for several seen by him a number of years ago seemed to have long, semi-transparent pinions, "like thim that grows on a dhraggin-fly." Barney's neighbors, however, contradicted him by stoutly denying the good people the attribute of wings, and intimated that at the time Barney saw the fairies he was too drunk to distinguish a pair of wings from a pair of legs, so this branch of the subject must remain in doubt.

With regard to their dress, the testimony is undisputed. Young lady fairies wear pure white robes and usually allow their hair to flow loosely over their shoulders; while fairy matrons bind up their tresses in a coil on the top or back of the head, also surrounding the temples with a golden band. Young gentlemen elves wear green jackets, with white breeches and stockings; and when a fairy of either sex has need of a cap or head-covering, the flower of the fox-glove is brought into requisition.

Male fairies are perfect in all military exercises, for, like the other inhabitants of Ireland, fairies are divided into factions, the objects of contention not, in most cases, being definitely known. In Kerry, a number of years ago, there was a great battle among the fairies, one party inhabiting a rath or sepulchral mound, the other an unused and lonely graveyard. Paddy O'Donohue was the sole witness of this encounter, the narrative being in his own words.

"I was lyin' be the road, bein' on me way home an' tired wid the walkin'. A bright moon was out that night, an' I heard a noise like a million av sogers, thrampin' on the road, so I riz me an' looked, an' the way was full av little men, the length o' me hand, wid grane coats on, an' all in rows like wan o' the ridgmints; aitch wid a pike on his showlder an' a shield on his arrum. Wan was in front, beway he was the ginral, walkin' wid his chin up as proud as a paycock. Jagers, but I was skairt an' prayed fasther than iver I did in me life, for it was too clost to me entirely they wor for comfort or convaynience aither. But they all went by, sorra the wan o' thim turnin' his head to raygard me at all, Glory be to God for that same; so they left me. Afther they were clane gone by, I had curosity for to see phat they were afther, so I folly'd thim, a good bit aff, an' ready to jump an' run like a hare at the laste noise, for I was afeared if they caught me at it, they 'd make a pig o' me at wanst or change me into a baste complately. They marched into the field bechuxt the graveyard an' the rath, an' there was another army there wid red coats, from the graveyard, an' the two armies had the biggest fight ye iver seen, the granes agin the reds. Afther lookin' on a bit, I got axcited, for the granes were batin' the reds like blazes, an' I up an' give a whilloo an' called out, 'At 'em agin! Don't lave wan o' the blâggards!' An' wid that word, the sight left me eyes an' I remimber no more till mornin', an' there was I, layin' on the road where I seen thim, as shtiff as a crutch."

The homes of the fairies are commonly in raths, tumuli of the pagan days of Ireland, and, on this account, raths are much dreaded, and after sundown are avoided by the peasantry. Attempts have been made to remove some of these raths, but the unwillingness of the peasants to engage in the work, no matter what inducements may be offered in compensation, has generally resulted in the abandonment of the undertaking. On one of the islands in the Upper Lake of Killarney there is a rath, and the proprietor, finding it occupied too much ground, resolved to have it levelled to increase the arable surface of the field. The work was begun, but one morning, in the early dawn, as the laborers were crossing the lake on their way to the island, they saw a procession of about two hundred persons, habited like monks, leave the island and proceed to the mainland, followed, as the workmen thought, by a long line of small, shining figures. The phenomenon was perhaps genuine, for the mirage is by no means an uncommon appearance in some parts of Ireland, but work on the rath was at once indefinitely postponed. Besides raths, old castles, deserted graveyards, ruined churches, secluded glens in the mountains, springs, lakes, and caves all are the homes and resorts of fairies, as is very well known on the west coast.

The better class of fairies are fond of human society and often act as guardians to those they love. In parts of Donegal and Galway they are believed to receive the souls of the dying and escort them to the gates of heaven, not, however, being allowed to enter with them. On this account, fairies love graves and graveyards, having often been seen walking to and fro among the grassy mounds. There are, indeed, some accounts of faction fights among the fairy bands at or shortly after a funeral, the question in dispute being whether the soul of the departed belonged to one or the other faction.

The amusements of the fairies consist of music, dancing, and ball-playing. In music their skill exceeds that of men, while their dancing is perfect, the only drawback being the fact that it blights the grass, "fairy-rings" of dead grass, apparently caused by a peculiar fungous growth, being common in Ireland. Although their musical instruments are few, the fairies use these few with wonderful skill. Near Colooney, in Sligo, there is a "knowlageable woman," whose grandmother's aunt once witnessed a fairy ball, the music for which was furnished by an orchestra which the management had no doubt been at great pains and expense to secure and instruct.

"It was the cutest sight alive. There was a place for thim to shtand on, an' a wondherful big fiddle av the size ye cud slape in it, that was played be a monsthrous frog, an' two little fiddles, that two kittens fiddled on, an' two big drums, baten be cats, an' two trumpets, played be fat pigs. All round the fairies were dancin' like angels, the fireflies givin' thim light to see by, an' the moonbames shinin' on the lake, for it was be the shore it was, an' if ye don't belave it, the glen 's still there, that they call the fairy glen to this blessed day."

The fairies do much singing, seldom, however, save in chorus, and their songs were formerly more frequently heard than at present. Even now a belated peasant, who has been at a wake, or is coming home from a fair, in passing a rath will sometimes hear the soft strains of their voices in the distance, and will hurry away lest they discover his presence and be angry at the intrusion on their privacy. When in unusually good spirits they will sometimes admit a mortal to their revels, but if he speaks, the scene at once vanishes, he becomes insensible, and generally finds himself by the roadside the next morning, "wid that degray av pains in his arrums an' legs an' back, that if sixteen thousand divils were afther him, he cud n't stir a toe to save the sowl av him, that's phat the fairies do be pinchin' an' punchin' him for comin' on them an' shpakin' out loud."

Kindly disposed fairies often take great pleasure in assisting those who treat them with proper respect, and as the favors always take a practical form, there is sometimes a business value in the show of reverence for them. There was Barney Noonan, of the County Leitrim, for instance, "An' sorra a betther boy was in the county than Barney. He 'd work as reg'lar as a pump, an' liked a bit av divarshun as well as annybody when he 'd time for it, that was n't aften, to be sure, but small blame to him, for he was n't rich be no manner o' manes. He 'd a power av ragârd av the good people, an' when he wint be the rath beyant his field, he 'd pull aff his caubeen an' take the dudheen out av his mouth, as p'lite as a dancin' masther, an' say, 'God save ye, ladies an' gintlemen,' that the good people always heard though they niver showed thimselves to him. He 'd a bit o' bog, that the hay was on, an' afther cuttin' it, he left it for to dhry, an' the sun come out beautiful an' in a day or so the hay was as dhry as powdher an' ready to put away.

"So Barney was goin' to put it up, but, it bein' the day av the fair, he thought he 'd take the calf an' sell it, an' so he did, an' comin' up wid the boys, he stayed over his time, bein' hindhered wid dhrinkin' an' dancin' an' palaverin' at the gurls, so it was afther dark when he got home an' the night as black as a crow, the clouds gatherin' on the tops av the mountains like avil sper'ts an' crapin' down into the glens like disthroyin' angels, an' the wind howlin' like tin thousand Banshees, but Barney did n't mind it all wan copper, bein' glorified wid the dhrink he 'd had. So the hay niver enthered the head av him, but in he wint an' tumbled in bed an' was shnorin' like a horse in two minnits, for he was a bach'ler, God bless him, an' had no wife to gosther him an' ax him where he 'd been, an' phat he 'd been at, an' make him tell a hunderd lies about not gettin' home afore. So it came on to thunder an' lighten like as all the avil daymons in the univarse were fightin' wid cannons in the shky, an' by an' by there was a clap loud enough to shplit ye skull an' Barney woke up.

"'Tattheration to me,' says he to himself, 'it 's goin' for to rain an' me hay on the ground. Phat'll I do?' says he.

"So he rowled over on the bed an' looked out av a crack for to see if it was raley rainin'. An there was the biggest crowd he iver seen av little men an' wimmin. They 'd built a row o' fires from the cow-house to the bog an' were comin' in a shtring like the cow goin' home, aitch wan wid his two arrums full o' hay. Some were in the cow-house, resayvin' the hay; some were in the field, rakin' the hay together; an' some were shtandin' wid their hands in their pockets beways they were the bosses, tellin' the rest for to make haste. An' so they did, for every wan run like he was after goin' for the docther, an' brought a load an' hurried back for more.

"Barney looked through the crack at thim a crossin' himself ivery minnit wid admiration for the shpeed they had. 'God be good to me,' says he to himself,' 'tis not ivery gossoon in Leitrim that 's got haymakers like thim,' only he never spake a work out loud, for he knewn very well the good people 'ud n't like it. So they brought in all the hay an' put it in the house an' thin let the fires go out an' made another big fire in front o' the dure, an' begun to dance round it wid the swatest music Barney iver heard.

"Now be this time he 'd got up an' feelin' aisey in his mind about the hay, begun to be very merry. He looked on through the dure at thim dancin', an' by an' by they brought out a jug wid little tumblers and begun to drink summat that they poured out o' the jug. If Barney had the sense av a herrin', he 'd a kept shtill an' let thim dhrink their fill widout openin' the big mouth av him, bein' that he was as full as a goose himself an' naded no more; but when he seen the jug an' the tumblers an' the fairies drinkin' away wid all their mights, he got mad an' bellered out like a bull, 'Arra-a-a-h now, ye little attomies, is it dhrinkin' ye are, an' never givin' a sup to a thirsty mortial that always thrates yez as well as he knows how,' and immedjitly the fairies, an' the fire, an' the jug all wint out av his sight, an' he to bed agin in a timper. While he was layin' there, he thought he heard talkin' an' a cugger-mugger goin' on, but when he peeped out agin, sorra a thing did he see but the black night an' the rain comin' down an' aitch dhrop the full av a wather-noggin. So he wint to slape, continted that the hay was in, but not plazed that the good people 'ud be pigs entirely, to be afther dhrinkin' undher his eyes an' not offer thim a taste, no, not so much as a shmell at the jug.

"In the mornin' up he gets an' out for to look at the hay an' see if the fairies put it in right, for he says, 'It 's a job they 're not used to.' So he looked in the cow-house an' thought the eyes

'ud lave him when there was n't a shtraw in the house at all.
'Holy Moses,' says he, 'phat have they done wid it?' an' he
could n't consave phat had gone wid the hay. So he looked in the
field an' it was all there; bad luck to the bit av it had the fairies
left in the house at all, but when he shouted at thim, they got
tarin' mad an' took all the hay back agin to the bog, puttin' every
shtraw where Barney laid it, an' it was as wet as a drownded cat.
But it was a lesson to him he niver forgot, an' I go bail that the
next time the fairies help him in wid his hay he 'll kape shtill an'
let thim dhrink thimselves to death if they plaze widout sayin' a
word."

The good people have the family relations of husband and
wife, parent and child, and although it is darkly hinted by some
that fairy husbands and wives have as many little disagreements
as are found in mortal households, "for, sure a woman's tongue
is longer than a man's patience, " and "a husband is bound for to
be gosthered day in an' day out, for a woman's jaw is sharpened
on the divil's grindshtone," yet opinions unfavorable to married
happiness among the fairies are not generally received. On the
contrary, it is believed that married life in fairy circles is
regulated on the basis of the absolute submission of the wife to
the husband. As this point was elucidated by a Donegal woman,
"They 're wan, that 's the husband an' the wife, but he 's more
the wan than she is."

The love of children is one of the most prominent traits of
fairy character, but as it manifests itself by stealing beautiful
babes, replacing them by young Leprechawns, the fairies are
much dreaded by west coast mothers, and many precautions are
taken against the elves. Thefts of this kind now rarely occur, but
once they were common, as "in thim owld times ye cud see tin
fairies where there is n't wan now, be razon o' thim lavin' the
counthry."

A notable case of baby stealing occurred in the family of
Termon Magrath, who had a castle, now in picturesque ruins, on

the shore of Lough Erne, in the Country Donegal. The narrator of the incident was "a knowledgable woman," who dwelt in an apology for a cabin, a thatched shed placed against the precipitous side of the glen almost beneath the castle. The wretched shelter was nearly concealed from view by the overhanging branches of a large tree and by thick undergrowth, and seemed unfit for a pig-pen, but, though her surroundings were poor beyond description, "Owld Meg," in the language of

one of her neighbors, "knew a dale av fairies an' witches an' could kape thim from a babby betther than anny woman that iver dhrew the breath av life." A bit of tobacco to enable her to take a "dhraw o' the pipe, an' that warms me heart to the whole worruld," brought forth the story.

"It 's a manny year ago, that Termon Magrath wint, wid all his army, to the war in the County Tyrone, an' while he was gone the babby was born an' they called her Eva. She was her mother's first, so she felt moighty onaisey in her mind about her 's knowin' that the good people do be always afther the first wan that comes, an' more whin it 's a girl that 's in it, that they thry to stale harder than they do a boy, bekase av belavin' they 're aisier fur to rare, though it 's mesilf that does n't belave that same, fur wan girl makes more throuble than tin boys an' is n't a haporth more good.

"So whin the babby was born they sent afther an owld struckawn av a widdy that set up for a wise woman, that knew no more o' doctherin' than a pig av Paradise, but they thought she could kape away the fairies, that 's a job that takes no ind av knowledge in thim that thries it. But the poor owld woman did the best she knew how, an' so, God be good to her, she was n't to be blamed fur that, but it 's the likes av her that do shame thim that 's larned in such things, fur they make people think all wise wimmin as ignerant as hersilf. So she made the sign o' the crass on the babby's face wid ashes, an' towld thim to bit aff its nails and not cut thim till nine weeks, an' held a burnin' candle afore its eyes, so it 'ud do the deeds av light an' not av darkness, an' mixed sugar an' salt an' oil, an' give it to her, that her life 'ud be swate an' long presarved an' go smooth, but the owld widdy forgot wan thing. She did n't put a lucky shamrock, that 's got four leaves, in a gospel an' tie it 'round the babby's neck wid a t'read pulled out av her gown, an' not mindin' this, all the rest was no good at all. No more did she tell the mother not to take her eyes aff the child till the ninth day; afther that the fairies cud n't take it.

"So the nurse tuk the babby in the next room an' laid it on the bed, an' wint away for a minnit, but thinkin' she heard it cry, back she come an' there was the babby, bedclothes an' all just goin' through the flure, bein' dhrawn be the fairies. The nurse scraiched an' caught the clothes an' the maid helped her, so that the two o' thim pulled wid all their mights an' got the bedclothes up agin, but while the child was out o' sight, the fairies changed it an' put a fairy child in its place, but the nurse did n't know phat the fairies done, no more did the owld struckawn, that shows she was an ignerant woman entirely. But the fairies tuk Eva away undher the lake where they trated her beautiful. Every night they gev her a dance, wid the loveliest music that was iver heard, wid big drums an' little drums, an' fiddles an' pipes an' thrumpets, fur such a band the good people do have when they give a dance.

"So she grew an' the quane said she should have a husband among the fairies, but she fell in love wid an owld Leprechawn, an' the quane, to sarcumvint her, let her walk on the shore o' the lake where she met Darby O'Hoolighan an' loved him an' married him be the quane's consint. The quane towld her to tell him if he shtruck her three blows widout a razon, she 'd lave him an' come back to the fairies. The quane gev her a power av riches, shape an' pigs widout number an' more oxen than ye cud count in a week. So she an' Darby lived together as happy as two doves, an' she had n't as much care as a blind piper's dog, morebetoken, they had two boys, good lookin' like their mother an' shtrong as their father.

"Wan day, afther they 'd been marred siventeen year, she an' Darby were goin' to a weddin', an' she was shlow, so Darby towld her fur to harry an' gev her a slap on the shouldher wid the palm av his hand, so she begun to cry. He axed her phat ailed he an' she towld him he 'd shtruck her the first av the three blows. So he was mighty sorry an' said he 'd be careful, but it was n't more than a year after, when he was taichin' wan o' the boys to use a shtick, that she got behind him an' got hit wid the shillaly. That was the second blow, an' made her lose her timper, an' they had a rale quarl. So he got mad, sayin' that nayther o' thim blows ought to be counted, bein' they both come be accident. So he flung the shtick agin the wall, 'Divil take the shtick,' says he, an' went out quick, an' the shtick fell back from the wall an' hit her an the head. 'That's the third,' says she, an' she kissed her sons an' walked out. Thin she called the cows in the field an' they left grazin' an' folly'd her; she called the oxen in the shtalls an' they quit atin' an' come out; an' she shpoke to the calf that was hangin' in the yard, that they 'd killed that mornin' an' it got down an' come along. The lamb that was killed the day afore, it come; an' the pigs that were salted an' thim hangin' up to dhry, they come, all afther her in a shtring. Thin she called to her things in the house, an' the chairs walked out, an' the tables, an' the chist av drawers, an' the boxes, all o' thim put out legs like bastes an' come along, wid the pots an' pans, an' gridiron, an' buckets, an' noggins, an' kish, lavin' the house as bare as a 'victed tinant's, an' all afther her to the lake, where they wint undher an' disappared, an' have n't been seen be man or mortial to this blessed day.

"Now, there 's thim that says the shtory aint thrue, fur, says they, how 'ud a woman do such a thrick as go aff that a way an' take ivery thing she had, just bekase av her husband hittin' her be accident thim three times. But thim that says it forgits that she was a young wan, aven if she did have thim boys I was afther tellin' ye av, an' faith, it 's no lie I 'm sayin', that it 's not in the power av the angels o' God to be knowin' phat a young wan 'ull be doin'. Afther they get owld, an' do be losin' their taythe, an' their beauty goes, thin they 're sober an' get over thim notions; but it takes a dale av time to make an owld wan out av a young wan.

"But she did n't forget the boys she 'd left, an' wanst in a

while she 'd come to the aidge av the lake whin they were clost
be the bank an' spake wid thim, fur aven, if she was half a fairy,
she 'd the mother's heart that the good God put in her bosom;
an' wan time they seen her wid a little attomy av a man alang
wid her, that was a Leprechawn, as they knewn be the look av
him, an' that makes me belave that the rale rayzon av her lavin'
her husband was to get back to the owld Leprechawn she was in
love wid afore she was marr'd to Darby O'Hoolighan."

Far Darrig in Donegal
Letitia Maclintock

PAT DIVER, the tinker, was a man well accustomed to a
wandering life, and to strange shelters; he had shared the
beggar's blanket in smoky cabins; he had crouched beside the
still in many a nook and corner where poteen was made on the
wild Innishowen mountains; he had even slept on the bare
heather, or on the ditch, with no roof over him but the vault of
heaven; yet were all his nights of adventure tame and commonplace when compared with one especial night.

During the day preceding that night, he had mended all the
kettles and saucepans in Moville and Greencastle, and was on
his way to Culdaff, when night overtook him on a lonely
mountain road.

He knocked at one door after another asking for a night's
lodging, while he jingled the halfpence in his pocket, but was

everywhere refused.

Where was the boasted hospitality of Innishowen, which he had never before known to fail? It was of no use to be able to pay when the people seemed so churlish. Thus thinking, he made his way toward a light a little further on, and knocked at another cabin door.

An old man and woman were seated one at each side of the fire.

"Will you be pleased to give me a night's lodging, sir?" asked Pat respectfully.

"Can you tell a story?" returned the old man.

"No, then, sir, I canna say I'm good at story-telling" replied the puzzled tinker.

"Then you maun just gang further, for none but them that can tell a story will get in here."

This reply was made in so decided a tone that Pat did not attempt to repeat his appeal, but turned away reluctantly to resume his weary journey.

"A story, indeed," muttered he. "Auld wives fables to please the weans!"

As he took up his bundle of tinkering implements, he observed a barn standing rather behind the dwelling house, and, aided by the rising moon, he made his way toward it.

It was a clean, roomy barn, with a piled-up heap of straw in one corner. Here was a shelter not to be despised; so Pat crept under the straw, and was soon asleep.

He could not have slept very long when he was awakened by the tramp of feet, and, peeping cautiously through a crevice in his straw covering, he saw four immensely tall men enter the barn, dragging a body, which they threw roughly upon the floor.

They next lighted a fire in the middle of the barn, and fastened the corpse by the feet with a great rope to a beam in the roof. One of them then began to turn it slowly before the fire. "Come on," said he, addressing a gigantic fellow, the tallest of the four—"I'm tired; you be to tak' your turn."

"Faix an' troth, I'll no turn him," replied the big man. "There's Pat Diver in under the straw, why wouldn't he tak' his turn?"

With hideous clamor the four men called the wretched Pat, who, seeing there was no escape, thought it was his wisest plan to come forth as he was bidden.

"Now, Pat," said they, "you'll turn the corpse, but if you let him burn you'll be tied up there and roasted in his place."

Pat's hair stood on end, and the cold perspiration poured from his forehead, but there was nothing for it but to perform his dreadful task.

Seeing him fairly embarked in it, the tall men went away.

Soon, however, the flames rose so high as to singe the rope, and the corpse fell with a great thud upon the fire, scattering the ashes and embers, and extracting a howl of anguish from the miserable cook, who rushed to the door, and ran for his life.

He ran on until he was ready to drop with fatigue, when, seeing a drain overgrown with tall, rank grass, he thought he would creep in there and lie hidden till morning.

But he was not many minutes in the drain before he heard the heavy tramping again, and the four men came up with their burthen, which they laid down on the edge of the drain.

"I'm tired," said one, to the giant; "it's your turn to carry him a piece now."

"Faix and troth, I'll no carry him," replied he, "but there's Pat Diver in the drain, why wouldn't he come out and tak' his turn?"

"Come out, Pat, come out," roared all the men, and Pat, almost dead with fright, crept out.

He staggered on under the weight of the corpse until he reached Kiltown Abbey, a ruin festooned with ivy, where the brown owl hooted all night long, and the forgotten dead slept around the walls under dense, matted tangles of brambles and ben-weed.

No one ever buried there now, but Pat's tall companions turned into the wild graveyard, and began digging a grave.

Pat, seeing them thus engaged, thought he might once more try to escape, and climbed up into a hawthorn tree in the fence, hoping to be hidden in the boughs.

"I'm tired," said the man who was digging the grave; "here, take the spade," addressing the big man, "it's your turn."

"Faix an' troth, it's no my turn," replied he, as before. "There's Pat Diver in the tree, why wouldn't he come down and tak' his turn?"

Pat came down to take the spade, but just then the cocks in the little farmyards and cabins round the abbey began to crow, and the men looked at one another.

"We must go," said they, "and well is it for you, Pat Diver, that the cocks crowed, for if they had not, you'd just ha' been bundled into that grave with the corpse."

Two months passed, and Pat had wandered far and wide over the county Donegal, when he chanced to arrive at Raphoe during a fair.

Among the crowd that filled the Diamond he came suddenly on the big man.

"How are you, Pat Diver?" said he, bending down to look into the tinker's face.

"You've the advantage of me, sir, for I havna' the pleasure of knowing you," faltered Pat.

"Do you not know me, Pat?" Whisper—"When you go back to Innishowen, you'll have a story to tell!"

The Brown Man
Gerald Griffin

IN A LONELY CABIN, in a lonely glen, on the shores of a lonely lough in one of the most lonesome districts of west Munster, lived a lone woman named Guare. She had a beautiful girl, a daughter named Nora. Their cabin was the only one within three miles round them every way. As to their mode of living, it was simple enough, for all they had was one little garden of white cabbage, and they had eaten that down to a few heads between them, a sorry prospect in a place where even a handful of *prishoc* weed was not to be had without sowing it.

It was a very fine morning in those parts, for it was only snowing and hailing, when Nora and her mother were sitting at the door of their little cottage, and laying out plans for the next day's dinner. On a sudden, a strange horseman rode up to the door. He was strange in more ways than one. He was dressed in brown, his hair was brown, his eyes were brown, his boots were brown, he rode a brown horse, and he was followed by a brown dog.

"I'm come to marry you, Nora Guare," said the Brown Man.

"Ax my mother fusht, if you plaise, sir," said Nora, dropping him a curtsy.

"You'll not refuse, ma'am," said the Brown Man to the old mother, "I have money enough, and I'll make your daughter a lady, with servants at her call, and all manner of fine doings about her." And so saying, he flung a purse of gold into the widow's lap.

"Why then the heavens speed you and her together, take her away with you, and make much of her," said the old mother, quite bewildered with all the money.

"Agh, agh," said the Brown Man, as he placed her on his horse behind him without more ado. "Are you all ready now?"

"I am!" said the bride. The horse snorted, and the dog barked, and almost before the word was out of her mouth, they were all whisked away out of sight. After traveling a day and a night, faster than the wind itself, the Brown Man pulled up his horse in the middle of the Mangerton mountain, in one of the most lonesome places that eye ever looked on.

"Here is my estate," said the Brown Man.

"A'then, is it this wild bog you call an estate?" said the bride.

"Come in, wife; this is my palace," said the bridegroom.

"What! a clay-hovel, worse than my mother's!"

They dismounted, and the horse and the dog disappeared in an instant, with a horrible noise, which the girl did not know whether to call snorting, barking, or laughing.

"Are you hungry?" said the Brown Man. "If so, there is your dinner."

"A handful of raw white-eyes [potatoes] and a grain of salt!"

"And when you are sleepy, here is your bed," he continued, pointing to a little straw in a corner, at sight of which Nora's limbs shivered and trembled again. It may be easily supposed that she did not make a very hearty dinner that evening, nor did her husband either.

In the dead of the night, when the clock of Muckross Abbey had just tolled one, a low neighing at the door and a soft barking at the window were heard. Nora feigned sleep. The Brown Man passed his hand over her eyes and face. She snored. "I'm coming," said he, and he arose gently from her side. In half an hour after she felt him by her side again. He was cold as ice.

The next night the same summons came. The Brown Man rose. The wife feigned sleep. He returned, cold. The morning came.

The next night came. The bell tolled at Muckross, and was heard across the lakes. The Brown Man rose again, and passed a light before the eyes of the feigning sleeper. None slumber so sound as they who *will* not wake. Her heart trembled, but her frame was quiet and firm. A voice at the door summoned the husband.

"You are very long coming. The earth is tossed up, and I am hungry. Hurry! Hurry! Hurry! if you would not lose all."

"I'm coming!" said the Brown Man. Nora rose and followed instantly. She beheld him at a distance winding through a lane of frost-nipped sallow trees. He often paused and looked back, and once or twice retraced his steps to within a few yards of the tree, behind which she had shrunk. The moonlight, cutting the shadow close and dark about her, afforded the best concealment. He again proceeded, and she followed. In a few minutes they reached the old Abbey of Muckross. With a sickening heart she saw him enter the churchyard. The wind rushed through the huge yew-tree and startled her. She mustered courage enough, however, to reach the gate of the churchyard and look in. The Brown Man, the horse, and the dog, were there seated by an open grave, eating something and glancing their brown, fiery eyes about in every direction. The moonlight shone full on them and her. Looking down towards her shadow on the earth, she started with horror to observe it move, although she was herself perfectly still. It waved its black arms, and motioned her back. What the feasters said, she understood not, but she seemed still fixed in the spot. She looked once more on her shadow; it raised one hand, and pointed the way to the lane; then slowly rising from the ground, and confronting her, it walked rapidly off in that direction. She followed as quickly as might be.

She was scarcely in her straw, when the door creaked behind, and her husband entered. He lay down by her side and started.

"Uf! Uf!" said she, pretending to be just awakened, "how cold you are, my love!"

"Cold, inagh? Indeed you're not very warm yourself, my dear, I'm thinking."

"Little admiration I shouldn't be warm, and you laving me alone this way at night, till my blood is snow broth, no less."

"Umph!" said the Brown Man, as he passed his arm round her waist. "Ha! your heart is beating fast?"

"Little admiration it should. I am not well, indeed. Them praties and salt don't agree with me at all."

"Umph!" said the Brown Man.

The next morning as they were sitting at the breakfast table together, Nora plucked up a heart and asked leave to go to see her mother. The Brown Man, who ate nothing, looked at her in a way that made her think he knew all. She felt her spirit die away within her.

"If you only want to see your mother," said he, "there is no occasion for your going home. I will bring her to you here. I didn't marry you to be keeping you gadding."

The Brown Man then went out and whistled for his dog and his horse. They both came; and in a very few minutes they pulled up at the old widow's cabin-door.

The poor woman was very glad to see her son-in-law, though she did not know what could bring him so soon.

"Your daughter sends her love to you, mother," says the Brown Man, the villain, "and she'd be obliged to you for a *loand* of a *shoot* of your best clothes, as she's going to give a grand party, and the dressmaker has disappointed her."

"To be sure and welcome," said the mother; and making up a bundle of clothes, she put them into his hands.

"Whogh! whogh!" said the horse as they drove off, "that was well done. Are we to have a mail of her?"

"Easy, ma-coppuleen, and you'll get your 'nough before night," said the Brown Man, "and you likewise, my little dog."

"Boh!" cried the dog, "I'm in no hurry—I hunted down a doe this morning that was fed with milk from the horns of the moon."

Often in the course of that day did Nora Guare go to the door, and cast her eye over the weary flat before it, to discern, if possible, the distant figures of her bridegroom and mother. The dusk of the second evening found her alone in the desolate cot. She listened to every sound. At length the door opened, and an old woman, dressed in a new jock, and leaning on a staff, entered the hut. "O mother, are you come?" said Nora, and was about to rush into her arms, when the old woman stopped her.

"Whisht! whisht! my child!—I only stepped in before the man to know how you like him? Speak softly, in dread he'd hear you—he's turning the horse loose, in the swamp, abroad, over."

"O mother, mother! such a story!"

"Whisht! easy again—how does he use you?"

"Sarrow worse. That straw my bed, and them white-eyes — and bad ones they are—all my diet. And 'tisn't that same, only—"

"Whisht! easy, again! He'll hear you, maybe—Well?"

"I'd be easy enough only for his own doings. Listen, mother. The fusht night, I came about twelve o'clock—"

"Easy, speak easy, eroo!"

"He got up at the call of the horse and the dog, and out a good hour. He ate nothing next day. The second night, and the second day, it was the same story. The third—"

"Husht! husht! Well, the third night?"

"The third night I said I'd watch him. Mother, don't hold my hand so hard . . . He got up, and I got up after him . . . Oh, don't laugh, mother, for 'tis frightful . . . I followed him to Muckross churchyard . . . Mother, mother, you hurt my hand . . . I looked in at the gate—there was great moonlight there, and I could see everything as plain as day."

"Well, darling—husht! softly! What did you see?"

"My husband by the grave, and the horse, . . . Turn your head aside, mother, for your breath is very hot . . . and the dog and they eating.—Ah, you are not my mother!" shrieked the miserable girl, as the Brown Man flung off his disguise, and stood before her, grinning worse than a blacksmith's face through a horse-collar. He just looked at her one moment, and then darted his long fingers into her bosom, from which the red blood spouted in so many streams. She was very soon out of all pain, and a merry supper the horse, the dog, and the Brown Man had that night, by all accounts.

Satan as a Sculptor

D.R. McAnally, Jr.

NEAR ONE OF the fishing villages which abound on the Clare coast, a narrow valley runs back from the sea into the mountains, opening between two precipices that, ages ago, were rent asunder by the forces of nature. On entering the valley by the road leading from the seashore, nothing can be seen but barren cliffs and craggy heights, covered here and there by patches of the moss peculiar to the country. After making some progress, the gorge narrows, the moss becomes denser on the overhanging rocks; trees, growing out of clefts in the precipices, unite their branches above the chasm, and shroud the depths, so that, save an hour or two at noon, the rays of the sun do not penetrate to the crystal brook, rippling along at the bottom over its bed of moss-covered pebbles,—now flashing white as it leaps down a declivity, now hiding itself under the overreaching ferns, now coming again into the light, but always hurrying on as though eager to escape from the dark, gloomy retreat, and, for a moment, enjoy the sunshine of the wider valley beyond before losing its life in the sea.

At a narrow turn in the valley and immediately over the spot where the brook has its origin in a spring bursting out of a crevice in the rock and falling into a circular well partly scooped out, partly built up for the reception of the sparkling water, a cliff rises perpendicularly to the height of fifty feet, surmounted, after a break in the strata, by another, perhaps twenty feet higher, the upper portion being curiously wrought by nature's chisel into the shape of a human countenance. The forehead is shelving, the eyebrows heavy and menacing; the nose large and hooked like the beak of a hawk; the upper lip short, the chin prominent and pointed, while a thick growth of ferns in the shelter of the crag forming the nose gives the impression of a small mustache and goatee. Above the forehead a mass of tangled undergrowth and ferns bears a strong resemblance to an Oriental turban. An eye is plainly indicated by a bit of light-colored stone, and altogether the face has a sinister leer, that, in an ignorant age, might easily inspire the fears of a superstitious people.

On a level with the chin and to the right of the face is the mouth of a cave, reached by a path up the hillside, rude steps in the rock rendering easier the steep ascent. The cave can be entered only by stooping, but inside a room nearly seven feet high and about twelve feet square presents itself. Undoubtedly the cave was once the abode of an anchorite, for on each side of the entrance a Latin cross is deeply carved in the rock, while within, at the further side, and opposite the door, a block of stone four feet high was left for an altar. Above it, a shrine is hollowed out of the stone wall, and over the cavity is another cross, surmounted by the mystic I.H.S.

The legend of the cave was told by an old "wise woman" of the neighborhood with a minuteness of detail that rendered the narrative more tedious than graphic. A devout believer in the

truth of her own story, she told it with wonderful earnestness, combining fluency of speech with the intonations of oratory.

"'T is the cave av the saint, but phat saint I 'm not rightly sartain. Some say it was Saint Patrick himself, but 't is I don't belave that same. More say it was the blessed Saint Kevin, him that done owld King O'Toole out av his land in the bargain he made fur curin' his goose, but that 's not thrue aither, an' it 's my consate they 're right that say it was Saint Tigernach, the same that built the big Abbey av Clones in Monaghan. His Riverince, Father Murphy, says that same, an' sorra a wan has a chance av knowin' betther than him.

"An' the big head on the rock there is the divil's face that the saint made him put there, the time the blessed man was too shmart fur hi whin the Avil Wan thried to do him.

"A quare owld shtory it is, an' the quol'ty that come down here on the coast laugh if it 's towld thim, an' say it 's a t'underin' big lie that 's in it, bekase they don't undhershtand it, but if men belaved nothin' they did n't undhershtand, it 's a short craydo they 'd have. But I was afther tellin', Saint Tigernach lived in the cave, it bein' him an' no other; morebetoken, he was a good man an' shrewder than a fox. He made the cave fur himself an' lived there, an' ivery day he 'd say tin thousand paters, an' five thousand aves, an' a thousand craydos, an' thin go out among the poor. There was n't manny poor thin in Ireland, Glory be to God, fur the times was betther thin, but phat there was looked up to the saint, fur he was as good as a cupboard to thim, an' whin he begged fur the poor, sorra a man 'ud get from him till he 'd given him a copper or more, fur he 'd shtick like a constable to ye till he 'd get his money. An' all that were parshecuted, an' the hungry, an' naked, and God's poor, wint to the saint like a child to its mother an' towld him the whole o' their heart.

"While the blessed saint lived here, over acrass the hill an' beyant the peat-bog there was a hedger an' ditcher named

O'Connor. He was only a poor laborin' man, an' the owld woman helped him, while his girl, be the name o' Kathleen, tinded the house, fur I must tell ye, they kept a boord in the corner beways av a bar an' a jug wid potheen that they sowld to thim that passed, fur it was afore the days av the gaugers, bad cess to thim, an' ivery man dhrunk phat he plazed widout payin' a pinny to the govermint. So O'Connor made the potheen himself an' Kathleen sowld it to the turf-cutters, an' mighty little did they buy, bekase they 'd no money. She was a fine girl, wid a pair av eyes that 'ud dint the hearts av owld an' young, an' wid a dacint gown fur the week an' a clane wan fur the Sunday, an' just such a girl as 'ud make an owld felly feel himself young agin. Sorra the taste av divilmint was there in the girl at all, fur she was good as the sunshine in winther an' as innycent as a shpring lamb, an' wint to church an' did her jooty reglar.

"She was afther fallin' in love wid a young felly that done ditchin' an' they were to be marr'd whin he got his house done an' his father gev him a cow. He was n't rich be no manes, but as fur feelin' poverty, he never dhreamt o' such a thing, fur he 'd the love o' Kathleen an' thought it a forchune.

"In thim thimes the castle at the foot o' the hill was kept be a lord, that wid roomytisms an' panes in his jints was laid on his bed all the time, and the son av him, Lord Robert, was the worst man to be runnin' afther girls iver seen in the County Clare. He was the dandy among thim an' broke the hearts o' thim right an' lift like he was shnappin' twigs undher his feet. Manny a wan he desaved an' let go to the gods, as they did at wanst, fur whin the divil gets his foot on a woman's neck, she niver lifts her head agin.

"Wan day, Lord Robert's father's roomytism got the betther av him an' laid him out, an' they gev him an iligant wake an' berryin', an' while they were at the grave Lord Robert looked up an' seen Kathleen shtandin' among the people an' wondhered who she was. So he come into the eshtate an' got a stable full av horses an' dogs, an' did a power o' huntin', an' as he was a sojer, he 'd a shwarm av throopers at the cassel, all the like av himself. But not long afther the berryin', Lord Robert was huntin' in the hills, an' he come down towards the bog an' seen O'Connor's cabin, an' says to his man, 'Bedad, I wondher if they 've a dhrop to shpare here, I 'm mortial dhry.' So in they wint, an' axed an' got thim their dhrink, an' thin he set the wicked eyes av him on the girl an' at wanst remimbered her.

"'It 's a mighty fine girl ye are,' says he to Kathleen thin, an' fit fur the house av a prince.'

"'None o' yer deluderhin' talk to me, Sorr,' says Kathleen to him. "I know ye, an' it 's no good I know av ye,' says she to him. 'T was the good girl she was an' as firm as a landlord in a bad year when she thought there was anny avil intinded.

"So he wint away that time an' come agin an' agin when he was huntin' an' always had some impidince to say at her. She towld her parrents av it, an' though they did n't like it at all, they was n't afeared fur the girl, an' he 'd spind more in wan dhrinkin' than they 'd take in in a week, so they were not sorry to see him come, but ivery time he come he wint away more detarmined to have the girl, an' whin he found he cud n't get her be fair manes he shwore he 'd do it be foul. So wanst, whin she 'd been cowlder to him than common an' would n't have a prisint he brought her, he says to her, 'Begob, I 'll bring ye to terms. If ye won't accept me prisints, I 'll make ye bend yer will widout prisints,' an' he wint away. She got frighted, an' whin she saw Tim Maccarty, she towld him av Lord Robert an' phat he said. Well, it made Tim mighty mad. 'Tatther an' agers,' says he, 'be the powers, I 'll break every bone in his body if he lays a finger on yer showlder; but, fur all that, whin Tim got to thinkin', he got skairt av Kathleen.

"'Sure,' says he to himself, 'ain't wimmin like glass jugs, that 'll break wid the laste touch? I 'll marry her immejitly an' take out av Clare into Kerry,' says he, 'an' let him dare to come afther her there,' says he, for he knewn that if Lord Robert came into the Kerry mountains, the boys 'ud crack his shkull wid the same compuncshusness that they 'd have to an egg shell. So he left aff the job an' convaynienced himself to go to Kathleen that night an' tell her his belafe.

"'Am n't I afeared fur ye, me darlin',' says he, 'and would n't I dhrowned me in the say if anny harm 'ud come to ye, so I think we 'd betther be married at wanst.'

"So Kathleen consinted an' made a bundle av her Sunday gown, an' they shtarted fur the saint's cave, that bein' the nearest place they cud be marr'd at, an' being' marr'd be him was like bein' marr'd be a priest.

"So they wint alang the road to where the foot-path laves it be the oak-tree, then up the path an' through the boreen to where Misther Dawson's black mare broke her leg jumpin' the hedge, an' whin they rached that shpot they heard a noise on the road behint thim an' stud be the hedge, peepin' through to have a look at it an' see phat it was. An' there was Lord Robert an' a dozen av his bad min, wid their waypons an' the armor on thim shinin' in the moonlight. It was ridin' to O'Connor's they were, an' whin Tim an' Kathleen set their eyes on thim, they seen they 'd made a narrer eshcape.

"Howandiver, as soon as Lord Robert an' his min were out o' sight, they ran wid all their shpeed, an' lavin' the path where Dennis Murphy fell into the shtrame lasht winter comin' back from Blanigan's wake whin he 'd had too much, they tuk the rise o' the hill, an' that was a mishtake. If they 'd kep be the hedge an' 'round be the foot-bridge, then up the footway the other side o' the brook an' ferninst the mill, they 'd have kep out o' sight, an' been safe enough; but as they were crassin' the hill, wan av Robert's min saw thim, fur it was afther the girl he was sure enough, an' whin he found from her father her an' Tim were gone, they rode aff here an' there sarchin' afther thim. Whin the sojer shpied thim on the top o' the hill, he blew his thrumpet, an' here come all the rest shtreelin' along on the run, round the hill as fast as their bastes 'ud take thim, fur they guessed where the two 'ud be goin'. An' Katleen an' Tim come tumblin' down the shlope, an' bad luck to the minnit they 'd to shpare whin they got into the cave before there was the whole gang, wid their horses puffin', an' their armors rattlin' like a pedler's tins.

"The saint was on a pile av shtraw in the corner, shnorin' away out av his blessed nose, fur it was as sound aslape as a pig he was, bein' tired entirely wid a big day's job, an' did n't wake up wid their comin' in. So Lord Robert an' his min left their horse below an' climbed up an' looked in, but cud see nothin' be razon av the darkness.

"'Arrah now,' says he, 'Kathleen, come along out o' that now, fur I 've got ye safe an' sound.'

"They answered him niver a word, but he heard a noise that was the saint turnin' over on his bed bein' onaisey in his slape.

"'Come along out o' that,' he repaited; 'an' you, Tim Maccarty, if ye come out, ye may go back to yer ditchin', but if ye wait fur me to fetch ye, the crows 'ull be atin' ye at sunrise. Shtrike a light,' says he. So they did, an' looked in an' saw Tim an' Kathleen, wan on aitch side o' the althar, holdin' wid all their mights to the crass that was on it.

"'Dhrag thim out av it,' says Lord Robert, an' the min went in, but afore they come near thim, Saint Tigernach shtopped shnorin', bein' wakened wid the light an' jabberin', an' shtud up on the flure.

"'Howld on now,' says the blessed saint, 'phat 's the matther here? Phat 's all this murtherin' noise about?' says he.

"Lord Robert's min all dhrew back, for there was a power o' fear av the saint in the county, an' Lord Robert undhertuk to axplain that the girl was a sarvint av his that run away wid that thafe av a ditcher, but Saint Tigernach seen through the whole thrick at wanst.

"'Lave aff,' says he. 'Don't offer fur to thrape thim lies on

me. pack aff wid yer murtherers, or it 's the curse ye 'll get afore
ye can count yer fingers,' an' wid that all the min went out, an'
Lord Robert afther thim, an' all he cud say 'ud n't pervail on the
sojers to go back afther the girl.

"'No, yer Anner,' says they to him; 'we ate yer Anner's
mate, an' dhrink yer Anner's dhrink, an' 'ull do yer Anner's
biddin' in all that 's right. We 're parfectly willin' to wait till
mornin' an' murther the ditcher an' shtale the girl whin they
come out an' get away from the saint, but he mus n't find it out.
It 's riskin' too much. Begorra, we 've got sowls to save,' says
they, so they all got on their horses an' shtarted back to the
cassel.

"Lord Robert folly'd thim a bit, but the avil heart av him
was so set on Kathleen that he cud n't bear the thought av lettin'
her go. So whin he got to the turn av the road, 'T'underation,'
says he, ''t is the wooden head that 's set on me showldhers, that
I did n't think av the witch afore.'

"Ye see, in the break av the mountains beyant the mill,
where the rath is, there was in thim times the cabin av a great
witch. 'T was a dale av avil she done the County Clare wid
shtorms an' rainy sayzons an' cows lavin' aff their milk, an' she
'd a been dhrownded long afore, but fur fear av the divil, her
masther, that was at her elbow, whinever she 'd crook her finger.
So to her Lord Robert wint, an' gev a rap on the dure, an' in.
There she sat wid a row av black cats on aitch side, an' the full
av a shkillet av sarpints a-shtewin' on the fire. He knew her well,
fur she 'd done jobs fur him afore, so he made bowld to shtate
his arriant widout so much as sayin' good day to ye. The owld
fagot made a charm to call her masther, an' that minnit he was
shtandin' be her side, bowin' an' schrapin' an' shmilin' like a
gintleman come to tay. He an' Lord Robert fell to an' had a
power av discoorse on the bargain, fur Robert was a sharp wan
an' wanted the conthract onsartain-like, hopin' to chate the divil
at the end, as we all do, be the help av God, while Satan thried to

make it shtronger than a tinant's lace. Afther a dale av palatherin', they aggrade that the divil was to do all that Lord Robert axed him fur twinty years, an' then to have him sowl an' body; but if he failed, there was an end av the bargain. But there was a long face on the owld felly whin the first thing he was bid to do was to bring Kathleen out o' the cave an' carry her to the cassel.

"'By Jayminny,' says Satan, 'it 's no aisey job fur to be takin' her from the power av a great sant like him,' a-scratchin' his head. 'But come on, we 'll thry.'

"So the three av thim mounted on the wan horse, Lord Robert in the saddle, the divil behind, an' the witch in front av him, an' away like the wind to the cave. Whin they got to the turn o' the hill, they got aff an' hid in the bushes bechune the cave an' the shpring, bekase, as Satan axplained to Lord Robert, ivery night, just at midnight, the saint wint to get him a dhrink av wather, bein' dhry wid the devotions, an' 'ud bring the full av a bucket back wid him.

"'We 'll shtop him be the shpring,' says the divil, 'wid the witch, an' you an' me 'ull shtale the girl while he 's talkin'.

"So while the clock was shtrikin' fur twilve, out come the saint wid the wather-bucket an' shtarted to the shpring. Whin he got there an' was takin' his dhrink, up comes the witch an' begins tellin' him av a son she had (she was purtindin', ye ondhershtand, an' lyin' to him) that was as lazy as a câr-horse an' as much in the way as a sore thumb, an' axin' the saint's advice phat to do wid him, while Satan an' Lord Robert ran into the cave. The divil picked up Kathleen in his arrums, but he dar n't have done that same, only she was on the other side av the cave an' away from the althar, but Tim was shtandin' by it, an' shtarted out wid her kickin' an' schraichin'. Tim ran to grip him, but Satan tossed him back like a ball an' he fell on the flure.

"'Howld on till I shtick him,' says Lord Robert, pullin' out his soord.

"'Come on, ye bosthoon,' says Satan to him. 'Sure the saint 'ull be on us if we don't get away quick,' an' bedad, as he said thim words, the dure opened, an' in come Saint Tigernach wid a bucket av wather on his arrum an' in a hurry, fur he misthrusted something.

"'God's presince be about us,' says the blessed saint, whin he saw the divil, an' the turkey-bumps begun to raise on his blessed back an' the shweat a-comin' o his face, fur he knewn Satan well enough, an' consaved the owld felly had come fur himself be razon av a bit o' mate he ate that day, it bein' av a Friday; axceptin' he did n't ate the mate but only tasted it an' then spit it out agin to settle a quarl bechune a butcher an' a woman that bought the mate an' said it was bad, only he was afeared Satan did n't see him when he sput it out agin. 'God's presince be about us,' says the saint, a-crossin' himself as fast as he cud. In a minnit though, he seen it was n't him, but Kathleen, that was in it, an' let go the wather an' caught the blessed crass that was hangin' on him wid his right hand an' gripped Satan be the throat wid his lift, a-pushin' the crass in his face.

"The divil dhropped Kathleen like it was a bag av male she was, an' she rolled over an' over on the flure like a worrum till she raiched the althar an' stuck to it as tight as the bark on a tree. An' a fine thing it was to see the inimy av our sowls a-lyin' there trimblin', wid the saint's fut on his neck.

"'Glory be to God,' says the saint. 'Lie you there till I make an example av ye,' says he, an' turned to look fur Lord Robert, bekase he knewn the two o' thim 'ud be in it. But the Sassenagh naded no invitation to be walkin' aff wid himself, but whin he seen phat come to the divil, he run away wid all the legs he had, an' the witch wid him, an' Tim afther thim wid a whoop an' a fishtful av shtones. But they left him complately an' got away disconsarted, an' Tim come back.

"'Raise up,' says Saint Tigernach to the divil, 'an' shtand in the corner,' makin' the blessed sign on the ground afore him.

'I'm afther marryin' these two at wanst, widout fee or license, an' you shall be the witness.'

"So he married thim there, while the divil looked on. Faix, it 's no lie I 'm tellin' ye; it 's not the onliest marryin' the divil 's been at, but he 's not aften seen at thim when he 's in as low sper'ts as he was at that. But it was so that they were married wid Satan fur a witness, an' some says the saint thransported thim to Kerry through the air, but 't is n't meself that belaves that same, but that they walked to Kilrush an' wint to Kerry in a fisherman's boat.

"Afther they 'd shtarted, the saint turns to Satan an' says, 'No more av yer thricks wid them two, me fine felly, fur I mane to give you a job that 'll kape ye out av mischief fur wan time at laste,' fur he was mightily vexed wid him a-comin' that-a-way right into his cave the same as if the place belonged to him.

"'Go you to work,' says he, 'an' put yer face on the rock over the shpring, so that as long as the mountain shtands min can come an' see phat sort av a dirthy lookin' baste ye are.'

"So Satan wint out an' looked up at the rock, shmilin', as fur to say that was not great matther, an' whin the blessed man seen the grin that was on him, he says, 'None av yer inchantmints will I have at all, at all. It 's honest work ye 'll do, an' be the same token, here 's me own hammer an' chisel that ye 'll take,' an' wid that the divil looked mighty sarious, an' left aff grinnin' for he parsaived the clift was granite.

"'Sure it 's jokin' yer Riverince is,' says he, 'ye don't mane it. Sorra the harder bit av shtone bechuxt this an' Donegal,' an' it was thrue for him, fur he knewn the coast well.

"'Bad luck to the taste av a lie 's in it,' says the saint. 'So take yer waypons an' go at it, owld Buck-an'-Whye, fur the sooner ye begin, the quicker ye 'll be done, an' the shtone won't soften be yer watin'. Mind ye kape a civil tongue in yer head while ye 're at the job, or it'll be a holiday to the wan I 'll find ye,' says he, lookin' at him very fierce.

"So wid great displazemint, Satan tuk the hammer an' chisel, an' climbed up an' wint to work a cuttin' his own face on the shtone, an' it was as hard as iron it was, an whin he 'd hit it a couple av cracks, he shtopped an' shuck his head an' thin scratched over his year wid the chisel an' looked round at the saint as fur to say somethin', but the blessed saint looked at him agin so fayroshus, that he made no raimark at all, but turned back to the clift quick an' begun to hammer away in airnest till the shweat shtud on his haythenish face like the dhrops on a wather-jug.

"On the next day, Lord Robert thought he 'd call the owld Inimy, an' remind him that, bein' as he 'd failed to get Kathleen, their bargain was aff. So he made the charm Satan gev him, but he did n't come fur anny thrial he 'd make.

"'Bad scran to the Imp,' says he. 'Sure he must be mighty busy or maybe he 's forgot entirely.'

"So he out an' wint to see the witch, bu she was n't in, an' while he was waitin' for her, bein' not far away from the saint's cave, he thought he 'd have a peep, an' see if Tim an' Kathleen were shtill there. So he craweled over the top o' the hill beyant the cave like the sarpint that he was, an' whin he come down a little, he seen the owld Pooka on the clift, wid the hammer in wan hand an' the chisel in the other a poundin' away at the rock an' hangin' on be his tail to a tree. Lord Robert thought the eyes 'ud lave his head, fur he seen it was the divil sure enough, but he cud n't rightly make out phat he was doin'. So he crawled down till he seen, an' thin, when he undhershtood, he riz an' come an' took a sate on a big shtone ferninst the clift, a shlappin' his legs wid his hands, an' roarin' an' the wather bilin' out av his eyes wid laughin'.

"'Hilloo Nickey,' says he, when he 'd got his breath agin an' cud shpake. "Is it yerself that 's in it?' Mind the impidince av him, shpakin' that familiar to the inimy av our sowls, but faix, he 'd a tongue like a jews harp, an' cud use it too.

"'Kape from me,' says Satan to him agin, as crass as two shticks, an' widout turnin' his head fur to raigârd him. 'Lave me! Begorra, I 'll wipe the clift aff wid yer carkidge if ye come anny closter,' says he.

"'A-a-a-h, woorroo, now. Aisey, ye desayvin' owld blaggârd,' says Lord Robert, as bowld as a ram, fur he knewn that Satan dare n't lave the job to come at him. 'Will ye kape yer timper? Sure ye have n't the manners av a goat; to be shpakin' to a gintleman like that. I 've just come to tell ye that bein' ye failed, our bargain 's aff,' says he.

"'Out wid ye,' says the divil, turnin' half round an' howldin' be wan hand to the big shtone nose he 'd just done, an' shakin' the other fist wid the chisel in it at Lord Robert. 'D' ye think I want to be aggervated wid the likes av ye, ye whey-faced shpalpeen, an' me losin' the whole day, an' business pressin' at this saison, an' breakin' me back on the job, an' me fingers sore wid the chisel, an' me tail shkinned wid howldin' on? Bad luck to the shtone, it 's harder than a Scotchman's head, it is, so it is,' says he, turnin' back agin when he seen the saint at the dure av the cave. An' thin he begun a peckin' away at the clift fur dear life, shwearin' to himself, so the saint cud n't hear him, every time he give his knuckles an onlucky crack wid the hammer.

"'Ye 're not worth the throuble,' says he to Lord Robert; he was that full av rage he cud n't howld in. 'It 's a paltherin' gossoon I was fur thriflin' wid ye whin I was sure ave ye annyhow.'

"'Yer a liar,' says Lord Robert, 'ye desaivin' nagurly Haythen. If ye was sure o' me phat did ye want to make a bargain fur?'

"'Yer another,' says Satan. 'Is n't a sparrer in yer hand betther than a goose on a shtring?'

"So they were goin' on wid the blaggârdin' match, whin the blessed saint, that come out whin he heard thim begin, an' thin set on the dure a-watchin', to see that owld Nick did n't schamp the job, interfared.

"'Howld yer pace, Satan, an' kape at yer work,' says he. 'An' for you, ye blatherin', milk-faced villin, wid the heart as black as a crow, walk aff wid ye an' go down on yer hard-hearted onbelavin' knees, or it 's no good 'ull come o' ye.' An' so he did.

"Do I belave the shtory? Troth, I dunno. It 's quare things happened in them owld days, an' there 's the face on the clift as ugly as the divil cud be an' the hammer an' chisel are in the church an' phat betther proof cud ye ax?

"Phat come av the lovers? No more do I know that, barrin' they grew owld an' shtayed poor an' forgot the shpringtime av youth in the winter av age, but if they lived a hunderd years, they niver forgot the marryin' in the saint's cave, wid the black face av the Avil Wan lookin' on from the dark corner."

Donald and His Neighbors
Traditional

HUDDEN AND DUDDEN and Donald O'Nery were near neighbors
in the barony of Balinconlig, and plowed with three bullocks;
but the two former, envying the present prosperity of the latter,
determined to kill his bullock, to prevent his farm from being
properly cultivated and labored, that going back in the world he
might be induced to sell his lands, which they meant to get
possession of. Poor Donald, finding his bullock killed,
immediately skinned it, and throwing the skin over his shoulder,
with the fleshy side out, set off to the next town with it, to
dispose of it to the best of his advantage. Going along the road a
magpie flew on the top of the hide, and began picking it,
chattering all the time. The bird had been taught to speak, and
imitate the human voice, and Donald, thinking he understood
some words it was saying, put round his hand and caught hold

of it. Having got possession of it, he put it under his greatcoat, and so went on to town. Having sold the hide, he went into an inn to take a dram, and following the landlady into the cellar, he gave the bird a squeeze which made it chatter some broken accents that surprised her very much. "What is that I hear?" said she to Donald. "I think it is talk and yet I do not understand." "Indeed," said Donald, "it is a bird I have that tells me everything, and I always carry it with me to know when there is any danger. "Faith," says he, "it says you have far better liquor than you are giving me." "That is strange," said she, going to another cask of better quality, and asking him if he would sell the bird. "I will," said Donald, "if I get enough for it." "I will fill your hat with silver if you leave it with me." Donald was glad to hear the news, and taking the silver, set off, rejoicing at his good luck. He had not been long at home until he met with Hudden and Dudden. "Mr.," said he, "you thought you had done me a bad turn, but you could not have done me a better; for look here, what I have got for the hide," showing them a hatful of silver; "you never saw such a demand for hides in your life as there is at present." Hudden and Dudden that very night killed their bullocks, and set out the next morning to sell their hides. On coming to the place they went through all the merchants, but could only get a trifle for them; at last they had to take what they could get, and came home in a great rage, and vowing revenge on poor Donald. He had a pretty good guess how matters would turn out, and he being under the kitchen window, he was afraid they would rob him, or perhaps kill him when asleep, and on that account when he was going to bed he left his old mother in his place, and lay down in her bed, which was in the other side of the house, and they taking the old woman for Donald, choked her in her bed, but he making some noise, they had to retreat, and leave the money behind them, which grieved them very much. However by daybreak, Donald got his mother on his back, and carried her to town. Stopping at a well, he fixed his mother with her staff, as if she was stooping for a drink, and then went into a public house convenient and called for a dram. "I wish," said he to a woman that stood near him, "you would tell my mother to come in; she is at yon well trying to get a drink, and she is hard of hearing; if she does not observe you, give her a little shake and tell her that I want her." The woman called her several times, but she seemed to take no notice; at length she went to her and shook her by the arm, but when she let her go again, she tumbled on her head into the well, and, as the woman thought, was drowned. She, in her great surprise and fear at the accident, told Donald what had happened. "O mercy," said he, "what is this?" He ran and pulled her out of the well, weeping and lamenting all the time, and acting in such a manner that you would imagine that he had lost his senses. The woman, on the other hand, was far worse than Donald, for his grief was only feigned, but she imagined herself to be the cause of the old woman's death. The inhabitants of the town, hearing what had happened, agreed to make Donald up a good sum of money for his loss, as the accident happened in their place, and Donald brought a greater sum home with him than he got for the magpie. They buried Donald's mother, and as soon as he saw Hudden and Dudden he showed them the last purse of money he had got. "You thought to kill me last night," said he, "but it was good for me it happened on my mother, for I got all that purse for her to make gunpowder."

That very night Hudden and Dudden killed their mothers, and the next morning set off with them to town. On coming to the town with their burthen on their sacks, they went up and down crying, "Who will buy old wives for gunpowder?" so that everyone laughed at them, and the boys at last clotted them out of the place. They then saw the cheat, and vowed revenge on Donald, buried the old women, and set off in pursuit of him. Coming to his house, they found him sitting at his breakfast, and seizing him, put him in a sack, and went to drown him in a river at some distance. As they were going along the highway they raised a hare, which they saw had but three feet, and throwing off the sack, ran after her, thinking by her appearance she would be easily taken. In their absence there came a drover that way, and hearing Donald singing in the sack, wondered greatly what could be the matter. "What is the reason," said he, "that you are singing, and you confined?" "Oh, I am going to heaven," said Donald, "and in a short time I expect to be free from trouble." "O dear," said the drover, "what will I give you if you let me to your place?" "Indeed, I do not know," said he, "it would take a good sum." "I have not much money," said the drover, "but I have twenty head of fine cattle, which I will give you to exchange places with me." "Well," says Donald, "I do not care if I should loose the sack, and I will come out." In a moment the drover liberated him, and went into the sack himself, and Donald drove home the fine heifers, and left them in his pasture. Hudden and Dudden, having caught the hare, returned, and getting the sack on one of their backs, carried Donald, as they thought, to the river and threw him in, where he immediately sank. They then marched home, intending to take immediate possession of Donald's property, but how great was their surprise when they found him safe at home before them with such a fine herd of cattle, whereas they knew he had none before. "Donald," said they, "what is all this? We thought you were drowned, and yet you are here before us." "Ah !" said he, "if I had but help along with me when you threw me in, it would have been the best job ever I met with, for of all the sight of cattle and gold that ever was seen is there, and no one to own

them, but I was not able to manage more than what you see, and I could show you the spot where you might get hundreds." They both swore they would be his friend, and Donald accordingly led them to a very deep part of the river, and lifted up a stone. "Now," said he, "Watch this," throwing it into the stream; "there is the very place, and go in, one of you first, and if you want help, you have nothing to do but call." Hudden jumping in, and sinking to the bottom, rose up again, and making a bubbling noise, as those do that are drowning, attempted to speak, but could not. "What is that he is saying now?" says Dudden "Faith," says Donald, "he is calling for help; don't you hear him?" "Stand about," said he, running back, "till I leap in. I know how to do it better than any of you." Dudden, to have the advantage of him, jumped in off the bank, and was drowned along with Hudden, and this was the end of Hudden and Dudden.

The Eyes of the Dead
Daniel Corkery

I

IF HE had not put it off for three years John Spillane's homecoming would have been that of a famous man. Bonfires would have been lighted on the hill-tops of Rossamara, and the ships passing by, twenty miles out, would have wondered what they meant.

Three years ago, the *Western Star*, an Atlantic liner, one night tore her iron plates to pieces against the cliff-like face of an iceberg, and in less than an hour sank in the waters. Of the 789 human souls aboard her one only had been saved, John Spillane, able seaman, of Rossamara in the county of Cork. The name of the little fishing village, his own name, his picture, were in all the papers of the world, it seemed, not only because he alone had escaped, but by reason of the manner of that escape. He had clung to a drift of wreckage, must have lost consciousness for more than a whole day, floated then about on the ocean for a second day, for a second night, and had arrived at the threshold of another dreadful night when he was rescued. A fog was coming down on the waters. It frightened him more than the darkness. He raised a shout. He kept on shouting. When safe in the arms of his rescuers his breathy, almost inaudible voice was still forcing out some cry which they interpreted as Help! Help!

That was what had struck the imagination of men—the half-insane figure sending his cry over the waste of waters, the fog thickening, and the night falling. Although the whole world had read also of the groping rescue ship, of Spillane's bursts of hysterical laughter, of his inability to tell his story until he had slept eighteen hours on end, what remained in the memory was the lonely figure sending his cry over the sea.

And then, almost before his picture had disappeared from the papers, he had lost himself in the great cities of the States. To Rossamara no word had come from himself, nor for a long time from any acquaintance; but then, when about a year had gone by, his sister or mother as they went up the road to Mass of a Sunday might be stopped and informed in a whispering voice that John had been seen in Chicago, or, it might be, in New York, or Boston, or San Francisco, or indeed anywhere. And from the meagerness of the messages it was known, with only too much certainty, that he had not, in exchanging sea for land, bettered his lot. If once again his people had happened on such empty tidings of him, one knew it by their bowed and stilly attitude in the little church as the light whisper of the Mass rose and fell about them.

When three years had gone by he lifted the latch of his mother's house one October evening and stood awkwardly in the middle of the floor. It was nightfall and not a soul had seen him break down from the ridge and cross the roadway. He had come secretly from the ends of the earth.

And before he was an hour in their midst he rose up impatiently, timidly, and stole into his bed.

"I don't want any light," he said, and as his mother left him there in the dark, she heard him yield his whole being to a sigh of thankfulness. Before that he had told them he felt tired, a natural thing, since he had tramped fifteen miles from the railway station in Skibbereen. But day followed day without his showing any desire to rise from the bedclothes and go abroad among the people. He had had enough of the sea, it seemed; enough too of the great cities of the States. He was a pity, the neighbors said; and the few of them who from time to time caught glimpses of him, reported him as not yet having lost the scared look that the ocean had left on him. His hair was grey or nearly grey, they said, and, swept back fiercely from his forehead, a fashion strange to the place, seemed to pull his eyes open, to keep them wide open, as he looked at you. His moustache also was grey, they said, and his cheeks were grey too, sunken and dark with shadows. Yet his mother and sister, the only others in the house, were glad to have him back with them; at any rate, they said, they knew where he was.

They found nothing wrong with him. Of speech neither he nor they ever had had the gift; and as day followed day, and week week, the same few phrases would carry them through the day and into the silence of night. In the beginning they had thought it natural to speak with him about the wreck; soon, however, they came to know that it was a subject for which he had no welcome. In the beginning also, they had thought to rouse him by bringing the neighbor to his bedside, but such visits instead of cheering him only left him sunken in silence, almost in despair. The priest came to see him once in a while, and advised the mother and sister, Mary her name was, to treat him as normally as they could, letting on that his useless presence was no affliction to them nor even a burden. In time John Spillane was accepted by all as one of those unseen ones, or seldom-seen ones, who are to be found in every village in the world—the bedridden, the struck-down, the aged—forgotten of all except the few faithful creatures who bring the cup to the bedside of a morning, and open the curtains to let in the sun.

II

In the nearest house, distant a quarter-mile from them, lived Tom Leane. In the old days before John Spillane went to sea, Tom had been his companion, and now of a night-time he would drop in if he had any story worth telling or if, on the day following, he chanced to be going back to Skibbereen, where he might buy the Spillanes such goods as they needed, or sell a pig for them, slipping it in among his own. He was a quiet creature, married, and struggling to bring up the little family that was thickening about him. In the Spillanes' he would, dragging at the pipe, sit on the settle, and quietly gossip with the old woman while Mary moved about on the flags putting the household gear tidy for the night. But all three of them, as they kept up the simple talk, were never unaware of the silent listener in the lower room. Of that room the door was kept open; but no lamp was lighted within it; no lamp indeed was needed, for a shaft of light from the kitchen struck into it showing one or two of the religious pictures on the wall and giving sufficient light to move about in. Sometimes the conversation would drift away from the neighborly doings, for even to Rossamara tidings from the great world abroad would sometimes come; in the middle of such gossip, however, a sudden thought would strike Tom Leane, and, raising his voice, he would blurt out: "But sure 'tis foolish for the like of me to be talking about these far-off places, and that man inside after traveling the world, over and thither." The man inside, however, would give no sign whatever whether their gossip had been wise or foolish. They might hear the bed creak, as if he had turned with impatience at their mention of his very presence.

There had been a spell of stormy weather, it was now the middle of February, and for the last five days at twilight the gale seemed always to set in for a night of it. Although there was scarcely a house around that part of the southwest Irish coast that had not some one of its members, husband or brother or son, living on the sea, sailoring abroad or fishing the home waters or those of the Isle of Man—in no other house was the strain of a spell of disastrous weather so noticeable in the faces of its inmates. The old woman, withdrawn into herself, would handle her beads all day long, her voice every now and then raising itself, in forgetfulness, to a sort of moan not unlike the wind's, upon which the younger woman would chide her with a "Sh! sh!" and bend vigorously upon her work to keep bitterness from her thoughts. At such a time she might enter her brother's room and find him raised on his elbow in the bed, listening to the howling winds, scared it seemed, his eyes fixed and wide open. He would drink the warm milk she had brought him, and hand the vessel back without a word. And in the selfsame attitude she would leave him.

The fifth night instead of growing in loudness and fierceness the wind died away somewhat. It became fitful, promising the end of the storm; and before long they could distinguish between the continuous groaning and pounding of the sea and the sudden shout the dying tempest would fling among the treetops and the rocks. They were thankful to note such signs of relief; the daughter became more active, and the mother put by her beads. In the midst of a sudden sally of the wind's the latch was raised, and Tom Leane gave them greeting. His face was rosy and glowing under his sou'wester; his eyes were sparkling from the sting of the salty gusts. To see him, so sane, so healthy, was to them like a blessing. "How is it with ye?" he said, cheerily, closing the door to.

"Good, then, good, then," they answered him, and the mother rose almost as if she would take him by the hand. The reply meant that nothing unforeseen had befallen them. He understood as much. He shook a silent head in the direction of the listener's room, a look of inquiry in his eyes, and this look Mary answered with a sort of hopeless upswing of her face. Things had not improved in the lower room.

The wind died away, more and more; and after some time streamed by with a shrill steady undersong; all through, however, the crashing of the sea on the jagged rocks beneath kept up an unceasing clamor. Tom had a whole budget of news for them. Finny's barn had been stripped of its roof; a window in the chapel had been blown in; and Largy's store of fodder had been shredded in the wind; it littered all the bushes to the east. There were rumors of a wreck somewhere; but it was too soon yet to know what damage the sea had done in its five days' madness. The news he had brought them did not matter; what mattered was his company, the knitting of their half-distraught household once again to humankind. Even when at last he stood up to go, their spirits did not droop, so great had been the restoration.

"We're finished with it for a while anyhow," Tom said, rising for home.

"We are, we are; and who knows, it mightn't be after doing

all the damage we think."

He shut the door behind him. The two women had turned towards the fire when they thought they again heard his voice outside. They wondered at the sound; they listened for his footsteps. Still staring at the closed door, once more they heard his voice. This time they were sure. The door reopened, and he backed in, as one does from an unexpected slap of rain in the face. The light struck outwards, and they saw a white face advancing. Some anxiety, some uncertainty, in Tom's attitude as he backed away from that advancing face, invaded them so that they too became afraid. They saw the stranger also hesitating, looking down his own limbs. His clothes were dripping; they were clung in about him. He was bare-headed. When he raised his face again, his look was full of apology. His features were large and flat, and grey as a stone. Every now and then a spasm went through them, and they wondered what it meant. His clab of a mouth hung open; his unshaven chin trembled. Tom spoke to him: "You'd better come in; but 'tis many another house would suit you better than this."

They heard a husky, scarce-audible voice reply: "A doghouse would do, or a stable." Bravely enough he made an effort to smile.

"Oh, 'tisn't that at all. But come in, come in." He stepped in slowly and heavily, again glancing down his limbs. The water running from his clothes spread in a black pool on the flags. The young woman began to touch him with her finger tips as with some instinctive sympathy, yet could not think, it seemed, what was best to be done. The mother, however, vigorously set the fire-wheel at work, and Tom built up the fire with bog-timber and turf. The stranger meanwhile stood as if half-dazed. At last, as Mary with a candle in her hand stood pulling out dry clothes from a press, he blurted out in the same husky voice, Welsh in accent:

"I think I'm the only one!"

They understood the significance of the words, but it seemed wrong to do so.

"What is it you're saying?" Mary said, but one would not have recognized the voice for hers, it was so toneless. He raised a heavy sailor's hand in an awkward taproom gesture: "The others, they're gone, all of them."

The spasm again crossed his homely features, and his hand fell. He bowed his head. A coldness went through them. They stared at him. He might have thought them inhuman. But Mary suddenly pulled herself together, leaping at him almost: "Sh! Sh!" she said, "speak low, speak low, low," and as she spoke, all earnestness, she towed him first in the direction of the fire, and then away from it, haphazardly it seemed. She turned from him and whispered to Tom:

"Look, take him up into the loft, and he can change his clothes. Take these with you, and the candle, the candle." And she reached him the candle eagerly. Tom led the stranger up the stairs, it was more like a ladder, and the two of them disappeared into the loft. The old woman whispered:

"What was it he said?"

"'Tis how his ship is sunk."

"Did he say he was the only one?"

"He said that."

"Did himself hear him?" She nodded towards her son's room.

"No, didn't you see me pulling him away from it? But he'll hear him now. Isn't it a wonder Tom wouldn't walk easy on the boards!"

No answer from the old woman. She had deliberately seated herself in her accustomed place at the fire, and now moaned out:

"Aren't we in a cruel way, not knowing how he'd take a

thing!"

"Am I better tell him there's a poor seaman after coming in on us?"

"Do you hear them above! Do you hear them!"

In the loft the men's feet were loud on the boards. The voice they were half-expecting to hear they then heard break in on the clatter of the boots above:

"Mother! Mother!"

"Yes, child, yes."

"Who's aloft? Who's going around like that, or is it dreaming I am?"

The sounds from above were certainly like what one hears in a ship. They thought of this, but they also felt something terrible in that voice they had been waiting for: they hardly knew it for the voice of the man they had been listening to for five months.

"Go in and tell him the truth," the mother whispered. "Who are we to know what's right to be done. Let God have the doing of it." She threw her hands in the air.

Mary went in to her brother, and her limbs were weak and cold. The old woman remained seated at the fire, swung round from it, her eyes towards her son's room, fixed, as the head itself was fixed, in the tension of anxiety.

After a few minutes Mary emerged with a strange alertness upon her:

"He's rising! He's getting up! 'Tis his place, he says. He's quite good." She meant he seemed bright and well. The mother said:

"We'll take no notice of him, only just as if he was always with us."

"Yes."

They were glad then to hear the two men in the loft groping for the stair head. The kettle began to splutter in the boil, and

Mary busied herself with the table and tea cups.

The sailor came down, all smiles in his ill-fitting, haphazard clothes. He looked so overjoyed one might think he would presently burst into song.

III

"The fire is good," he said. "It puts life in one. And the dry clothes too. My word, I'm thankful to you, good people; I'm thankful to you." He shook hands with them all effusively.

"Sit down now; drink up the tea."

"I can't figure it out; less than two hours ago, out there . . . As he spoke he raised his hand towards the little porthole of a window, looking at them with his eyes staring. "Don't be thinking of anything, but drink up the hot tea," Mary said.

He nodded and set to eat with vigor. Yet suddenly he would stop, as if he were ashamed of it, turn half-round and look at them with beaming eyes, look from one to the other and back again; and they affably would nod back at him. "Excuse me, people," he would say, "excuse me." He had not the gift of speech, and his too-full heart could not declare itself. To make him feel at his ease, Tom Leane sat down away from him, and the women began to find something to do about the room. Then there were only little sounds in the room: the breaking of the eggs, the turning of the fire-wheel, the wind going by. The door of the lower room opened silently, so silently that none of them heard it, and before they were aware, the son of the house, with his clothes flung on loosely, was standing awkwardly in the middle of the floor, looking down on the back of the sailorman bent above the table. "This is my son," the mother thought of saying. "He was after going to bed when you came in."

The Welshman leaped to his feet, and impulsively, yet without many words, shook John Spillane by the hand, thanking him and all the household. As he seated himself again at the table John made his way silently towards the settle from which, across the room, he could see the sailor as he bent over his meal.

The stranger put the cup away from him, he could take no more; and Tom Leane and the womenfolk tried to keep him in talk, avoiding, as by some mutual understanding, the mention of what he had come through. The eyes of the son of the house were all the time fiercely buried in him. There came a moment's silence in the general chatter, a moment it seemed impossible to fill, and the sailorman swung his chair half-round from the table, a spoon held in his hand lightly: "I can't figure it out. I can't nohow figure it out. Here I am, fed full like a prize beast; and warm—Oh, but I'm thankful—and all my mates," with the spoon he was pointing towards the sea—"white, and cold like dead fish! I can't figure it out."

To their astonishment a voice traveled across the room from the settle

"Is it how ye struck?"

"Struck! Three times we struck! We struck last night, about this time last night. And off we went in a puff! Fine, we said. We struck again. 'Twas just coming light. And off again. But when we struck the third time, 'twas like that!" He clapped his hands together; "She went in matchwood! 'Twas dark. Why, it can't be two hours since!"

"She went to pieces?" the same voice questioned him.

"The *Nan Tidy* went to pieces, sir! No one knew what had happened or where he was. 'Twas too sudden. I found myself clung about a snag of rock. I hugged it. I hugged it."

He stood up, hoisted as from within.

"Is it you that was on the look-out?"

"Me! We'd all been on the look-out for three days. My word, yes, three days. We were stupefied with it!"

They were looking at him as he spoke, and they saw the shiver again cross his features; the strength and warmth that the food and comfort had given him fell from him, and he became in an instant the half-drowned man who had stepped in to them that night with the clothes sagging about his limbs, "Twas bad, clinging to that rock, with them all gone! 'Twas lonely! Do you know, I was so frightened I couldn't call out." John Spillane stood up, slowly, as if he too were being hoisted from within.

"Were they looking at you?"

"Who?"

"The rest of them. The eyes of them."

"No," the voice had dropped, "no, I didn't think of that!" The two of them stared as if fascinated by each other.

"You didn't!" It seemed that John Spillane had lost the purpose of his questioning. His voice was thin and weak; but he was still staring with unmoving, puzzled eyes at the stranger's face. The abashed creature before him suddenly seemed to gain as much eagerness as he had lost: his words were hot with anxiety to express himself adequately:

"But now, isn't it curious, as I sat there, there at that table, I thought somehow they would walk in, that it would be right for them, somehow, to walk in, all of them!"

His words, his eager lowered voice, brought in the darkness outside, its vastness, its terror. They seemed in the midst of an unsubstantial world. They feared that the latch would lift, yet dared not glance at it, lest that should invite the lifting. But it was all one to the son of the house, he appeared to have gone away into some mood of his own; his eyes were glaring, not looking at anything or anyone close at hand. With an instinctive groping for comfort, they all, except him, began to stir, to find some little homely task to do: Mary handled the tea ware, and Tom his pipe, when a rumbling voice, very indistinct, stilled them all again. Words, phrases, began to reach them—that a man's eyes will close and he on the lookout, close in spite of himself, that it wasn't fair, it wasn't fair, it wasn't fair! And lost in his agony, he began to glide through them, explaining, excusing the terror that was in him: "All round. Staring at me. Blaming me. A sea of them. Far, far! Without a word out of them, only their eyes in the darkness, pale like candles!"

Transfixed, they glared at him, at his round-shouldered sailor's back disappearing again into his den of refuge. They could not hear his voice any more, they were afraid to follow him.

Darby O'Gill and the Leprechaun
Herminie Kavanagh

THE NEWS that Darby O'Gill had spint six months with the Good People spread fast and far and wide.

At fair or hurlin' or market he would be backed be a crowd agin some convaynient wall and there for hours men, women, and childher, with jaws dhroppin' and eyes bulgin'd, stand feminst him listening to half-frightened questions or to bould, mystarious answers.

Alway, though, one bit of wise adwise inded his discoorse: "Nayther make nor moil nor meddle with the fairies," Darby'd say. "If you're going along the lonely boreen at night and you hear, from some fairy fort, a sound of fiddles, or of piping, or of sweet woices singing, or of little feet patthering in the dance, don't turn your head, but say your prayers an' hould on your way. The pleasures the Good People'll share with you have a sore sorrow hid in them, an' the gifts they'll offer are only made to break hearts with."

Things went this a-way till one day in the market, over among the cows, Maurteen Cavanaugh, the schoolmasther—a cross-faced, argifying ould man he was—conthradicted Darby pint blank. "Stay a bit," says Maurteen, catching Darby by the coat-collar. "You forget about the little fairy cobbler, the Leprechaun," he says. "You can't deny that to catch the Leprechaun is great luck entirely. If one only fix the glance of his eye on the cobbler, that look makes the fairy a presner—one can do anything with him as long as a human look covers the little lad and he'll give the favors of three wishes to buy his freedom," says Maurteen.

At that Darby, smiling high and knowledgeable, made answer over the heads of the crowd.

"God help your sinse, honest man!" he says. "Around the favors of thim same three wishes is a bog of thricks an' cajolories and con-ditions that'll defayt the wisest.

"First of all, if the look be taken from the little cobbler for as much as the wink of an eye, he's gone forever," he says. "Man alive, even when he does grant the favors of the three wishes, you're not safe, for, if you tell anyone you've seen the Leprechaun, the favors melt like snow, or if you make a fourth wish that day—whiff! they turn to smoke. Take my advice—nayther make nor moil nor meddle with the fairies."

"Thrue for ye," spoke up long Pether McCarthy, siding in with Darby. "Didn't Barney McBride, on his way to early mass one May morning, catch the fairy cobbler sewing an' workin' away under a hedge. 'Have a pinch of snuff, Barney agra,' says the Leprechaun, handing up the little snuff-box. But, mind ye, when my poor Barney bint to take a thumb an' finger full, what did the little villain do but fling the box, snuff and all, into

Barney's face. An' thin, whilst the poor lad was winkin' and blinkin', the Leprechaun gave one leap and was lost in the reeds.

"Thin, again, there was Peggy O'Rourke, who captured him fair an' square in a hawthorn-bush. In spite of his wiles she wrung from him the favors of the three wishes. Knowing, of course, that if she towld of what had happened to her the spell was broken and the wishes wouldn't come thrue, she hurried home, aching and longing to in some way find from her husband Andy what wishes she'd make.

"Throwing open her own door, she said, 'What would ye wish for most in the world, Andy dear? Tell me an' your wish'll come thrue,' says she. A peddler was crying his wares out in the lane. 'Lanterns, tin lanterns!' cried the peddler. 'I wish I had one of thim lanterns,' says Andy, careless, and bendin' over to get a coal for his pipe, when, lo and behold, there was the lantern in his hand.

"Well, so vexed was Peggy that one of her fine wishes should be wasted on a palthry tin lantern, that she lost all patience with him. 'Why thin, bad scran to you!' says she—not mindin' her own words —'I wish the lantern was fastened to the ind of your nose!'

"The word wasn't well out of her mouth till the lantern *was* hung swinging from the ind of Andy's nose in a way that the wit of man couldn't loosen. It took the third and last of Peggy's wishes to relayse Andy."

"Look at that, now!" cried a dozen voices from the admiring crowd. "Darby said so from the first."

Well, after a time people used to come from miles around to see Darby and sit undher the sthraw-stack beside the stable to adwise with our hayro about their most important business— what was the best time for the settin' of hins, or what was good to cure colic in childher, an' things like that.

Any man so parsecuted with admiration an' hayrofication might aisily feel his chest swell out a bit, so it's no wondher that Darby set himself up for a knowledgeable man.

He took to talkin' slow an' shuttin' one eye whin he listened, and he walked with a knowledgeable twist to his chowlders. He grew monsthrously fond of fairs and public gatherings where people made much of him, and he lost every ounce of liking he ever had for hard worruk.

Things wint on with him in this way from bad to worse, and where it would have inded no man knows, if one unlucky morning he hadn't rayfused to bring in a creel of turf his wife Bridget had axed him to fetch her. The unfortunate man said it was no work for the likes of him.

The last word was still on Darby's lips whin he rayalized his mistake, an' he'd have given the world to have the sayin' back again.

For a minute you could have heard a pin dhrop. Bridget, instead of being in a hurry to begin at him, was crool dayliberate. She planted herself in the door, her two fists on her hips, an' her lips shut.

The look Julius Sayser'd trow at a servant-girl he'd caught stealing sugar from the rile cupboard was the glance she waved up and down from Darby's toes to his head, and from his head to his brogues agin.

Thin she began an' talked steady as a fall of hail that has now an' then a bit of lightning an' tunder mixed in it.

The knowledgeable man stood purtendin' to brush his hat and tryin' to look brave, but the heart inside of him was meltin' like butther.

Bridget began aisily be carelessly mentioning a few of Darby's best known wakenesses. Afther that she took up some of them not so well known, being ones Darby himself had sayrious doubts about having at all. But on these last she was more savare than on the first. Through it all he daren't say a word—he only smiled lofty and bitther.

'Twas but natural next for Bridget to explain what a poor crachure her husband was the day she got him, an what she might have been if she had married ayther one of the six others who had axed her. The step for her was a little one, thin, to the shortcomings and misfortunes of his blood relaytions, which she follyed back to the blaggardisms of his fourth cousin, Phelim McFadden.

Even in his misery poor Darby couldn't but marvel at her wondherful memory.

By the time she began talking of her own family, and especially about her Aunt Honoria O'Shaughnessy, who had once shook hands with a Bishop, and who in the rebellion of '98 had trun a brick at a Lord Liftenant, whin he was riding by, Darby was as wilted and as forlorn-looking as a roosther caught out in the winther rain.

He lost more pride in those few minutes than it had taken months to gather an' hoard. It kept falling in great drops from his forehead.

Just as Bridget was lading up to what Father Cassidy calls a pur-roar-ration—that being the part of your wife's discoorse whin, after telling you all she's done for you, and all she's stood from your relaytions, she breaks down and cries, and so smothers you entirely—just as she was coming to that, I say, Darby scrooged his caubeen down on his head, stuck his fingers in his two ears, and, making one grand rush through the door, bolted as fast as his legs could carry him down the road toward Sleive-na-mon Mountains.

Bridget stood on the step looking afther him, too surprised for a word. With his fingers still in his ears, so that he couldn't hear her commands to turn back, he ran without stopping till he came to the willow-tree near Joey Hooligan's forge. There he slowed down to fill his lungs with the fresh, sweet air.

'Twas one of those warm-hearted, laughing autumn days which steals for a while the bonnet and shawl of the May. The sun, from a sky of feathery whiteness, laned over, telling jokes to the worruld, an' the goold harvest-fields and purple hills, lasy and continted, laughed back at the sun. Even the blackbird flying over the haw-tree looked down an' sang to those below, "God save all here"; an' the linnet from her bough answered back quick an' sweet, "God save you kindly, sir !"

With such pleasant sight and sounds an' twitterings at every side, our hayro didn't feel the time passing till he was on top of the first hill of the Sleive-na-mon Mountains, which, as everyone knows, is called the Pig's Head.

It wasn't quite lonesome enough on the Pig's Head, so our hayro plunged into the walley an' climbed the second mountain—the Divil's Pillow where 'twas lonesome and desarted enough to shuit anyone.

Beneath the shade of a tree, for the days was warm, he set himself down in the long, sweet grass, lit his pipe, and let his mind go free. But, as he did, his thoughts rose together like a flock of frightened, angry pheasants, an' whirred back to the owdacious things Bridget had said about his relations.

Wasn't she the mendageous, humbrageous woman, he thought, to say such things about as illegant stock, as the O'Gills and the O'Gradys?

Why, Wullum O'Gill, Darby's uncle, at that minute, was head butler at Castle Brophy, and was known far an' wide as being one of the foinest scholars an' as having the most beautiful pair of legs in all Ireland!

This same Wullum O'Gill had tould Bridget in Darby's own hearing, on a day when the three were going through the great picture-gallery at Castle Brophy, that the O'Gills at one time had been Kings in Ireland.

Darby never since could raymember whether this time was before the flood or afther the flood. Bridget said it was durin' the flood, but surely that sayin' was nonsinse.

Howsumever, Darby knew his Uncle Wullum was right, for he often felt in himself the signs of greatness. And now as he sat alone on the grass, he said out loud:

"If I had me rights I'd be doing nothing all day long but sittin' on a throne, an' playin' games of forty-five with the Lord Liftenant an' some of me generals. There never was a lord that likes good ating or dhrinking betther nor I, or who hates worse to get up airly in the morning. That last disloike I'm tould is a great sign entirely of gentle blood the worruld over," says he.

As for the wife's people, the O'Hagans an' the O'Shaughnessys, well—they were no great shakes, he said to himself, at laste so far as looks were concerned. All the handsomeness in Darby's childher came from his own side of the family. Even Father Cassidy said the childher took afther the O'Gills .

"If I were rich," said Darby, to a lazy ould bumble-bee who was droning an' tumbling in front of him, "I'd have a castle like Castle Brophy, with a great picture-gallery in it. On one wall I'd put the picture of the O'Gills and the O'Gradys, and on the wall ferninst them I'd have the O'Hagans an' the O'Shaughnessys."

At that ideah his heart bubbled in a new and fierce deloight. "Bridget's people," he says agin, scowling at the bee, "would look four times as common as they raylly are, whin they were compared in that way with my own relations. An' whenever Bridget got rampageous I'd take her in and show her the difference betwixt the two clans, just to punish her, so I would."

How long the lad sat that way warming the cowld thoughts of his heart with drowsy, pleasant dhrames an' misty longings he don't rightly know, whin—tack, tack, tack, tack, came the busy sound of a little hammer from the other side of a fallen oak.

"Be jingo!" he says to himself with a start, "'tis the Leprechaun that's in it."

In a second he was on his hands an' knees, the tails of his coat flung across his back, an' he crawling softly toward the sound of the hammer. Quiet as a mouse he lifted himself up on the mossy log to look over, and there before his two popping eyes was a sight of wondheration.

Sitting on a white stone an' working away like fury, hammering pegs into a little red shoe, half the size of your thumb, was a bald-headed ould cobbler of about twice the hoight of your hand. On the top of a round, snub nose was perched a pair of horn-rimmed spectacles, an' a narrow fringe of iron-gray whuskers grew undher his stubby chin. The brown leather apron he wore was so long that it covered his green knee-breeches an' almost hid the knitted gray stockings.

The Leprechaun—for it was he indade—as he worked, mumbled an' mutthered in great discontent:

"Oh, haven't I the hard, hard luck," he said. "I'll never have thim done in time for her to dance in tonight. So, thin, I'll be kilt entirely," says he. "Was there ever another quane of the fairies as wearing on shoes an' brogues an' dancin' slippers? Haven't I the—" Looking up, he saw Darby.

"The top of the day to you, dacint man!" says the cobbler, jumpin' up. Giving a sharp cry, he pinted quick at Darby's stomach. "But, wirra, wirra, what's that wooly, ugly thing you have crawling an' creepin' on your weskit?" he said, purtendin' to be all excited.

"Sorra thing on my weskit," answered Darby, cool as ice, "or anywhere else that'll make me take my two bright eyes off'n you—not for a second," says he.

"Well! Well! will you look at that, now?" laughed the cobbler. "Mark how quick an' handy he took me up! Will you have a pinch of snuff, clever man?" he axed, houlding up the little box.

"Is it the same snuff you gave Barney McBride a while ago?" axed Darby, sarcastic. "Lave off your foolishness," says our hayro, growin' fierce, "and grant me at once the favors of the three wishes, or I'll have you smoking like a herring in my own chimney before nightfall," says he.

At that the Leprechaun, seeing that he but wasted time on so knowledgeable a man as Darby O'Gill, surrendhered, and granted the favors of the three wishes.

"What is it you ask?" says the cobbler, himself turning on a sudden very sour an' sullen.

"First an' foremost," says Darby, "I want a home of my ansisthers, an' it must be a castle like Castle Brophy, with pictures of my kith an' kin on the wall, and then facing them pictures of my wife Bridget's kith an' kin on the other wall."

"That favor I give ye, that wish I grant ye," says the fairy, making the shape of a castle on the ground with his awl.

"What next?" he grunted.

"I want goold enough for me an' my generations to enjoy in grandeur the place forever."

"Always the goold," sneered the little man, bending to dhraw with his awl on the turf the shape of a purse.

"Now for your third and last wish. Have a care!"

"I want the castle set on this hill—the Divils Pillow—where we two stand," says Darby. Then sweeping with his arm, he says, "I want the land about to be my demesne."

The Leprechaun stuck his awl on the ground. "That wish I give you, that wish I grant you," he says. With that he straightened himself up, and grinning most aggravaytin' the while, he looked Darby over from top to toe. "You're a foine, knowledgeable man, but have a care of the fourth wish!" says he.

Bekase there was more of a challenge than friendly warning in what the small lad said, Darby snapped his fingers at him an' cried:

"Have no fear, little man! If I got all Ireland ground for making a fourth wish, however small, before midnight I'd not make it. I'm going home now to fetch Bridget an' the childher, and the only fear or unaisiness I have is that you'll not keep your word, so as to have the castle here ready before us when I come back."

"Oho! I'm not to be thrusted, amn't I?" screeched the little lad, flaring into a blazing passion. He jumped upon the log that was betwixt them, and with one fist behind his back shook the other at Darby.

"You ignorant, suspicious-minded blaggard!" says he. "How dare the likes of you say the likes of that to the likes of me!" cried the cobbler. "I'd have you to know," he says, " that I had a repitation for truth an' voracity ayquil if not shuperior to the best, before you were born!" he shouted. "I'll take no high talk from a man that's afraid to give words to his own wife if whin she's in a tantrum!" says the Leprechaun.

"It's aisy to know you're not a married man," says Darby, mighty scornful, "bekase if you—"

The lad stopped short, forgetting what he was going to say in his surprise an' aggaytation, for the far side of the mountain was waving up an' down before his eyes like a great green blanket that is being shook by two women, while at the same time high spots of turf on the hillside toppled sidewise to level themselves up with the low places. The enchantment had already begun to make things ready for the castle. A dozen foine trees that stood in a little grove bent their heads quickly together, and thin by some inwisible hand they were plucked up by the roots an' dhropped aside much the same as a man might grasp a handful of weeds an' fling them from his garden.

The ground under the knowledgeable man's feet began to rumble an' heave. He waited for no more. With a cry that was half of gladness an' half of fear, he turned on his heel an' started on a run down into the walley, leaving the little cobbler standing on the log, shouting abuse after him an' ballyraggin' him as he ran.

So excited was Darby that, going up the Pig's Head, he was nearly run over by a crowd of great brown building stones which were moving down slow an' ordherly like a flock of driven sheep—but they moved without so much as bruising a blade of grass or bendin' a twig, as they came.

Only once, and that at the top of the Pig's Head, he trew a look back.

The Divil's Pillow was in a great commotion; a whirlwind was sweeping over it—whether of dust or of mist he couldn't tell.

Afther this, Darby never looked back again or to the right or the left of him, but kept straight on till he found himself, panting and pufflng, at his own kitchen door. 'Twas tin minutes before he could spake, but at last, whin he tould Bridget to make ready herself and the childher to go up to the Divil's Pillow with him, for once in her life that raymarkable woman, without axing, How comes it so, What rayson have you, or Why should I do it, set to work washing the childer's faces.

Maybe she dabbed a little more soap in their eyes than was needful, for 'twas a habit she had; though this time if she did, not a whimper broke from the little hayros. For the matther of that, not one word, good, bad or indifferent, did herself spake till the whole family were trudging down the lane two by two, marching like sojers.

As they came near the first hill along its sides the evening twilight turned from purple to brown, and at the top of the Pig's Head the darkness of a black night swooped suddenly down on them. Darby hurried on a step or two ahead, an' resting his hand upon the large rock that crowns the hill, looked anxiously over to the Divil's Pillow. Although he was ready for something foine, yet the greatness of the foineness that met his gaze knocked the breath out of him.

Across the deep walley, and on top of the second mountain, he saw lined against the evening sky the roof of an imminse castle, with towers an' parrypets an' battlements. Undher the towers a thousand sullen windows glowed red in the black walls. Castle Brophy couldn't hould a candle to it.

"Behold!" says Darby, flinging out his arm, and turning to his wife, who had just come up—"behold the castle of my ansisthers who were my forefathers!"

"How," says Bridget, quick and scornful—"how could your aunt's sisters be your four fathers?"

What Darby was going to say to her he don't just raymember, for at that instant from the right-hand side of the mountain came a cracking of whips, a rattling of wheels, an' the rush of horses, and, lo and behold! a great dark coach with flashing lamps, and drawn by four coal-black horses, dashed up the hill and stopped beside them. Two shadowy men were on the driver's box.

"Is this Lord Darby O'Gill?" axed one of them, in a deep, muffled woice. Before Darby could reply, Bridget took the words out of his mouth.

"It is!" she cried, in a kind of a half cheer, "an' Lady O'Gill an' the childher."

"Then hurry up!" says the coachman. "Your supper's gettin' cowld."

Without waiting for anyone Bridget flung open the carriage door, an' pushin' Darby aside jumped in among the cushions. Darby, his heart sizzlin' with vexation at her audaciousness, lifted in one after another the childher, and then got in himself.

He couldn't undherstand at all the change in his wife, for she had always been the odherliest, modestist woman in the parish.

Well, he'd no sooner shut the door than crack went the whip, the horses gave a spring, the carriage jumped, and down the hill they went. For fastness there was never another carriage-ride like that before nor since. Darby hildt tight with both hands to the window, his face pressed against the glass. He couldn't tell whether the horses were only flying or whether the coach was falling down the hill into the walley. By the hollow feeling in his stomach he thought they were falling. He was striving to think of some prayers when there came a terrible jolt which sint his two heels against the roof an' his head betwixt the cushions. As he righted himself the wheels began to grate on a graveled road, an' plainly they were dashing up the side of the second mountain.

Even so, they couldn't have gone far whin the carriage dhrew up in a flurry, an' he saw through the gloom a high iron gate being slowly opened.

"Pass on," said a voice from somewhere in the shadows; "their supper's getting cowld."

As they flew undher the great archway, Darby had a glimpse of the thing which had opened the gate, and had said their supper was getting cowld. It was standing on its hind legs—in the darkness he couldn't be quite sure as to its shape, but it was ayther a Bear or a Loin.

His mind was in a pondher about this when, with a swirl an' a

bump, the carriage stopped another time, an' now it stood
before a broad flight of stone steps which led up to the main
door of the castle. Darby, half afraid, peering out through the
darkness, saw a square of light high above him which came
from the open hall door. Three sarvants in livery stood waiting
on the thrashol.

"Make haste, make haste!" says one, in a doleful voice; "their
supper's gettin' cowld."

Hearing these words, Bridget imagetly bounced out, an' was
halfway up the steps before Darby could ketch her an' hould her
till the childher came up.

"I never in all my life saw her so owdacious," he says, half
cryin', an' linkin' her arm to keep her back, an' thin, with the
childher following two by two, according to size, the whole
family payraded up the steps, till Darby, with a gasp of deloight,
stopped on the thrashol of a splendid hall. From a high ceiling
hung great flags from every nation an' domination, which
swung and swayed in the dazzlin' light. Two lines of men and
maid servants dhressed in silks an' satins an' brocades, stood
facing aich other, bowing an' smiling an' wavin' their hands in
welcome. The two lines stretched down to the goold stairway at
the far ind of the hall. For half of one minute Darby, every eye
in his head as big as a tay-cup, stood hesitaytin'. Thin he said,
"Why should it flutther me? Arrah, ain't it all mine? Aren't all
these people in me pay? I'll engage it's a pritty penny all this
grandeur is costing me to keep up this minute." He trew out his
chist. "Come on, Bridget!" he says; "let's go into the home of
my ansisthers."

Howandever, scarcely had he stepped into the beautiful place
whin two pipers with their pipes, two fiddlers with their fiddles,
two flute-players with their flutes, an' they dhressed in scarlet
an' goold, stepped out in front of him, and thus to maylodius

music the family proudly marched down the hall, climbed up the goolen stairway at its ind, an' thin turned to enter the biggest room Darby had ever seen.

Something in his sowl whuspered that this was the picture-gallery.

"Be the powers of Pewther!" says the knowledgeable man to himself, "I wouldn't be in Bridget's place this minute for a hatful of money! Wait, oh just wait, till she has to compare her own relations with my own foine people! I know how she'll feel, but I wondher what she'll say," he says.

The thought that all the unjust things, all the unraysonable things Bridget had said about his kith an' kin were just going to be disproved and turned against herself, made him proud an' almost happy.

But wirrasthrue! He should have raymembered his own adwise not to make nor moil nor meddle with the fairies, for here he was to get the first hard welt from the little Leprechaun.

It was the picture-gallery sure enough, but how terribly different everything was from what the poor lad expected. There on the left wall, grand an' noble, shone the pictures of Bridget's people. Of all the well-dressed, handsome, proud-appearing persons in the whole worruld, the O'Hagans an' the O'Shaughnessys would compare with the best. This was a hard enough crack, though a crushinger knock was to come. Ferninst them on the right wall glowered the O'Gills and the O'Gradys, and of all the ragged, sheep-stealing, hangdog-looking villains one ever saw in jail or out of jail, it was Darby's kindred.

The place of honor on the right wall was given to Darby's fourth cousin, Phelem McFadden, an' he was painted with a pair of handcuffs on him. Wullum O'Gill had a squint in his right eye, and his thin legs bowed like hoops on a barrel.

If you have ever at night been groping your way through a

dark room, and got a sudden, hard bump on the forehead from the edge of the door, you can undherstand the feelings of the knowledgeable man.

"Take that picture out!" he said, hoarsely, as soon as he could speak. "An' will someone kindly inthrojuice me to the man who med it? Bekase," he says, "I intend to take his life! There was never a crass-eyed O'Gill since the world began," says he.

Think of his horror an' surprise whin he saw the left eye of Wullum O'Gill twist itself slowly over toward his nose and squint worse than the right eye.

Purtending not to see this, an' hoping no one else did, Darby fiercely led the way over to the other wall.

Fronting him stood the handsome picture of Honoria O'Shaughnessy, an' she dhressed in a shuit of tin clothes like the knights of ould used to wear—armor I think they calls it.

She hildt a spear in her hand with a little flag on the blade, an' her smile was proud and high.

"Take that likeness out, too," says Darby, very spiteful; "that's not a dacint shuit of clothes for any woman to wear!"

The next minute you might have knocked him down with a feather, for the picture of Honoria O'Shaughnessy opened its mouth an' stuck out its tongue at him.

"The supper's getting cowld, the supper's getting cowld!" someone cried at the other ind of the picture gallery. Two big doors were swung open, an' glad enough was our poor hayro to folly the musicianers down to the room where the ating an' drinking were to be thransacted.

This was a little room with lots of looking-glasses, and it was bright with a thousand candles, and white with the shining-ist marble. On the table was biled beef an' reddishes an' carrots an' roast mutton an' all kinds of important ating an' drinking. Beside there stood fruits an' sweets an'—but, sure, what is the use in talkin'?

A high-backed chair stood ready for aich of the family, an' 'twas a lovely sight to see them all whin they were sitting there—Darby at the head, Bridget at the foot, the childher—the poor little paythriarchs —sitting bolt upright on aich side, with a bewigged and befrilled serving-man standing haughty behind every chair.

The atin' and dhrinkin' would have begun at once—in throth there was already a bit of biled beef on Darby's plate—only that he spied a little silver bell beside him. Sure, 'twas one like those the quality keep to ring whin they want more hot wather for their punch, but it puzzled the knowledgeable man, and 'twas the beginning of his misfortune.

"I wondher," he thought, "if 'tis here for the same raison as the bell is at the Curragh races—do they ring this one so that all at the table will start ating and dhrinking fair, an' no one will have the advantage, or is it," he says to himself agin, "to ring whin the head of the house thinks everyone has had enough. Haven't the quality quare ways! I'll be a long time learning them," he says.

He sat silent and puzzling an' staring at the biled beef on his plate, afeard to start in without ringing the bell, an' dhreadin' to risk ringing it. The grand sarvants towered cowldly on every side, their chins tilted, but they kep' throwing over their chowlders glances so scornful and haughty that Darby shivered at the thought of showing any uncultivaytion.

While our hayro sat thus in unaisy contimplation an' smouldherin' mortification an' flurried hesitaytion, a powdhered head was poked over his chowlder, and a soft, beguiling voice said, "Is there anything else you'd wish for?"

The foolish lad twisted in his chair, opened his mouth to spake, and gave a look at the bell; shame rushed to his cheeks, he picked up a bit of the biled beef on his fork, an' to consale his turpitaytion gave the misfortunit answer:

"I'd wish for a pinch of salt, if you plaze," says he.

'Twas no sooner said than came the crash. Oh, tunderation an' murdheration, what a roaring crash it was! The lights winked out together at a breath an' left a pitchy, throbbing darkness. Overhead and to the sides was a roaring, smashing, crunching noise, like the ocean's madness when the winthry storm breaks agin the Kerry shore, an' in that roar was mingled the tearing and the splitting of the walls and the fading of the chimneys. But through all this confusion could be heard the shrill, laughing woice of the Leprechaun. "The clever man med his fourth grand wish" it howled.

Darby—a thousand wild woices screaming an' mocking above him—was on his back kicking and squirming and striving to get up, but some load hilt him down, an' something bound his eyes shut.

"Are you kilt, Bridget asthore?" he cried; "Where are the childher?" he says.

Instead of answer there suddenly flashed a fierce an' angry silence, an' its quickness frightened the lad more than all the wild confusion before.

'Twas a full minute before he dared to open his eyes to face the horrors which he felt were standing about him; but when courage enough to look came, all he saw was the night-covered mountain, a purple sky, and a thin, new moon, with one trembling goold star a hand's space above its bosom.

Darby struggled to his feet. Not a stone of the castle was left, not a sod of turf but what was in its ould place; every sign of the little cobbler's work had melted like April snow. The very trees Darby had seen pulled up by the roots that same afternoon now stood a waving blur below the new moon, an' a nightingale was singing in their branches. A cricket chirped lonesomely on the same fallen log which had hidden the Leprechaun.

"Bridget! Bridget!" Darby called agin an' agin. Only a sleepy owl on a distant hill answered.

A shivering thought jumped into the boy's bewildered sowl—maybe the Leprechaun had stolen Bridget an' the childher.

The poor man turned, and for the last time darted down into the night-filled walley.

Not a pool in the road he waited to go around, not a ditch in his path he didn't leap over, but ran as he never ran before till he raiched his own front door.

His heart stood still as he peeped through the window. There were the childher croodled around Bridget, who sat with the youngest asleep in her lap before the fire, rocking back an' forth, an' she crooning a happy, continted baby-song.

Tears of gladness crept into Darby's eyes as he looked in upon her. "God bless her!" he says to himself. "She's the flower of the O'Hagans and the O'Shaughnessys, and she's a proud feather in the caps of the O'Gills and the O'Gradys."

'Twas well he had this happy thought to cheer him as he lifted the door-latch, for the manest of all the little cobbler's spiteful thricks waited in the house to meet Darby—nayther Bridget nor the childher raymembered a single thing of all that had happened to them during the day. They were willing to make their happydavitts that they had been no farther than their own petatie-patch since morning.

Daniel Crowley and the Ghosts
Traditional

THERE LIVED A MAN IN CORK whose name was Daniel Crowley. He was a coffin-maker by trade, and had a deal of coffins laid by, so that his apprentice might sell them when himself was not at home.

A messenger came to Daniel Crowley's shop one day and told him that there was a man dead at the end of the town, and to send up a coffin for him, or to make one.

Daniel Crowley took down a coffin, put it on a donkey cart, drove to the wake house, went in and told the people of the house that the coffin was there for them. The corpse was laid out on a table in a room next to the kitchen. Five or six women were keeping watch around it; many people were in the kitchen.

Daniel Crowley was asked to sit down and commence to shorten the night: that is, to tell stories, amuse himself and others. A tumbler of punch was brought, and he promised to do the best he could.

He began to tell stories and shorten the night. A second glass of punch was brought to him, and he went on telling tales. There was a man at the wake who sang a song: after him another was found, and then another. Then the people asked Daniel Crowley to sing, and he did. The song that he sang was of another nation. He sang about the good people, the fairies. The song pleased the company, they desired him to sing again, and he did not refuse.

Daniel Crowley pleased the company so much with his two songs that a woman who had three daughters wanted to make a match for one of them and get Daniel Crowley as a husband for her. Crowley was a bachelor, well on in years, and had never thought of marrying.

The mother spoke of the match to a woman sitting next to her. The woman shook her head, but the mother said:

"If he takes one of my daughters I'll be glad, for he has money laid by. Do you go and speak to him, but say nothing of me at first.'

The woman went to Daniel Crowley then, and told him that she had a fine, beautiful girl in view, and that now was his time to get a good wife; he'd never have such a chance again.

Crowley rose up in great anger. "There isn't a woman wearing clothes that I'd marry," said he. " There isn't a woman born that could bring me to make two halves of my loaf for her."

The mother was insulted now and forget herself. She began to abuse Crowley.

"Bad luck to you, you hairy little scoundrel," said she, "you might be a grandfather to my child. You are not fit to clean the shoes on her feet. You have only dead people for company day and night; 'tis by them you make your living."

"Oh, then," said Daniel Crowley, "I'd prefer the dead to the living any day if all the living were like you. Besides, I have nothing against the dead. I am getting employment by them and not by the living, for 'tis the dead that want coffins."

"Bad luck to you, 'tis with the dead you ought to be and not with the living; 'twould be fitter for you to go out of this altogether and go to your dead people."

"I'd go if I knew how to go to them," said Crowley.

"Why not invite them to supper?" retorted the woman.

He rose up then, went out, and called:

"Men, women, children, soldiers, sailors, all people that I have ever made coffins for, I invite you tonight to my house, and I'll spend what is needed in giving a feast."

The people who were watching the dead man on the table saw him smile when he heard the invitation. They ran out of the room in a fright and out of the kitchen, and Daniel Crowley hurried away to his shop as fast as ever his donkey could carry him. On the way he came to a public-house and, going in, bought a pint bottle of whiskey, put it in his pocket, and drove on.

The workshop was locked and the shutters down when he left that evening, but when he came near he saw that all the windows were shining with light, and he was in dread that the building was burning or that robbers were in it. When right there Crowley slipped into a corner of the building opposite, to know could he see what was happening, and soon he saw crowds of men, women, and children walking toward his shop and going in, but none coming out. He was hiding some time when a man tapped him on the shoulder and asked, "Is it here you are, and we waiting for you? 'Tis a shame to treat company this way. Come now."

Crowley went with the man to the shop, and as he passed the threshold he saw a great gathering of people. Some were neighbors, people he had known in the past. All were dancing, singing, amusing themselves. He was not long looking on when a man came up to him and said:

"You seem not to know me, Daniel Crowley."

"I don't know you," said Crowley. " How could I?"

"You might then, and you ought to know me, for I am the first man you made a coffin for, and 'twas I gave you the first start in business."

Soon another came up, a lame man: "Do you know me, Daniel Crowley?"

"I do not."

"I am your cousin, and it isn't long since I died."

"Oh, now I know you well, for you are lame. In God's name," said Crowley to the cousin, "how am I to get these people out o' this. What time is it?"

"'Tis early yet, it's hardly eleven o'clock, man."

Crowley wondered that it was so early.

"Receive them kindly," said the cousin; "be good to them, make merriment as you can."

"I have no money with me to get food or drink for them; 'tis night now, and all places are closed," answered Crowley.

"Well, do the best you can," said the cousin.

The fun and dancing went on, and while Daniel Crowley was looking around, examining everything, he saw a woman in the far-off comer. She took no part in the amusement, but seemed very shy in herself.

"Why is that woman so shy—she seems to be afraid?" asked he of the cousin. "And why doesn't she dance and make merry like others?"

"Oh, 'tis not long since she died, and you gave the coffin, as she had no means of paying for it. She is in dread you'll ask her for the money, or let the company know that she didn't pay," said the cousin.

The best dancer they had was a piper by the name of John Reardon from the city of Cork. The fiddler was one John Healy. Healy brought no fiddle with him, but he made one, and the way he made it was to take off what flesh he had on his body. He rubbed up and down on his own ribs, each rib having a different note, and he made the loveliest music that Daniel Crowley had ever heard. After that the whole company followed his example. All threw off what flesh they had on them and began to dance jigs and hornpipes in their bare bones. When by chance they struck against one another in dancing, you'd think it was Brandon Mountain that was sinking Mount Eagle, with the noise that was in it.

Daniel Crowley plucked up all his courage to know could he live through the night, but still he thought daylight would never come. There was one man, John Sullivan, that he noticed especially. This man had married twice in his life, and with him came the two women. Crowley saw him taking out the second wife to dance a breakdown, and the two danced so well that the company were delighted, and all the skeletons had their mouths open, laughing. He danced and knocked so much merriment out of them all that his first wife, who was at the end of the house, became jealous and very mad altogether. She ran down to where he was and told him she had a better right to dance with him than the second wife; "That's not the truth for you," said the second wife, "I have a better right than you. When he married me you were a dead woman and he was free, and, besides, I'm a better dancer than what you are, and I will dance with him whether you like it or not."

"Hold your tongue!" screamed the first wife. "Sure, you

couldn't come to this feast tonight at all but for the loan of another woman's shinbones."

Sullivan looked at his two wives and asked the second one:

"Isn't it your own shinbones you have?"

"No, they are borrowed. I borrowed a neighboring woman's shins from her, and 'tis those I have with me tonight."

"Who is the owner of the shinbones you have under you?" asked the husband.

"They belong to one Catherine Murray. She hadn't a very good name in life."

"But why didn't you come on your own feet?"

"Oh, I wasn't good myself in life, and I was put under a penalty, and the penalty is that whenever there is a feast or a ball I cannot go to it unless I am able to borrow a pair of shins."

Sullivan was raging when he found that the shinbones he had been dancing with belonged to a third woman, and she not the best, and he gave a slap to the wife that sent her spinning into a corner.

The woman had relations among the skeletons present, and they were angry when they saw the man strike their friend. "We'll never let that go with him," said they. "We must knock satisfaction out of Sullivan!"

The woman's friends rose up, and, as there were no clubs or weapons, they pulled off their left arms and began to slash and strike with them in terrible fashion. There was an awful battle in one minute.

While this was going on Daniel Crowley was standing below at the end of the room, cold and hungry, not knowing but he'd be killed. As Sullivan was trying to dodge the blows sent against him, he got as far as Daniel Crowley and stepped on his toe without knowing it; Crowley got vexed and gave Sullivan a blow with his fist that drove the head from him and sent it flying to the opposite corner.

When Sullivan saw his head flying off from the blow, he ran, and, catching it, aimed a blow at Daniel Crowley with the head, and aimed so truly that he knocked him under the bench; then, having him at a disadvantage, Sullivan hurried to the bench and began to strangle him. He squeezed his throat and held him so firmly between the bench and the floor that the man lost his senses and couldn't remember a thing more.

When Daniel Crowley came to himself in the morning, his apprentice found him stretched under the bench with an empty bottle under his arm. He was bruised and pounded. His throat was sore where Sullivan had squeezed it; he didn't know how the company broke up, nor when his guests went away.

The Defeat of the Widows

D.R. McAnally, Jr.

WHEN SUPERSTITIONS HAVE not yet been banished from any other part of the world it is not wonderful that they should still be found in the country districts of Ireland, rural life being especially favorable to the perpetuation of old ways of living and modes of thought, since in an agricultural district less change takes place in a century than may, in a city, be observed in a single decade. Country people preserve their old legends with their antique styles of apparel, and thus the relics of the pagan ages of Ireland have come down from father to son, altered and adapted to the changes in the country and its population. Thus, for instance, the old-fashioned witch is no longer found in any part of Ireland, her memory lingering only as a tradition, but her modern successor is frequently met with, and in many parishes a retired hovel in a secluded lane is a favorite resort of the neighboring peasants, for it is the home of the Pishogue, or wise woman, who collects herbs, and, in her way, doctors her patients sometimes with simple medicinal remedies, sometimes with charms, according to their gullibility and the nature of their ailments.

Not far from Ballinahinch, a fishing village on Birterbuy Bay, in the County Galway, and in the most lonely valley of the neighborhood, there dwells one of these wise women who supplant the ancient witches. The hovel which shelters her bears every indication of wretched poverty; the floor is mud, the smoke escapes through a hole in the thatch in default of a chimney; the bed is a scanty heap of straw in the corner, and two rude shelves, bearing a small assortment of cracked jars and broken bottles, constitute Moll's stock in trade.

The misery of her household surroundings, however, furnished to the minds of her patients no argument against the efficiency of her remedies, Moll being commonly believed to have "a power av goold," though no one had ever see any portion thereof. But with all her reputed riches she had no fear of robbers, for "she could aisily do for thim did they but come as many as the shtraws in the thatch," and would-be robbers, no doubt understanding that fact, prudently consulted their own safety by staying away from the vicinity of her cabin.

"Owld Moll," as she was known, was a power in the parish, and her help was sought in many emergencies. Did a cow go dry, Moll knew the reason and might possibly remove the spell; if a baby fell ill, Moll had an explanation of its ailment, and could tell at a glance whether the little one was or was not affected by the evil eye of a secret enemy. If a pig was stolen, she was shrewd in her conjectures as to the direction its wrathful owner must take in the search. But her forte lay in bringing about lovematches. Many were the charms at her command for this purpose, and equally numerous the successes with which she was accredited. Some particulars of her doings in this direction were furnished by Jerry Magwire, a jolly car-man of

Galway, who had himself been benefited by her services.

"Sure I was married meself be her manes," stated Jerry, "an' this is the way it was. Forty-nine years ago come next Mickelmas, I was a good-lookin' young felly, wid a nate cabin on the road from Ballinasloe to Ballinamore, havin' a fine câr an' a mare an' her colt, that was as good as two horses whin the colt grew up. I was afther payin' coort to Dora O'Callighan, that was the dawther av Misther O'Callighan that lived in the County Galway, an', be the same token, was a fine man. In thim times I used be comin' over here twict or three times a year wid a bagman, commerical thraveller, you 'd call him, an' I heard say av Owld Moll, an' she was n't owld thin, an' the next time I come, I wint to her an' got an inchantmint. Faix, some av it is gone from me, but I mind that I was to change me garthers, an' tie on me thumb a bit o' bark she gev me, an' go to the churchyard on Halloween, an' take the first chilla-ca-pooka (snail) I found on a tombshtone, an' begob, it was that same job that was like to be the death o' me, it bein' dark an' I bendin' to look clost, a hare jumped in me face from undher the shtone. 'Jagers,' says I, an' me fallin' on me back on the airth an' the life lavin' me. 'Presince o' God be about me,' says I, for I knewn the inchantmint was n't right, no more I ought n't to be at it, but the hare was skairt like meself an' run, an' I found the shnail an' run too wid the shweat pourin' aff me face in shtrames.

"So I put the shnail in a plate that I covered wid another, an' av the Sunday, I opened it fur to see phat letters it writ, an' bad luck to the wan o' thim cud I rade at all, fur in thim days I cud n't tell A from any other letther. I tuk the plate to Misther O'Callighan, fur he was a fine scholar an' cud rade both books an' writin', an' axed him phat the letters was.

"'A-a-ah, ye ignerant gommoch,' says he to me, 'yer head 's as empty as a drum. Sure here 's no writin' at all, only marks that the shnail's afther makin' an' it crawlin' on the plate.'

"So I explained the inchantmint to him, an' he looked a little closter, an' thin jumped wid shurprise.

"'Oh,' says he. 'Is that thrue?' says he. 'Ye must axqueeze me, Misther Magwire. Sure the shnails does n't write a good hand, an' I 'm an owld man an' me eyes dim, but I see it betther now. Faith, the first letter 's a D,' says he, an' thin he shtudied awhile. 'An' the next is a O, an' thin there 's a C,' says he, 'only the D an' the C is bigger than the O, an' that 's all the letters there is,' says he.

"'An' phat does thim letters shpell?' says I, bekase I did n't know.

"'Ah, bad scran to 'em,' says he; 'there 's thim cows in me field agin,' says he. 'Ax Dora, here she comes,' an' away he wint as she come in, an' I axed her phat D.O.C. shpelt; an' she towld me her name, an' I go bail she was surprised to find the shnail had writ thim letters on the plate, so we marr'd the next Sunday.

"But Owld Moll is a knowledgeable woman an' has a power av shpells an' charms. There 's Tim Gallagher, him as dhrives the public câr out o' Galway, he 's bought his luck av her be the month, fur nigh on twinty year, barin' wan month, that he forgot, an' that time he shpilt his load in the ditch an' kilt a horse, bein' too dhrunk to dhrive.

"Whin me dawther Dora, that was named afther her mother, was ill afther she 'd been to the dance, whin O'Hoolighan's Peggy was married to Paddy Noonan (she danced too hard in the cabin an' come home in the rain), me owld woman wint to Moll an' found that Dora had been cast wid an avil eye. So she gev her a tay to dhrink an' a charm to wear agin it, an' afther she 'd dhrunk the tay an' put on the charm the faver lift her, an' she was well entirely.

"Sure Moll towld me wan magpie manes sorrow, two manes luck, three manes a weddin', an' four manes death; an' did n't I see four o' thim the day o' the fair in Ennis whin O'Dougherty was laid out? An' whin O'Riley cut his arrum wid a bill-hook, an' the blood was runnin', did n't she tie a shtring on the arrum an' dip a raven's feather into the blood av a black cat's tail, an' shtop the bleedin'? An' did n't she bid me take care o' meself the day I met a redheaded woman afore dinner, an' it was n't six months till I met the woman in the mornin', it a-rainin' an' ivery dhrop the full o' yer hat, an' me top-coat at home, an' that same night was I tuk wid the roomytics an' did n't shtir a toe fur a fortnight. Faix, she 's an owld wan is Moll; phat she can't do it n't worth thryin'. If she goes fur to make a match, all the fathers in Ireland cud n't purvint it, an' it 's no use o' their settin' theirselves agin her, fur her head 's as long as a summer day an' as hard as a shillalee.

"Did iver ye hear how she got a husband for owld Miss Rooney, the same that married Misther Dooley that kapes the Aygle Inn in Lisdoon Varna, an' tuk him clane away from the Widdy Mulligan an' two more widdy's that were comin' down upon him like kites on a young rabbit?

"Well, it's a mighty improvin' shtory, fur it shows that widdys can be baten whin they're afther a husband, that some does n't belave, but they do say it takes a witch, the divil, an' an owld maid to do it, an' some think that all o' thim is n't aiquel to a widdy, aven if there 's three o' thim an' but wan av her.

"The razon av it is this. Widdy wimmin are like lobsthers, whin they wanst ketch holt, begob, they 've no consate av lettin' go at all, but will shtick to ye tighter than a toenail, till ye 've aither to marry thim or murther thim, that 's the wan thing in the end; fur if ye marry thim ye 're talked to death, an' if ye murther thim ye 're only dacintly hanged out o' the front dure o' the jail. Whin they 're after a husband, they 're as busy as owld Nick, an' as much in airnest as a dog in purshoot av a flea. More-be-token, they 're always lookin' fur the proper man, an' if they see wan that they think will shuit, bedad, they go afther him as strait as an arrer, an' if he does n't take the alarum an' run like a shape-thief, the widdy 'ull have him afore the althar an' married fast an' tight while he 'd be sayin'a Craydo.

"They know so much be wan axpayrience av marryin', that, barrin' it 's a widdy man that 's in it, an' he nows as much as thimselves, they 'll do for him at wanst, bekase it 's well undhershtood that a bach'ler, aither young or owld, has as much show av outshtrappin' a widdy as a mouse agin a weasel.

"Now, this Misther Dooley was an owld bach'ler, nigh on five an' thirty, an' about fifteen years ago, come next Advint, he come from Cork wid a bit o' money, an' tuk the farm beyant Misther McCoole's on the lift as ye come out o' Galway. He was n't a bad lookin' felly, an' liked the ladies, an' the first time he was in chapel afther takin' the farm, aitch widdy an' owld maid set the two eyes av her on him, an' the Widdy Mulligan says to herself, says she, 'Faix, that 's just the man to take the place av me dear Dinnis,' fur, ye see the widdy's always do spake that-a-way av their husbands, a-givin' them the good word after they 're dead, so as to make up fur the tonge lashin's they give 'em whin they 're alive. It 's quare, so it is, phat widdys are like. Whin ye see a widdy at the wake schraimin' fit to shplit yer head wid the noise, an' flingin' herself acrass the grave at the berryin' like it was a bag o'male she was, an' thin spakin' all the time av 'me poor dear hushband,' I go bail they lived together as paceful as a barrel full o' cats an' dogs; no more is it sorrow that 's in it, but raimorse that 's tarin' at her, an' the shquailin' an' kickin' is beways av a pinnance fur the gostherin' she done him whin he was livin', fur the more there 's in a jug, the less noise it makes runnin' out, an' whin ye 've a heavy load to carry, ye nade all yer breath, an' so have none to waste tellin' how it 's breakin' yer back.

"So it was wid the Widdy Mulligan, that kept the Shamrock Inn, for her Dinnis was a little ottomy av a gossoon, an' her the full av a dure, an' the arrum on her like a smith an' the fut like a leg o' mutton. Och, she was big enough thin, but she 's a horse entirely now, wid the walk av a duck, an' the cheeks av her shakin' like a bowl av shtirabout whin she goes. Her poor Dinnis dar n't say his sowl belonged to him, but was conthrolled be her, an' they do say his last words were, 'I 'll have pace,' that was phat he niver had afther he married her, fur she was wan that 'ud be shmilin' an' shmilin' an' the tongue av her like a razer. She 'd a good bit o' property in the inn, siven beds in the house fur thravellers, an' six childher, the oldest nigh onto twelve, an' from him on down in reg'lar steps like thim in front o' the coort-house.

"Now, a bit up the shtrate from the Shamrock there was a little shop kept be Missis O'Donnell, the widdy av Tim O'Donnell, that died o' bein' mortified in his legs that broke be his fallin' aff his horse wan night whin he was comin' back from Athlone, where he 'd been to a fair. Missis O'Donnell was a wapin' widdy, that 's got eyes like a hydrant, where ye can turn on the wather whin ye plaze. Begorra, thim 's the widdys that 'ull do fur anny man, fur no more can ye tell phat 's in their minds be lookin' at their faces than phat kind av close they 've got on be lookin' at their shadders, an' whin they corner a man that 's tinder-hearted, an' give a shy look at him up out o' their eyes, an' thin look down an' sind two or three dhrops o' wather from undher their eye-lashers, the only salvation fur him is to get up an' run like it was a bag o' gun-powdher she was. So Missis O'Donnell, whin she seen Misther Dooley, tuk the same notion into her head that the Widdy Mulligan did, fur she 'd two childher, a boy an' a gurrul, that were growin' up, an' the shop was n't payin' well.

"There was another widdy in it, the Widdy McMurthry, that aftherwards married a sargeant av the polis, an' lives in Limerick. She was wan o' thim frishky widdy's that shtruts an' wears fine close an' puts on more airs than a paycock. She was a fine-lookin' woman thim times, an' had money in plinty that she got be marryin' McMurthry, that was owld enough to be a father to her an' died o' dhrinkin' too much whiskey at first, an' thin too much sulphur-wather at Lisdoon Varna to set him right agin.

She was always ready wid an answer to ye, fur it was quick witted she was, wid slathers o' talk that did n't mane annything, an' a giggle that she did n't nade to hunt fur whin she wanted it to make a show wid. An' she 'd a dawther that was a fine child, about siventeen, a good dale like her mother.

"Now, Misther Dooley has a kind heart in his body fur wimmin in gineral, an' as he liked a bit o' chaff wid thim on all occashuns, he was n't long in gettin' acquainted wid all the wimmin o' the parish, an' was well liked be thim, an', be the same token, was n't be the men, fur men, be nacher, doesn't like a woman's man anny more than wimmin like a man's woman. But, afther a bit, he begun to center himself on the three widdys, an' sorra the day' ud go by whin he come to town but phat he 'd give wan or another o' thim a pace av his comp'ny that was very plazin' to thim. Bedad, he done that same very well, for he made a round av it for to kape thim in suspince. He 'd set in the ale room o' the Shamrock an hour in the afthernoon an' chat wid the Widdy Mulligan as she was sarvin' the dhrink, an' shtop in the Widdy O'Donnell's shop as he was goin' by, to get a thrifle or a bit av shwates an' give to her childher beways av a complimint, an' thin go to Missis McMurthry's to tay, an' so got on well wid thim all. An' it 's me belafe he 'd be doin' that same to this blessed day only that the widdys begun to be pressin' as not likin' fur to wait any longer. Fur, mind ye, a widdy 's not like a young wan that 'll wait fur ye to spake an' if ye don't do it, 'ull go on foriver, or till she gets tired av waitin' an' takes some wan else that does spake, widout sayin' a word to ye at all; but the widdy 'ull be hintin' an' hintin', an' her hints 'ull be as shtrong as a donkey's kick, so that the head o' ye has to be harder than a pavin'-shtone if ye don't undhershtand, an' ye 've got to have more impidince than a monkey if ye don't spake up an' say something about marryin'.

"Well, as I was afther sayin', the widdys begun to be pressin' him clost: the Widdy Mulligan tellin' him how good her business was an' phat a savin' there 'd be if a farm an' a public were put together; the Widdy O'Donnell a-lookin' at him out av her tears an' sighin' an' tellin' him how lonely he must be out on a farm an' nobody but a man wid him in the house, fur she was lonesome in town, an' it was n't natheral at all, so it was n't, fur aither man or woman to be alone; an' the Widdy McMurthry a palatherin' to him that if he 'd a fine, good-lookin' woman that loved him, he 'd be a betther man an' a changed man entirely. So they wint on, the widdys a-comin' at him, an' he thryin' to kape wid thim all, as he might have knewn he could n't do (barrin' he married the three o' thim like a Turk), until aitch wan got to undhershtand, be phat he said to her, that he was goin' to marry her, an' the minnit they got this in their heads, aitch begged him that he 'd shtay away from the other two, fur aitch knewn he wint to see thim all. By jayminy, it bothered him thin, fur he liked to talk to thim all aiquelly, an' did n't want to confine his agrayable comp'ny to anny wan o' thim. So he got out av it thish-a-way. He promised the Widdy McMurthry that he 'd not go to the Shamrock more than wanst in the week, nor into the Widdy O'Donnell's barrin' he naded salt fur his cow; an' said to the Widdy Mulligan that he 'd not more than spake to Missis O'Donnell whin he wint in, an' that he 'd go no more at all to Missis McMurthry's; an' he towld Missis O'Donnell that whin he wint to the Shamrock he 'd get his sup an' thin lave at wanst, an' not go to the Widdy McMurthry's axceptin' whin his horse wanted to be shod, the blacksmith's bein' ferninst her dure that it 'ud be convaynient fur him to wait at. So he shmiled wid himself thinkin' he 'd done thim complately, an' made up his mind that whin his pitaties were dug he 'd give up the farm an' get over into County Clare, away from the widdys.

"But thim that think widdys are fools are desaved entirely, an' so was Misther Dooley, fur instead av his troubles bein' inded, begob, they were just begun. Ivery time he wint into the Shamrock Missis O'Donnell heard av it an' raymonshtrated wid

him, an' 'ud cry at him beways it was dhrinkin' himself to death
he was; afther lavin' the Shamrock, the Widdy Mulligan 'ud set
wan av her boys to watch him up the strate an' see if he
shtopped in the shop. Av coorse he cud n't go by, an' whin he
come agin, the Widdy Mulligan 'ud gosther him about it, an'
thin he 'd promise not to do it agin. No more cud he go in the
Widdy O'Donnell's shop widout meetin' Missis McMurthry's
dawther that was always shtreelin' on the strate, an' thin her
mother 'ud say to him it was a power o' salt his cow was atin',
an' the Widdy O'Donnell towld him his horse must be an
axpensive baste fur to nade so much shooin'.

"Thin he 'd tell thim a lot o' lies that they purtinded to
belave an' did n't, bekase they 're such desavers thimselves that
it is n't aisey fur to do thim, but Dooley begun to think if it got
anny hotter fur him he 'd lave the pitaties to the widdys to divide
bechune thim as a raytribution fur the loss av himself, an' go to
Clare widout delay.

"While he 'd this bother on him he got to know owld Miss
Rooney, that lived wid her mother an' father on the farm next
but wan to his own, but on the other side o' the way, an' the
manes be which he got to know her was this. Wan mornin', whin
Dooley's man, Paddy, wint to milk the cow, bad scran to the
dhrop she 'd to shpare, an' he pullin' an' pullin', like it was
ringin' the chapel bell he was, an' she kickin', an' no milk
comin', faix not as much as 'ud blind the eye av a midge. So he
wint an' towld Misther Dooley.

"'I can get no milk,' says he. 'Begorra the cow 's as dhry as
a fiddler's troat,' says he.

"'Musha, thin,' says Misther Dooley, 'it 's the lazy
omadhawn ye are. I don't belave it. Can ye milk at all?' says he.

"'I can,' says Paddy, 'as well as a calf,' says he. 'But phat 's
the use ov pullin'? Ye 'd get the same quantity from a rope,' says
he.

"So Dooley wint out an' thried himself an' did n't get as

much as a shmell of milk.

"'Phat 's the matther wid the baste?' says he, 'an' her on the grass from sun to sun.'

"'Be jakers,' says Paddy, 'it 's my consate that she 's bewitched.'

"'It 's thrue fur ye,' says Dooley, as the like was aften knewn. 'Go you to Misther Rooney's wid the pail an' get milk fur the calf, an' ax if there 's a Pishogue hereabouts.'

"So Paddy wint an' come back sayin' that the young lady towld him there was.

"'So there 's a young lady in it,' thinks Dooley. Faix, the love av coortin' was shtrong on him. 'Did ye ax her how to raich the woman?'

"'Bedad, I did n't. I forgot,' says Paddy.

"'That 's yerself entirely,' says Dooley to him agin. 'I 'd betther thrust me arriants to a four-legged jackass as to wan wid two. He 'd go twict as fast an' remimber as much. I 'll go meself,' says he, only wantin' an axcuse, an' so he did. He found Miss Rooney thried to be plazin', an' it bein' convainient, he wint agin, an' so it was ivery day whin he 'd go fur the calf's milk he 'd have a chat wid her, an' sometimes come over in the avenin', bekase it was n't healthy fur him in town just thin.

"But he wint to Owld Moll about the cow, an' the charm she gev him soon made the baste all right agin, but, be that time, he 'd got used to goin' to Rooney's an' liked it betther than the town, bekase whinever he wint to town he had to make so many axcuses he was afeared the widdys 'ud ketch him in a lie.

"So he shtayed at home most times and wint over to Rooney's the rest, fur it was n't a bad job at all, though she was about one an' forty, an' had give up the fight fur a husband an' so saiced strugglin'. As long as they 've anny hope, owld maids are the most prayposptherous craythers alive, fur they' ll fit thimselves wid the thrappin's av a young gurrul an' look as onaisey in thim as a boy wid his father's britches on. But whin they 've consinted to the sitiwation an' saiced to struggle, thin they begin to be happy an' enjoy life a bit, but there 's no aise in the worruld fur thim till thin. Now Miss Rooney had gev up the contist an' plasthered her hair down on aitch side av her face so smooth ye 'd shwear it was ironed it was, an' begun to take the worruld aisey.

"But there 's thim that says an owld maid niver does give up her hope, only lets on to be continted so as to lay in amboosh fur anny onsuspishus man that happens to shtray along, an' faix, it looks that-a-way from phat I 'm goin' to tell ye, bekase as soon as Misther Dooley begun to come over an' palather his fine talk to her an' say shwate things, thin she up an' begins shtrugglin' harder nor iver, bekase it was afther she 'd let go, an' comin' onexpected-like she thought it was a dispinsation av Providence, whin rayly it was only an accident it was, beways av Dooley's cow goin' dhry an' the calf too young to lave suckin' an' ate grass.

"Annyhow, wan day, afther Misther Dooley had talked purty nice the avenin' afore, she put an her cloak, an' wint to Owld Moll an' in an' shut the dure.

"'Now, Moll,' she says to the owld cuillean, 'it 's a long time since I 've been to ye, barrin' the time the goat was lost, fur, sure, I lost me confidince in ye. Ye failed me twict, wanst whin John McCune forgot me whin he wint to Derry an' thin come back an' married that Mary O'Niel, the impidint young shtrap, wid the air av her as red as a glowin' coal; an' wanst whin Misther McFinnigan walked aff from me an' married the Widdy Bryan. Now ye must do yer besht, fur I 'm thinkin' that, wid a little industhry, I cud get Misther Dooley, the same that the town widdys is so flusthrated wid.'

"'An' does he come to see ye, at all?' says Moll.

"'Faith he does, an' onless I 'm mishtaken is mightily plazed wid his comp'ny whin it 's me that 's in it,' says Miss Rooney.

"'An' phat widdys is in it,' says Moll, as she did n't know, bekase sorra a step did the widdys go to her wid their love doin's, as they naded no help, an' cud thransact thim affairs thimselves as long as their tongues held out.

"So Miss Rooney towld her, an' Moll shuk her head. 'Jagers,' says she, 'I 'm afeared yer goose is cooked if all thim widdys is after him. I won't thry,' says she.

"But Miss Rooney was as much in airnest as the widdys, troth, I 'm thinkin', more, bekase she was fairly aitchin' fur a husband now she 'd got her mind on it.

"'Sure, Moll,' says she, 'ye would n't desart me now an' it me last show. Thim widdys can marry who they plaze, bad scran to 'em, but if Misther Dooley gets from me, divil fly wid the husband I 'll get at all, at all,' beginnin' to cry.

"So, afther a dale av palatherin', Moll consinted to thry, bein' it was the third time Miss Rooney had been to her, besides, she wanted to save her charackther for a knowledgeable woman. So she aggrade to do her best, an' gev her a little bag to carry wid 'erbs in it, an' writ some words on two bits av paper an' the same in Latin. It was an awful charm, no more do I remimber it, fur it was niver towld me, nor to anny wan else, fur it was too dreadful to say axceptin' in Latin an' in a whisper fur fear the avil sper'ts 'ud hear it, that don't undhershtand thim dape langwidges.

"'Now, darlint,' says owld Moll, a-givin' her wan, 'take you this charm an' kape it on you an' the bag besides, an' ye must manage so as this other paper 'ull be on Misther Dooley, an' if it fails an he don't marry ye I 'll give ye back yer money an' charge ye nothing at all,' says she.

"So Miss Rooney tuk the charms an' paid Owld Moll one pound five, an' was to give her fifteen shillins more afther she was married to Dooley.

"She wint home, bothered entirely how she 'd get the charm on Dooley, an' the avenin' come, an' he wid it, an' shtill she did n't know. So he set an' talked an' talked, an' by an' by he dhrunk up the rest av the whiskey an' wather in his glass an' got up to go.

"'Why, Misther Dooley,' says she, bein' all at wanst shtruck be an idee. 'Was iver the like seen av yer coat?' says she. 'Sure it 's tore in the back. Sit you down agin wan minnit an' I 'll mend it afore ye can light yer pipe. Take it aff,' says she.

"'Axqueeze me,' says Dooley. 'I may be a bigger fool than I look, or I may look a bigger fool than I am, but I know enough to kape the coat on me back whin I 'm wid a lady,' says he.

"'Then take a sate an' I 'll sow it on ye,' says she to him agin, so he set down afore the fire, an' she, wid a pair av shizzors an' a nadle, wint behind him an' at the coat. 'T was a sharp thrick av her, bekase she took the shizzors, an' whin she was lettin' on to cut aff the t'reads that she said were hangin', she ripped the collar an' shlipped in the bit o' paper, an' sowed it up as nate as a samesthress in less than no time.

"'It 's much beholden to ye I am,' say Dooley, risin' wid his pipe lit. 'An' it 's a happy man I 'd be if I 'd a young woman av yer size to do the like to me ivery day.'

"'Glory be to God,' says Miss Rooney to herself, fur she thought the charm was beginnin' to work. But she says to him, 'Oh, it 's talkin' ye are. A fine man like you can marry who he plazes.'

"So Dooley wint home, an' she, think' the business as good as done, towld her mother that night she was to marry Misther Dooley. The owld lady cud n't contain herself or the saycret aither, so the next mornin' towld it to her sister, an' she to her dawther that wint to school wid Missis McMurthry's gurrul. Av coorse the young wan cud n't howld her jaw anny more than the owld wans, an' up an' towld the widdy's dawther an' she her mother an' the rest o' the town, so be the next day every wan knew that Dooley was goin' to marry Miss Rooney: that shows, if ye want to shpread a bit o' news wid a quickness aiquel to the tellygraph, ye 've only to tell it to wan woman as a saycret.

"Well, me dear, the noise the widdys made 'ud shtun a dhrummer. Dooley had n't been in town fur a week, an' widdys bein' nacherly suspishus, they misthrusted that somethin' was wrong, but divil a wan o' thim thought he' d do such an onmannerly thrick as that. But they all belaved it, bekase widdys judge iverybody be themselves, so they were mighty mad.

"The Widdy McMurthry was first to hear the news, as her dawther towld her, an' she riz in a fury. 'Oh the owdashus villin,' says she; 'to think av him comin' her an' me listenin' at him that was lyin' fasther than a horse 'ud throt. But I 'll have justice, so I will, an' see if there 's a law for a lone widdy. I 'll go to the judge,' fur, I forgot to tell ye, it was jail delivery an' the coort was settin' an' the judge down from Dublin wid a wig on him the size av a bar'l.

"Whin they towld Missis O'Donnell, she bust out cryin' an' says, 'Sure it can't be thrue. It is n't in him to desave a poor widdy wid only two childer, an' me thrustin' on him' so she wint into the back room an' laid on the bed.

"But whin the Widdy Mulligan learned it, they thought she'd take a fit, the face av her got so red an' she chokin' wid rage. 'Tatther an' agers,' says she. 'If I only had that vagabone here five minnits, it 's a long day it 'ud be afore he 'd desave another tinder-hearted faymale.'

"'Oh, be aisey,' says wan to her, 'faix, you 're not the onliest wan that 's in it. Sure there 's the Widdy O'Donnell an' Missis McMurthry that he 's desaved aiquelly wid yerself.'

"'Is that thrue?' says she; 'by this an' by that I 'll see thim an' we 'll go to the judge an' have him in the prision. Sure the Quane 's a widdy herself an' knows how it feels, an' her judge 'ull take the part av widdys that 's misconshtrewed be a nagurly blaggârd like owld Dooley. Bad luck to the seed, breed, an' generation av him. I cud mop up the flure wid him, the divil roast him, an' if I lay me hands on him, I 'll do it,' says she, an' so she would; an' a blessin it was to Misther Dooley he was not in town just thin, but at home, diggin' pitaties as fast as he cud, an' chucklin' to himself how he 'd send the pitaties to town be Paddy, an' himself go to Clare an' get away from the whole tribe av widdys an' owld maids.

"So the Widdy Mulligan wint afther the Widdy O'Donnell an' tuk her along, an' they towld thim av the Widdy McMurthry an' how she was done be him, an they got her too, fur they all said, 'Sure we would n't marry him fur him, but only want to see him punished fur misconshtructing phat we said to him an' lying to us.' Be this time half the town was ready an' aiger to go wid thim to the coort, an' so they did, an' in, wid the offishers thryin' to kape thim out, an' the wimmin shovin' in, an' all their frinds wid 'em, an' the shur'f callin' out 'Ordher in the coort,' an' the judge lookin' over his shpectacles at thim.

"'Phat 's this at all?' says the judge, wid a solemnious voice. 'Is it a riat it is, or a faymale convulsion?'—whin he seen all the wimmin. 'Phat 's the matther?' says he, an' wid that all the wimmin begun at wanst, so as the noise av thim was aiquel to a 'viction.

"'Marcy o' God,' says the judge, 'phat 's in the faymales at all? Are they dishtracted entirely, or bewitched, or only dhrunk?' says he.

"'We 're crazy wid graif, yer Lordshap,' they schraimed at him at wanst. 'It 's justice we want agin the uppresser.'

"'Phat 's the uppresser been a-doin'?' axed the judge.

"'Disthroyin' our pace, an' that av our families,' they said to him.

"'Who is the oppresser?' he axed.

"'Owld Dooley,' they all shouted at him at the wan time, like it was biddin' at an auction they were.

"So at first the judge cud n't undhershtand at all, till some wan whishpered the truth to him an' thin he scrotched his chin wid a pen.

"'Is it a man fur to marry all thim widdys? By me wig, he 's a bowld wan. Go an' fetch him,' he says to a constable. 'Be sated, ladies, an' ye 'll have justice,' he says to the widdys, very p'lite. 'Turn out thim other blaggârds,' he says to the shur'f, an' away wint the polisman afther Dooley.

"He found him at home, wid his coat aff, an' him an' Paddy diggin' away at the pitaties for dear life, bekase he wanted to get thim done.

"'Misther Dooley,' says the consthable to him, 'ye 're me prish'ner. Come along, ye must go wid me at wanst.'

"At first, Dooley was surprised in that degray he thought the life 'ud lave him, as the consthable come up behind him on the quiet, so as to give him no show to run away.

"'Phat for?' says Dooley to him, whin he 'd got his wind agin.

"'Faix, I 'm not sartain,' says the polisman, that was n't a bad felly; 'but I belave it 's along o' thim widdys that are so fond o' ye. The three o' thim 's in the coort an' all the faymales in town, an' the judge sint me afther ye, an' ye must come at wanst, so make ready to go immejitly.'

"'Don't go wid him,' says Paddy, wid his sleeves rowled up an' spitting in his hands. 'Lave me at him,' says he, but Dooley would n't, bekase he was a paceable man. But he was n't anxshus to go to the coort at all; begob, he 'd all the coortin' he naded, but bein' there was no help fur it, he got his coat, the same that Miss Rooney sowed the charm in, an' shtarted wid the consthable.

"Now, it was that mornin' that owld Rooney was in town, thryin' to sell a goat he had, that gev him no end o' throuble be losin' itself part of the time an' the rest be jumpin' on the thatch an' stickin' its feet through. But he cud n't sell it, as ivery wan knew the bast as well as himself, an' so he was sober, that was n't common wid him. Whin he seen the widdys an' the other wimmin wid thim shtravigerin' through the strate on the way to the coort an' heard the phillaloo they were afther makin', he axed phat the matther was. So they towld him, an' says he, 'Be the powers, if it 's a question av makin' him marry some wan, me dawther has an inthrust in the matther,' so he dhropped the goat's shtring an' shtarted home in a lamplighter's throt to fetch her, an' got there about the time the polisman nabbed Dooley.

"'There, they 're afther goin' now,' says he to her. 'Make haste, or we'll lose thim,' an' aff they run, she wid her charm an' he widout his coat, grippin' a shillalee in his fisht, an' caught up wid Paddy that was follerin' the polisman an' Dooley.

"So they jogged along, comfortable enough, the polisman an' Dooley in the lade, afther thim owld Rooney an' Paddy, blaggârdin' the consthable ivery fut o' the way, an' offerin' fur to bate him so as he would n't know himself be lookin' in the glass, an' Miss Rooney in the rare, wondherin' if the charm 'ud work right. But Dooley did n't let a word out av his jaw, as knowin' he 'd nade all his breath afther gettin' into the coort.

"At the rise o' the hill the pursesshun was met be about a hunderd o' the town boys that come out fur to view thim, an' that yelled at Dooley how the widdys were waitin' to tare him in paces, an' that he was as good as a dead man a'ready, so he was; an' whin they got into town, all the men jined the show, roarin' wid laughter an' shoutin' at Dooley that the judge cud n't do anny more than hang him at wanst, an' to shtand it like a hayro, bekase they 'd all be at the hangin' an' come to the wake besides an' have a tundherin' big time. But he answered thim niver a word, so they all wint on to the coort, an' in, bringin' the other half o' the town wid 'em, the faymale half bein' there kapin' comp'ny wid the widdys.

"The minnit they come nie the dure, all the widdys an' wimmin begun in wan breath to make raimarks on thim.

"'A-a-a-ah, the hang-dog face he has,' says Missis McMurthry. 'Sure has n't he the look av a shape-thief on the road to the gallus?'

"'See the haythen vagabone,' says the Widdy Mulligan. 'If I

had me tin fingers on him for five minnits, it's all the satiswhackshun I 'd ax. Bad cess to the hair I 'd lave on the head av him or in his whushkers aither.'

"But the Widdy O'Donnell only cried, an' all the wimmin turned their noses up whin they seen Miss Rooney comin' in.

"'Look at that owld thing,' says they. 'Phat a power av impidince! Mind the consate av her to be comin' here wid him. Sure she has n't the shame av a shtone monkey,' says they av her.

"'Silence in the coort,' says the shur'f. 'Stop that laughin' be the dure. Git along down out o' thim windys,' says he to the mob that Dooley an' the consthable brought wid thim.

"'Misther Dooley,' says the judge, 'I'm axed to b'lave ye 're thryin' to marry four wimmin at wanst, three av the same aforeshed bein' widdys an' the other wan not. Is it thrue, or do ye plade not guilty?' says he.

"'It 's not thrue, yer Lordshap,' says Dooley, shpakin' up, bekase he seen he was in for it an' put on a bowld face. 'Thim widdys is crazy to get a husband, an' misconsayved the manin' o' me words,' says he, an' that minnit you 'd think a faymale lunattic ashylum broke loose in the coort.

"They all gabbled at wanst like a field av crows. They said he was a haythen, a Toork, a vulgar shpalpeen, a lyin' blaggârd, a uppresser av the widdy, a robber av the orphin, he was worse than a nagur, he was, so he was, an' they niver thought av belavin' him, nor av marryin' him aither till he axed thim, an' so on.

"The judge was a married man himself an' knewn it was no use thryin' to shtop the gostherin', for it was a joke av him to say that the differ bechuxt a woman an' a book was you cud shut up a book, so he let thim go on till they were spint an' out o' breath an' shtopped o' thimselves like an owld clock that 's run down.

"'The sintince av this coort, Misther Dooley, is, that ye

marry wan av 'em an' make compinsation to the other wans in a paycoonyary way be payin' thim siven poun' aitch.'

"'Have marcy, yer Lordshap,' says Dooley, bekase he seen himself shtripped av all he had. 'Make it five poun', an' that 's more than I 've got in money.'

"'Siven pound, not a haporth less,' says the judge. "if ye have n't the money ye can pay it in projuice. An' make yer chice bechune the wimmin who ye 'll marry, as it 's married ye 'll be this blessed day, bekase ye 've gone too long a'ready,' says the judge, very starn, an' thin the widdys all got quite, an' begun to be sorry they gev him so many hard names.

"'Is it wan o' the widdy's must I marry?' says Dooley, axin' the judge, an' the charm in his coller beginnin' to work hard an' remind him av Miss Rooney, that was settin' on wan side, trimblin'.

"'Tare an' 'ouns,' says the judge. 'Bad luck to ye, ye onmannerly idjit,' as he was gettin' vexed wid Dooley, that was shtandin', acrotchin' the head av him like he was thryin' to encourage his brains. 'Was n't it wan o' the wimmin that I tould ye to take?' says he.

"'If that 's phat yer Lordshap syas, axin' yer pardin an' not misdoubtin' ye, if it 's plazin' to ye, bedad, I 'll take the owld maid, bekase thim widdys have got a sight av young wans, an' childer are like toothpicks, ivery man wants his own an' not another felly's.' But he had another razon that he towld to me afther; says he, 'If I 've got to have a famly, be jakers, I want to have the raisin' av it meself,' an' my blessin' on him for that same.

"But whin he was spakin' an' said he 'd take Miss Rooney, wid that word she fainted away fur dead, an' was carried out o' the coort be her father an' Paddy.

"So it was settled, an' as Dooley did n't have the money, the widdys aggrade to take their pay some other way. The Widdy Mulligan tuk the pitaties he was diggin' whin the polisman gripped him, as she said they 'd kape the inn all winter. The Widdy McMurthry got his hay, which come convaynient, bekase her brother kep post horses an' tuk the hay av her at two shillins undher the market. Missis O'Donnell got the cow that made all the throuble be goin' dhry at the wrong time, an' bein' it was a good cow was vally'd at tin poun' so she geve him three poun', an' was to sind him the calf whin it was weaned. So the widdys were all paid for bein' wounded in their hearts be Misther Dooley, an' a good bargain they made av it, bekase a widdy's affections are like gârden weeds, the more ye thrample thim the fasther they grow.

"Misther Dooley got Miss Rooney, an' she a husband, fur they pulled her out av her faint wid a bucket o' wather, an' the last gossoon in town wint from the coort to the chapel wid Miss Rooney an Misther Dooley, the latther crassin' himself ivery minnit an' blessin' God ivery step he tuk that it was n't the jail he was goin' to, an' they were married there wid a roarin' crowd waitin' in the strate fur to show thim home. But they sarcumvinted thim, bekase they wint out the back way an' through Father O'Donohue's gârden, an' so home, lavin' the mob howlin' before the chapel dure like wild Ingines.

"An' that's the way the owld maid defated three widdys, that is n't often done, no more would she have done it but for owld Moll an' the charm in Dooley's coat. But he's very well plazed, an' that I know, for afther me first wife died, her I was tellin' ye av, I got the roomytics in me back like tin t'ousand divils clawin' at me backbone, an' I made me mind up that I 'd get another wife, bekase I wanted me back rubbed, sence it 'ull be chaper, says I, to marry some wan to rub it than to pay a boy to do that same. So I was lookin' roun' an' met Misther Dooley an' spake av it to him, an' good luk it 'ud have been if I 'd tuk his advice, but I did n't, bein' surrounded be a widdy afther, that 's rubbed me back well fur me only wid a shtick. But says he to me, 'Take you my advice Misther Magwire, an' whin ye marry, get you an owld maid, if there 's wan to be had in the counthry. Gurruls is flighty an' axpectin' too much av ye, an' widdys is greedy buzzards as ye 've seen by my axpayriences, but owld maids is humble, an' thankful for gettin' a husband at all, God bless 'em, so they shtrive to plaze an' do as ye bid thim widout grumblin' or axin' throublesome questions.'"

From The Crock of Gold
James Stephens

WHEN THE LEPRECAUN came through the pine wood on the following day he met the two children at a little distance from the house. He raised his open right hand above his head (this is both the fairy and the Gaelic form of salutation), and would have passed on but that a thought brought him to a halt. Sitting down before the two children he stared at them for a long time, and they stared back at him. At last he said to the boy:

"What is your name, a vic vig O?"

"Seumas Beg, sir," the boy replied.

"It's a little name," said the Leprecaun.

"It's what my mother calls me, sir," returned the boy.

"What does your father call you," was the next question.

"Seumas Eoghan Maelduin O'Carbhail Mac an Droid."

"It's a big name," said the Leprecaun, and he turned to the

little girl. "What is your name, a cailin vig O?"

"Brigid Beg, sir."

"And what does your father call you?"

"He never calls me at all, sir."

"Well, Seumaseen and Breedeen, you are good little children, and I like you very much. Health be with you until I come to see you again."

And then the Leprecaun went back the way he had come. As he went he made little jumps and cracked his fingers, and sometimes he rubbed one leg against the other.

"That's a nice Leprecaun," said Seumas.

"I like him too," said Brigid.

"Listen," said Seumas, "let me be the Leprecaun, and you be the two children, and I will ask you our names."

So they did that.

The next day the Leprecaun came again. He sat down beside the children and, as before, he was silent for a little time.

"Are you not going to ask us our names, sir?" said Seumas.

His sister smoothed out her dress shyly.

"My name, sir, is Brigid Beg," said she.

"Did you ever play Jackstones?" said the Leprecaun.

"No, sir," replied Seumas.

"I'll teach you how to play Jackstones," said the Leprecaun, and he picked up some pine cones and taught the children that game.

"Did you ever play Ball in the Decker?"

"No, sir," said Seumas.

"Did you ever play 'I can make a nail with my ree-ro-raddy-O, I can make a nail with my ree-ro-ray?'"

"No, sir," replied Seumas.

"It's a nice game," said the Leprecaun, "and so is Cap-on-the-back, and Twenty-four yards on the billy-goat's tail, and Towns,

and Relievo, and Leap-frog. I'll teach you all these games," said
the Leprecaun, "and I'll teach you how to play Knifey, and
Hole-and-taw, and Horneys and Robbers."

"Leap-frog is the best one to start with, so I'll teach it to you
at once. Let you bend down like this, Breedeen, and you bend
down like that a good distance away, Seumas. Now I jump over
Breedeen's back, and then I run and jump over Seumaseen's
back like this, and then I run ahead again and I bend down.
Now, Breedeen, you jump over your brother, and then you jump
over me, and run a good bit on and bend down again. Now,
Seumas, it is your turn; you jump over me and then over your
sister, and then you run on and bend down again and I jump.

"This is a fine game, sir," said Seumas.

"It is, a vic vig,—keep in your head," said the Leprecaun.
"That's a good jump, you couldn't beat that jump, Seumas."

"I can jump better than Brigid already," replied Seumas,
"and I'll jump as well as you do when I get more practice—
keep in your head, sir."

Almost without noticing it they had passed through the edge
of the wood, and were playing into a rough field which was
cumbered with big, gray rocks. It was the very last field in sight,
and behind it the rough, heather-packed mountain sloped
distantly away to the skyline. There was a raggedy blackberry
hedge all round the field, and there were long, tough, haggard-
looking plants growing in clumps here and there. Near a corner
of this field there was a broad, low tree, and as they played they
came near and nearer to it. The Leprecaun gave a back very
close to the tree. Seumas ran and jumped and slid down a hole
at the side of the tree. Then Brigid ran and jumped and slid
down the same hole

"Dear me!" said Brigid, and she flashed out of sight.

The Leprecaun cracked his fingers and rubbed one leg against the other, and then he also dived into the hole and disappeared from view.

When the time at which the children usually went home had passed, the Thin Woman of Inis Magrath became a little anxious. She had never known them to be late for dinner before. There was one of the children whom she hated; it was her own child, but as she had forgotten which of them was hers, and as she loved one of them, she was compelled to love both for fear of making a mistake, and chastising the child for whom her heart secretly yearned. Therefore, she was equally concerned about both of them.

Dinner time passed and supper time arrived, but the children did not. Again and again the Thin Woman went out through the dark pine trees and called until she was so hoarse that she could not even hear herself when she roared. The evening wore on to the night, and while she waited for the Philosopher to come in she reviewed the situation. Her husband had not come in, the children had not come in, the Leprecaun had not returned as arranged. . . . A light flashed upon her. The Leprecaun had kidnapped her children! She announced a vengeance against the Leprecauns, which would stagger humanity. While in the extreme center of her ecstasy the Philosopher came through the trees and entered the house.

The Thin Woman flew to him—

"Husband," said she, "the Leprecauns of Gort na Cloca Mora have kidnapped our children."

The Philosopher gazed at her for a moment.

"Kidnapping," said he, "has been for many centuries a favorite occupation of fairies, gypsies, and the brigands of the East. The usual procedure is to attach a person and hold it to ransom. If the ransom is not paid an ear or a finger may be cut from the captive and despatched to those interested, with the statement that an arm or a leg will follow in a week unless suitable arrangements are entered into."

"Do you understand," said the Thin Woman passionately, "that it is your own children who have been kidnapped?"

"I do not," said the Philosopher. "This course, however, is rarely followed by the fairy people: they do not ordinarily steal for ransom, but for love of thieving, or from some other obscure and possibly functional causes, and the victim is retained in their forts or duns until by the effluxion of time they forget their origin and become peaceable citizens of the fairy state. Kidnapping is not by any means confined to either humanity or the fairy people."

"Monster," said the Thin Woman in a deep voice, "will you listen to me?"

"I will not," said the Philosopher. "Many of the insectivora also practice this custom. Ants, for example, are a respectable race living in well-ordered communities. They have attained to a most complex and artificial civilization, and will frequently adventure far afield on colonizing or other expeditions from whence they return with a rich booty of aphides and other stock, who thenceforward become the servants and domestic creatures of the republic. As they neither kill nor eat their captives, this practice will be termed kidnapping. The same may be said of bees, a hardy and industrious race living in hexagonal cells which are very difficult to make. Sometimes, on lacking a queen of their own, they have been observed to abduct one from a less powerful neighbor, and use her for their own purposes without shame, mercy, or remorse."

"Will you not understand?" screamed the Thin Woman.

"I will not," said the Philosopher. "Semitropical apes have been rumored to kidnap children, and are reported to use them very tenderly indeed, sharing their coconuts, yams, plantains, and other equatorial provender with the largest generosity, and conveying their delicate captives from tree to tree (often at great distances from each other and from the ground) with the most guarded solicitude and benevolence."

"1 am going to bed," said the Thin Woman; "your stirabout is on the hob."

"Are there lumps in it, my dear?" said the Philosopher.

"I hope there are," replied the Thin Woman, and she leaped into bed. That night the Philosopher was afflicted with the most extraordinary attack of rheumatism he had ever known, nor did he get any ease until the gray morning wearied his lady into a reluctant slumber.

．　　　．　　　．　　　．　　　．

The Thin Woman of Inis Magrath slept very late that morning, but when she did awaken her impatience was so urgent that she could scarcely delay to eat her breakfast. Immediately after she had eaten she put on her bonnet and shawl and went through the pine wood in the direction of Gort na Cloca Mora. In a short time she reached the rocky field, and, walking over to the tree in the southeast corner, she picked up a small stone and hammered loudly against the trunk of the tree. She hammered in a peculiar fashion, giving two knocks and then three knocks, and then one knock. A voice came up from the hole.

"Who is that, please?" said the voice.

"Ban na Droid of Inis Magrath, and well you know it," was her reply.

"I am coming up, Noble Woman," said the voice, and in another moment the Leprecaun leaped out of the hole.

"Where are Seumas and Brigid Beg?" said the Thin Woman

sternly.

"How would I know where they are," replied the Leprecaun. "Wouldn't they be at home now?"

"If they were at home I wouldn't have come here looking for them," was her reply. "It is my belief that you have them."

"Search me," said the Leprecaun, opening his waistcoat.

"They are down there in your little house," said the Thin Woman angrily, "and the sooner you let them up the better it will be for yourself and your five brothers."

"Noble Woman," said the. Leprecaun, "you can go down yourself into our little house and look. I can't say fairer than that."

"I wouldn't fit down there," said she. " I'm too big."

"You know the way for making yourself little," replied the Leprecaun.

"But I mightn't be able to make myself big again," said the Thin Woman, "and then you and your dirty brothers would have it all your own way. If you don't let the children up," she continued, "I'll raise the Shee of Croghan Conghaile against you. You know what happened to the Cluricauns of Oilean na Glas when they stole the Queen's baby—It will be a worse thing than that for you. If the children are not back in my house before moonrise this night, I'll go round to my people. Just tell that to your five ugly brothers. Health with you," she added, and strode away.

"Health with yourself, Noble Woman," said the Leprecaun, and he stood on one leg until she was out of sight and then he slid down into the hole again.

*   *   *   *   *

When the children leaped into the hole at the foot of the tree they found themselves sliding down a dark, narrow slant which dropped them softly enough into a little room. This room was hollowed out immediately under the tree, and great care had been taken not to disturb any of the roots which ran here and there through the chamber in the strangest criss-cross, twisted fashion. To get across such a place one had to walk round, and jump over, and duck under perpetually. Some of the roots had formed themselves very conveniently into low seats and narrow, uneven tables, and at the bottom all the roots ran into the floor and away again in the direction required by their business. After the clear air outside this place was very dark to the children's eyes, so that they could not see anything for a few minutes, but after a little time their eyes became accustomed to the semiobscurity and they were able to see quite well. The first things they became aware of were six small men who were seated on low roots. They were all dressed in tight green clothes and little leathern aprons, and they wore tall green hats which wobbled when they moved. They were all busily engaged making shoes. One was drawing out wax ends on his knee, another was softening pieces of leather in a bucket of water, another was polishing the instep of a shoe with a piece of curved bone, another was paring down a heel with a short broad-bladed knife, and another was hammering wooden pegs into a sole. He had all the pegs in his mouth, which gave him a wide-faced, jolly expression, and according as a peg was wanted he blew it into his hand and hit it twice with his hammer, and then he blew another peg, and he always blew the peg with the right end uppermost, and never had to hit it more than twice. He was a person well worth watching.

 The children had slid down so unexpectedly that they almost forgot their good manners, but as soon as Seumas Beg discovered that he was really in a room he removed his cap and stood up.

"God be with all here," said he.

The Leprecaun who had brought them lifted Brigid from the floor to which amazement still constrained her.

"Sit down on that little root, child of my heart," said he, "and you can knit stockings for us."

"Yes, sir," said Brigid meekly.

The Leprecaun took four knitting needles and a ball of green wool from the top of a high, horizontal root. He had to climb over one, go round three, and climb up two roots to get at it, and he did this so easily that it did not seem a bit of trouble. He gave the needles and wool to Brigid Beg.

"Do you know how to turn the heel Brigid Beg?" said he.

"No, sir," said Brigid.

"Well, I'll show you how when you come to it."

The other six Leprecauns had ceased work and were looking at the children. Seumas turned to them.

"God bless the work," said he politely.

One of the Leprecauns, who had a gray, puckered face and a thin fringe of gray whisker very far under his chin, then spoke.

"Come over here, Seumas Beg," said he, "and I'll measure you for a pair of shoes. Put your foot up on that root."

The boy did so, and the Leprecaun took the measure of his foot with a wooden rule.

"Now, Brigid Beg, show me your foot," and he measured her also. "They'll be ready for you in the morning."

"Do you never do anything else but make shoes, sir?" said Seumas.

"We do not," replied the Leprecaun, "except when we want new clothes, and then we have to make them, but we grudge every minute spent making anything else except shoes, because that is the proper work for a Leprecaun. In the nighttime we go about the country into people's houses and we clip little pieces off their money, and so, bit by bit, we get a crock of gold together, because, do you see, a Leprecaun has to have a crock of gold so that if he's captured by menfolk he may be able to ransom himself. But that seldom happens, bccause it's a great disgrace altogether to be captured by a man, and we've practiced so long dodging among the roots here that we can easily get away from them. Of course, now and again we are caught; but men are fools, and we always escape without having to pay the ransom at all. We wear green clothes because it's the color of the grass and the leaves, and when we sit down under a bush or lie in the grass they just walk by without noticing us."

"Will you let me see your crock of gold?" said Seumas.

The Leprecaun looked at him fixedly for a moment.

"Do you like griddle bread and milk?" said he.

"I like it well," Seumas answered.

"Then you had better have some," and the Leprecaun took a piece of griddle bread from the shelf and filled two saucers with milk.

While the children were eating the Leprecauns asked them many questions—

"What time do you get up in the morning?"

"Seven o'clock," replied Seumas.

"And what do you have for breakfast?"

"Stirabout and milk," he replied.

"It's good food," said the Leprecaun. "What do you have for dinner?"

"Potatoes and milk," said Seumas.

"It's not bad at all," said the Leprecaun. "And what do you have for supper?"

Brigid answered this time because her brother's mouth was full.

"Bread and milk, sir," said she.

"There's nothing better," said the Leprecaun.

"And then we go to bed," continued Brigid.

"Why wouldn't you?" said the Leprecaun.

It was at this point the Thin Woman of Inis Magrath knocked on the tree trunk and demanded that the children should be returned to her.

When she had gone away the Leprecauns held a consultation, whereat it was decided that they could not afford to anger the Thin Woman and the Shee of Croghan Conghaile so they shook hands with the children and bade them good-bye. The Leprecaun who had enticed them away from home brought them back again, and on parting he begged the children to visit Gort na Cloca Mora whenever they felt inclined.

"There's always a bit of griddle bread or potato cake, and a noggin of milk for a friend," said he.

"You are very kind, sir," replied Seumas, and his sister said the same words.

As the Leprecaun walked away they stood watchlng him.

"Do you remember," said Seumas, "the way he hopped and waggled his leg the last time he was here?"

"I do so," replied Brigid.

"Well he isn't hopping or doing anything at all this time," said Seumas.

"He's not in good humor tonight," said Brigid, "but I like him."

"So do I," said Seumas.

When they went into the house the Thin Woman of Inis Magrath was very glad to see them, and she baked a cake with currants in it, and also gave them both stirabout and potatoes; but the Philosopher did not notice that they had been away at all. He said at last that "talking was bad wit, that women were always making a fuss, that children should be fed, but not fattened, and that beds were meant to be slept in." The Thin Woman replied "that he was a grisly old man without bowels, that she did not know what she had married him for, that he was three times her age, and that no one would believe what she had to put up with."

The Canterville Ghost
Oscar Wilde

I

WHEN MR. HIRAM B. OTIS, the American Minister, bought Canterville Chase, every one told him he was doing a very foolish thing, as there was no doubt at all that the place was haunted. Indeed, Lord Canterville himself, who was a man of the most punctilious honor, had felt it his duty to mention the fact to Mr. Otis when they came to discuss terms.

"We have not cared to live in the place ourselves," said Lord Canterville, "since my grandaunt, the Dowager Duchess of Bolton, was frightened into a fit, from which she never really recovered, by two skeleton hands being placed on her shoulders as she was dressing for dinner, and I feel bound to tell you, Mr. Otis, that the ghost has been seen by several living members of my family, as well as by the rector of the parish, the Rev. Augustus Dampier, who is a Fellow of King's College, Cambridge. After the unfortunate accident to the Duchess, none of our younger servants would stay with us, and Lady Canterville often got very little sleep at night, in consequence of the mysterious noises that came from the corridor and the library."

"My Lord," answered the Minister, "I will take the furniture and the ghost at a valuation. I have come from a modern country, where we have everything that money can buy; and with all our spry young fellows painting the Old World red, and carrying off your best actors and prima-donnas, I reckon that if there were such a thing as a ghost in Europe, we'd have it at home in a very short time in one of our public museums, or on the road as a show."

"I fear that the ghost exists," said Lord Canterville, smiling, "though it may have resisted the overtures of your enterprising impresarios. It has been well known for three centuries, since 1584 in fact, and always makes its appearance before the death of any member of our family."

"Well, so does the family doctor for that matter, Lord Canterville. But there is no such thing, sir, as a ghost, and I guess the laws of Nature are not going to be suspended for the British aristocracy."

"You are certainly very natural in America," answered Lord Canterville who did not quite understand Mr. Otis's last observation, "and if you don't mind a ghost in the house, it is all right. Only you must remember I warned you."

A few weeks after this, the purchase was concluded, and at the close of the season the Minister and his family went down to Canterville Chase. Mrs. Otis, who, as Miss Lucretia R. Tappan, of West 53d Street, had been a celebrated New York belle, was now a very handsome, middle-aged woman, with fine eyes, and a superb profile. Many American ladies on leaving their native land adopt an appearance of chronic ill-health, under the impression that it is a form of European refinement, but Mrs. Otis had never fallen into this error. She had a magnificent constitution, and a really wonderful amount of animal spirits. Indeed, in many respects, she was quite English, and was an excellent example of the fact that we have really everything in common with America nowadays, except, of course, language. Her eldest son, christened Washington by his parents in a moment of patriotism, which he never ceased to regret, was a fair-haired, rather good-looking young man, who had qualified himself for American diplomacy by leading the German at the Newport Casino for three successive seasons, and even in London was well known as an excellent dancer. Gardenias and the peerage were his only weaknesses. Otherwise he was extremely sensible. Miss Virginia E. Otis was a little girl of fifteen, lithe and lovely as a fawn, and with a fine freedom in her large blue eyes. She was a wonderful Amazon, and had once raced old Lord Bilton on her pony twice round the park, winning by a length and a half, just in front of the Achilles statue, to the huge delight of the young Duke of Cheshire, who proposed for her on the spot, and was sent back to Eton that very night by his guardians, in floods of tears. After Virginia came the twins, who were usually called "The Stars and Stripes," as they were always getting swished. They were delightful boys, and, with the exception of the worthy Minister, the only true republicans of the family.

As Canterville Chase is seven miles from Ascot, the nearest railway station, Mr. Otis had telegraphed for a waggonette to meet them, and they started on their drive in high spirits. It was a lovely July evening, and the air was dedicate with the scent of the pinewoods. Now and then they heard a wood-pigeon brooding over its own sweet voice, or saw, deep in the rustling fern, the burnished breast of the pheasant. Little squirrels peered at them from the beech-trees as they went by, and the rabbits scudded away through the brushwood and over the mossy knolls, with their white tails in the air. As they entered the avenue of Canterville Chase, however, the sky became suddenly overcast with clouds, a curious stillness seemed to hold the atmosphere, a great flight of rooks passed silently over their heads, and, before they reached the house, some big drops of rain had fallen.

Standing on the steps to receive them was an old woman, neatly dressed in black silk, with a white cap and apron. This was Mrs. Umney, the housekeeper, whom Mrs. Otis, at Lady Canterville's earnest request, had consented to keep in her former position. She made them each a low curtsey as they alighted, and said in a quaint, old-fashioned manner, "I bid you welcome to Canterville Chase." Following her, they passed through the fine Tudor hall into the library, a long, low room, panelled in black oak, at the end of which was a large stained glass window. Here they found tea left out for them, and, after taking off their wraps, they sat down and began to look round, while Mrs. Umney waited on them.

Suddenly Mrs. Otis caught sight of a dull red stain on the floor just by the fireplace, and, quite unconscious of what it really signified, said to Mrs. Umney, "I am afraid something has been spilt there."

"Yes, madam," replied the old housekeeper in a low voice, "blood has been spilt on that spot."

"How horrid!" cried Mrs. Otis; "I don't at all care for blood-stains in a sitting-room. It must be removed at once."

The old woman smiled, and answered in the same low,

mysterious voice, "It is the blood of Lady Eleanore de Canterville, who was murdered on that very spot by her own husband, Sir Simon de Canterville, in 1575. Sir Simon survived her nine years, and disappeared suddenly under very mysterious circumstances. His body has never been discovered, but his guilty spirit still haunts the Chase. The blood-stain has been much admired by tourists and others, and cannot be removed."

"That is all nonsense," cried Washington Otis; "Pinkerton's Champion Stain Remover and Paragon Detergent will clean it up in no time," and before the terrified housekeeper could interfere, he had fallen upon his knees and was rapidly scouring the floor with a small stick of what looked like a black cosmetic. In a few moments no trace of the blood-stain could be seen.

"I knew Pinkerton would do it," he exclaimed, triumphantly, as he looked round at his admiring family; but no sooner had he said these words than a terrible flash of lightning lit up the sombre room, a fearful peal of thunder made them all start to their feet, and Mrs. Umney fainted.

"What a monstrous climate!" said the American Minister, calmly, as he lit a long cheroot. "I guess the old country is so overpopulated that they have not enough decent weather for everybody. I have always been of opinion that emigration is the only thing for England."

"My dear Hiram," cried Mrs. Otis, "what can we do with a woman who faints ?"

"Charge it to her like breakages," answered the Minister; "she won't faint after that"; and in a few moments Mrs. Umney certainly came to. There was no doubt, however, that she was extremly upset, and she sternly warned Mr. Otis to beware of some trouble coming to the house.

"I have seen things with my own eyes, sir," she said, "that

would make any Christian's hair stand on end, and many and many a night I have not closed my eyes in sleep for the awful things that are done here." Mr. Otis, however, and his wife warmly assured the honest soul that they were not afraid of ghosts, and, after invoking the blessings of Providence on her new master and mistress, and making arrangements for an increase of salary, the old housekeeper tottered off to her own room.

II

THE STORM raged fiercely all that night, but nothing of particular note occurred. The next morning, however, when they came down to breakfast, they found the terrible stain of blood once again on the floor. "I don't think it can be the fault of the Paragon Detergent," said Washington, "for I have tried it with everything. It must be the ghost." He accordingly rubbed out the stain a second time, but the second morning it appeared again. The third morning also it was there, though the library had been locked up at night by Mr. Otis himself, and the key carried upstairs. The whole family were now quite interested; Mr. Otis began to suspect that he had been too dogmatic in his denial of the existence of ghosts, Mrs. Otis expressed her intention of joining the Psychical Society, and Washington prepared a long letter to Messrs. Myers and Podmore on the subject of the Permanence of Sanguineous Stains when connected with Crime. That night all doubts about the objective existence of phantasmata were removed for ever.

The day had been warm and sunny; and, in the cool of the evening, the whole family went out to drive. They did not return home till nine o'clock, when they had a light supper. The conversation in no way turned upon ghosts, so there were not even those primary conditions of receptive expectations which so often precede the presentation of psychical phenomena. The subjects discussed, as I have since learned from Mr. Otis, were merely such as form the ordinary conversation of cultured Americans of the better class, such as the immense superiority of Miss Fanny Devonport over Sarah Bernhardt as an actress; the difficulty of obtaining green corn, buckwheat cakes, and hominy, even in the best English houses; the importance of Boston in the development of the world-soul; the advantages of the baggage-check system in railway travelling; and the sweetness of the New York accent as compared to the London drawl. No mention at all was made of the supernatural, nor was

Sir Simon de Canterville alluded to in any way. At eleven o'clock the family retired, and by half-past all the lights were out. Some time after, Mr. Otis was awakened by a curious noise in the corridor, outside his room. It sounded like the clank of metal, and seemed to be coming nearer every moment. He got up at once, struck a match, and looked at the time. It was exactly one o'clock. He was quite calm, and felt his pulse, which was not at all feverish. The strange noise still continued, and with it he heard distinctly the sound of footsteps. He put on his slippers, took a small oblong phial out of his dressing-case, and opened the door. Right in front of him he saw, in the wan moonlight, an old man of terrible aspect. His eyes were as red burning coals; long grey hair fell over his shoulders in matted coils; his garments, which were of antique cut, were soiled and ragged, and from his wrists and ankles hung heavy manacles and rusty gyves.

"My dear sir," said Mr. Otis, "I really must insist on your oiling those chains, and have brought you for that purpose a small bottle of the Tammany Rising Sun Lubricator. It is said to be completely efficacious upon one application, and there are several testimonials to that effect on the wrapper from some of our most eminent native divines. I shall leave it here for you by the bedroom candles, and will be happy to supply you with more, should you require it." With these words the United States Minister laid the bottle down on a marble table, and, closing his door, retired to rest.

For a moment the Canterville ghost stood quite motionless in natural indignation; then, dashing the bottle violently upon the polished floor, he fled down the corridor, uttering hollow groans, and emitting a ghastly green light. Just, however, as he reached the top of the great oak staircase, a door was flung open, two little white-robed figures appeared, and a large pillow whizzed past his head! There was evidently no time to be lost, so, hastily adopting the Fourth dimension of Space as a means of escape, he vanished through the wainscoting, and the house became quite quiet.

On reaching a small secret chamber in the left wing, he leaned up against a moonbeam to recover his breath, and began to try and realize his position. Never in a brilliant and uninterrupted career of three hundred years, had he been so grossly insulted. He thought of the Dowager Duchess, whom he had frightened into a fit as she stood before the glass in her lace and diamonds; of the four housemaids, who had gone into hysterics when he merely grinned at them through the curtains on one of the spare bedrooms; of the rector of the parish, whose candle he had blown out as he was coming late one night from the library, and who had been under the care of Sir William Gull ever since, a perfect martyr to nervous disorders; and of old Madame de Tremouillac, who, having wakened up one morning early and seen a skeleton seated in an armchair by the fire reading her diary, had been confined to her bed for six weeks with an attack of brain fever, and, on her recovery, had become reconciled to the Church, and broken off her connection with that notorious sceptic, Monsieur de Voltaire. He remembered the terrible night when the wicked Lord Canterville was found choking in his dressing-room, with the knave of diamonds half-way down his throat, and confessed, just before he died, that he had cheated Charles James Fox out of £50,000 at Crockford's by means of that very card, and swore that the ghost had made him swallow it. All his great achievements came back to him again, from the butler who had shot himself in the pantry because he had seen a green hand tapping at the window-pane, to the beautiful Lady Stutfield, who was always obliged to wear a black velvet band round her throat to hide the mark of five fingers burnt upon her white skin, and who drowned herself at last in the carp-pond at the end of the King's Walk. With the enthusiastic egotism of the true artist, he went over his most celebrated performances, and smiled bitterly to himself as he recalled to mind his last appearance as "Red Reuben, or the Strangled Babe," his *début* as "Gaunt Gibeon, the Blood-sucker of Bexley Moor," and the *furore* he had excited one lovely June evening by merely playing ninepins with his own bones upon the lawn-tennis ground. And after all this some wretched modern Americans were to come and offer him the Rising Sun Lubricator, and throw pillows at his head! It was quite unbearable. Besides, no ghost in history had ever been treated in this manner. Accordingly, he determined to have vengeance, and remained till daylight in an attitude of deep thought.

III

THE next morning, when the Otis family met at breakfast, they discussed the ghost at some length. The United States Minister was naturally a little annoyed to find that his present had not been accepted. "I have no wish," he said, "to do the ghost any personal injury, and I must say that, considering the length of time he has been in the house I don't think it is at all polite to throw pillows at him"—a very just remark, at which, I am sorry to say, the twins burst into shouts of laughter. "Upon the other hand," he continued, "if he really declines to use the Rising Sun Lubricator, we shall have to take his chains from him. It would be quite impossible to sleep, with such a noise going on outside the bedrooms."

For the rest of the week, however, they were undisturbed, the only thing that excited any attention being the continual renewal of the blood-stain on the library floor. This certainly was very strange, as the door was always locked at night by Mr. Otis, and the windows kept closely barred. The chameleon-like color, also, of the stain excited a good deal of comment. Some mornings it was a dull (almost Indian) red, then it would be vermillion, then a rich purple, and once when they came down for family prayers, according to the simple rites of the Free American Reformed Episcopalian Church, they found it a bright emerald-green. These kaleidoscopic changes naturally amused the party very much, and bets on the subject were freely made every evening. The only person who did not enter into the joke was little Virginia, who, for some unexplained reason, was always a good deal distressed at the sight of the blood-stain, and very nearly cried the morning it was emerald-green.

The second appearance of the ghost was on Sunday night. Shortly after they had gone to bed they were suddenly alarmed by a fearful crash in the hall. Rushing down-stairs, they found that a large suit of old armor had become detached from its stand, and had fallen on the stone floor, while seated in a high-backed chair was the Canterville ghost, rubbing his knees with an expression of acute agony on his face. The twins, having brought their pea-shooters with them, at once discharged two pellets on him, with that accuracy of aim which can only be attained by long and careful practice on a writing-master, while the United States Minister covered him with his revolver, and called upon him, in accordance with Californian etiquette, to hold up his hands! The ghost started up with a wild shriek of rage, and swept through them like a mist, extinguishing Washington Otis's candle as he passed, and so leaving them all in total darkness. On reaching the top of the staircase he recovered himself, and determined to give his celebrated peal of demoniac laughter. This he had on more than one occasion found extremely useful. It was said to have turned Lord Raker's wig grey in a single night, and had certainly made three of Lady Canterville's French governesses give warning before their month was up. He accordingly laughed his most horrible laugh, till the old vaulted roof rang and rang again, but hardly had the fearful echo died away when a door opened, and Mrs. Otis came out in a light blue dressing-gown. "I am afraid you are far from well," she said, "and have brought you a bottle of Doctor Dobell's tincture. If it is indigestion, you will find it a most excellent remedy." The ghost glared at her in fury, and began at once to make preparations for turning himself into a large black dog, an accomplishment for which he was justly renowned, and to which the family doctor always attributed the permanent idiocy of Lord Canterville's uncle, the Hon. Thomas Horton. The sound of approaching footsteps, however, made him hesitate in his fell purpose, so he contented himself with becoming faintly phosphorescent, and vanished with a deep churchyard groan, just as the twins had come up to him.

On reaching his room he entirely broke down, and became a prey to the most violent agitation. The vulgarity of the twins, and the gross materialism of Mrs. Otis, were naturally extremely annoying, but what really distressed him most was that he had been unable to wear the suit of mail. He had hoped that even modern Americans would be thrilled by the sight of a Spectre in Armor, if for no more sensible reason, at least out of respect for their national poet Longfellow, over whose graceful and attractive poetry he himself had whiled away many a weary hour when the Cantervilles were up in town. Besides it was his own suit. He had worn it with great success at the Kenilworth tournament, and had been highly complimented on it by no less a person than the Virgin Queen herself. Yet when he had put it on, he had been completely overpowered by the weight of the huge breastplate and steel casque, and had fallen heavily on the stone pavement, barking both his knees severely, and bruising the knuckles of his right hand.

For some days after this he was extremely ill, and hardly stirred out of his room at all, except to keep the blood-stain in proper repair. However, by taking great care of himself, he recovered, and resolved to make a third attempt to frighten the United States Minister and his family. He selected Friday, August 17th, for his appearance, and spent most of that day in looking over his wardrobe, ultimately deciding in favor of a large slouched hat with a red feather, a winding-sheet frilled at the wrists and neck, and a rusty dagger. Towards evening a violent storm of rain came on, and the wind was so high that all the windows and doors in the old house shook and rattled. In fact, it was just such weather as he loved. His plan of action was this. He was to make his way quietly to Washington Otis's room, gibber at him from the foot of the bed, and stab himself three times in the throat to the sound of low music. He bore Washington a special grudge, being quite aware that it was he who was in the habit of removing the famous Canterville blood-stain by means of Pinkerton's Paragon Detergent. Having reduced the reckless and foolhardy youth to a condition of abject terror, he was then to proceed to the room occupied by the United States Minister and his wife, and there to place a clammy hand on Mrs. Otis's forehead, while he hissed into her trembling husband's ear the awful secrets of the charnel-house. With regard to little Virginia, he had not quite made up his mind. She had never insulted him in any way, and was pretty and gentle. A few hollow groans from the wardrobe, he thought, would be more than sufficient, or, if that failed to wake her, he might grabble at the counterpane with palsy-twitching fingers. As for the twins, he was quite determined to teach them a lesson. The first thing to be done was, of course, to sit upon their chests, so as to produce the stifling sensation of nightmare. Then, as their beds were quite close to each other, to stand between them in the form of a green, icy-cold corpse, till they became paralyzed with fear, and finally, to throw off the winding-sheet, and crawl round the room, with white, bleached bones and one rolling eyeball, in the character of "Dumb Daniel, or the Suicide's Skeleton," a *rôle* in which he had on more than one occasion produced a great effect, and which he considered quite equal to his famous part of "Martin the Maniac, or the Masked Mystery." At half-past ten he heard the family going to bed. For some time he was disturbed by wild shrieks of laughter from the twins, who, with the light-hearted gaiety of schoolboys, were evidently amusing themselves before they retired to rest, but at a quarter-past eleven all was still and as midnight sounded, he sallied forth. The owl beat against the windowpanes, the raven croaked from the old yew-tree, and the wind wandered moaning round the house like a lost soul; but the Otis family slept unconscious of their doom, and high above the rain and storm he could hear the steady snoring of the Minister for the United States. He stepped stealthily out of the wainscoting, with an evil smile on his cruel, wrinkled mouth, and the moon hid her face in a cloud as he stole past the great oriel window, where his own arms and those of his murdered wife were blazoned in azure and gold. On and on he glided, like an evil shadow, the very darkness seeming to loathe him as he passed. Once he thought he heard something call, and stopped; but it was only the baying of a dog from the Red Farm, and he went on muttering strange sixteenth-century curses, and ever and anon brandishing the rusty dagger in the midnight air. Finally he reached the corner of the passage that led to luckless Washington's room. For a moment he paused there, the wind blowing his long grey locks about his head, and twisting into grotesque and fantastic folds the nameless horror of the dead man's shroud. Then the clock struck the quarter, and he felt the time was come. He chuckled to himself, and turned the corner; but no sooner had he done so than, with a piteous wail of terror, he fell back, and hid his blanched face in his long, bony hands. Right in front of him was standing a horrible spectre, motionless as a carven image, and monstrous as a madman's dream! Its head was bald and burnished; its face round, and fat, and white; and hideous laughter seemed to have writhed its features into an eternal grin. From the eyes streamed rays of scarlet light, the mouth was a wide well of fire, and a hideous garment, like to his own, swathed with its silent snows the Titan form. On its breast was a placard with strange writing in antique characters, some scroll of shame it seemed, some record of wild sins, some awful calendar of crime, and, with its right hand, it bore aloft a falchion of gleaming steel.

Never having seen a ghost before, he naturally was terribly frightened, and, after a second hasty glance at the awful phantom, he fled back to his room, tripping up in his long winding-sheet as he sped down the corridor, and finally dropping the rusty dagger into the Minister's jackboots, where it was found in the morning by the butler. Once in the privacy of his own apartment, he flung himself down on a small pallet-bed, and hid his face under the clothes. After a time, however, the brave old Canterville spirit asserted itself, and he determined to go and speak to the other ghost as soon as it was daylight. Accordingly, just as the dawn was touching the hills with silver, he returned towards the spot where he had first laid eyes on the grisly phantom, feeling that, after all, two ghosts were better than one, and that, by the aid of his new friend, he might safely grapple with the twins. On reaching the spot, however, a terrible sight met his gaze. Something had evidently happened to the spectre, for the light had entirely faded from its hollow eyes, the gleaming falchion had fallen from its hand, and it was leaning up against the wall in a strained and uncomfortable attitude. He rushed forward and seized it in his arms, when, to his horror, the head slipped off and rolled on the floor, the body assumed a recumbent posture, and he found himself clasping a white dimity bed-curtain, with a sweeping brush, a kitchen cleaver, and a hollow turnip lying at his feet! Unable to understand this curious transformation, he clutched the placard with feverish haste, and there, in the grey morning light, he read these fearful words:—

> YE OTIS GHOSTE
> Ye Onlie True and Originale Spook
> Beware of Ye Imitationes.
> All others are counterfeite.

The whole thing flashed across him. He had been tricked, foiled, and outwitted! The old Canterville look came into his eyes; he ground his toothless gums together; and, raising his withered hands high above his head, swore according to the picturesque phraseology of the antique school, that, when

Chanticleer had sounded twice his merry horn, deeds of blood would be wrought, and murder walk abroad with silent feet.

Hardly had he finished this awful oath when, from the red-tiled roof of a distant homestead, a cock crew. He laughed a long, low, bitter laugh, and waited. Hour after hour he waited, but the cock, for some strange reason, did not crow again. Finally, at half-past seven, the arrival of the housemaids made him give up his fearful vigil, and he stalked back to his room, thinking of his vain oath and baffled purpose. There he consulted several books of ancient chivalry, of which he was exceedingly fond, and found that, on every occasion on which this oath had been used, Chanticleer had always crowed a second time. "Perdition seize the naughty fowl," he muttered, "I have seen the day when, with my stout spear, I would have run him through the gorge, and made him crow for me as 'twere in death!" He then retired to a comfortable lead coffin, and stayed there till evening.

IV

THE next day the ghost was very weak and tired. The terrible excitement of the last four weeks was beginning to have its effect. His nerves were completely shattered, and he started at the slightest noise. For five days he kept to his room, and at last made up his mind to give up the point of the blood-stain on the library floor. If the Otis family did not want it, they clearly did not deserve it. They were evidently people on a low, material plane of existence, and quite incapable of appreciating the symbolic value of sensuous phenomena. The question of phantasmic apparitions, and the development of astral bodies, was of course quite a different matter, and really not under his control. It was his solemn duty to appear in the corridor once a week, and to gibber from the large oriel window on the first and third Wednesdays in every month, and he did not see how he could honorably escape from his obligations. It is quite true that his life had been very evil, but, upon the other hand, he was most conscientious in all things connected with the supernatural. For the next three Saturdays, accordingly, he traversed the corridor as usual between midnight and three o'clock, taking every possible precaution against being either heard or seen. He removed his boots, trod as lightly as possible on the old worm-eaten boards, wore a large black velvet cloak, and was careful to use the Rising Sun Lubricator for oiling his chains. I am bound to acknowledge that it was with a good deal of difficulty that he brought himself to adopt this last mode of protection. However, one night, while the family were at dinner, he slipped into Mr. Otis's bedroom and carried off the bottle. He felt a little humiliated at first, but afterwards was sensible enough to see that there was a great deal to be said for the invention, and, to a certain degree, it served his purpose. Still, in spite of everything he was not left unmolested. Strings were continually being stretched across the corridor, over which he tripped in the dark, and on one occasion, while dressed for the part of "Black Isaac, or the Huntsman of Hogley Woods," he met with a severe fall, through treading on a butter-slide, which the twins had constructed from the entrance of the Tapestry Chamber to the top of the oak staircase. This last insult so enraged him, that he resolved to make one final effort to assert his dignity and social position, and determined to visit the insolent young Etonians the next night in his celebrated character of "Reckless Rupert, or the Headless Earl."

He had not appeared in this disguise for more than seventy years; in fact, not since he had so frightened pretty Lady Barbara Modish by means of it, that she suddenly broke off her engagement with the present Lord Canterville's grandfather, and ran away to Gretna Green with handsome Jack Castletown, declaring that nothing in the world would induce her to marry into a family that allowed such a horrible phantom to walk up and down the terrace at twilight. Poor Jack was afterwards shot in a duel by Lord Canterville on Wandsworth Common, and Lady Barbara died of a broken heart at Tunbridge Wells before the year was out, so, in every way, it had been a great success. It was, however, an extremely difficult "make-up," if I may use such a theatrical expression in connection with one of the greatest mysteries of the supernatural, or, to employ a more scientific term, the higher-natural world, and it took him fully three hours to make his preparations. At last everything was ready, and he was very pleased with his appearance. The big leather riding-boots that went with the dress were just a little too large for him, and he could only find one of the two horse-pistols, but, on the whole, he was quite satisfied, and at a quarter-past one he glided out of the wainscoting and crept down the corridor. On reaching the room occupied by the twins, which I should mention was called the Blue Bed Chamber, on account of the color of its hangings, he found the door just ajar. Wishing to make an effective entrance, he flung it wide open, when a heavy jug of water fell right down on him, wetting him to the skin, and just missing his left shoulder by a couple of inches. At the same moment he heard stifled shrieks of laughter proceeding from the four-post bed. The shock to his nervous system was so great that he fled back to his room as hard as he could go, and the next day he was laid up with a severe cold. The only thing that at all consoled him in the whole affair was the fact that he had not brought his head with him, for, had he done so, the consequences might have been very serious.

He now gave up all hope of ever frightening this rude American family, and contented himself, as a rule, with creeping about the passages in list slippers, with a thick red muffler round his throat for fear of drafts, and a small arquebuse, in case he should be attacked by the twins. The final blow he received occurred on the 19th of September. He had gone down-stairs to the great entrance-hall, feeling sure that there, at any rate, he would be quite unmolested, and was amusing himself by making satirical remarks on the large Saroni photographs of the United States Minister and his wife, which had now taken the place of the Canterville family pictures. He was simply but neatly clad in a long shroud, spotted with churchyard mould, had tied up his jaw with a strip of yellow linen, and carried a small lantern and a sexton's spade. In fact, he was dressed for the character of "Jonas the Graveless, or the Corpse-Snatcher of Chertsey Barn," one of his most remarkable impersonations, and one which the Cantervilles had every reason to remember, as it was the real origin of their quarrel with their neighbor, Lord Rufford. It was about a quarter-past two o'clock in the morning, and, as far as he could ascertain, no one was stirring. As he was strolling towards the library, however, to see if there were any traces left of the blood-stain, suddenly there leaped out on him from a dark corner two figures, who waved their arms wildly above their heads, and shrieked out "BOO!" in his ear.

Seized with a panic, which, under the circumstances, was only natural, he rushed for the staircase, but found Washington Otis waiting for him there with the big garden-syringe, and being thus hemmed in by his enemies on every side, and driven almost to bay, he vanished into the great iron stove, which, fortunately for him, was not lit, and had to make his way home through the flues and chimneys, arriving at his own room in a terrible state of dirt, disorder, and despair.

After this he was not seen again on any nocturnal expedition.

The twins lay in wait for him on several occasions, and strewed the passages with nutshells every night to the great annoyance of their parents and the servants, but it was of no avail. It was quite evident that his feelings were so wounded that he would not appear. Mr. Otis consequently resumed his great work on the history of the Democratic Party, on which he had been engaged for some years; Mrs. Otis organized a wonderful clam-bake, which amazed the whole county; the boys took to lacrosse, euchre, poker, and other American national games, and Virginia rode about the lanes on her pony, accompanied by the young Duke of Cheshire, who had come to spend the last week of his holidays at Canterville Chase. It was generally assumed that the ghost had gone away, and, in fact, Mr. Otis wrote a letter to that effect to Lord Canterville, who, in reply, expressed his great pleasure at the news, and sent his best congratulations to the Minister's worthy wife.

The Otises, however, were deceived, for the ghost was still in the house, and though now almost an invalid, was by no means ready to let matters rest, particularly as he heard that among the guests was the young Duke of Cheshire, whose grand-uncle, Lord Francis Stilton, had once bet a hundred guineas with Colonel Carbury that he would play dice with the Canterville ghost, and was found the next morning lying on the floor of the card-room in such a helpless paralytic state that, though he lived on to a great age, he was never able to say anything again but "Double Sixes." The story was well known at the time, though, of course, out of respect to the feelings of the two noble families, every attempt was made to hush it up, and a full account of all the circumstances connected with it will be found in the third volume of Lord Tattle's *Recollections of the Prince Regent and his Friends*. The ghost, then, was naturally very anxious to show that he had not lost his influence over the

Stiltons, with whom, indeed, he was distantly connected, his own first cousin having been married *en secondes noces* to the Sieur de Bulkeley, from whom, as every one knows, the Dukes of Cheshire are lineally descended. Accordingly, he made arrangements for appearing to Virginia's little lover in his celebrated impersonation of "The Vampire Monk, or the Bloodless Benedictine," a performance so horrible that when old Lady Startup saw it, which she did on one fatal New Year's Eve, in the year 1764, she went off into the most piercing shrieks, which culminated in violent apoplexy, and died in three days, after disinheriting the Cantervilles, who were her nearest relations, and leaving all her money to her London apothecary. At the last moment, however, his terror of the twins prevented his leaving his room, and the little Duke slept in peace under the great feathered canopy in the Royal Bedchamber, and dreamed of Virginia.

V

A few days after this, Virginia and her curly-haired cavalier went out riding on Brockley meadows, where she tore her habit so badly in getting through a hedge that, on their return home, she made up her mind to go up by the back staircase so as not to be seen. As she was running past the Tapestry Chamber, the door of which happened to be open, she fancied she saw someone inside, and thinking it was her mother's maid, who sometimes used to bring her work there, looked in to ask her to mend her habit. To her immense surprise, however, it was the Canterville Ghost himself! He was sitting by the window, watching the ruined gold of the yellowing trees fly through the air, and the red leaves dancing madly down the long avenue. His head was leaning on his hand, and his whole attitude was one of extreme depression. Indeed, so forlorn, and so much out of repair did he look, that little Virginia, whose first idea had been to run away and lock herself in her room, was filled with pity, and determined to try and comfort him. So light was her footfall, and so deep his melancholy, that he was not aware of her presence till she spoke to him.

"I am so sorry for you," she said, "but my brothers are going back to Eton to-morrow, and then, if you behave yourself, no one will annoy you."

"It is absurd asking me to behave myself," he answered, looking round in astonishment at the pretty little girl who had ventured to address him, "quite absurd. I must rattle my chains, and groan through keyholes, and walk about at night, if that is what you mean. It is my only reason for existing."

"It is no reason at all for existing, and you know you have been very wicked. Mrs. Umney told us, the first day we arrived here, that you had killed your wife."

"Well, I quite admit it," said the Ghost, petulantly, "but it was a purely family matter, and concerned no one else."

"It is very wrong to kill any one," said Virginia, who at times had a sweet puritan gravity, caught from some old New England ancestor.

"Oh, I hate the cheap severity of abstract ethics! My wife was very plain, never had my ruffs properly starched, and knew nothing about cookery. Why, there was a buck I had shot in Hogley Woods, a magnificent pricket, and do you know how she had it sent to table? However, it is no matter now, for it is all over, and I don't think it was very nice of her brothers to starve me to death, though I did kill her."

"Starve you to death? Oh, Mr. Ghost—I mean Sir Simon, are you hungry? I have a sandwich in my case. Would you like it?"

"No, thank you, I never eat anything now; but it is very kind of you, all the same, and you are much nicer than the rest of your horrid, rude, vulgar, dishonest family."

"Stop!" cried Virginia, stamping her foot, "it is you who are rude, and horrid, and vulgar, and as for dishonesty, you know you stole the paints out of my box to try and furbish up that ridiculous blood-stain in the library. First you took all my reds, including the vermilion, and I couldn't do any more sunsets, then you took the emerald green and the chrome-yellow, and finally I had nothing left but indigo and Chinese white, and could only do moonlight scenes, which are always depressing to look at, and not at all easy to paint. I never told on you, though I was very much annoyed, and it was most ridiculous, the whole thing; for who ever heard of emerald-green blood ?"

"Well, really," said the Ghost, rather meekly, "what was I to do? It is a very difficult thing to get real blood nowadays, and, as your brother began it all with his Paragon Detergent, I certainly saw no reason why I should not have your paints. As for color, that is always a matter of taste: the Cantervilles have blue blood, for instance, the very bluest in England; but I know you Americans don't care for things of this kind."

"You know nothing about it, and the best thing you can do is to emigrate and improve your mind. My father will be only too happy to give you a free passage, and though there is a heavy duty on spirits of every kind, there will be no difficulty about the Custom House, as the officers are all Democrats. Once in New York, you are sure to be a great success. I know lots of people there who would give a hundred thousand dollars to have a grandfather, and much more than that to have a family ghost."

"I don't think I should like America."

"I suppose because we have no ruins and no curiosities," said Virginia, satirically.

"No ruins! no curiosities!" answered the Ghost; "you have your navy and your manners."

"Good evening; I will go and ask papa to get the twins an extra week's holiday."

"Please don't go, Miss Virginia," he cried; "I am so lonely and so unhappy, and I really don't know what to do. I want to go to sleep and I cannot."

"That's quite absurd! You have merely to go to bed and blow out the candle. It is very difficult sometimes to keep awake, especially at church, but there is no difficulty at all about sleeping. Why, even babies know how to do that, and they are not very clever."

"I have not slept for three hundred years," he said sadly, and Virginia's beautiful blue eyes opened in wonder; "for three hundred years I have not slept, and I am so tired."

Virginia grew quite grave, and her little lips trembled like rose-leaves. She came towards him, and kneeling down at his side, looked up into his old withered face.

"Poor, poor Ghost," she murmured; "have you no place where you can sleep ?"

"Far away beyond the pinewoods," he answered, in a low, dreamy voice, "there is a little garden. There the grass grows long and deep, there are the great white stars of the hemlock flower, there the nightingale sings all night long. All night long he sings, and the cold crystal moon looks down, and the yew-tree spreads out its giant arms over the sleepers."

Virginia's eyes grew dim with tears, and she hid her face in her hands.

"You mean the Garden of Death," she whispered.

"Yes, death. Death must be so beautiful. To lie in the soft brown earth, with the grasses waving above one's head, and listen to silence. To have no yesterday, and no to-morrow. To forget time, to forget life, to be at peace. You can help me. You can open for me the portals of death's house, for love is always with you, and love is stronger than death is."

Virginia trembled, a cold shudder ran through her, and for a few moments there was silence. She felt as if she was in a terrible dream.

Then the Ghost spoke again, and his voice sounded like the sighing of the wind.

"Have you ever read the old prophecy on the library window?"

"Oh, often," cried the little girl, looking up; "I know it quite well. It is painted in curious black letters, and is difficult to read. There are only six lines:

> When a golden girl can win
> Prayer from out the lips of sin,
> When the barren almond bears,
> and a little child gives away its tears,
> Then shall all the house be still
> And peace come to Canterville.

But I don't know what they mean."

"They mean," he said, sadly, "that you must weep with me for my sins, because I have no tears, and pray with me for my soul, because I have no faith, and then, if you have always been sweet, and good, and gentle, the Angel of Death will have mercy on me. You will see fearful shapes in darkness, and wicked voices will whisper in your ear, but they will not harm you, for against the purity of a little child the powers of Hell cannot prevail."

Virginia made no answer, and the ghost wrung his hands in wild despair as he looked down at her bowed golden head. Suddenly she stood up, very pale, and with a strange light in her eyes. "I am not afraid," she said firmly, "and I will ask the Angel to have mercy on you."

He rose from his seat with a faint cry of joy, and taking her hand bent over it with old-fashioned grace and kissed it. His fingers were as cold as ice, and his lips burned like fire, but Virginia did not falter, as he led her across the dusky room. On the faded green tapestry were embroidered little huntsmen. They blew their tasselled horns and with their tiny hands waved to her to go back. "Go back! little Virginia," they cried, "go back!" but the Ghost clutched her hand more tightly, and she shut her eyes against them. Horrible animals with lizard tails and goggle eyes blinked at her from the carven chimneypiece, and murmured, "Beware! little Virginia, beware! we may never see you again," but the Ghost glided on more swiftly, and Virginia did not listen. When they reached the end of the room he stopped, and muttered some words she could not understand. She opened her eyes, and saw the wall slowly fading away like a mist, and a great black cavern in front of her. A bitter cold wind swept round them, and she felt something pulling at her dress. "Quick, quick," cried the Ghost, "or it will be too late," and in a moment the wainscoting had closed behind them, and the Tapestry Chamber was empty.

VI

ABOUT ten minutes later, the bell rang for tea, and, as Virginia did not come down, Mrs. Otis sent up one of the footmen to tell her. After a little time he returned and said that he could not find Miss Virginia anywhere. As she was in the habit of going out to the garden every evening to get flowers for the dinner-table, Mrs. Otis was not at all alarmed at first, but when six o'clock struck, and Virginia did not appear, she became really agitated, and sent the boys out to look for her, while she herself and Mr. Otis searched every room in the house. At half-past six the boys came back and said that they could find no trace of their sister anywhere. They were all now in the greatest state of excitement, and did not know what to do, when Mr. Otis suddenly remembered that, some few days before, he had given a band of gypsies permission to camp in the park. He accordingly at once set off for Blackfell Hollow, where he knew they were, accompanied by his eldest son and two of the farm-servants. The little Duke of Cheshire, who was perfectly frantic with anxiety, begged hard to be allowed to go too, but Mr. Otis would not allow him, as he was afraid there might be a scuffle. On arriving at the spot, however, he found that the gypsies had gone, and it was evident that their departure had been rather sudden, as the fire was still burning, and some plates were lying on the grass. Having sent off Washington and the two men to scour the district, he ran home, and despatched telegrams to all the police inspectors in the county, telling them to look out for a little girl who had been kidnapped by tramps or gypsies. He then ordered his horse to be brought round, and, after insisting on his wife and the three boys sitting down to dinner, rode off down the Ascot road with a groom. He had hardly, however, gone a couple of miles, when he heard somebody galloping after him, and, looking round, saw the little Duke coming up on his pony, with his face very flushed, and no hat. "I'm awfully sorry, Mr. Otis," gasped out the boy, "but I can't eat any dinner as long as Virginia is lost. Please, don't be angry with me; if you had let us be engaged last year, there would never have been all this trouble. You won't send me back, will you? I can't go! I won't go!"

The Minister could not help smiling at the handsome young scapegrace, and was a good deal touched at his devotion to Virginia, so leaning down from his horse, he patted him kindly on the shoulders, and said, "Well, Cecil, if you won't go back, I suppose you must come with me, but I must get you a hat at

Ascot."

"Oh, bother my hat! I want Virginia!" cried the little Duke, laughing, and they galloped on to the railway station. There Mr. Otis inquired of the station-master if any one answering to the description of Virginia had been seen on the platform, but could get no news of her. The station-master, however, wired up and down the line, and assured him that a strict watch would be kept for her, and, after having bought a hat for the little Duke from a linen-draper, who was just putting up his shutters, Mr. Otis rode off to Bexley, a village about four miles away, which he was told was a well-known haunt of the gypsies, as there was a large common next to it. Here they roused up the rural policeman, but could get no information from him, and, after riding all over the common, they turned their horses' heads homewards, and reached the Chase about eleven o'clock, dead-tired and almost heart-broken. They found Washington and the twins waiting for them at the gate-house with lanterns, as the avenue was very dark. Not the slightest trace of Virginia had been discovered. The gypsies had been caught on Brockley meadows, but she was not with them, and they had explained their sudden departure by saying that they had mistaken the date of Chorton Fair, and had gone off in a hurry for fear they should be late. Indeed, they had been quite distressed at hearing of Virginia's disappearance, as they were very grateful to Mr. Otis for having allowed them to camp in his park, and four of their number had stayed behind to help in the search. The carp-pond had been dragged, and the whole case thoroughly gone over, but without any result. It was evident that, for that night at any rate, Virginia was lost to them; and it was in a state of the deepest depression that Mr. Otis and the boys walked up to the house, the groom following behind with the two horses and the pony. In the hall they found a group of frightened servants, and lying on a sofa in the library was poor Mrs. Otis, almost out of her mind with terror and anxiety, and having her forehead bathed with eau de cologne by the old housekeeper. Mr. Otis at once insisted on her having something to eat, and ordered up supper for the whole party. It was a melancholy meal, as hardly any one spoke, and even the twins were awe-struck and subdued, as they were very fond of their sister. When they had finished, Mr. Otis, in spite of the entreaties of the little Duke, ordered them all to bed, saying that nothing more could be done that night, and that he would telegraph in the morning to Scotland Yard for some detectives to be sent down immediately. Just as they were passing out of the dining-room, midnight began to boom from the clock tower, and when the last stroke sounded they heard a crash and a sudden shrill cry; a dreadful peal of thunder shook the house, a strain of unearthly music floated through the air, a panel at the top of the staircase flew back with a loud noise, and out on the landing, looking very pale and white, with a little casket in her hand, stepped Virginia. In a moment they had all rushed up to her. Mrs. Otis clasped her passionately in her arms, the Duke smothered her with violent kisses, and the twins executed a wild war-dance round the group.

"Good heavens! child, where have you been?" said Mr. Otis, rather angrily, thinking that she had been playing some foolish trick on them. "Cecil and I have been riding all over the country looking for you, and your mother has been frightened to death. You must never play these practical jokes any more."

"Except on the Ghost! except on the Ghost!" shrieked the twins, as they capered about.

"My own darling, thank God you are found; you must never leave my side again," murmured Mrs. Otis, as she kissed the trembling child, and smoothed the tangled gold of her hair.

"Papa," said Virginia, quietly, "I have been with the Ghost.

He is dead, and you must come and see him. He had been very wicked, but he was really sorry for all that he had done, and he gave me this box of beautiful jewels before he died."

The whole family gazed at her in mute amazement, but she was quite grave and serious; and, turning round, she led them through the opening in the wainscoting down a narrow secret corridor, Washington following with a lighted candle, which he had caught up from the table. Finally, they came to a great oak door, studded with rusty nails. When Virginia touched it, it swung back on its heavy hinges, and they found themselves in a little low room, with a vaulted ceiling, and one tiny grated window. Imbedded in the wall was a huge iron ring, and chained to it was a gaunt skeleton, that was stretched out at full length on the stone floor, and seemed to be trying to grasp with its long fleshless fingers an old-fashioned trencher and ewer, that were placed just out of its reach. The jug had evidently been once filled with water, as it was covered inside with green mould. There was nothing on the trencher but a pile of dust. Virginia knelt down beside the skeleton, and, folding her little hands together, began to pray silently, while the rest of the party looked on in wonder at the terrible tragedy whose secret was now disclosed to them.

"Hallo!" suddenly exclaimed one of the twins, who had been looking out of the window to try and discover in what wing of the house the room was situated. "Hallo! the old withered almond-tree has blossomed. I can see the flowers quite plainly in the moonlight."

"God has forgiven him," said Virginia, gravely, as she rose to her feet, and a beautiful light seemed to illumine her face.

"What an angel you are!" cried the young Duke, and he put his arm round her neck, and kissed her.

VII

FOUR days after these curious incidents, a funeral started from Canterville Chase at about eleven o'clock at night. The hearse was drawn by eight black horses, each of which carried on its head a great tuft of nodding ostrich-plumes, and the leaden coffin was covered by a rich purple pall, on which was embroidered in gold the Canterville coat-of-arms. By the side of the hearse and the coaches walked the servants with lighted torches, and the whole procession was wonderfully impressive. Lord Canterville was the chief mourner, having come up specially from Wales to attend the funeral, and sat in the first carriage along with little Virginia. Then came the United States Minister and his wife, then Washington and the three boys, and in the last carriage was Mrs. Umney. It was generally felt that, as she had been frightened by the ghost for more than fifty years of her life, she had a right to see the last of him. A deep grave had been dug in the corner of the churchyard, just under the old yew-tree, and the service was read in the most impressive manner by the Rev. Augustus Dampier. When the ceremony was over, the servants, according to an old custom observed in the Canterville family, extinguished their torches, and, as the coffin was being lowered into the grave, Virginia stepped forward, and laid on it a large cross made of white and pink almond-blossoms. As she did so, the moon came out from behind a cloud, and flooded with its silent silver the little churchyard, and from a distant copse a nightingale began to sing. She thought of the ghost's description of the Garden of Death, her eyes became dim with tears, and she hardly spoke a word during the drive home.

The next morning, before Lord Canterville went up to town, Mr. Otis had an interview with him on the subject of the jewels the ghost had given to Virginia. They were perfectly magnificent, especially a certain ruby necklace with old Venetian setting, which was really a superb specimen of sixteenth-century work, and their value was so great that Mr. Otis felt considerable scruples about allowing his daughter to accept them.

"My lord," he said, "I know that in this country mortmain is held to apply to trinkets as well as to land, and it is quite clear to me that these jewels are, or should be, heirlooms in your family. I must beg you, accordingly, to take them to London with you, and to regard them simply as a portion of your property which has been restored to you under certain strange conditions. As for my daughter, she is merely a child, and has as yet, I am glad to say, but little interest in such appurtenances of idle luxury, I am also informed by Mrs. Otis, who, I may say, is no mean authority upon Art,—having had the privilege of spending several winters in Boston when she was a girl,—that these gems are of great monetary worth, and if offered for sale would fetch a tall price. Under these circumstances, Lord Canterville, I feel sure that you will recognize how impossible it would be for me to allow them to remain in the possession of any member of my family; and, indeed, all such vain gauds and toys, however suitable or necessary to the dignity of the British aristocracy, would be completely out of place among those who have been brought up on the severe, and I believe immortal, principles of Republican simplicity. Perhaps I should mention that Virginia is very anxious that you should allow her to retain the box, as a memento of your unfortunate but misguided ancestor. As it is extremely old, and consequently a good deal out of repair, you may perhaps think fit to comply with her request. For my own part, I confess I am a good deal surprised to find a child of mine expressing sympathy with medievalism in any form, and can only account for it by the fact that Virginia was born in one of your London suburbs shortly after Mrs. Otis had returned from a trip to Athens."

Lord Canterville listened very gravely to the worthy Minister's speech, pulling his grey moustache now and then to hide an involuntary smile, and when Mr. Otis had ended, he shook him cordially by the hand, and said: "My dear sir, your charming little daughter rendered my unlucky ancestor, Sir Simon, a very important service, and I and my family are much indebted to her for her marvellous courage and pluck. The jewels are clearly hers, and, egad, I believe that if I were heartless enough to take them from her, the wicked old fellow would be out of his grave in a fortnight, leading me the devil of a life. As for their being heirlooms, nothing is an heirloom that is not so mentioned in a will or legal document, and the existence of these jewels has been quite unknown. I assure you I have no more claim on them than your butler, and when Miss Virginia grows up, I dare say she will be pleased to have pretty things to wear. Besides, you forget, Mr. Otis, that you took the furniture and the ghost at a valuation, and anything that belonged to the ghost passed at once into your possession, as, whatever activity Sir Simon may have shown in the corridor at night, in point of law he was really dead, and you acquired his property by purchase."

Mr. Otis was a good deal distressed at Lord Canterville's refusal, and begged him to reconsider his decision, but the good-natured peer was quite firm, and finally induced the Minister to allow his daughter to retain the present the ghost had given her, and when, in the spring of 1890, the young Duchess of Cheshire was presented at the Queen's first drawing-room on the occasion of her marriage, her jewels were the universal theme of admiration. For Virginia received the coronet, which is the reward of all good little American girls, and was married to her boy-lover as soon as he came of age. They were both so charming, and they loved each other so much, that everyone was delighted at the match, except the old Marchioness of Dumbleton, who had tried to catch the Duke for one of her seven unmarried daughters, and had given no less than three expensive dinner-parties for that purpose, and, strange to say, Mr. Otis himself. Mr. Otis was extremely fond of the young Duke personally, but, theoretically, he objected to titles, and, to use his own words, "was not without apprehension lest, amid the enervating influences of a pleasure-loving aristocracy, the true principles of Republican simplicity should be forgotten." His objections, however, were completely overruled, and I believe that when he walked up the aisle of St. George's, Hanover Square, with his daughter leaning on his arm, there was not a prouder man in the whole length and breadth of England.

The Duke and Duchess, after the honeymoon was over, went down to Canterville Chase, and on the day after their arrival they walked over in the afternoon to the lonely churchyard by the pine woods. There had been a great deal of difficulty at first about the inscription on Sir Simon's tombstone, but finally it had been decided to engrave on it simply the initials of the old gentleman's name, and the verse from the library window. The Duchess had brought with her some lovely roses, which she strewed upon the grave, and after they had stood by it for some time they strolled into the ruined chancel of the old abbey. There the Duchess sat down on a fallen pillar while her husband lay at her feet smoking a cigarette and looking up at her beautiful eyes. Suddenly he threw his cigarette away, took hold of her hand, and said to her, "Virginia, a wife should have no secrets from her husband."

"Dear Cecil! I have no secrets from you."

"Yes, you have," he answered, smiling, "you have never told me what happened to you when you were locked up with the ghost."

"I have never told anyone, Cecil," said Virginia, gravely.

"I know that, but you might tell me."

"Please don't ask me, Cecil, I cannot tell you. Poor Sir Simon! I owe him a great deal. Yes, don't laugh, Cecil, I really do. He made me see what Life is, and what Death signifies, and why Love is stronger than both."

The Duke rose and kissed his wife lovingly.

"You can have your secret as long as I have your heart," he murmured.

"You have always had that, Cecil."

"And you will tell our children some day, won't you ?"

Virginia blushed.

The Haunted Cellar
Thomas Crofton Croker

THERE ARE FEW people who have not heard of the Mac-
Carthys—one of the real old Irish families, with the true
Milesian blood running in their veins as thick as buttermilk.
Many were the clans of this family in the south; as the Mac
Carthymore—and the Mac Carthy-reagh—and the Mac Carthy
of Muskerry; and all of them were noted for their hospitality to
strangers, gentle and simple.

But not one of that name, or of any other, exceeded Justin
Mac Carthy, of Ballinacarthy, at putting plenty to eat and drink
upon his table; and there was a right hearty welcome for
everyone who should share it with him. Many a wine cellar
would be ashamed of the name if that at Ballinacarthy was the
proper pattern for one. Large as that cellar was, it was crowded
with bins of wine, and long rows of pipes, and hogsheads, and

casks, that it would take more time to count than any sober man could spare in such a place, with plenty to drink about him, and a hearty welcome to do so.

There are many, no doubt, who will think that the butler would have little to complain of in such a house; and the whole country round would have agreed with them, if a man could be found to remain as Mr. MacCarthy's butler for any length of time worth speaking of; yet not one who had been in his service gave him a bad word.

"We have no fault," they would say, "to find with the master, and if he could but get anyone to fetch his wine from the cellar, we might everyone of us have grown gray in the house and have lived quiet and contented enough in his service until the end of our days."

"'Tis a queer thing that, surely," thought young Jack Leary, a lad who had been brought up from a mere child in the stables of Ballinacarthy to assist in taking care of the horses, and had occasionally lent a hand in the butler's pantry:—"'Tis a mighty queer thing, surely, that one man after another cannot content himself with the best place in the house of a good master, but that everyone of them must quit, all through the means, as they say, of the wine cellar. If the master, long life to him! would but make me his butler, I warrant never the word more would be heard of grumbling at his bidding to go to the wine cellar."

Young Leary, accordingly, watched for what he conceived to be a favorable opportunity of presenting himself to the notice of his master.

A few mornings after, Mr. Mac Carthy went into his stableyard rather earlier than usual, and called loudly for the groom to saddle his horse, as he intended going out with the hounds. But there was no groom to answer, and young Jack Leary led Rainbow out of the stable.

"Where is William?" inquired Mr. Mac Carthy.

"Sir?" said Jack; and Mr. Mac Carthy repeated the question.

"Is it William, please your honor?" returned Jack; "why, then, to tell the truth, he had just *one* drop too much last night."

"Where did he get it?" said Mr. Mac Carthy; "for since Thomas went away the key of the wine cellar has been in my pocket, and I have been obliged to fetch what was drunk myself."

"Sorrow a know I know," said Leary, "unless the cook might have give him the *least taste* in life of whiskey. But," continued he, performing a low bow by seizing with his right hand a lock of hair, and pulling down his head by it, while his left leg, which had been put forward, was scraped back against the ground, "may I make so bold as just to ask your honor one question?"

"Speak out, Jack," said Mr. Mac Carthy.

"Why, then, does your honor want a butler?"

"Can you recommend me one," returned his master, with the smile of good-humor upon his countenance, "and one who will not be afraid of going to my wine cellar?"

"Is the wine cellar all the matter?" said young Leary; "devil a doubt I have of myself then for that."

"So you mean to offer me your services in the capacity of butler?" said Mr. Mac Carthy, with some surprise.

"Exactly so," answered Leary, now for the first time looking up from the ground.

"Well, I believe you to be a good lad, and have no objection to give you a trial."

"Long may your honor reign over us, and the Lord spare you to us!" ejaculated Leary, with another national bow, as his master rode off; and he continued for some time to gaze after him with a vacant stare, which slowly and gradually assumed a look of importance.

"Jack Leary," said he, at length, "Jack—is it Jack?" in a tone of wonder; "faith, 'tis not Jack now, but Mr. John, the butler;" and with an air of becoming consequence he strided out of the stable-yard towards the kitchen.

It is of little purport to my story, although it may afford an instructive lesson to the reader, to depict the sudden transition of nobody into somebody. Jack's former stable companion, a poor superannuated hound named Bran, who had been accustomed to receive many an affectionate pat on the head, was spurned from him with a kick and an "Out of the way, sirrah." Indeed, poor Jack's memory seemed sadly affected by this sudden change of situation. What established the point beyond all doubt was his almost forgetting the pretty face of Peggy, the kitchen wench, whose heart he had assailed but the preceding week by the offer of purchasing a gold ring for the fourth finger of her right hand, and a lusty imprint of good-will upon her lips.

When Mr. Mac Carthy returned from hunting, he sent for Jack Leary—so he still continued to call his new butler. "Jack," said he, "I believe you are a trustworthy lad, and here are the keys of my cellar. I have asked the gentlemen with whom I hunted today to dine with me, and I hope they may be satisfied at the way in which you will wait on them at table; but, above all, let there be no want of wine after dinner."

Mr. John having a tolerably quick eye for such things, and being naturally a handy lad, spread his cloth accordingly, laid his plates and knives and forks in the same manner he had seen his predecessors in office perform these mysteries, and really, for the first time, got through attendance on dinner very well.

It must not be forgotten, however, that it was at the house of an Irish country squire, who was entertaining a company of booted and spurred fox-hunters, not very particular about what are considered matters of infinite importance under other circumstances and in other societies.

For instance, few of Mr. Mac Carthy's guests (though all excellent and worthy men in their way) cared much whether the punch produced after soup was made of Jamaica or Antigua rum; some even would not have been inclined to question the correctness of good old Irish whiskey; and, with the exception of their liberal host himself, every one in company preferred the port which Mr. Mac Carthy put on his table to the less ardent flavor of claret—a choice rather at variance with modern sentiment.

It was waxing near midnight, when Mr. Mac Carthy rung the bell three times. This was a signal for more wine; and Jack proceeded to the cellar to procure a fresh supply, but it must be confessed not without some little hesitation.

The luxury of ice was then unknown in the south of Ireland; but the superiority of cool wine had been acknowledged by all men of sound judgment and true taste.

The grandfather of Mr. Mac Carthy, who had built the mansion of Ballinacarthy upon the site of an old castle which had belonged to his ancestors, was fully aware of this important fact; and in the construction of his magnificent wine cellar had availed himself of a deep vault, excavated out of the solid rock in former times as a place of retreat and security. The descent to this vault was by a flight of steep stone stairs, and here and there in the wall were narrow passages—I ought rather to call them crevices; and also certain projections, which cast deep shadows, and looked very frightful when anyone went down the cellar stairs with a single light: indeed, two lights did not much improve the matter, for though the breadth of the shadows became less, the narrow crevices remained as dark and darker than ever.

Summoning up all his resolution, down went the new butler,

bearing in his right hand a lantern and the key of the cellar, and in his left a basket, which he considered sufficiently capacious to contain an adequate stock for the remainder of the evening: he arrived at the door without any interruption whatever; but when he put the key, which was of an ancient and clumsy kind—for it was before the days of Bramah's patent—and turned it in the lock, he thought he heard a strange kind of laughing within the cellar, to which some empty bottle that stood upon the floor outside vibrated so violently that they struck against each other: in this he could not be mistaken, although he may have been deceived in the laugh, for the bottles were just at his feet, and he saw them in motion.

Leary paused for a moment, and looked about him with becoming caution. He then boldly seized the handle of the key, and turned it with all his strength in the lock, as if he doubted his own power of doing so; and the door flew open with a most tremendous crash, that if the house had not been built upon the solid rock would have shook it from the foundation.

To recount what the poor fellow saw would be impossible, for he seems not to have known very clearly himself: but what he told the cook next morning was, that he heard a roaring and bellowing like a mad bull, and that all the pipes and hogsheads and casks in the cellar went rocking backwards and forwards with so much force that he thought everyone would have been staved in, and that he should have been drowned or smothered in wine.

When Leary recovered, he made his way back as well as he could to the dining room, where he found his master and the company very impatient for his return.

"What kept you?" said Mr. Mac Carthy in an angry voice; "and where is the wine? I rung for it half an hour since."

"The wine is in the cellar, I hope, sir," said Jack, trembling violently; "I hope 'tis not all lost."

"What do you mean, fool?" exclaimed Mr. Mac Carthy in a still more angry tone: "why did you not fetch some with you?"

Jack looked wildly about him, and only uttered a deep groan.

"Gentlemen," said Mr. Mac Carthy to his guests, "this is too much. When I next see you to dinner, I hope it will be in another house, for it is impossible I can remain longer in this, where a man has no command over his own wine cellar, and cannot get a butler to do his duty. I have long thought of moving from Ballinacarthy; and I am now determined, with the blessing of God, to leave it tomorrow. But wine shall you have were I to go myself to the cellar for it." So saying, he rose from table, took the key and lantern from his half-stupified servant, who regarded him with a look of vacancy, and descended the narrow stairs, already described, which led to his cellar.

When he arrived at the door, which he found open, he thought he heard a noise, as if of rats or mice scrambling over the casks, and on advancing perceived a little figure, about six inches in height, seated astride upon the pipe of the oldest port in the place, and bearing a spigot upon his shoulder. Raising the lantern, Mr. Mac Carthy contemplated the little fellow with wonder: he wore a red night-cap on his head; before him was a short leather apron, which now, from his attitude, fell rather on one side; and he had stockings of a light blue color, so long as nearly to cover the entire of his leg; with shoes, having huge silver buckles in them, and with high heels (perhaps out of vanity to make him appear taller). His face was like a withered winter apple; and his nose, which was of a bright crimson color, about the tip wore a delicate purple bloom, like that of a plum; yet his eyes twinkled

> "like those mites
> Of candied dew in money nights—"

and his mouth twitched up at one side with an arch grin.

"Ha, scoundrel!" exclaimed Mr. Mac Carthy, "have I found you at last? disturber of my cellar—what are you doing there?"

"Sure, and master," returned the little fellow, looking up at him with one eye, and with the other throwing a sly glance towards the spigot on his shoulder, "a'n't we going to move tomorrow? and sure you would not leave your own little Cluricaune Naggeneen behind you?"

"Oh!" thought Mr. MacCarthy, "if you are to follow me, master Naggeneen, I don't see much use in quitting Ballinacarthy." So filling with wine the basket which young Leary in his fright had left behind him, and locking the cellar door, he rejoined his guests.

For some years after Mr. Mac Carthy had always to fetch the wine for his table himself, as the little Cluricaune Naggeneen seemed to feel a personal respect towards him. Notwithstanding the labor of these journeys, the worthy lord of Ballinacarthy lived in his paternal mansion to a good round age, and was famous to the last for the excellence of his wine, and conviviality of his company; but at the time of his death, the same conviviality had nearly emptied his wine cellar; and as it was never so well filled again, nor so often visited, the revels of master Naggeneen became less celebrated, and are now only spoken of among the legendary lore of the country. It is even said that the poor little fellow took the declension of the cellar so to heart, that he became negligent and careless of himself, and that he has been sometimes seen going about with hardly a *skreed* to cover him.

The Henpecked Giant

D.R. McAnally, Jr.

No LOCALITY OF Ireland is fuller of strange bits of fanciful legend than the neighborhood of the Giant's Causeway. For miles along the coast the geological strata resemble that of the Causeway, and the gradual disintegration of the stone has wrought many peculiar and picturesque effects among the basaltic pillars, while each natural novelty has woven round it a tissue of traditions and legends, some appropriate, others forced, others ridiculous misapplications of commonplace tales. Here, a long straight row of columns known as the "Giant's Organ," and tradition pictures the scene when the giants of old, with their gigantic families, sat on the Causeway and listened to the music; there, a group of isolated pillars is called the "Giant's Chimneys," since they once furnished an exit for the smoke of the gigantic kitchen. A solitary pillar, surrounded by the crumbling remains of others, bears a distant resemblance to a seated female figure, the "Giant's Bride," who slew her husband and attempted to flee, but was overtaken by the power of a magician, who changed her into stone as she was seated by the shore, waiting for the boat that was to carry her away. Further on, a cluster of columns forms the "Giant's Pulpit," where a presumably outspoken gigantic preacher denounced the sins of a gigantic audience. The Causeway itself, according to legend, formerly extended to Scotland, being originally constructed by Finn Maccool and his friends, this notable giant having invited Benandoner, a Scotch giant of much celebrity, to come over and fight him. The invitation was accepted, and Maccool, out of politeness, built the Causeway the whole distance, the big Scotchman thus walking over dryshod to receive his beating.

Some distance from the mainland is found the Ladies' Wishing Chair, composed of blocks in the Great Causeway, wishes made while seated here being certain of realization. To the west of the Wishing Chair a solitary pillar rises from the sea, the "Gray Man's Love." Look to the mainland, and the mountain presents a deep, narrow cleft, with perpendicular sides, the "Gray Man's Path." Out in the sea, but unfortunately not often in sight, is the "Gray Man's Isle," at present inhabited only by the Gray Man himself. As the island, however, appears but once in seventeen years, and the Gray Man is never seen save on the eve of some awful calamity, visitors to the Causeway have a very slight chance of seeing either island or man. There can be no doubt though of the existence of both, for everybody knows he was one of the greatest of the giants during his natural lifetime, nor could any better evidence be asked than the facts that his sweetheart, turned into stone, still stands in sight of the Causeway; the precipice, from which she flung herself into the sea, is still known by the name of the "Lovers' Leap;" and the path he made through the mountain is still used by him when he leaves his island and comes on shore.

It is not surprising that so important a personage as the Gray

Man should be the central figure of many legends, and indeed over him the story-makers seem to have had vigorous competition, for thirty or forty narratives are current in the neighborhood concerning him and the principal events of his life. So great a collection of legendary lore on one topic rendered the choice of a single tradition which should fairly cover the subject a matter of no little difficulty. As sometimes happens in grave undertakings, the issue was determined by accident. A chance boat excursion led to the acquaintance of Mr. Barney O'Toole, a fisherman, and conversation developed the fact that this gentleman was thoroughly posted in the local legends, and was also the possessor of a critical faculty which enabled him to differentiate between the probable and the improbable, and thus to settle the historical value of a tradition. In his way, he was also a philosopher, having evidently given much thought to social issues, and expressing his conclusions thereupon with the ease and freedom of a master mind.

Upon being informed of the variety and amount of legendary material collected about the Gray Man and his doings, Barney unhesitatingly pronounced the entire assortment worthless, and condemned all the gathered treasures as the creations of petty intellects, which could not get out of the beaten track, but sought in the supernatural a reason for and explanation of every fact that seemed at variance with the routine of daily experience. In his opinion, the Gray Man is never seen at all in our day and generation, having been gathered to his fathers ages ago; nor is there any enchanted island; to use his own language, "all thim shtories bein' made be thim blaggârd guides that set up av a night shtringin' out laigends for to enthertain the quol'ty."

"Now, av yer Anner wants to hear it, I can tell ye the thrue shtory av the Gray Man, no more is there anny thing wondherful in it, but it 's just as I had it from me grandfather, that towld it to the childher for to entertain thim.

"It 's very well beknownst that in thim owld days there were gionts in plinty hereabouts, but they did n't make the Causeway at all, for that 's a work o' nacher, axceptin' the Gray Man's Path, that I 'm goin' to tell ye av. But ivery wan knows that there were giants, bekase if there was n't, how cud we know o' thim at all, but wan thing 's sartain, they were just like us, axceptin' in the matther o' size, for wan ov thim 'ud make a dozen like the men that live now.

"Among the giants that lived about the Causeway there was wan, a young giont named Finn O'Goolighan, that was the biggest av his kind, an' none o' them cud hide in a kish. So Finn, for the size av him, was a livin' terror. His little finger was the size av yer Anner's arrum, an' his wrist as big as yer leg, an' so he wint, bigger an' bigger. Whin he walked he carried an oak-tree for a shtick, ye cud crawl into wan av his shoes, an' his caubeen 'ud cover a boat. But he was a good-humored young felly wid a laugh that 'ud deefen ye, an' a plazin' word for all he met, so as if ye run acrass him in the road, he 'd give ye 'good morrow kindly,' so as ye 'd feel the betther av it all day. He 'd work an' he 'd play an' do aither wid all the might that was in him. Av a week day you 'd see him in the field or on the shore from sun to sun as busy as a hen wid a dozen chicks; an' av a fair-day or av a Sunday, there he 'd be, palatherin' at the girls, an' dancin' jigs that he done wid extrame nateness, or havin' a bout wid a shtick on some other felly's head, an' indade, at that he was so clever that it was a delight for to see him, for he 'd crack a giont's shkull that was as hard as a pot wid wan blow an' all the pleasure in life. So he got to be four or five an' twinty an' not his betther in the County Antrim.

"Wan fine day, his father, Bryan O'Goolighan, that was as big a giont as himself, says to him, says he, 'Finn, me Laddybuck, I 'm thinkin' ye 'll want to be gettin' marr'd.'

"'Not me,' says Finn.

"'An' why not?' says his father.

"'I've no consate av it,' says Finn.

"'Ye 'd be the betther av it,' says his father.

"'Faix, I 'm not sure o' that,' says Finn; 'gettin' marr'd is like turnin' a corner, ye don't know phat ye 're goin' to see,' says he.

"'Thrue for ye,' says owld Bryan, for he 'd had axpayrience himself, 'but if ye 'd a purty woman to make the stir-about for ye av a mornin' wid her won white hands, an' to watch out o' the dure for ye in the avenin',' an' put on a sod o' turf whin she sees ye comin', ye 'd be a betther man,' says he.

"'Bedad, it 's not aisey for to conthravene that same,' says Finn, 'barrin' I might n't git wan like that. Wimmin is like angels,' says he. 'There 's two kinds av 'em, an' the wan hat shmiles like a dhrame o' heaven afore she 's marr'd, is the wan that gits to be a tarin' divil afther her market 's made an' she 's got a husband.'

"Ye see Finn was a mighty smart young felly, if he was a giont, but his father did n't give up hope av gettin' him marr'd, for owld folks that 's been through a dale o' throuble that-a-way always thries to get the young wans into the same thrap, beways, says they, av taichin' them to larn something. But Bryan was a wise owld giont, an' knewn, as the Bible says, there 's time enough for all things. So he quit him, an' that night he spake wid the owld woman an' left it wid her, as knowin' that whin it 's a matther o' marryin', a woman is more knowledgable an' can do more to bring on that sort o' mis'ry in wan day than a man can in all the years God gives him.

"Now, in ordher that ye see the pint, I 'm undher the needcessity av axplainin' to yer Anner that Finn did n't be no manes have the hathred at wimmin that he purtinded, for indade he liked them purty well, but he thought he undhershtood thim well enough to know that the more ye talk swate to thim, the more they don't like it, barrin' the 're fools, that sometimes happens. So whin he talked wid 'em or about thim, he spake o' thim shuperskillious, lettin' on to despize the lasht wan o' thim, that was a takin' way he had, for wimmin love thimselves a dale betther than ye 'd think, unless yer Anner 's marr'd an' knows, an' that Finn knew, so he always said o' thim the manest things he cud get out av his head, an' that made thim think av him, that was phat he wanted. They purtinded to hate him for it, but he did n't mind that, for he knewn it was only talk, an' there was n't wan o' thim that would n't give the lasht tooth out av her jaw to have him for a husband.

"Well, as I was sayin', afther owld Bryan give Finn up, his mother tuk him in hand, throwin' a hint at him wanst in a while, sighin' to him how glad she 'd be to have a young lady giont for a dawther, an' dhroppin' a word about phat an iligant girl Burthey O'Ghallaghy was, that was the dawther av wan o' the naburs, that she got Finn, unbeknownst to himself, to be thinkin' about Burthey. She was a fine young lady giont, about tin feet high, as broad as a cassel dure, but she was good size for Finn, as ye know be phat I said av him. So when Finn's mother see him takin' her home from church afther benediction, an' the nabers towld her how they obsarved him lanin' on O'Ghallaghy's wall an' Burthey lightin' his pipe wid a coal, she thought to herself, 'fair an' aisey goes far in a day,' an' made her mind up that Finn 'ud marry Burthey. An' so, belike, he 'd a' done, if he had n't gone over, wan onlucky day, to the village beyant, where the common people like you an' me lived.

"When he got there, in he wint to the inn to get him his dhrink, for it 's a mishtake to think that thim gionts were all blood-suckin' blaggârds as the Causeway guides say, but, barrin' they were in dhrink, were as paceable as rabbits. So when Finn wint in, he says, 'God save ye,' to thim settin', an' gev the table a big crack wid his shillaylah as for to say he wanted his glass. But instead o' the owld granny that used for to fetch him his potheen, out shteps a nate little woman wid hair an' eyes as black as a crow an' two lips on her as red as a cherry an' a quick sharp way like a cat in a hurry.

"'An' who are you, me Dear?' says Finn, lookin' up.

"'I 'm the new barmaid, Sorr, av it 's plazin' to ye,' says she, makin' a curchey, an' lookin' shtrait in his face.

"'It is plazin',' says Finn. ''T is I that 's glad to be sarved be wan like you. Only,' says he, 'I know be the look o' yer eye ye 've a timper.'

"'Dade I have,' says she, talkin' back at him, 'an' ye 'd betther not wake it.'

"Finn had more to say an' so did she, that I won't throuble yer Anner wid, but when he got his fill av dhrink an' said all he 'd in his head, an' she kep' aven wid him at ivery pint, he wint away mightily plazed. The next Sunday but wan he was back agin, an' the Sunday afther, an' afther that agin. By an' by, he 'd come over in the avenin' afther the work was done, an' lane on the bar or set on the table, talkin' wid the barmaid, for she was as sharp as a thornbush, an' sorra a word Finn 'ud say to her in impidince or anny other way, but she 'd give him his answer afore he cud get his mouth shut.

"Now, be this time, Finn's mother had made up her mind that Finn 'ud marry Burthey, an' so she sent for the matchmaker, an' they talked it all over, an' Finn's father seen Burthey's father, an' they settled phat Burthey 'ud get an' phat Finn was to have, an' were come to an agraymint about the match, onbeknownst to Finn, bekase it was in thim days like it is now, the matches bein' made be the owld people, an' all the young wans did was to go an' be marr'd an' make the best av it. Afther all, maybe that 's as good a way as anny, for whin ye 've got all the throuble on yer back ye can stagger undher, there 's not a haporth o' differ whether ye got undher it yerself or whether it was put on ye, an' so it is wid gettin' marr'd, at laste so I 'm towld.

"Annyhow, Finn's mother was busy wid preparin' for th weddin' whin she heard how Finn was afther puttin' in his time at the village.

"'Sure that won't do,' she says to herself; 'he ought to know betther than to be spendin' ivery rap he 's got in dhrink an' gostherin' at that black-eyed huzzy, an' he to be marr'd to the best girl in the county.' So that night, when Finn come in, she spake fair an' soft to him that he 'd give up goin' to the inn, an' get ready for to be marr'd at wanst. An' that did well enough till she got to the marryin', when Finn riz up aff his sate, an' shut his taith so hard he bruk his pipestem to smithereens.

"'Say no more, mother,' he says to her. 'Burthey's good enough, but I would n't marry her if she was made av goold. Begob, she 's too big. I want no hogs'ead av a girl like her,' says he. 'If I 'm to be marr'd, I want a little woman. They 're betther o' their size, an' it don't take so much to buy gowns for thim, naither do they ate so much,' says he.

"'A-a-ah, baithershin,' says his mother to him; 'phat d'ye mane be talkin' that-a-way, an' me workin' me fingers to the bone clanin' the house for ye, an' relavn' ye av all the coortin' so as ye 'd not be bothered in the laste wid it.'

"'Shmall thanks to ye,' says Finn, 'sure is n't the coortin' the best share o' the job?'

"'Don't ye mane to marry her?' says his mother.

"'Divil a toe will I go wid her,' says Finn.

"'Out, ye onmannerly young blaggârd, I 'd tell ye to go to the divil, but ye 're on the way fast enough, an' bad luck to the fut I 'll shtir to halt ye. Only I 'm sorry for Burthey,' says she, 'wid her new gown made. When her brother comes back, begob 't is he that 'll be the death av ye immedjitly afther he dhrops his two eyes on ye.'

"'Aisey now,' says Finn, 'if he opens his big mouth at me, I 'll make him wondher why he was n't born deef an' dumb,' says he, an' so he would, for all that he was so paceable.

"Afther that, phat was his mother to do but lave aff an' go to bed, that she done, givin' Finn all the talk in her head an' a million curses besides, for she was mightily vexed at bein' bate that way an' was in a divil av a timper along o' the house-clanin', that always puts wimmin into a shtate av mind.

"So the next day the news was towld, an' Finn got to be a holy show for the nabers, bekase av not marryin' Burthey an' wantin' the barmaid. They were afeared to say annything to himself about it, for he 'd an arm on him the thick o' yer waist, an' no wan wanted to see how well he cud use it, but they 'd whisper afther him, an' whin he wint along the road, they 'd pint afther him, an' by an' by a giont like himself, an uncle av him towld him he 'd betther lave the counthry, an' so he thought he 'd do an' made ready for to shtart.

"But poor Burthey pined wid shame an' grief at the loss av him, for she loved im wid all the heart she had, an' that was purty big. So she fell aff her weight, till from the size av a hogs'ead she got no bigger round than a barrel an' was like to die. But all the time she kept on hopin' that he 'd come to her, but whin she heard for sartain he was goin' to lave the counthry she let go an' jumped aff that clift into the say an' committed shooicide an' drownded herself. She was n't turned into a pillar at all, that 's wan o' thim guides' lies; she just drownded like annybody that fell into the wather would, an' was found afther an' berrid be the fishermen, an' a hard job av it they had, for she weighed a ton. But they called the place the Lovers' Lape, bekase she jumped from it, an' lovin' Finn the way she did, the lape she tuk made the place be called afther her an' that 's razon enough.

"Finn was showbogher enough afore, but afther that he seen it was no use thryin' for to live in Ireland at all, so he got the barmaid, that was aiquel to goin' wid him, the more that ivery wan was agin him, that 's beway o' the conthrariness av wimmin, that are always ready for to do annything ye don't want thim to do, an' wint to Scotland an' was n't heard av for a long time.

"About twelve years afther, there was a great talk that Finn had got back from Scotland wid his wife an' had taken the farm over be the village, the first on the left as ye go down the mountain. At first there was no end av the fuss that was, for Burthey's frinds had n't forgotten, but it all come to talk, so Finn settled down quite enough an' wint to work. But he was an althered man. His hair an' beard were gray as a badger, so they called him the Gray Man, an' he 'd a look on him like a shape-stalin' dog. Everybody wondhered, but they did n't wondher long, for it was aisely persaived he had cause enough, for the tongue o' Missis Finn wint like a stame-ingine, kapin' so far ahead av her branes that she 'd have to shtop an' say 'an'-uh, an'-uh,' to give the latther time for to ketch up. Jagers, but she was the woman for to talk an' schold an' clack away till ye 'd want to die to be rid av her. When she was young she was a purty nice girl, but as she got owlder her nose got sharp, her lips were as thin as the aidge av a sickle, an' her chin was as pinted as the bow av a boat. The way she managed Finn was beautiful to see, for he was that afeared av her tongue that he dar n't say his sowl belonged to him when she was by.

"When he got up airly in the mornin', she'd ax, "Now phat are ye raisin' up so soon for, an' me just closin' me eyes in slape?' an' if he 'd lay abed, she 'd tell him to 'get along out o' that now, ye big gossoon; if it was n't for me ye 'd do nothin' at all but slape like a pig.' If he'd go out, she'd gosther him about where he was goin' an' phat he meant to do when he got there; if he shtayed at home, she'd raymark that he done nothin' but set in the cabin like a boss o' shtraw. When he thried for to plaze her, she 'd grumble at him bekase he did 't thry sooner; when he let her be, she 'd fall into a fury an' shtorm till his hair shtud up like it was bewitched it was.

"She 'd more thricks than a showman's dog. If scholdin' did n't do for Finn, she 'd cry at him, an' had tin childher that she larned to cry at him too, an' when she begun, the tin o' thim 'ud set up a yell that 'ud deefen a thrumpeter, so Finn 'ud give in.

"She cud fall ill on tin minnits notice, an' if Finn was

obsthreperous in that degray that she cud n't do him no other way, she 'd let on her head ached fit to shplit, so she 'd go to bed an' shtay there till she 'd got him undher her thumb agin. So she knew just where to find him whin she wanted him; that wimmin undhershtand, for there 's more divilmint in wan woman's head about gettin' phat she wants than in tin men's bodies.

"Sure, if iver annybody had raison to remimber the ould song, "When I was single," it was Finn.

"So, ye see, Finn, the Gray Man, was afther havin' the divil's own time, an' that was beways av a mishtake he made about marryin'. He thought it was wan o' thim goold bands the quol'ty ladies wear on their arrums, but he found it was a handcuff it was. Sure wimmin are quare craythers. Ye think life wid wan o' thim is like a sunshiny day an' it 's nothing but drizzle an' fog from dawn to dark, an' it 's my belafe that Misther O'Day was n't far wrong when he said wimmin are like the owld gun he had in the house an' that wint aff an the shly wan day an' killed the footman. 'Sure it looked innycent enough,' says he, 'but it was loaded all the same an' only waitin' for an axcuse to go aff at some wan, an' that 's like a woman, so it is,' he 'd say, an' ivery wan 'ud laugh when he towld that joke, for he was the landlord, 'that 's like a woman, for she 's not to be thrusted avin when she 's dead."

"But it 's me own belafe that the most sarious mishtake av Finn's was in marryin' a little woman. There 's thim that says all wimmin is a mishtake be nacher, but there 's a big differ bechuxt a little woman an' a big wan, the little wans have sowls too big for their bodies, so are always lookin' out for a big man to marry, an' the bigger he is, the betther they like him, as knowin' they can manage him all the aisier. So it was wid Finn an' his little wife, for be hook an' be crook she rejuiced him in that obejince that if she towld him for to go an' shtand on his head in the corner, he 'd do it wid the rish av his life, bekase he 'd wanted to die an' go to heaven as he heard the priest say there was no marryin' there, an' though he did n't dare to hint it, he belaved in his sowl that the rayzon was the wimmin did n't get that far.

"Afther they 'd been living here about a year, Finn thought he 'd fish a bit an' so help along, considherin' he 'd a big family

an' none o' the childher owld enough for to work. So he got a boat an' did purty well an' his wife used to come acrass the hill to the shore to help him wid the catch. But it was far up an' down agin an' she 'd get tired wid climbin' the hill an' jawing at Finn on the way.

"So wan day as they were comin' home, they passed a cabin an' there was the man that lived there, that was only a ditcher, a workin' away on the side av the hill down the path to the shpring wid a crowbar, movin' a big shtone, an' the shweat rollin' in shtrames aff his face.

"'God save ye,' says Finn to him.

"God save ye kindly,' says he to Finn.

"'It 's a bizzy man ye are,' says Finn.

"'Thrue for ye,' says the ditcher. 'It 's along o' the owld woman. "The way to the shpring is too stape an' shtoney," says she to me, an' sure, I 'm afther makin' it aisey for her.'

"'Ye 're the kind av a man to have,' says Missis Finn, shpakin' up. 'Sure all wimmin is n't blessed like your wife,' says she, lookin' at Finn, who let on to laugh when he wanted to shwear. They had some more discoorse, thin Finn an' his wife wint on, but it put a big notion into her head. If the bogthrotter, that was only a little ottommy, 'ud go to work like that an' make an aisey path for his owld woman to the shpring, phat 's the rayzon Finn cud n't fall to an' dig a path through the mountains, so she cud go to the say an' to the church on the shore widout breakin' her back climbin' up an' then agin climbin' down. 'T was the biggest consate iver in the head av her, an' she was n't wan o' thim that 'ud let it cool aff for the want o' talkin' about it, so she up an' towld it to Finn, an' got afther him to do it. Finn was n't aiger for to thry, bekase it was Satan's own job, so he held out agin all her scholdin' an' beggin' an' cryin'. Then she got sick on him, wid her headache, an' wint to bed, an' whin Finn was about she 'd wondher out loud phat she was iver born for an' why she cud n't die. Then she 'd pray, so as Finn 'ud hear her, to all the saints to watch over her big gossoon av a husband an' not forget him just bekase he was a baste, an' if Finn 'ud thry to quiet her, she 'd pray all the louder, an' tell him it did n't matther, she was dyin' an' 'ud soon be rid av him an' his brutal ways, so as Finn got half crazy wid her an' was ready to do annything in the worruld for to get her quiet.

"Afther about a week av this thratemint, Finn give in an' wint to work wid a pick an' shpade on the Gray Man's Path. But thim that says he made it in wan night is ignerant, for I belave it tuk him a month at laste; if not more. So that 's the thrue shtory av the Gray Man's Path, as me grandfather towld it, an' shows that a giont's size is n't a taste av help to him in a contist wid a woman's jaw.

"But to be fair wid her, I belave the onliest fault Finn's wife had was, she was possist be the divil, an' there 's thim that thinks that 's enough. I mind me av a young felly wan time tatt was in love, an' so to be axcused, that wished he 'd a hunderd tongues so to do justice to his swateheart. So after that he marr'd her, an' whin they 'd been marr'd a while an' she 'd got him undher her fisht, says they to him, 'An' how about yer hunderd tongues?' 'Begorra,' says he to thim agin, 'wid a hunderd I 'd get along betther av coorse than wid wan, but to be ayquel to the waggin' av her jaw I 'd nade a hunderd t'ousand.'

"So it 's a consate I have that Missis Finn was not a haporth worse nor the rest o' thim, an' that 's phat me grandfather said too, that had been marr'd twict, an' so knewn phat he was talkin' about. An' whin he towld the shtory av the Gray Man, he 'd always end it wid a bit av poethry:—-

> "'The first rib did bring in ruin
> As the rest have since been doin';
> Some be wan way, some another,
> Woman shtill is mischief's mother.
>
> "'Be she good or be she avil,
> Be she saint or be she divil,
> Shtill unaisey is his life
> That is marr'd wid a wife.'"

John Reardon and the Sister Ghosts

Traditional

ONCE THERE WAS A FARMER, a widower, Tom Reardon, who lived near Castlemain. He had an only son, a fine strong boy, who was almost a man, and the boy's name was John. This farmer married a second time, and the stepmother hated the boy and gave him neither rest nor peace. She was turning the father's mind against the son, till at last the farmer resolved to put the son in a place where a ghost was, and this ghost never let any man go without killing him.

One day the father sent the son to the forge with some chains belonging to a plow; he would have two horses plowing next day.

The boy took the chains to the forge; and it was nearly

evening when the father sent him, and the forge was four miles away.

The smith had much work and he hadn't the chains mended till close on to midnight. The smith had two sons, and they didn't wish to let John go, but he said he must go, for he had promised to be home and the father would kill him if he stayed away. They stood before him in the door, but he went in spite of them.

When two miles from the forge a ghost rose up before John, a woman; she attacked him and they fought for two hours, when he put the plow chain round her. She could do nothing then, because what belongs to a plow is blessed. He fastened the chain and dragged the ghost home with him, and told her to go to the bedroom and give the father and stepmother a rough handling, not to spare them.

The ghost beat them till the father cried for mercy, and said if he lived till morning he'd leave the place, and that the wife was the cause of putting John in the way to be killed.

John put food on the table and told the ghost to sit down and eat for herself, but she refused and said he must take her back to the very spot where he found her. John was willing to do that, and he went with her. She told him to come to that place on the following night, that there was a sister of hers, a ghost, a deal more determined and stronger than what herself was.

John told her that maybe the two of them would attack and kill him. She said that they would not, that she wanted his help against the sister, and that he would not be sorry for helping her. He told her he would come, and when he was leaving her she said not to forget the plow chains.

Next morning the father was going to leave the house, but the wife persuaded him to stay. "That ghost will never walk the way again," said she. John went the following night, and the ghost was waiting before him on the spot where he fought with her. They walked on together two miles by a different road, and halted. They were talking in that place a while when the sister came and attacked John Reardon, and they were fighting two hours and she was getting the better of the boy, when the first sister put the plow chains around her. He pulled her home with the chains, and the first sister walked along behind them. When John came to the house, he opened the door, and when the father saw the two ghosts he said that if morning overtook him alive he'd leave the son everything, the farm and the house.

The son told the second ghost to go down and give a good turn to the stepmother; "Let her have a few strong knocks," said he.

The second ghost barely left life in the stepmother. John had food on the table, but they would not take a bite, and the second sister said he must take her back to the very spot where he met her first. He said he would. She told him that he was the bravest man that ever stood before her, and that she would not threaten him again in the world, and told him to come the next night. He said he would not, for the two might attack and get the better of him. They promised they would not attack, but would help him, for it was to get the upper hand of the youngest and strongest of the sisters that they wanted him, and that he must bring the plow chains, for without them they could do nothing.

He agreed to go if they would give their word not to harm him. They said they would give their word and would help him the best they could.

The next day, when the father was going to leave the place, the wife would not let him. "Stay where you are," she said, "they'll never trouble us again."

John went the third night, and, when he came, the two sisters were before him, and they walked till they travelled four miles

then told him to stop on the green grass at one side and not to be
on the road.

They weren't waiting long when the third sister came, and red
lightning flashing from her mouth. She went at John, and with
the first blow that she gave him put him on his knees. He rose
with the help of the two sisters, and for three hours they fought,
and the youngest sister was getting the better of the boy when
the two others threw the chains around her. The boy dragged her
away home with him then, and, when the stepmother saw the
three sisters coming, herself and John's father were terrified
and they died of fright, the two of them

John put food on the table and told the sisters to come and eat,
but they refused, and the youngest told him that he must take
her to the spot where he fought with her. All four went to that
place, and at parting they promised never to harm him and to
put him in the way that he would never need to do a day's work,
nor his children after him, if he had any. The eldest sister told
him to come on the following night, and to bring a spade with
him; she would tell him, she said, her whole history from first to
last.

He went, and what she told him was this: Long ago her father
was one of the richest men in all Ireland: her mother died when
the three sisters were very young, and ten or twelve years after
the father died, and left the care of all the wealth and treasures
in the castle to herself, telling her to make three equal parts of it,
and to let herself and each of the other two sisters have one of
those parts. But she was in love with a young man unknown to
her father, and one night when the two sisters were fast asleep,
and she thought if she killed them she would have the whole
fortune for herself and her husband, she took a knife and cut
their throats, and when she had them killed she got sorry and
did the same to herself. The sentence put on them was that none

of the three was to have rest or peace till some man without fear would come and conquer them, and John was the first to attempt this.

She took him then to her father's castle—only the ruins of it were standing, no roof and only some of the walls, and showed where all the riches and treasures were. John, to make sure, took his spade and dug away, dug with what strength was in him, and just before daybreak he came to the treasure. That moment the three sisters left good health with him, turned into three doves, and flew away.

He had riches enough for himself and for seven generations after him.

The Leprechawn
D.R. McAnally, Jr.

EVERY MYTHOLOGY HAS its good and evil spirits which are objects of adoration and subjects of terror, and often both classes are worshipped from opposite motives; the good, that the worshipper may receive benefit; the evil, that he may escape harm. Sometimes good deities are so benevolent that they are neglected, superstitious fear directing all devotion towards the evil spirits to propitiate them and avert the calamities they are ever ready to bring upon the human race; sometimes the malevolent deities have so little power that the prayer of the pious is offered up to the good spirits that they may pour out still further favors, for man is a worshipping being, and will prostrate himself with equal fervor before the altar whether the deity be good or bad.

Midway, however, between the good and evil beings of all mythologies there is often one whose qualities are mixed; not wholly good nor entirely evil, but balanced between the two, sometimes doing a generous action, then descending to a petty meanness, but never rising to nobility of character nor sinking to the depths of depravity; good from whim, and mischievous from caprice.

Such a being is the Leprechawn of Ireland, a relic of the pagan mythology of that country. By birth the Leprechawn is of low descent, his father being an evil spirit and his mother a degenerate fairy; by nature he is a mischief-maker, the Puck of the Emerald Isle. He is of diminutive size, about three feet high, and is dressed in a little red jacket or roundabout, with red breeches buckled at the knee, gray or black stockings, and a hat, cocked in the style of a century ago, over a little, old, withered face. Round his neck is an Elizabethan ruff, and frills of lace are at his wrists. On the wild west coast, where the Atlantic winds bring almost constant rains, he dispenses with ruff and frills and wears a frieze overcoat over his pretty red suit, so that, unless on the lookout for the cocked hat, "ye might pass a Leprechawn on the road and never know it 's himself that 's in it at all."

In Clare and Galway, the favorite amusement of the Leprechawn is riding a sheep or goat, or even a dog, when the other animals are not available, and if the sheep look weary in the morning or the dog is muddy and worn out with fatigue, the peasant understands that the local Leprechawn has been going on some errand that lay at a greater distance than he cared to travel on foot. Aside from riding the sheep and dogs almost to death, the Leprechawn is credited with much small mischief about the house. Sometimes he will make the pot boil over and put out the fire, then again he will make it impossible for the pot to boil at all. He will steal the bacon-flitch, or empty the potato-kish, or fling the baby down on the floor, or occasionally will throw the few poor articles of furniture about the room with a strength and vigor altogether disproportioned to his diminutive size. But his mischievous pranks seldom go further than to drink up all the milk or despoil the proprietor's bottle of its poteen, sometimes, in sportiveness, filling the bottle with water, or, when very angry, leading the fire up to the thatch, and then startling the inmates of the cabin with his laugh as they rise, frightened, to put out the flames.

To offset these troublesome attributes, the Leprechawn is very domestic, and sometimes attaches himself to a family, always of the "rale owld shtock," accompanying its representatives from the castle to the cabin and never deserting them unless driven away by some act of insolence or negligence, "for, though he likes good atin', he wants phat he gets to come wid an open hand, an' 'ud laver take the half av a pratee that 's freely given than the whole av a quail that 's begrudged him." But what he eats must be specially intended for him, an instance being cited by a Clare peasant of a Leprechawn that deserted an Irish family, because, on one occasion, the dog having left a portion of his food, it was set by for the Leprechawn. "Jakers, 't was as mad as a little wasp he was, an' all that night they heard him workin' away in the cellar as busy as a nailer an' a sound like a catheract av wather goin' widout sayein'. In the mornin' they wint to see phat he 'd been at, but he was gone, an' whin they come to thry for the wine, bad loock to the dhrop he 'd left, but all was gone from ivory cask an' bottle, and they were filled wid say-wather, beways av rayvinge o' phat they done him."

In different country districts the Leprechawn has different names. In the northern counties he is the Logheryman; in Tipperary, he is the Lurigadawne; in Kerry, the Luricawne; in Monaghan, the Cluricawne. The dress also varies. The Logheryman wears the uniform of some British infantry regiments, a red coat and white breeches, but instead of a cap, he wears a broad-brimmed, high, pointed hat, and after doing some trick more than usually mischievous, his favorite position is to poise himself on the extreme point of his hat, standing at the top of a wall or on a house, feet in the air, then laugh heartily and disappear. The Lurigadawne wears an antique slashed jacket of red, with peaks all round and a jockey cap, also sporting a sword, which he uses as a magic wand. The Luricawne is a fat, pursy little fellow whose jolly round face rivals in redness the cutaway jacket he wears, that always has seven rows of seven buttons in each row, though what use they are has never been determined, since his jacket is never buttoned, nor, indeed, can it be, but falls away from a shirt invariably white as the snow. When in full dress he wears a helmet several sizes too large for him, but, in general, prudently discards this article of headgear as having a tendency to render him conspicuous in a country where helmets are obsolete, and wraps his head in a handkerchief that he ties over his ears.

The Cluricawne of Monaghan is a little dandy, being gorgeously arrayed in a swallow-tailed evening coat of red with green vest, white breeches, black stockings, and shoes that "fur the shine av 'em 'ud shame a lookin'-glass." His hat is a long cone without a brim, and is usually set jauntily on one side of his curly head. When greatly provoked, he will sometimes take vengeance by suddenly ducking and poking the sharp point of his hat into the eye of the offender. Such conduct is, however, exceptional, as he commonly contents himself with soundly abusing those at whom he has taken offence, the objects of his anger hearing his voice but seeing nothing of his person.

One of the most marked peculiarities of the Leprechawn family is their intense hatred of schools and schoolmasters, arising, perhaps, from the ridicule of them by teachers, who affect to disbelieve in the existence of the Leprechawn and thus insult him, for "it 's very well beknownst, that unless ye belave in him an' thrate him well, he 'll lave an' come back no more." He does not even like to remain in the neighborhood where a national school has been established, and as such schools are now numerous in Ireland, the Leprechawns are becoming scarce. "Wan gineration of taichers is enough for thim, bekase the families where the little fellys live forgit to set thim out the bit an' sup, an' so they lave." The few that remain must have a hard time keeping soul and body together for nowhere do they now receive any attention at meal-times, nor is the anxiety to see one by any means so great as in the childhood of men still living. Then, to catch a Leprechawn was certain fortune to him who had the wit to hold the mischief-maker a captive until demands for wealth were complied with.

"Mind ye," said a Kerry peasant, "the onliest time ye can ketch the little vagabone is whin he 's settin' down, an' he niver sets down axceptin' whin his brogues want mendin'. He runs about so much he wears thim out, an' whin he feels his feet on the ground, down he sets undher a hidge or behind a wall, or in the grass, an' takes thim aff an' mends thim. Thin comes you by, as quiet as a cat an' sees him there, that ye can aisily, be his red coat, an' you shlippin' up on him, catches him in yer arrums.

"'Give up yer goold,' says you.

"'Begob, I 've no goold,' says he.

"'Then outs wid yer magic purse,' says you.

"But it 's like pullin' a hat full av taith to get aither purse or goold av him. He 's got goold be the ton, an' can tell ye where ye can put yer finger on it, but he wont, till ye make him, an' that ye must do be no aisey manes. Some cuts aff his wind be chokin' him, an' some bates him, but don't for the life o' ye take yer eyes aff him, fur if ye do, he 's aff like a flash an' the same man niver sees him agin, an' that 's how it was wid Michael O'Dougherty.

"He was afther lookin' for wan nigh a year, fur he wanted to get married an' had n't anny money, so he thought the aisiest was to ketch a Luricawne. So he was lookin' an' watchin' an' the fellys makin' fun av him all the time. Wan night he was comin' back afore day from a wake he 'd been at, an' on the way home he laid undher the hidge an' shlept awhile, thin riz an' walked on. So as he was walkin', he seen a Luricawne in the grass be the road a-mendin' his brogues. So he shlipped up an' got him fast enough, an' thin made him tell him where was his goold. The Luricawne tuk him to nigh the place in the break o' the hills an' was goin' fur to show him, when all at wanst Mike heard the most outprobrious scraich over the head av him that 'ud make the hairs av ye shtand up like a mad cat's tail.

"'The saints defind me,' says he, 'phat 's that?' an' he looked up from the Luricawne that he was carryin' in his arrums. That minnit the little attomy wint out av his sight, fur he looked away from it an' it was gone, but he heard it laugh when it wint an' he niver got the goold but died poor, as me father knows, an' he a boy when it happened."

Although the Leprechawns are skilful in evading curious eyes, and, when taken, are shrewd in escapng from their captors, their tricks are sometimes all in vain, and after resorting to every device in their power, they are occasionally compelled to yield up their hidden stores, one instance of which was narrated by a Galway peasant.

"It was Paddy Donnelly av Connemara. He was always hard at work as far as anny wan seen, an' bad luck to the day he 'd miss, barrin' Sundays. When all 'ud go to the fair, sorra a fut he 'd shtir to go near it, no more did a dhrop av dhrink crass his lips. When they 'd ax him why he did n't take divarshun, he 'd laugh an' tell thim his field was divarshun enough fur him, an' by an' by he got rich, so they knewn that when they were at the fair or wakes or shports, it was lookin' fur a Leprechawn he was an' not workin', an' he got wan too, fur how else cud he get rich at all."

And so it must have been, in spite of the denials of Paddy Donnelly, though, to do him justice, he stoutly affirmed that his small property was acquired by industry, economy, and temperance. But according to the opinions of his neighbors, "bad scran to him 't was as greedy as a pig he was, fur he knewn where the goold was, an' wanted it all fur himself, an' so lied about it like the Leprechawns, that 's known to be the biggest liars in the world."

The Leprechawn is an old bachelor elf who successfully resists all efforts of scheming fairy mammas to marry him to young and beautiful fairies, persisting in single blessedness even in exile from his kind, being driven off as a punishment for his heterodoxy on matrimonial subjects. This is one explanation of the fact that Leprechawns are always seen alone, though other authorities make the Leprechawn solitary by preference, he having learned the hollowness of fairy friendship and the deceitfulness of fairy femininity, and left the society of his kind in disgust at its lack of sincerity.

It must be admitted that the latter explanation seems the more reasonable, since whenever the Leprechawn has been captured and forced to engage in conversation with his captor he displayed conversational powers that showed an ability to please, and as woman kind, even among fairy circles, are, according to an Irish proverb, "aisily caught be an oily tongue," the presumption is against the expulsion of the Leprechawn and in favor of his voluntary retirement.

However this may be, one thing is certain to the minds of all wise women and fairy-men, that he is the "thrickiest little divil that iver wore a brogue," whereof abundant proof is given. There was Tim O'Donovan, of Kerry, who captured a Leprechawn and forced him to disclose the spot where the "pot o' goold" was concealed. Tim was going to make the little rogue dig up the money for him, but, on the Leprechawn advancing the plea that he had no spade, released him, marking the spot by driving a stick into the ground and placing his hat on it. Returning the next morning with a spade, the spot pointed out by the "little ottomy av a desaver" being in the centre of a large bog, he found, to his unutterable disgust, that the Leprechawn was too smart for him, for in every direction innumerable sticks rose out of the bog, each bearing aloft an old "caubeen" so closely resembling his own that poor Tim, after long search, was forced to admit himself baffled and give up the gold that, on the evening before, had been fairly within his grasp, if "he 'd only had the brains in his shkull to make the Leprechawn dig it for him, shpade or no shpade."

Even when caught, therefore, the captor must outwit the captive, and the wily little rascal, having a thousand devices, generally gets away without giving up a penny, and sometimes succeeds in bringing the eager fortune hunter to grief, a notable instance of which was the case of Dennis O'Bryan, of Tipperary, as narrated by an old woman of Crusheen.

"It 's well beknownst that the Leprechawn has a purse that 's got the charmed shillin'. Only wan shillin', but the wondher av the purse is this: No matther how often ye take out a shillin' from it, the purse is niver empty at all, but whin ye put yer finger in agin, ye always find wan there, fur the purse fills up when ye take wan from it, so ye may shtand all day countin' out the shillin's an' they comin', that 's a thrick av the good peoples an' be magic.

"Now Dinnis was a young blaggârd that was always afther peepin' about undher the hidge fur to ketch a Leprechawn, though they do say that thim that does n't sarch afther thim see thim oftener that thim that does, but Dinnis made his mind up that if there was wan in the counthry, he 'd have him, fur he hated work worse than sin, an' did be settin' in a shebeen day in an' out till you 'd think he 'd grow on the sate. So wan day he was comin' home, an' he seen something red over in the corner o' the field, an' in he goes, as quiet as a mouse, an' up on the Leprechawn an' grips him be the collar an' down's him on the ground.

"'Arrah, now, ye ugly little vagbone,' says he, 'I 've got ye at last. Now give up yer goold, or by jakers I 'll choke the life out av yer pin-squazin' carkidge, ye owld cobbler, ye,' says he, shakin' him fit to make his head dhrop aff.

"The Leprechawn begged, and scritched, an' cried, an' said he was n't a rale Leprechawn that was in it, but a young wan that had n't anny goold, but Dinnis would n't let go av him, an' at last the Leprechawn said he 'd take him to the pot ov goold that was hid be the say, in a glen in Clare. Dinnis did n't want to go so far, bein' afeared the Leprechawn 'ud get away, an' he thought the divilish baste was afther lyin' to him, bekase he knewn there was goold closter than that, an' so he was chokin' him that his eyes stood out till ye cud knock 'em aff wid a shtick, an' the Leprechawn axed him would he lave go if he 'd give him the magic purse. Dinnis thought he 'd betther do it, fur he was mortially afeared the oudacious little villin 'ud do him so thrick an' get away, so he tuk the purse, afther lookin' at it to make sure it was red shilk, an' had the shillin' in it, but the minnit he tuk his two eyes aff the Leprechawn, away wint the rogue wid a laugh that Dinnis did n't like at all.

"But he was feelin' very comfortable be razon av gettin' the purse, an' says to himself, 'Begorra, 't is mesilf that 'll ate the full av me waistband fur wan time, an' dhrink till a stame-ingine can't squaze wan dhrop more down me neck,' says he, and aff he goes like a quarther-horse fur Miss Clooney's sheebeen, that 's where he used fur to go. In he goes, an' there was Paddy Grogan, an' Tim O'Donovan, an' Mike Conathey, an' Bryan Flaherty, an' a shtring more av 'om settin' on the table, an' he pulls up a sate an' down he sets, a-callin' to Miss Clooney to bring her best.

"'Where 's yer money?' says she to him, fur he did n't use to have none barrin' a tuppence or so.

"'Do you have no fear,' says he, 'fur the money,' says he, 'ye pinny-schrapin' owld shkeleton,' this was beways av a shot at her, fur it was the size av a load o' hay she was, an' weighed a ton. 'Do you bring yer best,' says he. 'I 'm a gintleman av forchune, bad loock to the job o' work I 'll do till the life laves me. Come, jintlemen, dhrink at my axpinse.' An' so they did an' more than wanst, an' afther four or five guns apace, Dinnis ordhered dinner fur thim all, but Miss Clooney towld him sorra the bit or sup more 'ud crass the lips av him till he paid fur that he had. So out he pulls the magic purse fur to pay, an' to show it thim an' towld thim phat it was an' where he got it.

"'And was it the Leprechawn gev it ye?' says they.

"'It was,' says Dinnis, 'an' the varchew av this purse is sich, that if ye take shillin's out av it be the handful all day long, they 'll be comin' in a shtrame like whiskey out av a jug,' says he, pullin' out wan.

"And thin, me jewel, he put in his fingers afther another, but it was n't there, for the Leprechawn made a ijit av him, an' instid o' givin' him the right purse, gev him wan just like it, so as onless ye looked clost, ye cud n't make out the differ betune thim. But the face on Dinnis was a holy show when he seen the Leprechawn had done him, an' he wid only a shillin', an' half a crown av dhrink down the troats av thim.

"'To the divil wid you an' yer Leprechawns, an' purses, an'

magic shillin's,' schreamed Miss Clooney, belavin', an' small blame to her that's, that it was lyin' to her he was. 'Ye 're a thafe, so ye are, dhrinkin' up me dhrink, wid a lie on yer lips about the purse, an' insultin' me into the bargain,' says she, thinkin' how he called her a shkeleton, an' her a load fur a waggin. 'Yer impidince bates owld Nick, so it does,' says she; so she up an' hits him a power av a crack on the head wid a bottle; an' the other felly's, a thinkin' sure that it was a lie he was afther tellin' them, an' he laving thim to pay fur the dhrink he 'd had, got on him an' belted him out av the face it was nigh onto dead he was. Then a consthable comes along an' hears the phillaloo they did be makin' an' comes in.

"'Tatther an' agers,' says he, 'lave aff. I command the pace. Phat 's the matther here?'

"So they towld him an' he consayved that Dinnis shtole the purse an' tuk him be the collar.

"'Lave go,' says Dinnis. 'Sure phat 's the harrum o' getting the purse av a Leprechawn?'

"'None at all,' says the polisman, 'av ye projuice the Leprechawn an' make him teshtify he gev it ye an' that ye have n't been burglarious an' sacrumvinted another man's money,' says he.

"But Dinnis cud n't do it, so the cunsthable tumbled him into the jail. From that he wint to corrt an' got thirty days at hard labor, that he niver done in this life afore, an' afther he got out, he said he 'd left lookin' for Leprechawns, fur they were too shmart fur him entirely, an' it 's thrue fur him, bekase I belave they were."

The Dead Smile
Francis Marion Crawford

I

SIR HUGH OCKRAM SMILED as he sat by the open window of his study, in the late August afternoon, and just then a curiously yellow cloud obscured the low sun, and the clear summer light turned lurid, as if it had been suddenly poisoned and polluted by the foul vapors of a plague. Sir Hugh's face seemed, at best, to be made of fine parchment drawn skin-tight over a wooden mask, in which two eyes were sunk out of sight, and peered from far within through crevices under the slanting. wrinkled lids, alive and watchful like two toads in their holes, side by side and exactly alike. But as the light changed, then a little yellow glare flashed in each. Nurse Macdonald said once that when Sir Hugh smiled he saw the faces of two women in hell—

two dead women he had betrayed. (Nurse Macdonald was a hundred years old.) And the smile widened, stretching the pale lips across the discolored teeth in an expression of profound self-satisfaction, blended with the most unforgiving hatred and contempt for the human soul. The hideous disease of which he was dying had touched his brain. His son stood beside him, tall, white, and delicate as an angel in a primitive picture, and though there was deep distress in his violet eyes as he looked at his father's face, he felt the shadow of that sickening smile stealing across his own lips and parting them and drawing them against his will. And it was like a bad dream, for he tried not to smile and smiled the more. Beside him, strangely like him in her wan, angelic beauty, with the same shadowy golden hair, the same sad violet eyes, the same luminously pale face, Evelyn Warburton rested one hand upon his arm. And as she looked into her uncle's eyes, and could not turn her own away, she knew that the deathly smile was hovering on her own red lips, drawing them tightly across her little teeth, while two bright tears ran down her cheeks to her mouth, and dropped from the upper to the lower lip while she smiled—and the smile was like the shadow of death and the seal of damnation upon her pure, young face.

"Of course," said Sir Hugh very slowly, and still looking out at the trees, 'if you have made up your mind to be married, I cannot hinder you, and I don't suppose you attach the smallest importance to my consent—"

"Father!" exclaimed Gabriel reproachfully.

"No, I do not deceive myself," continued the old man, smiling terribly. "You will marry when I am dead, though there is a very good reason why you had better not—why you had better not," he repeated very emphatically, and he slowly turned his toad eyes upon the lovers.

"What reason?" asked Evelyn in a frightened voice.

"Never mind the reason, my dear. You will marry just as if it did not exist." There was a long pause. "Two gone," he said, his voice lowering strangely, "and two more will be four—all together—for ever and ever, burning, burning, burning bright."

At the last words his head sank slowly back, and the little glare of the toad eyes disappeared under the swollen lids, and the lurid cloud passed from the westering sun, so that the earth was green again and the light pure. Sir Hugh had fallen asleep, as he often did in his last illness, even while speaking.

Gabriel Ockram drew Evelyn away, and from the study they went out into the dim hall, softly closing the door behind them, and each audibly drew breath, as though some sudden danger had been passed. They laid their hands each in the other's and their strangely-alike eyes met in a long look, in which love and perfect understanding were darkened by the secret terror of an unknown thing. Their pale faces reflected each other's fear.

"It is his secret," said Evelyn at last. "He will never tell us what it is."

"If he dies with it," answered Gabriel, "let it be on his own head!"

"On his head!" echoed the dim hall. It was a strange echo, and some were frightened by it, for they said that if it were a real echo it should repeat everything and not give back a phrase here and there, now speaking, now silent. But Nurse Macdonald said that the great hall would never echo a prayer when an Ockram was to die, though it would give back curses ten for one.

"On his head!" it repeated quite softly, and Evelyn started and looked round.

"It is only the echo." said Gabriel, leading her away.

They went out into the late afternoon light, and sat upon a stone seat behind the chapel, which was built across the end of the east wing. It was very still, not a breath stirred, and there was no sound near them. Only far off in the park a song-bird was whistling the high prelude to the evening chorus.

"It is very lonely here," said Evelyn, taking Gabriel's hand nervously, and speaking as if she dreaded to disturb the silence. "If it were dark. I should be afraid."

"Of what? Of me?" Gabriel's sad eyes turned to her.

"Oh no! How could I be afraid of you? But of the old Ockrams—they say they are just under our feet here in the north vault outside the chapel, all in their shrouds, with no coffins, as they used to bury them."

"As they always will—as they will bury my father, and me. They say an Ockram will not lie in a coffin."

"But it cannot be true—these are fairy tales—ghost stories!" Evelyn nestled nearer to her companion, grasping his hand more tightly, and the sun began to go down.

"Of course. But there is a story of old Sir Vernon, who was beheaded for treason under James II. The family brought his body back from the scaffold in an iron coffin with heavy locks, and they put it in the north vault. But ever afterwards, whenever the vault was opened to bury another of the family, they found the coffin wide open, and the body standing upright against the wall, and the head rolled away in a corner, smiling at it."

"As Uncle Hugh smiles?" Evelyn shivered.

"Yes, I suppose so," answered Gabriel, thoughtfully. "Of course I never saw it, and the vault has not been opened for thirty years—none of us have died since then."

"And if—if Uncle Hugh dies—shall you—" Evelyn stopped, and her beautiful thin face was quite white.

"Yes. I shall see him laid there too—with his secret, whatever it is." Gabriel sighed and pressed the girl's little hand.

"I do not like to think of it," she said unsteadily. "O Gabriel, what can the secret be? He said we had better not marry—not that he forbade it—but he said it so strangely, and he smiled—ugh!" Her small white teeth chattered with fear, and she looked over her shoulder while drawing still closer to Gabriel. "And, somehow, I felt it in my own face—"

"So did I," answered Gabriel in a low, nervous voice. "Nurse Macdonald—" He stopped abruptly.

"What? What did she say?"

"Oh—nothing. She has told me things—they would frighten you, dear. Come, it is growing chilly." He rose, but Evelyn held his hand in both of hers, still sitting and looking up into his face.

"But we shall be married, just the same—Gabriel! Say that we shall!"

"Of course, darling—of course. But while my father is so very ill it is impossible—"

"O Gabriel, Gabriel dear! I wish we were married now!" cried Evelyn in sudden distress. "I know that something will prevent it and keep us apart."

"Nothing shall!"

"Nothing?"

"Nothing human," said Gabriel Ockram, as she drew him down to her.

And their faces, that were so strangely alike, met and touched—and Gabriel knew that the kiss had a marvelous savor of evil. but on Evelyn's lips it was like the cool breath of a sweet and mortal fear. And neither of them understood, for they were innocent and young. Yet she drew him to her by her lightest touch, as a sensitive plant shivers and waves its thin leaves, and bends and closes softly upon what it wants, and he let himself be drawn to her willingly, as he would if her touch had been deadly and poisonous; for she strangely loved that half voluptuous breath of fear and he passionately desired the nameless evil something that lurked in her maiden lips.

"It is as if we loved in a strange dream," she said.

"I fear the waking," he murmured.

"We shall not wake, dear—when the dream is over it will have already turned into death, so softly that we shall not know it. But until then—"

She paused, and her eyes sought his, and their faces slowly came nearer. It was as if they had thoughts in their red lips that foresaw and foreknew the deep kiss of each other.

"Until then—" she said again, very low, and her mouth was nearer to his.

"Dream—till then," murmured his breath.

II

NURSE MACDONALD was a hundred years old. She used to sleep sitting all bent together in a great old leathern arm-chair with wings, her feet in a bag footstool lined with sheepskin. and many warm blankets wrapped about her, even in summer. Beside her a little lamp always burned at night by an old silver cup, in which there was something to drink.

Her face was very wrinkled. but the wrinkles were so small and fine and near together that they made shadows instead of lines. Two thin locks of hair, that was turning from white to a smoky yellow again, were drawn over her temples from under her starched white cap. Every now and then she woke, and her eyelids were drawn up in tiny folds like little pink silk curtains, and her queer blue eyes looked straight before her through doors and walls and worlds to a far place beyond. Then she slept again, and her hands lay one upon the other on the edge of the blanket; the thumbs had grown longer than the fingers with age, and the joints shone in the low lamplight like polished crab-apples.

It was nearly one o'clock in the night, and the summer breeze was blowing the ivy branch against the panes of the window with a hushing caress. In the small room beyond, with the door ajar, the girl-maid who took care of Nurse Macdonald was fast asleep. All was very quiet. The old woman breathed regularly, and her indrawn lips trembled each time as the breath went out, and her eyes were shut.

But outside the closed window there was a face, and violet eyes were looking steadily at the ancient sleeper, for it was like the face of Evelyn Warburton, though there were eighty feet from the sill of the window to the foot of the tower. Yet the cheeks were thinner than Evelyn's, and as white as a gleam, and her eyes stared, and the lips were not red with life, they were dead and painted with new blood.

Slowly Nurse Macdonald's wrinkled eyelids folded themselves back. and she looked straight at the face at the window while one might count ten.

"Is it time?" she asked in her little old, far-away voice.

While she looked the face at the window changed, for the eyes opened wider and wider till the white glared all round the bright violet, and the bloody lips opened over gleaming teeth. and stretched and widened and stretched again, and the shadowy golden hair rose and streamed against the window in the night breeze. And in answer to Nurse Macdonald's question came the sound that freezes the living flesh.

That low moaning voice that rises suddenly, like the scream of a storm, from a moan to a wail, from a wail to a howl, from a howl to the fear-shriek of the tortured dead—he who had heard knows, and he can bear witness that the cry of the banshee is an evil cry to hear alone in the deep night. When it was over and the face was gone, Nurse Macdonald shook a little in her great chair, and still she looked at the black square of the window, but there was nothing more there. nothing but the night, and the whispering ivy branch. She turned her head to the door that was ajar, and there stood the girl in her white gown, her teeth chattering with fright.

"It is time, child." said Nurse Macdonald. "I must go to him, for it is the end."

She rose slowly, leaning her withered hands upon the arms of the chair, and the girl brought her a woolen gown and a great mantle, and her crutch-stick, and made her ready. But very often the girl looked at the window and was unjointed with fear, and often Nurse Macdonald shook her head and said words which the maid could not understand.

"It was like the face of Miss Evelyn," said the girl at last, trembling.

But the ancient woman looked up sharply and angrily, and her queer blue eyes glared. She held herself by the arm of the great chair with her left hand, and lifted up her crutch-stick to strike the maid with all her might. But she did not.

"You are a good girl," she said. "but you are a fool. Pray for wit, child, pray for wit—or else find service in another house than Ockram Hall. Bring the lamp and help me under my left arm."

The crutch-stick clacked on the wooden floor, and the low heels of the woman's slippers clappered after her in slow triplets as Nurse Macdonald got toward the door. And down the stairs each step she took was a labor in itself, and by the clacking noise the waking servants knew that she was coming, very long before they saw her.

No one was sleeping now, and there were lights and whisperings and pale faces in the corridors near Sir Hugh's bedroom, and now someone went in, and now someone came out, but everyone made way for Nurse Macdonald, who had nursed Sir Hugh's father more than eighty years ago.

The light was soft and clear in the room. There stood Gabriel Ockram by his father's bedside, and there knelt Evelyn Warburton, her hair lying like a golden shadow down her shoulders, and her hands clasped nervously together. And opposite Gabriel, a nurse was trying to make Sir Hugh drink. But he would not, and though his lips were parted, his teeth were set. He was very, very thin and yellow now, and his eyes caught the light sideways and were as yellow coals.

"Do not torment him," said Nurse Macdonald to the woman who held the cup. "Let me speak to him, for his hour is come."

"Let her speak to him," said Gabriel in a dull voice.

So the ancient woman leaned to the pillow and laid the feather-weight of her withered hand, that was like a brown moth, upon Sir Hugh's yellow fingers, and she spoke to him earnestly, while only Gabriel and Evelyn were left in the room to hear.

"Hugh Ockram," she said, "this is the end of your life; and as I saw you born. and saw your father born before you, I am come to see you die. Hugh Ockram, will you tell me the truth?"

The dying man recognized the little far-away voice he had known all his life, and he very slowly turned his yellow face to Nurse Macdonald; but he said nothing. Then she spoke again.

"Hugh Ockram, you will never see the daylight again. Will you tell the truth? "

His toad-like eyes were not dull yet. They fastened themselves on her face.

"What do you want of me?" he asked, and each word struck hollow on the last. "I have no secrets. I have lived a good life."

Nurse Macdonald laughed—a tiny, cracked laugh, that made her old head bob and tremble a little, as if her neck were on a steel spring. But Sir Hugh's eyes grew red, and his pale lips began to twist.

"Let me die in peace," he said slowly.

But Nurse Macdonald shook her head. and her brown, moth-like hand left his and fluttered to his forehead.

"By the mother that bore you and died of grief for the sins you did, tell me the truth!"

Sir Hugh's lips tightened on his discolored teeth.

"Not on earth," he answered slowly.

"By the wife who bore your son and died heartbroken, tell me the truth!"

"Neither to you in life, nor to her in eternal death."

His lips writhed, as if the words were coals between them, and a great drop of sweat rolled across the parchment of his forehead. Gabriel Ockram bit his hand as he watched his father die. But Nurse Macdonald spoke a third time.

"By the woman whom you betrayed, and who waits for you this night, Hugh Ockram, tell me the truth!"

"It is too late. Let me die in peace."

The writhing lips began to smile across the set yellow teeth, and the toad eyes glowed like evil jewels in his head.

"There is time," said the ancient woman. "Tell me the name of Evelyn Warburton's father. Then I will let you die in peace."

Evelyn started back, kneeling as she was, and stared at Nurse Macdonald. and then at her uncle.

"The name of Evelyn's father?" he repeated slowly, while the awful smile spread upon his dying face.

The light was growing strangely dim in the great room. As Evelyn looked, Nurse Macdonald's crooked shadow on the wall grew gigantic. Sir Hugh's breath came thick, rattling in his throat, as death crept in like a snake and choked it back. Evelyn prayed aloud, high and clear.

Then something rapped at the window, and she felt her hair

rise upon her head in a cool breeze, as she looked around in spite of herself. And when she saw her own white face looking in at the window, and her own eyes staring at her through the glass, wide and fearful, and her own hair streaming against the pane, and her own lips dashed with blood. she rose slowly from the floor and stood rigid for one moment, till she screamed once and fell back into Gabriel's arms. But the shriek that answered hers was the fear-shriek of the tormented corpse, out of which the soul cannot pass for shame of deadly sins, though the devils fight in it with corruption, each for their due share.

Sir Hugh Ockram sat upright in his deathbed, and saw and cried aloud:

"Evelyn!" His harsh voice broke and rattled in his chest as he sank down. But still Nurse Macdonald tortured him, for there was a little life left in him still.

"You have seen the mother as she waits for you, Hugh Ockram. Who was this girl Evelyn's father? What was his name?"

For the last time the dreadful smile came upon the twisted lips, very slowly, very surely now, and the toad eyes glared red, and the parchment face glowed a little in the flickering light. For the last time words came.

"They know it in hell."

Then the glowing eyes went out quickly, the yellow face turned waxen pale, and a great shiver ran through the thin body as Hugh Ockram died.

But in death he still smiled, for he knew his secret and kept it still, on the other side, and he would take it with him, to lie with him for ever in the north vault of the chapel where the Ockrams lie uncoffined in their shrouds—all but one. Though he was dead, he smiled, for he had kept his treasure of evil truth to the end, and there was none left to tell the name he had spoken, but there was all the evil he had not undone left to bear fruit.

As they watched—Nurse Macdonald and Gabriel, who held Evelyn still unconscious in his arms while he looked at the father—they felt the dead smile crawling along their own lips— the ancient crone and the youth with the angel's face. Then they shivered a little, and both looked at Evelyn as she lay with her head on his shoulder, and, though she was very beautiful, the same sickening smile was twisting her mouth too, and it was like the foreshadowing of a great evil which they could not understand.

But by and by they carried Evelyn out, and she opened her eyes and the smile was gone. From far away in the great house the sound of weeping and crooning came up the stairs and echoed along the dismal corridors, for the women had begun to mourn the dead master, after the Irish fashion, and the hall had echoes of its own all that night, like the far-off wail of the banshee among forest trees.

When the time was come they took Sir Hugh in his winding-sheet on a trestle bier, and bore him to the chapel and through the iron door and down the long descent to the north vault, with tapers, to lay him by his father. And two men went in first to prepare the place and came back staggering like drunken men, and white, leaving their lights behind them.

But Gabriel Ockram was not afraid, for he knew. And he went in alone and saw that the body of Sir Vernon Ockram was leaning upright against the stone wall, and that his head lay on the ground near by with the face turned up, and the dried leathern lips smiled horribly at the dried-up corpse, while the iron coffin, lined with black velvet, stood open on the floor.

Then Gabriel took the thing in his hands, for it was very light, being quite dried by the air of the vault, and those who peeped in from the door saw him lay it in the coffin again, and it rustled a little, like a bundle of reeds, and sounded hollow as it touched the sides and the bottom. He also placed the head upon the shoulders and shut down the lid, which fell to with a rusty spring that snapped.

After that they laid Sir Hugh beside his father, with the trestle bier on which they had brought him, and they went back to the chapel.

But when they saw one another's faces, master and men, they were all smiling with the dead smile of the corpse they had left in the vault, so that they could not bear to look at one another until it had faded away.

III

GABRIEL OCKRAM became Sir Gabriel, inheriting the baronetcy with the half-ruined fortune left by his father, and still Evelyn Warburton lived at Ockham Hall, in the south room that had been hers ever since she could remember anything. She could not go away, for there were no relatives to whom she could have gone, and besides there seemed to be no reason why she should not stay. The world would never trouble itself to care what the Ockrams did on their Irish estates. as it was long since the Ockrams had asked anything of the world.

So Sir Gabriel took his father's place at the dark old table in the dining room, and Evelyn sat opposite to him, until such time as their mourning should be over, and they might be married at last. And meanwhile their lives went on as before, since Sir Hugh had been a hopeless invalid during the last year of his life, and they had seen him but once a day for the little while, spending most of their time together in a strangely perfect companionship.

But though the late summer saddened into autumn, and autumn darkened into winter, and storm followed storm, and rain poured on rain through the short days and the long nights, yet Ockram Hall seemed less gloomy since Sir Hugh had been laid in the north vault beside his father. And at Christmastide Evelyn decked the great hall with holly and green boughs, and huge fires blazed on every hearth. Then the tenants were all bidden to a New Year's dinner, and they ate and drank well, while Sir Gabriel sat at the head of the table. Evelyn came in when the port wine was brought, and the most respected of the tenants made a speech to propose her health.

It was long, he said, since there had been a Lady Ockram. Sir Gabriel shaded his eyes with his hand and looked down at the table, but a faint color came into Evelyn's transparent cheeks. But, said the grey-haired farmer, it was longer still since there had been a Lady Ockram so fair as the next was to be. and he gave the health of Evelyn Warburton.

Then the tenants all stood up and shouted for her, and Sir Gabriel stood up likewise, beside Evelyn. And when the men gave the last and loudest cheer of all, there was a voice not theirs, above them all, higher, fiercer, louder—a scream not earthly, shrieking for the bride of Ockram Hall. And the holly and the green boughs over the great chimney piece shook and slowly waved as if a cool breeze were blowing over them. But the men turned very pale, and many of them sat down their glasses, but others let them fall upon the floor for fear. And looking into one another's faces, they were all smiling strangely, a dead smile, like dead Sir Hugh's. One cried out words in Irish, and the fear of death was suddenly upon them all so that they fled in panic, falling over one another like wild beasts in the burning forest, when the thick smoke runs along the flame, and the tables were overset, and drinking glasses and bottles were broken in heaps, and the dark red wine crawled like blood upon the polished floor.

Sir Gabriel and Evelyn stood alone at the head of the table before the wreck of the feast, not daring to turn to see each other, for each knew that the other smiled. But his right arm held her and his left hand clasped her right as they stared before them, and but for the shadows of her hair one might not have told their two faces apart. They listened long, but the cry came not again, and the dead smile faded from their lips, while each remembered that Sir Hugh Ockram lay in the north vault, smiling in his winding-sheet, in the dark, because he had died with his secret.

So ended the tenants' New Year's dinner. But from that time on Sir Gabriel grew more and more silent, and his face grew even paler and thinner than before. Often without warning and without words, he would rise from his seat, as if something moved him against his will, and he would go out into the rain or the sunshine to the north side of the chapel, and sit on the stone bench, staring at the ground as if he could see through it, and through the vault below, and through the white winding-sheet in the dark, to the dead smile that would not die.

Always when he went out in that way Evelyn came out presently and sat beside him. Once, too, as in summer, their beautiful faces came suddenly near, and their lids drooped, and their red lips were almost joined together. But as their eyes met, they grew wide and wild, so that the white showed in a ring all round the deep violet, and their teeth chattered, and their hands were like hands of corpses, each in the other's for the terror of what was under their feet, and of what they knew but could not see.

Once, also, Evelyn found Sir Gabriel in the Chapel alone, standing before the iron door that led down to the place of death, and in his hand there was the key to the door, but he had not put it in the lock. Evelyn drew him away, shivering, for she had also been driven in waking dreams to see that terrible thing again, and to find out whether it had changed since it had lain there.

"I'm going mad," said Sir Gabriel, covering his eyes with his hand as he went with her. "I see it in my sleep, I see it when I am awake—it draws me to it, day and night—and unless I see it I shall die!"

"I know," answered Evelyn, "I know. It is as if threads were spun from it, like a spider's, drawing us down to it." She was silent for a moment, and then she stared violently and grasped his arm with a man's strength, and almost screamed the words she spoke. "But we must not go there!" she cried. "We must not go!"

Sir Gabriel's eyes were half shut, and he was not moved by the agony on her face.

"I shall die unless I see it again," he said, in a quiet voice not like his own. And all that day and that evening he scarcely spoke, thinking of it, always thinking, while Evelyn Warburton quivered from head to foot with a terror she had never known.

She went alone, on a grey winter's morning, to Nurse Macdonald's room in the tower, and sat down beside the great leathern easy chair, laying her thin white hand upon the withered fingers.

"Nurse," she said, "what was it that Uncle Hugh should have told you, that night before he died? It must have been an awful secret—and yet, though you asked him, I feel somehow that you know it, and that you know why he used to smile so dreadfully."

The old woman's head moved slowly from side to side.

"I can only guess—I shall never know," she answered slowly in her cracked little voice.

"But what do you guess? Who am I? Why did you ask who my father was? You know I am Colonel Warburton's daughter, and my mother was Lady Ockram's sister, so that Gabriel and I are cousins. My father was killed in Afghanistan. What secret can there be?"

"I do not know. I can only guess."

"Guess what?" asked Evelyn imploringly, and pressing the soft withered hands, as she leaned forward. But Nurse Macdonald's wrinkled lids dropped suddenly over her queer blue eyes, and her lips shook a little with her breath as if she were asleep.

Evelyn waited. By the fire the Irish maid was knitting fast, and the needles clicked like three or four clocks ticking against each other. And the real clock on the wall solemnly ticked alone, checking off the seconds of the woman who was a hundred years old, and had not many days left. Outside the ivy branch beat the window in the wintry blast, as it had beaten against the glass a hundred years ago.

Then as Evelyn sat there she felt again the waking of a horrible desire—the sickening wish to go down, down to the thing in the north vault, and to open the winding-sheet, and see whether it had changed, and she held Nurse Macdonald's hands as if to keep herself in her place and fight against the appalling attraction of the evil dead.

But the old cat that kept Nurse Macdonald's feet warm, lying aways on the bag footstool, got up and stretched itself, and looked up into Evelyn's eyes, while its back arched, and its tail thickened and bristled, and its ugly pink lips drew back in a devilish grin, showing its sharp teeth. Evelyn stared at it, half fascinated by its ugliness. Then the creature suddenly put out one paw with all its claws spread, and spat at the girl, and all at once the grinning cat was like the smiling corpse far down below, so that Evelyn shivered down to her small feet and covered her face with her free hand lest Nurse Macdonald should wake and see the dead smile there, for she could feel it.

The old woman had already opened her eyes again, and she touched her cat with the end of her crutch-stick, whereupon its back went down and its tail shrunk, and it sidled back to its place in the bag footstool. But its yellow eyes looked up sideways at Evelyn, between the slits of its lids.

"What is it that you guess, Nurse?" asked the young girl again.

"A bad thing—a wicked thing. But I dare not tell you, lest it might not be true, and the very thought should blast your life. For if I guess right, he meant that you should not know, and that you two should marry, and pay for his old sin with your souls."

"He used to tell us that we ought not to marry—"

"Yes—he told you that, perhaps—but it was as if a man put poisoned meat before a starving beast, and said 'do not eat', but never raised his hand to take the meat away. And if he told you that you should not marry, it was because he hoped you would, for of all men living or dead, Hugh Ockram was the falsest man that ever told a cowardly lie and the cruelest that ever hurt a weak woman, and the worst that ever loved a sin."

"But Gabriel and I love each other," said Evelyn very sadly.

Nurse Macdonald's old eyes looked far away, at sights seen long ago, and that rose in the grey winter air amid the mists of an ancient youth.

"If you love, you can die together," she said very slowly. "Why should you live, if it is true? I am a hundred years old. What has life given me? The beginning is fire, the end is a heap of ashes, and between the end and the beginning lies all the pain in the world. Let me sleep, since I cannot die."

Then the old woman's eyes closed again, and her head sank a little lower upon her breast.

So Evelyn went away and left her asleep. with the cat asleep on the bag footstool; and the young girl tried to forget Nurse Macdonald's words, but she could not, for she heard them over and over again in the wind, and behind her on the stairs. And as she grew sick with fear of the frightful unknown evil to which her soul was bound, she felt a bodily something pressing her, and pushing her, and forcing her on, and from the other side she felt the threads that drew her mysteriously, and when she shut her eyes, she saw in the chapel behind the altar the low iron door through which she must pass to go to the thing.

And as she lay awake at night, she drew the sheet over her face, lest she should see shadows on the wall beckoning her, and the sound of her own warm breath made whisperings in her ears, while she held the mattress with her hands to keep from getting up and going to the chapel. It would have been easier if there had not been a way thither through the library, by a door which was never locked. It would be fearfully easy to take her candle and go softly through the sleeping house. And the key of the vault lay under the altar behind a stone that turned. She knew the little secret. She could go alone and see.

But when she thought of it, she felt her hair rise on her head, and first she shivered so that the bed shook, and then the horror went through her in a cold thrill that was agony again, like myriads of icy needles boring into her nerves.

IV

THE OLD CLOCK in Nurse Macdonald's tower struck midnight. From her room she could hear the creaking chains and weights in their box in the corner of the staircase, and overheard the jarring of the rusty lever that lifted the hammer. She had heard it all her life. It struck eleven strokes clearly and then came the twelfth, with a dull half stroke, as though the hammer were too weary to go on, and had fallen asleep against the bell.

The old cat got up from the bag footstool and stretched itself, and Nurse Macdonald opened her ancient eyes and looked slowly round the room by the dim light of the night lamp. She touched the cat with her crutch-stick and it lay down upon her feet. She drank a few drops from her cup and went to sleep again.

But downstairs Sir Gabriel sat straight up as the clock struck, for he had dreamed a fearful dream of horror, and his heart stood still. till he awoke at its stopping, and it beat again furiously with his breath, like a wild thing set free. No Ockram had ever known fear waking, but sometimes it came to Sir Gabriel in his sleep.

He pressed his hands on his temples as he sat up in bed, and his hands were icy cold, but his head was hot. The dream faded far, and in its place there came the sick twisting of his lips in the dark that would have been a smile. Far off, Evelyn Warburton dreamed that the dead smile was on her mouth, and awoke, starting with a little moan, her face in her hands shivering.

But Sir Gabriel struck a light and got up and began to walk up and down his great room. It was midnight, and he had barely slept an hour, and in the north of Ireland the winter nights are long.

"I shall go mad," he said to himself, holding his forehead. He knew that it was true. For weeks and months the possession of the thing had grown upon him like a disease, till he could think of nothing without thinking first of that. And now all at once it outgrew his strength, and he knew that he must be its instrument or lose his mind—that he must do the deed he hated and feared if he could fear anything, or that something would snap in his brain and divide him from life while he was yet alive. He took the candlestick in his hand, the old-fashioned heavy candlestick that had always been used by the head of the house. He did not think of dressing. but went as he was, in his silk nightclothes and his slippers, and he opened the door. Everything was very still in the great old house. He shut the door behind him and walked noiselessly on the carpet through the long corridor. A cool breeze blew over his shoulder and blew the flame of his candle straight out from him. Instinctively he stopped and looked round, but all was still, and the upright flame burned steadily. He walked on, and instantly a strong draft was behind him, almost extinguishing the light. It seemed to blow him on his way, ceasing whenever he turned, coming again when he went on—invisible, icy.

Down the great staircase to the echoing hall he went, seeing nothing but the flame of the candle standing away from him over the guttering wax, while the cold wind blew over his shoulder and through his hair. On he passed through the open door into the library. dark with old books and carved bookcases, on through the door in the shelves, with painted shelves on it, and the imitated backs of books, so that one needed to know where to find it—and it shut itself after him with a soft click. He entered the low-arched passage, and though the door was shut behind him and fitted tightly in its frame, still the cold breeze blew the flame forward as he walked. And he was not afraid, but his face was very pale, and his eyes were wide and bright, looking before him, seeing already in the dark air the picture of the thing beyond. But in the chapel he stood still, his hand on the little turning stone tablet in the back of the stone altar. On the tablet were engraved words, *"Clavis sepulchri Clarissimorum Dominorum De Ockram"*—("the key to the vault of the most illustrious lord of Ockram"). Sir Gabriel paused and listened. He fancied that he heard a sound far off in the great house where all had been so still, but it did not come again. Yet he waited at the last, and looked at the low iron door.

Beyond it, down the long descent, lay his father uncoffined, six months dead, corrupt, terrible in his clinging shroud. The strangely preserving air of the vault could not yet have done its work completely. But on the thing's ghastly features, with their half-dried, open eyes, there would still be the frightful smile with which the man had died—the smile that haunted.

As the thought crossed Sir Gabriel's mind, he felt his lips writhing. and he struck his own mouth in wrath with the back of his hand so fiercely that a drop of blood ran down his chin and another, and more, falling back in the gloom upon the chapel pavement. But still his bruised lips twisted themselves. He turned the tablet by the simple secret. It needed no safer fastening, for had each Ockram been confined in pure gold, and had the door been wide, there was not a man in Tyrone brave enough to go down to the place, saving Gabriel Ockram himself, with his angel's face and his thin, white hands, and his sad unflinching eyes. He took the great gold key and set it into the lock of the iron door, and the heavy, rattling noise echoed down the descent beyond like footsteps, as if a watcher had stood behind the iron and were running away within, with heavy dead feet. And though he was standing still, the cool wind was from behind him, and blew the flame of the candle against the iron panel. He turned the key.

Sir Gabriel saw that his candle was short. There were new ones on the altar, with long candlesticks, and he lit one and left his own burning on the floor. As he set it down on the pavement his lip began to bleed again, and another drop fell upon the stones.

He drew the iron door open and pushed it back against the chapel wall, so that it should not shut of itself while he was within, and the horrible draft of the sepulcher came up out of the depths in his face, foul and dark. He went in, but though the fetid air met him, yet the flame of the tall candle was blown straight from him against the wind while he walked down the easy incline with steady steps, his loose slippers slapping the pavement as he trod.

He shaded the candle with his hand, and his fingers seemed to be made of wax and blood as the light shone through them. And in spite of him the unearthly draft forced the flame forward, till it was blue over the black wick, and it seemed as if it must go out. But he went straight on, with shining eyes.

The downward passage was wide, and he could not always see the walls by the struggling light, but he knew when he was in the place of death by the larger, drearier echo of his steps in the greater space and by the sensation of a distant blank wall. He stood still, almost enclosing the flame of the candle in the hollow of his hand. He could see a little, for his eyes were growing used to the gloom. Shadowy forms were outlined in the dimness, where the biers of the Ockrams stood crowded together, side by side, each with its straight, shrouded corpse, strangely preserved by the dry air, like the empty shell that the locust sheds in summer. And a few steps before him he saw clearly the dark shape of headless Sir Vernon's iron coffin, and he knew that nearest to it lay the thing he sought.

He was as brave as any of those dead men had been, and they were his fathers, and he knew that sooner or later he should lie there himself, beside Sir Hugh, slowly drying to a parchment shell. But he was still alive, and he closed his eyes a moment, and three great drops stood on his forehead.

Then he looked again, and by the whiteness of the winding-sheet he knew his father's corpse, for all the others were brown with age; and, moreover, the flame of the candle was blown towards it. He made four steps till he reached it, and suddenly the light burned straight and high, shedding a dazzling yellow glare upon the fine linen that was all white, save over the face, and where the joined hands were laid on the breast. And at those places ugly stains had spread, darkened with outlines of the features and of the tight-clasped fingers. There was a frightful stench of drying death.

As Sir Gabriel looked down, something stirred behind him, softly at first, then more noisily, and something fell to the stone floor with a dull thud and rolled up to his feet; he started back, and saw a withered head lying almost face upward on the pavement, grinning at him. He felt the cold sweat standing on his face, and his heart beat painfully.

For the first time in all his life that evil thing which men call fear was getting hold of him, checking his heart strings as a cruel driver checks a quivering horse, clawing at his backbone with icy hands, lifting his hair with freezing breath climbing up and gathering in his midriff with leaden weight.

Yet presently he bit his lip and bent down, holding the candle in one hand, to lift the shroud back from the head of the corpse with the other. Slowly he lifted it.

Then it clove to the half-dried skin of the face, and his hand shook as if someone had struck him on the elbow, but half in fear and half in anger at himself, he pulled it, so that it came away with a little ripping sound. He caught his breath as he held it, not yet throwing it back. and not yet looking. The horror was working in him, and he felt that old Vernon Ockram was standing up in his iron coffin, headless, yet watching him with the stump of his severed neck.

While he held his breath he felt the dead smile twisting his lips. In sudden wrath at his own misery, he tossed the death-stained linen backward, and looked at last. He ground his teeth lest he should shriek aloud.

There it was, the thing that haunted him, that haunted Evelyn

Warburton, that was like a blight on all that came near him.

The dead face was blotched with dark stains, and the thin, grey hair was matted about the discolored forehead. The sunken lids were half open, and the candle light gleamed on something foul where the toad eyes had lived.

But yet the dead thing smiled, as it had smiled in life; the ghastly lips were parted and drawn wide and tight upon the wolfish teeth, cursing still, and still defying hell to do its worst—defying, cursing, and always and for ever smiling alone in the dark.

Sir Gabriel opened the winding-sheet where the hands were, and the blackened, withered fingers were closed upon something stained and mottled. Shivering from head to foot, but fighting like a man in agony for his life, he tried to take the package from the dead man's hold. But as he pulled at it the claw-like fingers seemed to close more tightly, and when he pulled harder the shrunken hands and arms rose from the corpse with a horrible look of life following his motion—then as he wrenched the sealed packet loose at last, the hands fell back into their place still folded.

He set down the candle on the edge of the bier to break the seals from the stout paper. And, kneeling on one knee, to get a better light, he read what was within, written long ago in Sir Hugh's queer hand.

He was no longer afraid.

He read how Sir Hugh had written it all down that it might perchance be a witness of evil and of his hatred; how he had loved Evelyn Warburton, his wife's sister; and how his wife had died of a broken heart with his curse upon her, and how Warburton and he had fought side by side in Afghanistan, and Warburton had fallen; but Ockram had brought his comrade's wife back a full year later, and little Evelyn, her child, had been born in Ockram Hall. And next, how he had wearied of the mother, and she had died like her sister with his curse on her. And then, how Evelyn had been brought up as his niece, and how he had trusted that his son Gabriel and his daughter, innocent and unknowing, might love and marry, and the souls of the women he had betrayed might suffer another anguish before eternity was out. And, last of all, he hoped that some day, when nothing could be undone, the two might find his writing and live on, not daring to tell the truth for their children's sake and the world's word, as man and wife.

This he read, kneeling beside the corpse in the north vault, by the light of the altar candle; and when he had read it all, he thanked God aloud that he had found the secret in time. But when he rose to his feet and looked down at the dead face it was changed, and the smile was gone from it for ever, and the jaw had fallen a little, and the tired dead lips were relaxed. And then there was a breath behind him and close to him, not cold like that which had blown the flame of the candle as he came, but warm and human. He turned suddenly.

There she stood, all in white, with her shadowy golden hair— for she had risen from her bed and had followed him noiselessly, and had found him reading, and had herself read over his shoulder. He started violently when he saw her, for his nerves were unstrung—and then he cried out her name in the still place of death:

"Evelyn!"

"My brother!" she answered, softly and tenderly, putting out both hands to meet his.

The Blood-Drawing Ghost
Jeremiah Curtin

THERE WAS A YOUNG MAN in the parish of Drimoleague, county Cork, who was courting three girls at one time, and he didn't know which of them would he take; they had equal fortunes, and any of the three was as pleasing to him as any other. One day when he was coming home from the fair with his two sisters, the sisters began:

"Well, John," said one of them, "why don't you get married? Why don't you take either Mary, or Peggy, or Kate?"

"I can't tell you that," said John, "till I find which of them has the best wish for me."

"How will you know?" asked the other.

"I will tell you that as soon as any person will die in the parish."

In three weeks' time from that day an old man died. John

went to the wake and then to the funeral. While they were burying the corpse in the graveyard, John stood near a tomb which was next to the grave, and when all were going away, after burying the old man, he remained standing a while by himself, as if thinking of something; then he put his blackthorn stick on top of the tomb, stood a while longer, and on going from the graveyard left the stick behind him. He went home and ate his supper. After supper John went to a neighbor's house where young people used to meet of an evening, and the three girls happened to be there that time. John was very quiet, so that everyone noticed him.

"What is troubling you this evening, John?" asked one of the girls.

"Oh, I am sorry for my beautiful blackthorn," said he.

"Did you lose it?"

"I did not," said John; "but I left it on the top of the tomb next to the grave of the man who was buried today and whichever of you three will go for it is the woman I'll marry. Well, Mary, will you go for my stick?" asked he.

"Faith, then, I will not," said Mary.

"Well, Peggy, will you go?"

"If I were without a man forever," said Peggy, "I wouldn't go."

"Well, Kate," said he to the third, "will you go for my stick? If you go I'll marry you."

"Stand to your word," said Kate, " and I'll bring the stick."

"Believe me, that I will," said John.

Kate left the company behind her, and went for the stick. The graveyard was three miles away and the walk was a long one. Kate came to the place at last and made out the tomb by the fresh grave. When she had her hand on the blackthorn, a voice called from the tomb:

"Leave the stick where it is and open this tomb for me."

Kate began to tremble and was greatly in dread, but something was forcing her to open the tomb—she couldn't help herself.

"Take the lid off now," said the dead man when Kate had the door open and was inside in the tomb, "and take me out of this—take me on your back."

Afraid to refuse, she took the lid from the coffin, raised the dead man on her back, and walked on in the way he directed. She walked about the distance of a mile. The load, being very heavy, was near breaking her back and killing her. She walked half a mile farther and came to a village; the houses were at the side of the road.

"Take me to the first house," said the dead man.

She took him.

"Oh, we cannot go in here," said he, when they came near. "The people have clean water inside, and they have holy water, too. Take me to the next house."

She went to the next house.

"We cannot go in there," said he, when she stopped in front of the door. "They have clean water, but there is holy water as well."

She went to the third house.

"Go in here," said the dead man. "There is neither clean water nor holy water in this place; we can stop in it."

They went in.

"Bring a chair now and put me sitting at the side of the fire. Then find me something to eat and to drink."

She placed him in a chair by the hearth, searched the house, found a dish of oatmeal and brought it. "I have nothing to give you to drink but dirty water," said she.

"Bring me a dish and a razor."

She brought the dish and the razor.

"Come, now," said he, "to the room above."

They went up to the room, where three young men, sons of the man of the house, were sleeping in bed, and Kate had to hold the dish while the dead man was drawing their blood.

"Let the father and mother have that," said he, "in return for the dirty water," meaning that if there was clean water in the house he wouldn't have taken the blood of the young men. He closed their wounds in the way that there was no sign of a cut on them. "Mix this now with the meal, get a dish of it for yourself and another for me."

She got two plates and put the oatmeal in it after mixing it, and brought two spoons. Kate wore a handkerchief on her head; she put this under her neck and tied it; she was pretending to eat, but she was putting the food to hide in the handkerchief till her plate was empty.

"Have you your share eaten?" asked the dead man.

"I have," answered Kate.

"I'll have mine finished this minute," said he, and soon after he gave her the empty dish. She put the dishes back in the dresser and didn't mind washing them. "Come, now," said he, "and take me back to the place where you found me."

"Oh, how can I take you back; you are too great a load; 'twas killing me you were when I brought you." She was in dread of going from the houses again.

"You are stronger after that food than what you were in coming; take me back to my grave."

She went against her will. She rolled up the food inside in the handkerchief. There was a deep hole in the wall of the kitchen by the door, where the bar was slipped in when they barred the door; into this hole she put the handkerchief. In going back she shortened the road by going through a big field at command of the dead man. When they were at the top of the field she asked, was there any cure for those young men whose blood was drawn?

"There is no cure," said he, "except one. If any of that food had been spared, three bits of it in each young man's mouth would bring them to life again, and they'd never know of their death."

"Then," said Kate in her own mind, "that cure is to be had."

"Do you see this field?" asked the dead man.

"I do."

"Well there is as much gold buried in it as would make rich people of all who belong to you. Do you see the three *leachtans* [piles of small stones]? Underneath each pile of them is a pot of gold."

The dead man looked around for a while; then Kate went on, without stopping, till she came to the wall of the graveyard, and just then they heard the cock crow.

"The cock is crowing," said Kate; "it's time for me to be going home."

"It is not time yet," said the dead man; "that is a bastard cock."

A moment after that another cock crowed. "There the cocks are crowing a second time," said she. "No," said the dead man, "that is a bastard cock again; that's no right bird." They came to the mouth of the tomb and a cock crowed the third time.

"Well," said the girl, "that must be the right cock."

"Ah, my girl, that cock has saved your life for you. But for him I would have you with me in the grave for evermore, and if I knew this cock would crow before I was in the grave you wouldn't have the knowledge you have now of the field and the gold. Put me into the coffin where you found me. Take your time and settle me well. I cannot meddle with you now, and 'tis sorry I am to part with you."

"Will you tell me who you are?" asked Kate.

"Have you ever heard your father or mother mention a man called Edward Derrihy or his son Michael?"

"It's often I heard tell of them," replied the girl.

"Well, Edward Derrihy was my father; I am Michael. That blackthorn that you came for tonight to this graveyard was the lucky stick for you, but if you had any thought of the danger that was before you, you wouldn't be here. Settle me carefully and close the tomb well behind you."

She placed him in the coffin carefully, closed the door behind her, took the blackthorn stick, and away home was Kate. The night was far spent when she came. She was tired, and it's good reason the girl had. She thrust the stick into the thatch above the door of the house and rapped. Her sister rose up and opened the door.

"Where did you spend the night?" asked the sister. "Mother will kill you in the morning for spending the whole night from home."

"Go to bed," answered Kate, "and never mind me."

They went to bed, and Kate fell asleep the minute she touched the bed, she was that tired after the night.

When the father and mother of the three young men rose next morning, and there was no sign of their sons, the mother went to the room to call them, and there she found the three dead. She began to screech and wring her hands. She ran to the road screaming and wailing. All the neighbors crowded around to know what trouble was on her. She told them her three sons were lying dead in their bed after the night. Very soon the report spread in every direction. When Kate's father and mother heard it, they hurried off to the house of the dead men. When they came home Kate was still in bed; the mother took a stick and began to beat the girl for being out all the night and in bed all the day.

"Get up now, you lazy stump of a girl," said she, "and go to the wake-house; your neighbor's three sons are dead."

Kate took no notice of this. "I am very tired and sick," said she. "You'd better spare me and give me a drink."

The mother gave her a drink of milk and a bite to eat, and in the middle of the day she rose up.

"'Tis a shame for you not to be at the wake-house yet," said the mother; "hurry over now."

When Kate reached the house, there was a great crowd of people before her and great wailing. She did not cry, but was looking on. The father was as if wild, going up and down the house wringing his hands.

"Be quiet," said Kate. "Control yourself."

"How can I do that, my dear girl, and my three fine sons lying dead in the house?"

"What would you give," asked Kate, "to the person who would bring life to them again?"

"Don't be vexing me," said the father.

"It's neither vexing you I am nor trifling," said Kate. "I can put the life in them again."

"If it was true that you could do that, I would give you all that I have inside the house and outside as well."

"All I want from you," said Kate, "is the eldest son to marry and *Gort na Leachtan* [the field of the stone heaps] as fortune."

"My dear, you will have that from me with the greatest blessing."

"Give me the field in writing, from yourself, whether the son will marry me or not."

He gave her the field in his handwriting. She told all who were inside in the wake house to go outside the door, every man and woman of them. Some were laughing at her and more were crying, thinking it was mad she was. She bolted the door inside, and went to the place where she left the handkerchief, found it, and put three bites of the oatmeal and the blood in the mouth of each young man, and as soon as she did that the three got their natural color, and they looked like men sleeping. She opened the door, then called on all to come inside, and told the father to go and wake his sons.

He called each one by name, and as they woke they seemed very tired after their night's rest; they put on their clothes, and were greatly surprised to see all the people around. "How is this?" asked the eldest brother.

"Don't you know of anything that came over you in the night?" asked the father.

"We do not," said the sons. "We remember nothing at all since we fell asleep last evening."

The father then told them everything, but they could not believe it. Kate went away home and told her father and mother of her night's journey to and from the graveyard, and said that she would soon tell them more.

That day she met John.

"Did you bring the stick?" asked he.

"Find your own stick," said she, "and never speak to me again in your life."

In a week's time she went to the house of the three young men, and said to the father, "I have come for what you promised me."

"You'll get that with my blessing," said the father. He called the eldest son aside then and asked would he marry Kate, their neighbor's daughter. "I will," said the son. Three days after that the two were married and had a fine wedding. For three weeks they enjoyed a pleasant life without toil or trouble; then Kate said, "This will not do for us; we must be working. Come with me tomorrow and I'll give yourself and brothers plenty to do, and my own father and brothers as well."

She took them next day to one of the stone heaps in *Gort na Leachtan*. "Throw these stones to one side," said she.

They thought that she was losing her senses, but she told them that they'd soon see for themselves what she was doing. They went to work and kept at it till they had six feet deep of a hole dug; then they met with a flat stone three feet square and an iron hook in the middle of it.

"Sure there must be something underneath this," said the men. They lifted the flag, and under it was a pot of gold. All were very happy then. "There is more gold yet in the place," said Kate. "Come, now, to the other heap." They removed that heap, dug down, and found another pot of gold. They removed the third pile and found a third pot full of gold. On the side of the third pot was an inscription, and they could not make out what it was. After emptying it, they placed the pot by the side of the door.

About a month later a poor scholar walked the way, and as he was going in at the door he saw the old pot and the letters on the side of it. He began to study the letters.

"You must be a good scholar if you can read what's on that pot," said the young man.

"I can," said the poor scholar, "and here it is for you. There is a deal more at the south side of each pot."

The young man said nothing, but putting his hand in his pocket, gave the poor scholar a good day's hire. When he was gone, they went to work and found a deal more of gold in the south side of each stone heap. They were very happy then and very rich, and bought several farms and built fine houses, and it was supposed by all of them in the latter end that it was

Derrihy's money that was buried under the *leachtans*, but they could give no correct account of that, and sure why need they care? When they died, they left property to make their children rich to the seventh generation.

Master and Man
Thomas Crofton Croker

BILLY MAC DANIEL was once as likely a young man as ever shook his brogue at a patron,* emptied a quart or handled a shillelagh; fearing for nothing but the want of drink; caring for nothing but who should pay for it; and thinking of nothing but how to make fun over it; drunk or sober, a word and a blow was ever the way with Billy Mac Daniel; and a mighty easy way it is of either getting into or of ending a dispute. More is the pity that, through the means of his thinking, and fearing, and caring for nothing, this same Billy Mac Daniel fell into bad company; for surely the good people are the worst of all company anyone could come across.

It so happened that Billy was going home one clear frosty

* A festival held in honor of some patron saint.

night not long after Christmas; the moon was round and bright; but although it was as fine a night as heart could wish for, he felt pinched with cold. "By my word," chattered Billy, "a drop of good liquor would be no bad thing to keep a man's soul from freezing in him; and I wish I had a full measure of the best."

"Never wish it twice, Billy," said a little man in a three-cornered hat, bound all about with gold lace, and with great silver buckles in his shoes, so big that it a wonder how he could carry them, and he held out a glass as big as himself, filled with as good liquor as eye ever looked on or lip tasted.

"Success, my little fellow," said Billy Mac Daniel nothing daunted, though well he knew the little man to belong to the *good people*; "here's your health, anyway, and thank you kindly; no matter who pays for the drink"; and he took the glass and drained it to the very bottom without ever taking a second breath to it.

"Success," said the little man; "and you're heartily welcome, Billy; but don't think to cheat me as you have done others—out with your purse and pay me like a gentleman."

"Is it I pay you?" said Billy; "could I not just take you up and put you in my pocket as easily as a blackberry?"

"Billy Mac Daniel," said the little man, getting very angry, "you shall be my servant for seven years and a day, and that is the way I will be paid; so make ready to follow me."

When Billy heard this he began to be very sorry for having used such bold words toward the little man; and he felt himself, yet could not tell how, obliged to follow the little man the live-long night about the country, up and down, and over hedge and ditch, and through bog and brake, without any rest.

When morning began to dawn the little man turned round to him and said, "You may now go home, Billy, but on your peril don't fail to meet me in the Fort-field tonight; or if you do it may be the worse for you in the long run. If I find you a good servant, you will find me an indulgent master."

Home went Billy Mac Daniel; and though he was tired and weary enough, never a wink of sleep could he get for thinking of the little man; but he was afraid not to do his bidding, so up he got in the evening, and away he went to the Fort-field. He was not long there before the little man came towards him and said, "Billy, I want to go a long journey tonight; so saddle one of my horses, and you may saddle another for yourself, as you are to go along with me, and may be tired after your walk last night."

Billy thought this very considerate of his master, and thanked him accordingly: "But," said he, "if I may be so bold, sir, I would ask which is the way to your stable, for never a thing do I see but the fort here, and the old thorn tree in the corner of the field, and the stream running at the bottom of the hill, with the bit of bog over against us."

"Ask no questions, Billy," said the little man, "but go over to that bit of bog, and bring me two of the strongest rushes you can find."

Billy did accordingly, wondering what the little man would be at; and he picked two of the stoutest rushes he could find, with a little bunch of brown blossom stuck at the side of each, and brought them back to his master.

"Get up, Billy," said the little man, taking one of the rushes from him and striding across it.

"Where shall I get up, please your honor?" said Billy.

"Why, upon horseback, like me, to be sure," said the little man.

"Is it after making a fool of me you'd be," said Billy, "bidding me get a horseback upon that bit of a rush? Maybe you want to persuade me that the rush I pulled but a while ago out of the bog over there is a horse?"

"Up! up! and no words," said the little man, looking very angry; "the best horse you ever rode was but a fool to it." So Billy, thinking all this was in joke, and fearing to vex his master, straddled across the rush. "Borram! Borram! Borram!" cried the little man three times (which, in English, means to become great), and Billy did the same after him; presently the rushes swelled up into fine horses, and away they went full speed; but Billy, who had put the rush between his legs, without much minding how he did it, found himself sitting on horseback the wrong way, which was rather awkward, with his face to the horse's tail; and so quickly had his steed started off with him that he had no power to turn round, and there was therefore nothing for it but to hold on by the tail.

At last they came to their journey's end, and stopped at the gate of a fine house. "Now, Billy," said the little man, "do as you see me do, and follow me close; but as you did not know your horse's head from his tail, mind that your own head does not spin round until you can't tell whether you are standing on it or your heels; for remember that old liquor, though able to make a cat speak, can make a man dumb."

The little man then said some queer kind of words, out of which Billy could make no meaning; but he contrived to say them after him for all that; and in they both went through the keyhole of the door, and through one keyhole after another, until they got into the wine-cellar, which was well stored with all kinds of wine.

The little man fell to drinking as hard as he could, and Billy noway disliking the example, did the same. "The best of masters are you, surely," said Billy to him; "no matter who is the next; and well pleased will I be with your service if you continue to give me plenty to drink."

"I have made no bargain with you," said the little man, "and will make none; but up and follow me." Away they went, through keyhole after keyhole; and each mounting upon the rush which he left at the hall door, scampered off, kicking the clouds before them like snowballs, as soon as the words, "Borram, Borram, Borram," had passed their lips.

When they came back to the Fort-field the little man dismissed Billy, bidding him to be there the next night at the same hour. Thus did they go on, night after night, shaping their course one night here, and another night there; sometimes north, and sometimes east, and sometimes south, until there was not a gentleman's wine-cellar in all Ireland they had not visited, and could tell the flavor of every wine in it as well, ay, better than the butler himself.

One night when Billy Mac Daniel met the little man as usual in the Fort-field, and was going to the bog to fetch the horses for their journey, his master said to him, "Billy, I shall want another horse tonight, for maybe we may bring back more company than we take." So Billy, who now knew better than to question any order given to him by his master, brought a third rush, much wondering who it might be that would travel back in their company, and whether he was about to have a fellow-servant. "If I have," thought Billy, "he shall go and fetch the horses from the bog every night; for I don't see why I am not, every inch of me, as good a gentleman as my master."

Well, away they went, Billy leading the third horse, and never stopped until they came to a snug farmer's house, in the county Limerick, close under the old castle of Carrigogunniel, that was built, they say, by the great Brian Boru. Within the house there was great carousing going forward, and the little man stopped outside for some time to listen; then turning round all of a sudden, said, "Billy, I will be a thousand years old tomorrow!"

"God bless us, sir," said Billy; "will you?"

"Don't say these words again, Billy," said the little old man, "or you will be my ruin forever. Now Billy, as I will be a thousand years in the world tomorrow, I think it is full time for me to get married."

"I think so too, without any kind of doubt at all," said Billy, "if ever you mean to marry."

"And to that purpose," said the little man, "have I come all the way to Carrigogunniel; for in this house, this very night, is young Darby Riley going to be married to Bridget Rooney; and as she is a tall and comely girl, and has come of decent people, I think of marrying her myself, and taking her off with me."

"And what will Darby Riley say to that?" said Billy.

"Silence" said the little man, putting on a mighty severe look; "I did not bring you here with me to ask questions," and without holding further argument, he began saying the queer words which had the power of passing him through the keyhole as free as air, and which Billy thought himself mighty clever to be able to say after him.

In they both went; and for the better viewing the company, the little man perched himself up as nimbly as a cocksparrow upon one of the big beams which went across the house over all their heads, and Billy did the same upon another facing him; but not being much accustomed to roosting in such a place, his legs hung down as untidy as may be, and it was quite clear he had not taken pattern after the way in which the little man had bundled himself up together. If the little man had been a tailor all his life, he could not have sat more contentedly upon his haunches.

There they were, both master and man, looking down upon the fun that was going forward; and under them were the priest and piper, and the father of Darby Riley, with Darby's two brothers and his uncle's son; and there were both the father and the mother of Bridget Rooney, and proud enough the old couple were that night of their daughter, as good right they had; and her four sisters, with brand-new ribbons in their caps, and her three brothers all looking as clean and as clever as any three boys in Munster, and there were uncles and aunts, and gossips and cousins enough besides to make a full house of it; and plenty was there to eat and drink on the table for everyone of them, if they had been double the number.

Now it happened, just as Mrs. Rooney had helped his reverence to the first cut of the pig's head which was placed before her, beautifully bolstered up with white savoys, that the bride gave a sneeze, which made everyone at the table start, but not a soul said "and bless us." All thinking that the priest would have done so, as he ought if he had done his duty, no one wished to take the word out of his mouth, which, unfortunately, was preoccupied with pig's head and greens. And after a moment's pause the fun and merriment of the bridal feast went on without the pious benediction.

Of this circumstance both Billy and his master were no inattentive spectators from their exalted stations. "Ha!" exclaimed the little man, throwing one leg from under him with a joyous flourish, and his eye twinkled with a strange light, while his eyebrows became elevated into the curvature of Gothic arches; "Ha!" said he, leering down at the bride, and then up at Billy, "I have half of her now, surely. Let her sneeze but twice more, and she is mine, in spite of priest, mass-book, and Darby Riley."

Again the fair Bridget sneezed; but it was so gently, and she blushed so much, that few except the little man took, or seemed to take, any notice; and no one thought of saying "God bless us."

Billy all this time regarded the poor girl with a most rueful expression of countenance; for he could not help thinking what a terrible thing it was for a nice young girl of nineteen, with large blue eyes, transparent skin, and dimpled cheeks, suffused with health and joy, to be obliged to marry an ugly little bit of a man, who was a thousand years old, barring a day.

At this critical moment the bride gave a third sneeze, and Billy roared out with all his might, "God save us!" Whether this exclamation resulted from his soliloquy, or from the mere force of habit, he never could tell exactly himself; but no sooner was it uttered than the little man, his face glowing with rage and disappointment, sprung from the beam on which he had perched himself, and shrieking out in the shrill voice of a cracked bagpipe, "I discharge you from my service, Billy Mac Daniel— take *that* for your wages," gave poor Billy a most furious kick in the back, which sent his unfortunate servant sprawling upon his face and hands right in the middle of the supper table.

If Billy was astonished, how much more so was everyone of the company into which he was thrown with so little ceremony. But when they heard his story, Father Cooney laid down his knife and fork, and married the young couple out of hand with all speed; and Billy Mac Daniel danced the Rinka at their wedding, and plenty he did drink at it too, which was what he thought more of than dancing.

The Ghosts and the Game of Football

Patrick Kennedy

THERE WAS ONCE a poor widow woman's son that was going to look for service, and one winter's evening he came to a strong farmer's house, and this house was very near an old castle. "God save all here," says he, when he got inside the door. "God save you kindly," says the farmer. "Come to the fire." "Could you give me a night's lodging?" says the boy.

"That we will, and welcome, if you will only sleep in a comfortable room in the old castle above there; and you must have a fire and candlelight, and whatever you like to drink; and if you're alive in the morning I'll give you ten guineas." "Sure I'll be 'live enough if you send no one to kill me." "I'll send no one to kill you, you may depend. The place is haunted ever since my father died, and three or four people that slept in the same room were found dead next morning. If you can banish the spirits I'll give you a good farm and my daughter, so that you like one another well enough to be married." "Never say't twice. I've a middling safe conscience, and don't fear any evil spirit that ever smelled of brimstone."

Well and good, the boy got his supper, and then they went up with him to the old castle, and showed him into a large kitchen, with a roaring fire in the grate, and a table, with a bottle and glass, and tumbler on it, and the kettle ready on the hob. They bade him good night and Godspeed, and went off as if they didn't think their heels were half swift enough. "Well," says he to himself, "if there's any danger, this prayer-book will be usefuller than either the glass or tumbler." So he kneeled down and read a good many prayers, and then sat by the fire, and waited to see what would happen. In about a quarter of an hour, he heard something bumping along the floor overhead till it came to a hole in the ceiling. There it stopped, and cried out, "I'll fall, I'll fall." "Fall away," says Jack, and down came a pair of legs on the kitchen floor. They walked to one end of the room, and there they stood, and Jack's hair had like to stand upright on his head along with them. Then another crackling and whacking came to the hole, and the same words passed between the thing above and Jack, and down came a man's body, and went and stood upon the legs. Then comes the head and shoulders, till the whole man, with buckles in his shoes and knee-breeches, and a big flapped waistcoat and a three-cocked hat, was standing in one corner of the room. Not to take up your time for nothing, two more men, more old-fashioned dressed than the first, were soon standing in two other corners. Jack was a little cowed at first; but found his courage growing stronger every moment, and what would you have of it, the three old gentlemen began to kick a *puckeen* [football] as fast as they could, the man in the three-cocked hat playing again' the other two.

"Fair play is bonny play," says Jack, as bold as he could; but the terror was on him, and the words came out as if he was frightened in his sleep; "so I'll help *you*, sir." Well and good, he joined the sport, and kicked away till his shirt was ringing wet, savin' your presence, and the ball flying from one end of the room to the other like thunder, and still not a word was exchanged. At last the day began to break, and poor Jack was dead beat, and he thought, by the way the three ghosts began to look at himself and themselves, that they wished him to speak.

So, says he, "Gentlemen, as the sport is nearly over, and I done my best to please you, would you tell a body what is the reason of yous coming here night after night, and how could I give you rest, if it is rest you want?" "Them is the wisest words," says the ghost with the three-cocked hat, "you ever said in your life. Some of those that came before you found courage enough to take a part in our game, but no one had *misnach* [energy] enough to speak to us. I am the father of the good man of the next house, that man in the left corner is my father, and the man on my right is my grandfather. From father to son we were too fond of money. We lent it at ten times the honest interest it was worth; we never paid a debt we could get over, and almost starved our tenants and laborers."

"Here," says he, lugging a large drawer out of the wall; "here is the gold and notes that we put together, and we were not honestly entitled to the one-half of it; and here," says he, opening another drawer, "are bills and memorandums that'll show who were wronged, and who are entitled to get a great deal paid back to them. Tell my son to saddle two of his best horses for himself and yourself, and keep riding day and night, till every man and woman we ever wronged be rightified. When that is done, come here again some night; and if you don't hear or see anything, we'll be at rest, and you may marry my granddaughter as soon as you please."

Just as he said these words, Jack could see the wall through his body, and when he winked to clear his sight, the kitchen was as empty as a noggin turned upside down. At that very moment the farmer and his daughter lifted the latch, and both fell on their knees when they saw Jack alive. He soon told them everything that happened, and for three days and nights did the farmer and himself ride about, till there wasn't a single wronged person left without being paid to the last farthing.

The next night Jack spent in the kitchen he fell asleep before he was after sitting a quarter of an hour at the fire, and in his sleep he thought he saw three white birds flying up to heaven from the steeple of the next church.

Jack got the daughter for his wife, and they lived comfortably in the old castle; and if ever he was tempted to hoard up gold, or keep for a minute a guinea or a shilling from the man that earned it through the nose, he bethought him of the ghosts and the game of football.

How The Lakes Were Made

D.R. McAnally, Jr.

AMONG THE WEIRD legends of the Irish peasantry is found a class
of stories peculiar both in the nature of the subject and in the
character of the tradition. From the dawn of history, and even
before, the island has been crowded with inhabitants, and as the
centres of population changed, towns and cities were deserted
and fell into ruins. Although no longer inhabited, their sites are
by no means unknown or forgotten, but in many localities where
now appear only irregular heaps of earth and stones to which the
archæologist sometimes finds difficulty in attributing an
artificial origin there linger among the common people tales of
the city that once stood on the spot; of its walls, its castles, its
palaces, its temples, and the pompous worship of the deities
there adored. Just as, in Palestine, the identification of Bible
localities has, in many instances, been made complete by the
preservation among the Bedouins of the Scriptural names, so, in
Ireland, the cities of pagan times are now being located through

the traditions of the humble tillers of the soil, who transmit from father to son the place-names handed down for untold generations.

Instances are so abundant as to defy enumeration, but a most notable one is Tara, the greatest as it was the holiest city of pagan Ireland. Now it is a group of irregular mounds that the casual observer would readily mistake for natural hills, but for ages the name clung to the place until at last the attention of antiquaries was attracted, interest was roused, investigation made, excavation begun, and the site of Tara made a certainty.

Not all ancient Irish cities, however, escaped the hand of time as well as Tara, for there are geological indications of great natural convulsions in the island at a date comparatively recent, and not a few of the Irish lakes, whose name is legion, were formed by depression or upheaval, almost within the period of written history. A fertile valley traversed by a stream, a populous city by the little river, an earthquake-upheaval lower down the watercourse, closing the exist from the valley, a rising and spreading of the water, an exodus of the inhabitants, such has undoubtedly been the history of Lough Derg and Lough Ree, which are but reservoirs in the course of the River Shannon, while the upper and lower Erne lakes are likewise simply expansions of the river Erne. Lough Neag had a similar origin, the same being also true of Loughs Allen and Key. The Killarney Lakes give indisputable evidence of the manner in which they were formed, being enlargements of the Laune, and Loughs Carra and Mask, in Mayo, are believed to have a subterranean outlet to Lough Carrib, the neighborhood of all three testifying in the strongest possible manner to the sudden closing of the natural outlet for the contributing streams.

The towns which at one time stood on ground now covered by the waters of these lakes were not forgotten. The story of their fate was told by one generation to another, but in course of ages the natural cause, well known to the unfortunates at the time of the calamity, was lost to view, and the story of the disaster began to assume supernatural features. The destruction of the city became sudden; the inhabitants perished in their dwellings; and, as a motive for so signal an event was necessary, it was found in the punishment of duty neglected or crime committed.

Lough Allen is a small body of water in the County Leitrim, and on its shores, partly covered by the waves, are several evidences of human habitation, indications that the waters at present are much higher than formerly. Among the peasants in the neighborhood there is a legend that the little valley once contained a village. In the public square there was a fountain guarded by spirits, fairies, elves, and leprechawns, who objected to the building of the town in that locality, but upon an agreement between themselves and the first settlers permitted the erection of the houses on condition that the fountain be covered with an elegant stone structure, the basin into which the water flowed from the spring to be protected by a cover never to be left open, under pain of the town's destruction, "the good people being that nate an' clane that they did n't want the laste speck av dust in the wather they drunk." So a decree was issued, by the head man of the town, that the cover be always closed by those resorting to the fountain for water, and that due heed might be taken, children, boys under age, and unmarried women, were forbidden under any circumstances to raise the lid of the basin.

For many years things went on well, the fairies and the townspeople sharing alike the benefits of the fountain, till, on one unlucky day, preparations for a wedding were going on in a house close by, and the mother of the bride stood in urgent need of a bucket of water. Not being able to bring it herself, the alleged reason being "she was scholdin' the house in ordher," she commanded her daughter, the bride expectant, to go in her stead.

The latter objected, urging the edict of the headman already mentioned, but was overcome, partly by her mother's argument, that "the good people know ye 're the same as married now that the banns are cried," but principally by the more potent consideration, "Av ye hav n't that wather here in a wink, I 'll not lave a whole bone in yer body, ye lazy young shtrap, an' me breaking me back wid the work," she took the bucket and proceeded to the fountain with the determination to get the water and "shlip out agin afore the good people 'ud find her out." Had she adhered to this resolution, all would have been well, as the fairies would have doubtless overlooked this infraction of the city ordinance. But as she was filling the pail, her lover came in. Of course the two at once began to talk of the all-important subject, and having never before taken water from the fountain, she turned away, forgetting to close the cover of the well. In an instant, a stream, resistless in force, burst forth, and though all the married women of the town ran to put down the cover, their efforts were in vain, the flood grew mightier, the village was submerged, and, with two exceptions, all the inhabitants were drowned. The girl and her lover violated poetic justice by escaping; for, seeing the mischief they had done, they were the first to run away, witnessed the destruction of the town from a neighboring hill, and were afterwards married, the narrator of this incident coming to the sensible conclusion that "it was too bad entirely that the wans that got away were the wans that, be rights, ought to be droonded first."

Upper Lough Erne has a legend, in all important particulars identical with that of Lough Allen, the catastrophe being, however, in the former case brought about by the carelessness of a woman who left her baby at home when she went after water and hearing it scream, "as aven the best babies do be doin', God bless 'em, for no betther rayson than to lishen at thimselves," she hurried back, forgetting to cover the well, with a consequent calamity like that which followed similar forgetfulness at Lough Allen.

In the County Mayo is found Lough Conn, once, according to local storytellers, the site of a village built within and around the enclosure of a castle. The lord of the castle, being fond of fish, determined to make a fishpond, and as the spot selected for the excavation was covered by the cabins of his poorest tenants, he ordered all the occupants to be turned out forthwith, an order at once carried out "wid process-sarvers, an' bailiffs, an' consthables, an' sogers, an' polis, an' the people all shtandin' 'round." One of the evicted knelt on the ground and cursed the chief with "all the seed, breed and gineration av 'im," and prayed "that the throut-pond 'ud be the death av 'im." The prayer was speedily answered, for no sooner was the water turned into the newly-made pond, than an overflow resulted; the valley was filled; the waves climbed the walls of the castle, nor ceased to rise till they had swept the chief from the highest tower, where "he was down an his hard-hearted knees, sayin' his baids as fast as he cud, an' bawlin' at all the saints aither to bring him a boat or taiche him how to swim quick." Regard for the unfortunate tenants, however, prevented any interference by the saints thus vigorously and practically supplicated, so the chief was drowned and went, as the storyteller concluded, to a locality where he "naded more wather than he 'd left behind him, an' had the comp'ny av a shwarm av other landlords that turned out the poor to shtarve."

Lough Gara, in Sligo, flows over a once thriving little town, the City of Peace, destroyed by an overflow on account of the lack of charity for strangers. A poor widow entered it one night leading a child on each side and carrying a baby at her breast. She asked alms and shelter, but in vain; from door to door she went, but the customary Irish hospitality, so abundant alike to the deserving and to the unworthy, was lacking. At the end of the village "she begun to scraich, yer Anner, wid that shtrength you 'd think she 'd shplit her troat. " At this provocation, all the inhabitants at once ran to ascertain the reason of so unusual a noise, upon which, when they were gathered 'round her, the woman pronounced the curse of the widow and orphan on the people and their town. They laughed at her and returned home, but that night, the brook running through the village became a torrent, the outlet was closed, the waters rose, and "ivery wan o' them oncharitable blaggârds wor drownded, while they wor aslape. Bad cess to the lie that 's in it, for, sure there 's the lake to this blessed day."

In County Antrim there lies Lough Neag, one of the largest and most beautiful bodies of water on the island. The waters of the lake are transparently blue, and even small pebbles on the bottom can be seen at a considerable depth. Near the southern end, a survey of the bottom disclosed hewn stones laid in order, and careful observations have traced the regular walls of a structure of considerable dimensions. Tradition says it was a castle, surrounded by the usual village, and accounts for its destruction by the lake in this wise. In ancient times, the castle was owned by an Irish chief named Shane O'Donovan, noted for his bad traits of character, being merciless in war, tyrannical in peace, feared by his neighbors, hated by his dependents, and detested by everybody for his inhospitality and want of charity. His castle then stood by the bank of the lake, on an elevated promontory, almost an island, being joined to the mainland by a narrow isthmus, very little above the water level.

By chance there came into that part of Ireland an angel who had been sent from heaven to observe the people and note their piety. In the garb and likeness of a man, weary and footsore with travel, the angel spied the castle from the hills above the lake, came down, and boldly applied for a night's lodging. Not only was his request refused, "but the oncivil Shane O'Donovan set an his dogs fur to bite him." The angel turned away, but no sooner had he left the castle gate than the villagers ran 'round him and a contest ensued as to which of them should entertain the traveller. He made his choice, going to the house of a cobbler who was "that poor that he 'd but the wan pitatee, and when he wanted another he broke wan in two." The heavenly visitor shared the cobbler's potato and slept on the cobbler's floor, "puttin' his feet into the fire to kape thim warrum," but at daylight he rose, and calling the inhabitants of the village, led them out, across the isthmus to a hill near by, and bid them look back. They did so, beholding the castle and promontory separated from the mainland and beginning to subside into the lake. Slowly, almost imperceptibly, the castle sank, while the waters rose around, but stood like a wall on every side of the castle, not wetting a stone from turret to foundation. At length the wall of water was higher than the battlements, the angel waved his hand, the waves rushed over the castle and its sleeping inmates, and the O'Donovan inhospitality was punished. The angel pointed to a spot near by, told the villagers to build and prosper there; then, as the awe-stricken peasants kneeled before him, his clothing became white and shining, wings appeared on his shoulders, he rose into the air and vanished from their sight.

Of somewhat different origin is the pretty Lough Derryclare, in Connemara, south of the Joyce Country. The ferocious O'Flahertys frequented this region in past ages, and, with the exception of Oliver Cromwell, no historical name is better known in the west of Ireland than O'Flaherty. One of this doughty race was, it seems, a model of wickedness. "He was as proud as a horse wid a wooden leg, an' so bad, that, savin' yer presince, the divil himself was ashamed av him." This O'Flaherty had sent a party to devastate a neighboring village, but as the men did not return promptly, he started with a troop of horse in the direction they had taken. On the way he was passing through a deep ravine at the bottom of which flowed a tiny brook, when he met his returning troops, and questioning them as to the thoroughness with which their bloody work had been done, found, to his great wrath, that they had spared the church and those who took refuge in its sacred precincts.

"May God drownd me where I shtand," said he, "if I don't shlay thim all an the althar," and no doubt he would have done so, but the moment the words passed his lips, the rivulet became a seething torrent, drowned him and his men, and the lake was formed over the spot where they stood when the curse was pronounced. "An' sometimes, they say, that when the lake is quite shtill, ye may hear the groans av the lost sowls chained at the bottom."

The fairies are responsible for at least two of the Irish lakes, Lough Key and the Upper Lough Killarney. The former is an enlargement of the River Boyle, a tributary of the Shannon, and is situated in Roscommon. At a low stage of water, ruins can be discerned at the bottom of the river, and are reported to be those of a city whose inhabitants injudiciously attempted to swindle the "good people" in a land bargain. The city was built, it seems, by permission of the fairies, the understanding being that all raths were to be left undisturbed. For a long time the agreement was respected, fairies and mortals living side by side, and neither class interfering with the other. But, as the necessity for more arable land became evident, it was determined by the townspeople to level several raths and mounds that interfered with certain fields and boundary lines. The dangers of such a course were plainly pointed out by the local "fairy-man," and all the "knowledgeable women" lifted their voices against it, but in vain; down the raths must come and down they came, to the consternation of the knowing ones, who predicted no end of evil from so flagrant a violation of the treaty with the fairies.

The night after the demolition of the raths, one of the townsmen was coming through the gorge below the city, when, "Millia, murther, there wor more than a hundherd t'ousand little men in grane jackets bringin' shtones an' airth an' buildin' a wall acrass the glen. Begob, I go bail but he was the skairt man when he seen phat they done, an' run home wid all the legs he had an' got his owld woman an' the childher. When she axed him phat he was afther, he towld her to howld her whisht or he 'd pull the tongue out av her an' to come along an' not spake a word. So they got to the top o' the hill an then they seen the wathers swapin' an the city an' niver a sowl was there left o' thim that wor in it. So the good people had their rayvinge, an' the like o' that makes men careful wid raths, not to displaze their betthers, for there 's no sayin' phat they 'll do."

The Upper Killarney lake was created by the fairy queen of Kerry to punish her lover, the young Prince O'Donohue. She was greatly fascinated by him, and, for a time, he was as devoted to her as woman's heart could wish. But things changed, for, in the language of the boatman, who told the legend, "whin a woman loves a man, she 's satisfied wid wan, but whin a man loves a woman, belike he 's not contint wid twinty av her, an' so was it wid O'Donohue." No doubt, however, he loved the fairy queen as long as he could, but in time tiring of her, "he concluded to marry a foine lady, and when the quane rayproached him wid forgittin' her, at first he said it was n't so, an' whin she proved it an him, faith he 'd not a word left in his jaw. So afther a dale o' blasthogue bechuxt thim, he got as mad as Paddy Monagan's dog when they cut his tail aff, an' towld her he wanted no more av her, an' she towld him agin for to go an' marry his redheaded gurrul, 'but mârk ye,' says she to him, 'ye shall niver resave her into yer cassel.' No more did he, for the night o' the weddin', while they were all dhrinkin' till they were ready to burst, in comes the waither an' says, 'Here 's the wather,' says he. 'Wather,' says O'Donohue, 'we want no wather to-night. Dhrink away.' 'But the wather 's risin',' says the waither. 'Arrah, ye Bladdherang,' says O'Donohue, 'phat d' ye mane be inthrudin' an agrayble frinds an such an outspishus occasion wid yer presince? Be aff, or be the powdhers o' war I 'll wather ye,' says he, risin' up for to shlay the waither. But wan av his gintlemin whuspered the thruth in his year an' towld him to run. So he did an' got away just in time, for the cassel was half full o' wather whin he left it. But the quane did n't want to kill him, so he got away an' built another cassel an the hill beyant where he lived wid his bride."

Still another origin for the Irish lakes is found in Mayo, where Lough Carra is attributed to a certain "giont," by name unknown, who formerly dwelt in the neighborhood, and, with one exception, found everything necessary for comfort and convenience. He was a cleanly "giont," and desirous of performing his ablutions regularly and thoroughly. The streams in the neighborhood were ill adapted to his use, for when he entered any one of them for bathing purposes "bad scran to the wan that 'ud take him in furder than to the knees." Obviously this was not deep enough, so one day when unusually in need of a bath and driven desperate by the inadequacy of the means, "he spit an his han's an' went to work an' made Lough Carra. 'Bedad,' says he, 'I 'll have a wash now,' an' so he did," and doubtless enjoyed it, for the lake is deep and the water clear and pure.

Just below Lough Carra is Lough Mask, a large lake between Mayo and Galway. Concerning its origin, traditionary authorities differ, some maintain that the lake was the work of fairies, others holding that it was scooped out by a rival of the cleanly gigantic party already mentioned, a theory apparently confirmed by the fact that it has no visible outlet, though several streams pour into it, its waters, it is believed, escaping by a subterranean channel to Lough Corrib, thence to the sea. Sundry unbelievers, however, stoutly assert a conviction that "it 's so be nacher entirely an' thim that says it 's not is ignerant gommochs that don't know," and in the face of determined scepticism the question of the origin of the lake must remain unsettled.

Thus far, indeed, it is painful to be compelled to state that scarcely one of the narratives of this chapter passes undisputed among the veracious tradition-mongers of Ireland. Like most other countries in this practical, poetry-decrying age, the Emerald Isle has scientists and sceptics, and among the peasants are found many men who have no hesitation in proclaiming their disbelief in "thim owld shtories," and who even openly affirm that "laigends about fairies an' giants is all lies complately." In the face of this growing tendency towards materialism and the disposition to find in natural causes an explanation of wonderful events, it is pleasant to be able to conclude this chapter with an undisputed account of the origin of Lough Ree in the River Shannon, the accuracy of the information being in every particular guaranteed by a boatman on the Shannon, "a respectable man," who solemnly asseverated "Sure, that 's no laigend, but the blessed truth as I 'm livin' this minnit, for I 'd sooner cut out me tongue be the root than desave yer Anner, when every wan knows there 's not a taste av a lie in it at all."

"When the blessed Saint Pathrick was goin' through Ireland from wan end to the other buildin' churches, an' Father Malone says he built three hundherd an' sixty foive, that 's a good manny, he come to Roscommon be the way av Athlone, where ye saw the big barracks an' the sojers. So he passed through Athlone, the counthry bein' full o' haythens entirely an' not av Crissans, and went up the Shannon, kapin' the river on his right hand, an' come to a big peat bog, that 's where the lake is now. There were more than a thousand poor omadhawns av haythens a-diggin' the peat, an' the blessed saint convarted thim at wanst afore he 'd shtir a toe to go anny furder. Then he built thim a church an the hill be the bog, an' gev thim a holy man fur a priest be the name o' Caruck, that I b'lave is a saint too or lasteways ought to be fur phat he done. So Saint Pathrick left thim wid the priest, givin' him great power on the divil an' avil sper'ts, and towld him to build a priest's house as soon as he cud. So the blessed Caruck begged an' begged as long as he got anny money, an' whin he 'd the last ha'penny he cud shtart, he begun the priest's house fur to kape monks in.

"But the divil was watchin' him ivery minnit, fur it made the owld felly tarin' mad to see himself bate out o' the face that-a-way in the country where he 'd been masther so long, an' he determined he 'd spile the job. So wan night, he goes to the bottom o' the bog, an' begins dammin' the shtrame, from wan side to the other, layin' the shtones shtrong an' tight, an' the wather begins a risin an the bog. Now it happened that the blessed Caruck was n't aslape as Satan thought, but up an' about, for he misthrusted that the Owld Wan was dodgin' round like a wayzel, an' was an the watch fur him. So when the blessed man saw the wather risin' on the bog an' not a taste o' rain fallin', 'Phat 's this?' says he. 'Sure it 's some o' Satan's deludherin'.'

"So down he goes bechuxt the hills an' kapin' from the river, an' comes up below where the divil was workin' away pilin' on the airth an' shtones. So he comes craipin' up on him an' when he got purty clost, he riz an' says, 'Hilloo, Nayber!' Now Belzebub was like to dhrop on the ground wid fright at the look av him, he was that astonished. But there was no gettin' away, so he shtopped on the job, wiped the shweat aff his face, an' says, 'Hilloo yerself.'

"'Ye 're at yer owld thricks,' says the blessed Caruck.

"'Shmall blame to me, that 's,' says Belzebub, 'wid yer churches an' saints an' convartin' thim haythens, ye 're shpiling me business entirely. Sure, have n't I got to airn me bread?' says he, spakin' up as bowld as a cock, and axcusin' himself.

"At first the blessed Caruck was goin' to be rough wid him for shtrivin' to interfare wid the church an' the priest's house be risin' the wather on thim, but that minnit the moon shone out as bright as day an' he looked back an' there was the beautifulest lake he iver set his blessed eyes on, an' the church wid its towers riz above it like a fairy cassel in a dhrame, an' he clasped his hands wid delight. So Satan looked too an' was mortefied to death wid invy when he seen how he bate himself at his own game.

"So the blessed Caruck twold Belzebub to lave the dam where it was, an' then, thinkin' av the poor bog-throtters that 'ud nade the turf, he ordhered him beways av a punishmint, to dig all the turf there was in the bog an' pile it up on the hill to dhry.

"'Don't you lave as much as a speck av it undher wather,' says he to him, 'or as sure as I 'm a saint I 'll make ye repint it to the end of' yer snakin' life,' says he, an' thin stud on the bank an' watched the Owld Deludher while he brought out the turf in loads on his back, an' ivery load as big as the church, till the hape av sods was as high as a mountain. So he got it done be mornin', an' glad enough was the divil to have the job aff his hands, fur he was as wet as a goose in May an' as tired as a pedler's donkey. So the blessed Caruck towld him to take himself aff an' not come back: that he was mighty well plazed to do.

"That 's the way the lake come to be here, an' the blessed Caruck come well out o' that job, fur he sold the turf an' built a big house on the shore wid the money, an' chated the divil besides, Glory be to God, when the Owld Wan was thryin' his best fur to sarcumvint a saint."

The Specter Lovers
Joseph Sheridan Le Fanu

THERE LIVED SOME FIFTEEN YEARS SINCE in a small and ruinous
house, little better than a hovel, an old woman who was
reported to have considerably exceeded her eightieth year, and
who rejoiced in the name of Alice, or popularly, Ally Moran.
Her society was not much courted, for she was neither rich, nor,
as the reader may suppose, beautiful. In addition to a lean cur
and a cat she had one human companion, her grandson, Peter
Brien, whom, with laudable good-nature, she had supported
from the period of his orphanage down to that of my story,
which finds him in his twentieth year. Peter was a good-natured
slob of a fellow much more addicted to wrestling, dancing, and
love-making, than to hard work, and fonder of whiskey punch
than good advice. His grandmother had a high opinion of his
accomplishments, which indeed was but natural, and also of his

genius, for Peter had of late years begun to apply his mind to politics; and as it was plain that he had a mortal hatred of honest labor, his grandmother predicted, like a true fortune-teller, that he was born to marry an heiress, and Peter himself (who had no mind to forego his freedom even on such terms) that he was destined to find a pot of gold. Upon one point both agreed, that being unfitted by the peculiar bias of his genius for work, he was to acquire the immense fortune to which his merits entitled him by means of a pure run of good luck. This solution of Peter's future had the double effect of reconciling both himself and his grandmother to his idle courses, and also of maintaining that even flow of hilarious spirits which made him everywhere welcome, and which was in truth the natural result of his consciousness of approaching affluence.

It happened one night that Peter had enjoyed himself to a very late hour with two or three choice spirits near Palmerstown. They had talked politics and love, sung songs, and told stories, and, above all, had swallowed, in the chastened disguise of punch, at least a pint of good whiskey, every man.

It was considerably past one o'clock when Peter bid his companions goodbye, with a sigh and a hiccough, and lighting his pipe set forth on his solitary homeward way.

The bridge of Chapelizod was pretty nearly the midway point of his night march, and from one cause or another his progress was rather slow, and it was past two o'clock by the time he found himself leaning over its old battlements, and looking up the river, over whose winding current and wooded banks the soft moonlight was falling.

The cold breeze that blew lightly down the stream was grateful to him. It cooled his throbbing head, and he drank it in at his hot lips. The scene, too, had, without his being well sensible of it, a secret fascination. The village was sunk in the profoundest slumber, not a mortal stirring, not a sound afloat, a soft haze covered it all, and the fairy moonlight hovered over the entire landscape.

In a state between rumination and rapture, Peter continued to lean over the battlements of the old bridge, and as he did so he saw, or fancied he saw, emerging one after another along the river bank in the little gardens and enclosures in the rear of the street of Chapelizod, the queerest little whitewashed huts and cabins he had ever seen there before. They had not been there that evening when he passed the bridge on the way to his merry tryst. But the most remarkable thing about it was the odd way in which these quaint little cabins showed themselves. First he saw one or two of them just with the corner of his eye, and when he looked full at them, strange to say, they faded away and disappeared. Then another and another came in view, but all in the same coy way, just appearing and gone again before he could well fix his gaze upon them; in a little while, however, they began to bear a fuller gaze, and he found, as it seemed to himself, that he was able by an effort of attention to fix the vision for a longer and a longer time, and when they waxed faint and nearly vanished, he had the power of recalling them into light and substance, until at last their vacillating indistinctness became less and less, and they assumed a permanent place in the moonlit landscape.

"Be the hokey," said Peter, lost in amazement, and dropping his pipe into the river unconsciously, "them is the quarist bits iv mud cabins I ever seen, growing up like musharoons in the dew of an evening, and poppin' up here and down again there, and up again in another place, like so many white rabbits in a warren; and there they stand at last as firm and fast as if they were there from the Deluge; bedad it's enough to make a man a'most believe in the fairies."

This latter was a large concession from Peter, who was a bit of a free-thinker, and spoke contemptuously in his ordinary conversation of that class of agencies.

Having treated himself to a long last stare at these mysterious fabrics, Peter prepared to pursue his homeward way; having crossed the bridge and passed the mill, he arrived at the corner of the main street of the little town, and casting a careless look up the Dublin road, his eye was arrested by a most unexpected spectacle.

This was no other than a column of foot-soldiers, marching with perfect regularity towards the village, and headed by an officer on horseback. They were at the far side of the turnpike, which was closed; but much to his perplexity he perceived that they marched on through it without appearing to sustain the least check from that barrier.

On they came at a slow march; and what was most singular in the matter was that they were drawing several cannons along with them; some held ropes, others spoked the wheels, and others again marched in front of the guns and behind them, with muskets shouldered, giving a stately character of parade and regularity to this, as it seemed to Peter, most unmilitary procedure.

It was owing either to some temporary defect in Peter's vision, or to some illusion attendant upon mist and moonlight, or perhaps to some other cause, that the whole procession had a certain waving and vapory character which perplexed and tasked his eyes not a little. It was like the pictured pageant of a phantasmagoria reflected upon smoke. It was as if every breath disturbed it; sometimes it was blurred, sometimes obliterated; now here, now there. Sometimes, while the upper part was quite distinct, the legs of the column would nearly fade away or vanish outright, and then again they would come out into clear relief, marching on with measured tread, while the cocked hats and shoulders grew, as it were, transparent, and all but disappeared.

Notwithstanding these strange optical fluctuations however, the column continued steadily to advance. Peter crossed the street from the corner near the old bridge, running on tip-toe, and with his body stooped to avoid observation, and took up a position upon the raised footpath in the shadow of the houses, where, as the soldiers kept the middle of the road, he calculated that he might, himself undetected, see them distinctly enough as they passed.

"What the div—, what on airth," he muttered, checking the irreligious ejaculation with which he was about to start, for certain queer misgivings were hovering about his heart, notwithstanding the factitious courage of the whiskey bottle. "What on airth is the manin' of all this? Is it the French that's landed at last to give us a hand and help us in airnest to this blessed repale? If it is not them, I simply ask who the div—, I mane who on airth are they, for such sogers as them I never seen before in my born days?"

By this time the foremost of them were quite near, and truth to say they were the queerest soldiers he had ever seen in the course of his life. They wore long gaiters and leather breeches, three-cornered hats, bound with silver lace, long blue coats, with scarlet facings and linings, which latter were shown by a fastening which held together the two opposite corners of the skirt behind; and in front the breasts were in like manner connected at a single point, where and below which they sloped back, disclosing a long-flapped waistcoat of snowy whiteness; they had very large, long cross-belts, and wore enormous pouches of white leather hung extraordinarily low, and on each of which a little silver star was glittering. But what struck him as most grotesque and outlandish in their costume was their extraordinary display of shirt-frill in front, and of ruffle about their wrists, and the strange manner in which their hair was frizzled out and powdered under their hats, and clubbed up into great rolls behind. But one of the party was mounted. He rode a tall white horse with high action and arching neck; he had a snow-white feather in his three-cornered hat, and his coat was shimmering all over with a profusion of silver lace. From these circumstances Peter concluded that he must be the commander of the detachment, and examined him as he passed attentively. He was a slight, tall man, whose legs did not half fill his leather breeches, and he appeared to be at the wrong side of sixty. He had a shrunken, weather-beaten, mulberry-colored face, carried a large black patch over one eye, and turned neither to the right nor to the left, but rode on at the head of his men, with a grim, military inflexibility.

The countenances of these soldiers, officers as well as men, seemed all full of trouble, and, so to speak, scared and wild. He watched in vain for a single contented or comely face. They had, one and all, a melancholy and hang-dog look; and as they passed by, Peter fancied that the air grew cold and thrilling.

He had seated himself upon a stone bench, from which, staring with all his might, he gazed upon the grotesque and noiseless procession as it filed by him. Noiseless it was; he could neither hear the jingle of accoutrements, the tread of feet, nor the rumble of the wheels; and when the old colonel turned his horse a little, and made as though he were giving the word of command, and a trumpeter, with a swollen blue nose and white feather fringe round his hat, who was walking beside him, turned about and put his bugle to his lips, still Peter heard nothing, although it was plain the sound had reached the soldiers, for they instantly changed their front to three abreast.

"Botheration!" muttered Peter, "is it deaf I'm growing?"

But that could not be, for he heard the sighing of the breeze and the rush of the neighboring Liffey plain enough.

"Well," said he, in the same cautious key, "by the piper, this bangs Banagher fairly! It's either the Frinch army that's in it, come to take the town iv Chapelizod by surprise, an' makin' no noise for feard iv wakenin' the inhabitants; or else it's—it's—what it's—somethin' else. But, tundher-an-ouns, what's gone wid Fitzpatrick's shop across the way?"

The brown, dingy stone building at the opposite side of the street looked newer and cleaner than he had been used to see it; the front door of it stood open, and a sentry, in the same grotesque uniform, with shouldered musket, was pacing noiselessly to and fro before it. At the angle of this building, in like manner, a wide gate (of which Peter had no recollection whatever) stood open, before which, also, a similar sentry was gliding, and into this gateway the whole column gradually passed, and Peter finally lost sight of it.

"I'm not asleep; I'm not dhramin'," said he, rubbing his eyes, and stamping slightly on the pavement, to assure himself that he was wide awake. "It is a quare business, whatever it is; an' it's not alone that, but everything about the town looks strange to me. There's Tresham's house new painted, bedad, an' them flowers in the windies! An' Delany's house, too, that had not a whole pane of glass in it this morning, and scarce a slate on the roof of it! It is not possible it's what it's dhrunk I am. Sure there's the big tree, and not a leaf of it changed since I passed, and the stars overhead, all nght. I don't think it is in my eyes it is."

And so looking about him, and every moment finding or fancying new food for wonder, he walked along the pavement, intending, without further delay, to make his way home.

But his adventures for the night were not concluded. He had nearly reached the angle of the short lane that leads up to the church, when for the first time he perceived that an officer, in the uniform he had just seen, was walking before, only a few yards in advance of him.

The officer was walking along at an easy, swinging gait, and carried his sword under his arm, and was looking down on the pavement with an air of reverie.

In the very fact that he seemed unconscious of Peter's presence, and disposed to keep his reflections to himself, there was something reassuring. Besides, the reader must please to remember that our hero had a *quantum sufficit* of good punch before his adventure commenced, and was thus fortified against those qualms and terrors under which, in a more reasonable state of mind, he might not impossibly have sunk.

The idea of the French invasion revived in full power in Peter's fuddled imagination, as he pursued the nonchalant swagger of the officer.

"Be the powers iv Moll Kelly, I'll ax him what it is," said Peter, with a sudden accession of rashness. "He may tell me or not, as he plases, but he can't be offinded, anyhow."

With this reflection having inspired himself, Peter cleared his voice and began—

"Captain!" said he, "I ax your pardon, captain, an' maybe you'd be so condescindin' to my ignorance as to tell me, if it's plasin' to yer honor, whether your honor is not a Frinchman, if it's plasin' to you."

This he asked, not thinking that, had it been as he suspected, not one word of his question in all probability would have been intelligible to the person he addressed. He was, however, understood, for the officer answered him in English, at the same time slackening his pace and moving a little to the side of the pathway, as if to invite his interrogator to take his place beside him.

"No; I am an Irishman," he answered.

"I humbly thank your honor,' said Peter, drawing nearer — for the affability and the nativity of the officer encouraged him— "but maybe your honor is in the sarvice of the King of France?"

"I serve the same King as you do," he answered, with a sorrowful significance which Peter did not comprehend at the time, and, interrogating in turn, he asked, "But what calls you forth at this hour of the day?"

"The *day*, your honor!—the night, you mane."

"It was always our way to turn night into day, and we keep to it still," remarked the soldier. "But, no matter, come up here to my house; I have a job for you, if you wish to earn some money easily. I live here."

As he said this, he beckoned authoritatively to Peter, who followed almost mechanically at his heels, and they turned up a little lane near the old Roman Catholic chapel, at the end of which stood, in Peter's time, the ruins of a tall, stonebuilt house.

Like everything else in the town, it had suffered a metamorphosis. The stained and ragged walls were now erect, perfect, and covered with pebble-dash; windowpanes glittered coldly in every window; the green hall-door had a bright brass knocker on it. Peter did not know whether to believe his previous or his present impressions; seeing is believing, and Peter could not dispute the reality of the scene. All the records of his memory seemed but the images of a tipsy dream. In a trance of astonishment and perplexity, therefore, he submitted himself to the chances of his adventure.

The door opened, the officer beckoned with a melancholy air of authority to Peter, and entered. Our hero followed him into a sort of hall, which was very dark, but he was guided by the steps of the soldier, and, in silence, they ascended the stairs. The moonlight, which shone in at the lobbies, showed an old, dark wainscoting, and a heavy oak banister. They passed by closed doors at different landing-places, but all was dark and silent as, indeed, became that late hour of the night.

Now they ascended to the topmost floor. The captain paused for a minute at the nearest door, and, with a heavy groan, pushing it open, entered the room. Peter remained at the threshold. A slight female form in a sort of loose white robe, and with a great deal of dark hair hanging loosely about her, was standing in the middle of the floor, with her back towards them.

The soldier stopped short before he reached her, and said, in a voice of great anguish, "Still the same, sweet bird—sweet bird! still the same." Whereupon, she turned suddenly and threw her arms about the neck of the officer, with a gesture of fondness and despair, and her frame was agitated as if by a burst of sobs. He held her close to his breast in silence; and honest Peter felt a strange terror creep over him, as he witnessed these mysterious sorrows and endearments.

"Tonight, tonight—and then ten years more—ten long years—another ten years."

The officer and the lady seemed to speak these words together; her voice mingled with his in a musical and fearful wail, like a distant summer wind, in the dead hour of night wandering through ruins. Then he heard the officer say alone, in a voice of anguish—

"Upon me be it all, for ever, sweet birdie, upon me."

And again they seemed to mourn together in the same soft and desolate wail, like sounds of grief heard from a great distance.

Peter was thrilled with horror, but he was also under a strange fascination; and an intense and dreadful curiosity held him fast.

The moon was shining obliquely into the room, and through the window Peter saw the familiar slopes of the Park, sleeping mistily under its shimmer. He could also see the furniture of the room with tolerable distinctness—the old balloon-backed chairs, a four-post bed in a sort of recess and a rack against the wall, from which hung some military clothes and accoutrements; and the sight of all these homely objects reassured him somewhat, and he could not help feeling unspeakably curious to see the face of the girl whose long hair was streaming over the officer's epaulet.

Peter, accordingly, coughed, at first slightly, and afterward more loudly, to recall her from her reverie of grief; and, apparently, he succeeded; for she turned round, as did her companion, and both, standing hand in hand, gazed upon him fixedly. He thought he had never seen such large, strange eyes in all his life; and their gaze seemed to chill the very air around him, and arrest the pulses of his heart. An eternity of misery and remorse was in the shadowy faces that looked upon him.

If Peter had taken less whiskey by a single thimbleful, it is probable that he would have lost heart altogether before these figures, which seemed every moment to assume a more marked and fearful, though hardly definable, contrast to ordinary human shapes.

"What is it you want with me?" he stammered.

"To bring my lost treasure to the churchyard," replied the lady, in a silvery voice of more than mortal desolation.

The word "treasure" revived the resolution of Peter, although a cold sweat was covering him, and his hair was bristling with horror; he believed, however, that he was on the brink of fortune, if he could but command nerve to brave the interview to its close.

"And where," he gasped, "is it hid—where will I find it?"

They both pointed to the sill of the window, through which the moon was shining at the far end of the room, and the soldier said—

"Under that stone."

Peter drew a long breath, and wiped the cold dew from his face, preparatory to passing to the window, where he expected to secure the reward of his protracted terrors. But looking steadfastly at the window, he saw the faint image of a new-born child sitting upon the sill in the moonlight, with its little arms stretched toward him, and a smile so heavenly as he never beheld before.

At sight of this, strange to say, his heart entirely failed him; he looked on the figures that stood near, and beheld them gazing on the infantine form with a smile so guilty and distorted, that he felt as if he were entering alive among the scenery of hell, and shuddering, he cried in an irrepressible agony of horror—

"I'll have nothing to say with you, and nothing to do with you; I don't know what yez are or what yez want iv me, but let me go this minute, every one of yez, in the name of God."

With these words there came a strange rumbling and sighing about Peter's ears; he lost sight of everything, and felt that peculiar and not unpleasant sensation of falling softly, that sometimes supervenes in sleep, ending in a dull shock. After that he had neither dream nor consciousness till he wakened, chill and stiff, stretched between two piles of old rubbish, among the black and roofless walls of the ruined house.

We need hardly mention that the village had put on its wonted air of neglect and decay, or that Peter looked around him in vain for traces of those novelties which had so puzzled and distracted him upon the previous night.

"Ay, ay," said his grandmother, removing her pipe, as he ended his description of the view from the bridge, "sure enough I remember myself, when I was a slip of a girl, these little white cabins among the gardens by the river side. The artillery sogers that was married, or had not room in the barracks, used to be in them, but they're all gone long ago."

"The Lord be merciful to us!" she resumed, when he had described the military procession, "it's often I seen the regiment marchin' into the town, jist as you saw it last night, acushla. Oh, voch, but it makes my heart sore to think iv them days; they were pleasant times, sure enough; but is not it terrible, avick, to think it's what it was the ghost of the rigiment you seen? The Lord betune us an' harm, for it was nothing else, as sure as I'm sittin' here."

When he mentioned the peculiar physiognomy and figure of the old officer who rode at the head of the regiment—

"*That*," said the old crone, dogmatically, "was ould Colonel Grimshaw, the Lord presarve us! he's buried in the churchyard iv Chapelizod, and well I remember him, when I was a young thing, an' a cross ould floggin' fellow he was wid the men, an' a devil's boy among the girls—rest his soul!"

"Amen!" said Peter; "it's often I read his tombstone myself; but he's a long time dead."

"Sure, I tell you he died when I was no more nor a slip iv a girl—the Lord betune us and harm!"

"I'm afeard it is what I'm not long for this world myself, afther seeing such a sight as that," said Peter, fearfully.

"Nonsinse, avourneen," retorted his grandmother, indignantly, though she had herself misgivings on the subject; "sure there was Phil Doolan, the ferryman, that seen black Ann Scanlan in his own boat, and what harm ever kem of it?"

Peter proceeded with his narrative, but when he came to the

description of the house, in which his adventure had had so sinister a conclusion, the old woman was at fault.

"I know the house and the ould walls well, an' I can remember the time there was a roof on it, and the doors an' windows in it, but it had a bad name about being haunted, but by who, or for what, I forget intirely."

"Did you ever hear was there gold or silver there?" he inquired.

"No, no, avick, don't be thinking about the likes; take a fool's advice, and never go next or near them ugly black walls again the longest day you have to live; an' I'd take my davy, it's what it's the same word the priest himself I'd be afther sayin' to you if you wor to ax his raverence consarnin' it, for it's plain to be seen it was nothing good you seen there, and there's neither luck nor grace about it."

Peter's adventure made no little noise in the neighborhood, as the reader may well suppose; and a few evenings after it, being on an errand to old Major Vandeleur, who lived in a snug old-fashioned house, close by the river, under a perfect bower of ancient trees, he was called on to relate the story in the parlor.

The Major was, as I have said, an old man; he was small, lean, and upright, with a mahogany complexion, and a wooden inflexibility of face; he was a man, besides, of few words, and if *he* was old, it follows plainly that his mother was older still. Nobody could guess or tell *how* old, but it was admitted that her own generation had long passed away, and that she had not a competitor left. She had French blood in her veins, and although she did not retain her charms quite so well as Niñon de l'Enclos, she was in full possession of all her mental activity, and talked quite enough for herself and the Major.

"So, Peter," she said, "you have seen the dear, old Royal Irish again in the streets of Chapelizod. Make him a tumbler of punch, Frank; and Peter, sit down, and while you take it let us have the story."

Peter accordingly, seated near the door, with a tumbler of the nectarian stimulant steaming beside him, proceeded with marvelous courage, considering they had no light but the uncertain glare of the fire, to relate with minute particularity his awful adventure. The old lady listened at first with a smile of good-natured incredulity; her cross-examination touching the drinking-bout at Palmerstown had been teasing, but as the narrative proceeded she became attentive, and at length absorbed, and once or twice she uttered ejaculations of pity or awe. When it was over, the old lady looked with a somewhat sad and stern abstraction on the table, patting her cat assiduously meanwhile, and then suddenly looking upon her son, the Major, she said—

"Frank, as sure as I live he has seen the wicked Captain Devereux."

The Major uttered an inarticulate expression of wonder.

"The house was precisely that he has described. I have told you the story often, as I heard it from your dear grandmother, about the poor young lady he ruined, and the dreadful suspicion about the little baby. *She*, poor thing, died in that house heartbroken, and you know he was shot shortly after in a duel."

This was the only light that Peter ever received respecting his adventure. It was supposed, however, that he still clung to the hope that treasure of some sort was hidden about the old house, for he was often seen lurking about its walls, and at last his fate overtook him, poor fellow, in the pursuit; for climbing near the summit one day, his holding gave way, and he fell upon the hard uneven ground, fracturing a leg and a rib, and after a short interval died, and he, like the other heroes, lies buried in the little churchyard of Chapelizod.

The Crucifixion of the Outcast

W. B. Yeats

A MAN, with thin brown hair and a pale face, half ran, half walked, along the road that wound from the south to the town of Sligo. Many called him Cumhal, the son of Cormac, and many called him the Swift Wild Horse; and he was a gleeman, and he wore a short particolored doublet, and had pointed shoes, with a bulging wallet. Also he was of the blood of the Ernaans, and his birthplace was the Field of Gold; but his eating and sleeping places were in the five kingdoms of Eri, and his abiding place was not upon the ridge of the earth. His eyes strayed from the tower of what was later the Abbey of the White Friars to a row of crosses which stood out against the sky upon a hill a little to the eastward of the town, and he clenched his fist, and shook it at the crosses. He knew they were not empty, for the birds were fluttering about them; and he thought how, as like it as not, just such another vagabond as himself had been mounted on one of them; and he muttered: "If it were hanging or bow-stringing, or stoning or beheading, it would be bad enough. But to have the birds pecking your eyes and the wolves eating your feet! I would that the red wind of the Druids had withered in his cradle the soldier of Dathi, who brought the tree of death out of barbarous lands, or that the lightning, when it smote Dathi at the foot of the mountain, had smitten him also, or that his grave had been dug by the green-haired and green-toothed merrows deep at the roots of the deep sea."

While he spoke, he shivered from head to foot, and the sweat came out upon his face, and he knew not why, for he had looked upon many crosses. He passed over two hills and under the battlemented gate, and then round by a left-hand way to the door of the Abbey. It was studded with great nails, and when he knocked at it he roused the lay brother who was the porter, and of him he asked a place in the guest-house. Then the lay brother took a glowing turf on a shovel, and led the way to a big and naked outhouse strewn with very dirty rushes; and lighted a rush-candle fixed between two of the stones of the wall, and set the glowing turf upon the hearth and gave him two unlighted sods and a wisp of straw, and showed him a blanket hanging from a nail, and a shelf with a loaf of bread and a jug of water, and a tub in a far corner. Then the lay brother left him and went back to his place by the door. And Cumhal the son of Cormac began to blow upon the glowing turf that he might light the two sods and the wisp of straw; but the sods and the straw would not light, for they were damp. So he took off his pointed shoes, and drew the tub out of the corner with the thought of washing the dust of the highway from his feet; but the water was so dirty that he could not see the bottom. He was very hungry, for he had not eaten all that day, so he did not waste much anger upon the tub, but took up the black loaf, and bit into it, and then spat out the bite, for the bread was hard and mouldy. Still he did not give way to his anger, for he had not drunken these many hours; having a hop of heath beer or wine at his day's end, he had left the brooks untasted, to make his supper the more delightful. Now he put the jug to his lips, but he flung it from him straightway, for the water was bitter and ill-smelling. Then he gave the jug a kick, so that it broke against the opposite wall, and he took down the blanket to wrap it about him for the night. But no sooner did he touch it than it was alive with skipping fleas. At this, beside himself with anger, he rushed to the door of the guest-house, but the lay brother, being well accustomed to such outcries, had locked it on the outside; so he emptied the tub and began to beat the door with it, till the lay brother came to the door and asked what ailed him, and why he woke him out of sleep. "What ails me!" shouted Cumhal; "are not the sods as wet as the sands of the Three Rosses? and are not the fleas in the blanket as many as the waves of the sea and as lively? and is not the bread as hard as the heart of a lay brother who has forgotten God? and is not the water in the jug as bitter and as ill-smelling as his soul? and is not the foot-water the color that shall be upon him when he has been charred in the Undying Fires?" The lay brother saw that the lock was fast, and went back to his niche, for he was too sleepy to talk with comfort. And Cumhal went on beating at the door, and presently he heard the lay brother's foot once more, and cried out at him. "O cowardly and tyrannous race of monks, persecutors of the bard and the gleeman, haters of life and joy! O race that does not draw the sword and tell the truth! O race that melts the bones of the people with cowardice and with deceit!"

"Gleeman," said the lay brother, "I also makes rhymes; I make many while I sit in my niche by the door, and I sorrow to hear the bards railing upon the monks. Brother, I would sleep, and therefore I make known to you that it is the head of the monastery, our gracious abbot, who orders all things concerning the lodging of travelers."

"You may sleep," said Cumhal, "I will sing a bard's curse on the abbot." And he set the tub upside down under the window, and stood upon it, and began to sing in a very loud voice. The singing awoke the abbot, so that he sat up in bed and blew a silver whistle until the lay brother came to him. "I cannot get a wink of deep with that noise," said the abbot. What is happening?"

"It is a gleeman," said the lay brother, "who complains of the sods, of the bread. of the water in the jug, of the foot-water, and of the blanket. And now he is singing a bard's curse upon you, O brother abbot, and upon your father and your mother, and your grandfather and your grandmother, and upon all your relations."

"Is he cursing in rhyme?"

"He is cursing in rhyme, and with two assonances in every line of his curse."

The abbot pulled his nightcap off and crumpled it in his hands, and the circular grey patch of hair in the middle of his bald head looked like the cairn upon Knocknarea, for in Connaught they had not yet abandoned the ancient tonsure. "Unless we do somewhat," he said, "he will teach his curses to the children in the street, and the girls spinning at the doors, and to the robbers upon Ben Bulben."

"Shall I go, then," said the other, "and give him dry sods, a fresh loaf, clean water in a jug, clean foot-water, and a new blanket, and make him swear by the blessed Saint Benignus, and by the sun and moon, that no bond be lacking, not to tell his rhymes to the children in the street, and the girls spinning at the doors, and the robbers upon Ben Bulben?"

"Neither our Blessed Patron nor the sun and moon would avail at all," said the abbot; "for tomorrow or the next day the mood to curse would come upon him, or a pride in those rhymes would move him, and he would teach his lines to the children, and the girls, and the robbers. Or else he would tell another of his craft how he fared in the guest-house, and he in his turn would begin to curse, and my name would wither. For learn there is no steadfastness of purpose upon the roads, but only under roofs and between four walls. Therefore I bid you go and awaken Brother Kevin, Brother Dove, Brother Little Wolf, Brother Bald Patrick, Brother Bald Brandon, Brother James, and Brother Peter. And they shall take the man, and bind him with ropes, and dip him in the river that he shall cease to sing. And in the morning, lest this but make him curse the louder, we will crucify him."

"The crosses are all full," said the lay brother.

"Then we must make another cross. If we do not make an end to him another will, for who can eat and sleep in peace while men like him are going about the world? We would stand shamed indeed before blessed Saint Benignus, and sour would be his face when he comes to judge us at the Last Day, were we to spare an enemy of his when we had him under our thumb! Brother, there is not one of these bards and gleemen who has not scattered his bastards through the five kingdoms, and if they slit a purse or a throat, and it is always one or the other, it never comes into their heads to confess and do penance. Can you name one that is not heathen at heart, always longing after the Son of Lir, and Aengus, and Bridget, and the Dagda, and Dana the Mother, and all the false gods of the old days; always making poems in praise of those kings and queens of the demons, Finvaragh, whose home is under Cruachmaa, and Red Aodh of Cnocna-Sidhe, and Cleena of the Wave, and Aoibhell of the Grey Rock, and him they call Donn of the Vats of the Sea; and railing against God and Christ and the blessed Saints." While he was speaking he crossed himself, and when he had finished he drew the nightcap over his ears to shut out the noise, and closed his eyes and composed himself to sleep.

The lay brother found Brother Kevin, Brother Dove, Brother Little Wolf, Brother Bald Patrick, Brother Bald Brandon, Brother James, and Brother Peter sitting up in bed, and he made them get up. Then they bound Cumhal, and they dragged him to the river, and they dipped him in it at the place which was afterwards called Buckley's Ford.

"Gleeman," said the lay brother, as they led him back to the guest-house, "why do you ever use the wit which God has given you to make blasphemous and immoral tales and verses? For such is the way of your craft. I have, indeed. many such tales and verses well-nigh by rote, and so I know that I speak true! And why do you praise with rhyme those demons, Finvaragh, Red Aodh, Cleena, Aoibhell and Donn? I, too, am a man of great wit and learning, but I ever glorify our gracious abbot, and Benignus our Patron, and the princes of the province. My soul is decent and orderly, but yours is like the wind among the salley gardens. I said what I could for you, being also a man of many thoughts, but who could help such a one as you?"

"Friend," answered the gleeman, "my soul is indeed like the wind, and it blows me to and fro, and up and down, and puts many things into my mind and out of my mind, and therefore am I called the Swift Wild Horse." And he spoke no more that night, for his teeth were chattering with the cold.

The abbot and the monks came to him in the morning, and

bade him get ready to be crucified, and led him out of the guest-house. And while he still stood upon the step, a flock of great grass-barnacles passed high above him with clanking cries. He lifted his arms to them and said, "O great grass-barnacles, tarry a little, and mayhap my soul will tread with you to the waste places of the shore and to the ungovernable sea!" At the gate a crowd of beggars gathered about them. being come there to beg from any traveler or pilgrim who might have spent the night in the guest-house. The abbot and the monks led the gleeman to a place in the woods at some distance, where many straight young trees were growing, and they made him cut one down and fashion it to the right length, while the beggars stood round them in a ring, talking and gesticulating. The abbot then bade him cut off another and shorter piece of wood, and nail it upon the first. So there was his cross for him, and they put it upon his shoulder, for his crucifixion was to be on the top of the hill where the others were. A half-mile on the way he asked them to stop and see him juggle for them; for he knew, he said, all the tricks of Aengus the Sublehearted. The old monks were for pressing on, but the young monks would see him: so he did many wonders for them, even to the drawing of live frogs out of his ears. But after a while he turned on him, and said his tricks were dull and a little unholy, and set the cross on his shoulders again. Another half-mile on the way and he asked them to stop and hear him jest for them, for he knew, he said, all the jests of Conan the Bald, upon whose back a sheep's wool grew. And the young monks, when they had heard his merry tales, again bade him take up his cross, for it ill became them to listen to such follies. Another half-mile on the way, he asked them to stop and hear him sing the story of White-breasted Deirdre, and how she endured many sorrows, and how the sons of Usna died to serve her. And the young monks were mad to hear him, but when he had ended they grew angry, and beat him for waking forgotten longings in their hearts. So they set the cross upon his back and hurried him to the hill.

When he was come to the top, they took the cross from him, and began to dig a hole for it to stand in, while the beggars gathered round, and talked among themselves. "I ask a favor before I die," says Cumhal.

"We will grant you no more delays," says the abbot.

"I ask no more delays, for I have drawn the sword, and told the truth, and lived my dream. and am content."

"Would you, then, confess?"

"By sun and moon, not I; I ask but to be let eat the food I carry in my wallet. I carry food in my wallet whenever I go upon a journey, but I do not taste of it unless I am well-nigh starved. I have not eaten now these two days."

"You may eat, then," says the abbot, and he turned to help the monks dig the hole.

The gleeman took a loaf and some strips of cold fried bacon out of his wallet and laid them upon the ground. "I will give a tithe to the poor," says he, and he cut a tenth part from the loaf and the bacon. "Who among you is the poorest?" And thereupon was a great clamor, for the beggars began the history of their sorrows and their poverty, and their yellow faces swayed like Gara Lough when the floods have filled it with water from the bogs.

He listened for a little, and, says he, "I am myself the poorest, for I have traveled the bare road, and by the edges of the sea; and the tattered doublet of particolored cloth upon my back and the torn pointed shoes upon my feet have ever irked me, because of the towered city full of noble raiment which was in my heart. And I have been the more alone upon the roads and by the sea because I heard in my heart the rustling of the rose-bordered dress of her who is more subtle than Aengus the Subtlehearted, and more full of the beauty of laughter than Conan the Bald, and more full of wisdom of tears than White-breasted Deirdre, and more lovely than a bursting dawn to them that are lost in the darkness. Therefore, I award the tithe to myself; but yet, because I am done with all things, I give it unto you."

So he flung the bread and the strips of bacon among the beggars, and they fought with many cries until the last scrap was eaten. But meanwhile the monks nailed the gleeman to his cross, and set it upright in the hole, and shoveled the earth into the hole and trampled it level and hard. So then they went away, but the beggars stayed on, sitting round the cross. But when the sun was sinking, they also got up to go, for the air was getting chilly. And as soon as they had gone a little way, the wolves, who had been showing themselves on the edge of a neighboring coppice, came nearer, and the birds wheeled closer and closer. "Stay, outcasts, yet a little while," the crucified one called in a weak voice to the beggars, "and keep the beasts and the birds from me." But the beggars were angry because he had called them outcasts, so they threw stones and mud at him, and one that had a child held it up before his eyes and said that he was its father, and cursed him, and thereupon they left him. Then the wolves gathered at the foot of the cross, and the birds flew lower and lower. And presently the birds lighted all at once upon his head and arms and shoulders, and began to peck at him, and the wolves began to eat his feet."Outcasts," he moaned, "have you all turned against the outcast?"

The Witch Hare
Dublin University Magazine (1839)

ABOUT the commencement of the last century there lived in the vicinity of the once famous village of Aghavoe a wealthy farmer, named Bryan Costigan. This man kept an extensive dairy and a great many milch cows and every year made considerable sums by the sale of milk and butter. The luxuriance of the pasture lands in this neighborhood has always been proverbial; and, consequently, Bryan's cows were the finest and most productive in the country, and his milk and butter the richest and sweetest, and brought the highest price at every market at which he ordered these articles for sale.

Things continued to go on thus prosperously with Bryan Costigan, when, one season all at once, he found his cattle declining in appearance, and his dairy almost entirely profitless. Bryan, at first, attributed this change to the weather, or some such cause, but soon found or fancied reasons to assign it to a far different source. The cows, without any visible disorder, daily declined, and were scarcely able to crawl about on their pasture; many of them, instead of milk, gave nothing but blood; and the scanty quantity of milk which some of them continued to supply was so bitter that even the pigs would not drink it; while the butter which it produced was of such a bad quality, and stunk so horribly, that the very dogs would not eat it. Bryan applied for remedies to all the quacks and "fairy-women" in the country—but in vain. Many of the imposters declared that the mysterious malady in his cattle went beyond *their* skill; while others, although they found no difficulty in tracing it to superhuman agency, declared that they had no control in the matter, as the charm under the influence of which his property was made away with, was too powerful to be dissolved by anything less than the special interposition of Divine Providence. The poor farmer became almost distracted; he saw ruin staring him in the face; yet what was he to do? Sell his cattle and purchase others! No; that was out of the question, as they looked so miserable and emaciated that no one would even take them as a present, while it was also impossible to sell to a butcher, as the flesh of one which he killed for his own family was as black as a coal, and stunk like any putrid carrion.

The unfortunate man was thus completely bewildered. He knew not what to do; he became moody and stupid; his sleep forsook him by night, and all day he wandered about the fields, among his "fairy-stricken" cattle like a maniac.

Affairs continued in this plight, when one very sultry evening in the latter days of July, Bryan Costigan's wife was sitting at her own door, spinning at her wheel, in a very gloomy and agitated state of mind. Happening to look down the narrow green lane which led from the high road to her cabin, she espied a little old woman barefoot, and enveloped in an old scarlet cloak, approaching slowly, with the aid of a crutch which she carried in one hand, and a cane or walking-stick in the other. The farmer's wife felt glad at seeing the odd-looking stranger; she smiled, and yet she knew not why, as she neared the house. A vague and indefinable feeling of pleasure crowded on her imagination; and, as the old woman gained the threshold, she bade her "welcome" with a warmth which plainly told that her lips gave utterance but to the genuine feelings of her heart.

"God bless this good house and all belonging to it," said the stranger as she entered.

"God save you kindly, and you are welcome, whoever you are," replied Mrs. Costigan.

"Hem, I thought so," said the old woman with a significant grin. "I thought so, or I wouldn't trouble you."

The farmer's wife ran, and placed a chair near the fire for the stranger, but she refused, and sat on the ground near where Mrs. Costigan had been spinning. Mrs. Costigan had now time to survey the old hag's person minutely. She appeared of great age; her countenance was extremely ugly and repulsive; her skin was rough and deeply embrowned as if from long exposure to the effects of some tropical climate; her forehead was low, narrow, and indented with a thousand wrinkles; her long gray hair fell in matted elf-locks from beneath a white linen skull cap; her eyes were bleared, bloodsotten, and obliquely set in their sockets, and her voice was croaking, tremulous, and, at times, partially inarticulate. As she squatted on the floor, she looked round the house with an inquisitive gaze; she peered pryingly from corner to corner, with an earnestness of look, as if she had the faculty, like the Argonaut of old, to see through the very depths of the earth, while Mrs. C. kept watching her motions with mingled feelings of curiosity, awe, and pleasure.

"Mrs.," said the old woman, at length breaking silence, "I am dry with the heat of the day; can you give me a drink?"

"Alas!" replied the farmer's wife, "I have no drink to offer you except water, else you would have no occasion to ask me for it."

"Are you not the owner of the cattle I see yonder?" said the old hag, with a tone of voice and manner of gesticulation which plainly indicated her foreknowledge of the fact.

Mrs. Costigan replied in the affirmative, and briefly related to her every circumstance connected with the affair, while the old woman still remained silent, but shook her gray head repeatedly and still continued gazing round the house with an air of importance and self-sufficiency.

When Mrs. C. had ended, the old hag remained a while as if in a deep reverie; at length she said:

"Have you any of the milk in the house?"

"I have," replied the other.

"Show me some of it."

She filled a jug from a vessel and handed it to the old sybil, who smelled it, then tasted it, and spat out what she had taken on the floor.

"Where is your husband?" she asked.

"Out in the fields," was the reply.

"I must see him."

A messenger was despatched for Bryan, who shortly after made his appearance.

"Neighbor," said the stranger, "your wife informs me that your cattle are going against you this season."

"She informs you right," said Bryan.

"And why have you not sought a cure?"

"A cure!" re-echoed the man; "why, woman, I have sought cures until I was heartbroken, and all in vain; they get worse every day."

"What will you give me if I cure them for you?"

"Anything in our power," replied Bryan and his wife, both speaking joyfully, and with a breath.

"All I will ask from you is a silver sixpence, and that you will do everything which I will bid you," said she.

The farmer and his wife seemed astonished at the moderation of her demand. They offered her a large sum of money.

"No," said she, "I don't want your money; I am no cheat, and I would not even take sixpence, but that I can do nothing till I handle some of your silver."

The sixpence was immediately given her, and the most implicit obedience promised to her injunctions by both Bryan and his wife, who already began to regard the old beldame as their tutelary angel.

The hag pulled off a black silk ribbon or filet which encircled her head inside her cap, and gave it to Bryan, saying:

"Go, now, and the first cow you touch with this ribbon, turn her into the yard, but be sure you don't touch the second, nor speak a word until you return; be also careful not to let the ribbon touch the ground, for, if you do, all is over."

Bryan took the talismanic ribbon and soon returned, driving a red cow before him.

The old hag went out, and, approaching the cow, commenced pulling hairs out of her tail, at the same time singing some verse in the Irish language, in a low, wild, and unconnected strain. The cow appeared restive and uneasy, but the old witch still continued her mysterious chant until she had the ninth hair extracted. She then ordered the cow to be drove back to her pasture, and again entered the house.

"Go, now," said she to the woman, "and bring me some milk from every cow in your possession."

She went, and soon returned with a large pail filled with a frightful-looking mixture of milk, blood, and corrupt matter. The old woman got it into the churn, and made preparations for churning.

"Now," she said, "you both must churn, make fast the door and windows, and let there be no light but from the fire; do not open your lips until I desire you, and by observing my direction, I make no doubt but, ere the sun goes down, we will find out the infernal villain who is robbing you."

Bryan secured the doors and windows, and commenced churning. The old sorceress sat down by a blazing fire which had been specially lighted for the occasion, and commenced singing the same wild song which she had sung at the pulling of the cow hairs, and after a little time she cast one of the nine hairs into the fire, still singing her mysterious strain, and watching, with intense interest, the witching process.

A loud cry, as if from a female in distress, was now heard approaching the house; the old witch discontinued her incantations, and listened attentively. The crying voice approached the door.

"Open the door quickly," shouted the charmer.

Bryan unbarred the door, and all three rushed out the yard, when they heard the same cry down the *boreheen*, but could see nothing.

"It is all over," shouted the old witch; "something has gone amiss, and our charm for the present is ineffectual."

They now turned back quite crestfallen, when, as they were entering the door, the sybil cast her eyes downward, and perceiving a piece of horseshoe nailed on the threshold, she vociferated:

"Here I have it; no wonder our charm was abortive. The person that was crying abroad is the villain who has your cattle bewitched; I brought her to the house, but she was not able to come to the door on account of that horseshoe. Remove it instantly, and we will try our luck again."

Bryan removed the horseshoe from the doorway, and by the hag's directions placed it on the floor under the churn, having previously reddened it in the fire.

They again resumed their manual operations. Bryan and his wife began to churn, and the witch again to sing her strange verses, and casting her cow hairs into the fire until she had them all nearly exhausted. Her countenance now began to exhibit evident traces of vexation and disappoitment. She got quite pale, her teeth gnashed, her hand trembled, and as she cast the ninth and last hair into the fire, her person exhibited more the appearance of a female demon than of a human being.

Once more the cry was heard, and an aged red-haired woman was seen approaching the house quickly.

"Ho, ho!" roared the sorceress, "I knew it would be so; my charm has succeeded; my expectations are realized, and here she comes, the villain who has destroyed you."

"What are we to do now?" asked Bryan.

"Say nothing to her," said the hag; "give her whatever she demands, and leave the rest to me."

The woman advanced screeching vehemently, and Bryan went out to meet her. She was a neighbor, and she said that one of her best cows was drowning in a pool of water—that there was no one at home but herself, and she implored Bryan to go rescue the cow from destruction.

Bryan accompanied her without hesitation; and having rescued the cow from her perilous situation, was back again in a quarter of an hour.

It was now sunset, and Mrs. Costigan set about preparing supper.

During supper they reverted to the singular transactions of the day. The old witch uttered many a fiendish laugh at the success of her incantations, and inquired who was the woman whom they had so curiously discovered.

Bryan satisfied her in every particular. She was the wife of a neighboring farmer; her name was Rachel Higgins; and she had been long suspected to be on familiar terms with the spirit of darkness. She had five or six cows; but it was observed by her sapient neighbors that she sold more butter every year than other farmers' wives who had twenty. Bryan had, from the commencement of the decline in his cattle, suspected her for being the aggressor, but as he had no proof, he held his peace.

"Well," said the old beldame, with a grim smile, "it is not enough that we have merely discovered the robber; all is in vain if we do not take steps to punish her for the past, as well as to prevent her inroads for the future."

"And how will that be done?" said Bryan.

"I will tell you; as soon as the hour of twelve o'clock arrives tonight, do you go to the pasture, and take a couple of swift-running dogs with you; conceal yourself in some place convenient to the cattle; watch them carefully; and if you see anything, whether man or beast, approach the cows, set on the dogs, and if possible make them draw the blood of the intruder; then *all* will be accomplished. If nothing approaches before sunrise, you may return, and we will try something else."

Convenient there lived the cowherd of a neighboring squire. He was a hardy, courageous young man, and always kept a pair of very ferocious bulldogs. To him Bryan applied for assistance, and he cheerfully agreed to accompany him, and, moreover, proposed to fetch a couple of his master's best grayhounds, as his own dogs, although extremely fierce and bloodthirsty, could not be relied on for swiftness. He promised Bryan to be with him before twelve o'clock, and they parted.

Bryan did not seek sleep that night; he sat up anxiously awaiting the midnight hour. It arrived at last, and his friend, the herdsman, true to his promise, came at the time appointed. After some further admonitions from the *Collough*, they departed. Having arrived at the field, they consulted as to the best position they could choose for concealment. At last they pitched on a small brake of fern, situated at the extremity of the field, adjacent to the boundary ditch, which was thickly studded with large, old white-thorn bushes. Here they crouched themselves, and made the dogs, four in number, lie down beside them, eagerly expecting the appearance of their as yet unknown and mysterious visitor.

Here Bryan and his comrade continued a considerable time in nervous anxiety, still nothing approached, and it became manifest that morning was at hand; they were beginning to grow impatient, and were talking of returning home, when on a sudden they heard a rushing sound behind them, as if proceeding from something endeavoring to force a passage through the thick hedge in their rear. They looked in that direction, and judge of their astonishment, when they perceived a large hare in the act of springing from the ditch, and leaping on the ground quite near them. They were now convinced that this was the object which they had so impatiently expected, and they were resolved to watch her motions narrowly.

After arriving to the ground, she remained motionless for a few moments, looking around her sharply. She then began to skip and jump in a playful manner, now advancing at a smart pace toward the cows and again retreating precipitately, but still drawing nearer and nearer at each sally. At length she advanced up to the next cow, and sucked her for a moment; then on to the next, and so respectively to every cow on the field—the cows all the time lowing loudly, and appearing extremely frightened and agitated. Bryan, from the moment the hare commenced sucking the first, was with difficulty restrained from attacking her; but his more sagacious companion suggested to him that it was better to wait until she would have done, as she would then be much heavier, and more unable to effect her escape than at present. And so the issue proved; for being now done sucking them all, her belly appeared enormously distended, and she made her exit slowly and apparently with difficulty. She advanced toward the hedge where she had entered, and as she arrived just at the clump of ferns where her foes were couched, they started up with a fierce yell, and hallooed the dogs upon her path.

The hare started off at a brisk pace, squirting up the milk she had sucked from her mouth and nostrils, and the dogs making after her rapidly. Rachel Higgins's cabin appeared, through the gray of the morning twilight, at a little distance; and it was evident that puss seemed bent on gaining it, although she made a considerable circuit through the fields in the rear. Bryan and his comrade, however, had their thoughts, and made toward the cabin by the shortest route, and had just arrived as the hare came up panting and almost exhausted, and the dogs at her very scut. She ran round the house, evidently confused and disappointed at the presence of the men, but at length made for the door. In the bottom of the door was a small, semi-circular aperture, resembling those cut in fowl-house doors for the ingress and egress of poultry. To gain this hole, puss now made a last and desperate effort, and had succeeded in forcing her head and shoulders through it, when the foremost of the dogs made a spring and seized her violently by the haunch. She uttered a loud and piercing scream, and struggled desperately to free herself from his grip, and at last succeeded, but not until she left a piece of her rump in his teeth. The men now burst open the door; a bright turf fire blazed on the hearth, and the whole floor was streaming with blood. No hare, however, could be found, and the men were more than ever convinced that it was old Rachel, who had, by the assistance of some demon, assumed the form of the hare, and they now determined to have her if she were over the earth. They entered the bedroom, and heard some smothered groaning, as if proceeding from someone in extreme agony. They went to the corner of the room from whence the moans proceeded, and there, beneath a bundle of freshly-cut rushes, found the form of Rachel Higgins, writhing in the most excruciating agony, and almost smothered in a pool of blood. The men were astounded; they addressed the wretched old woman, but she either could not, or would not, answer them. Her wound still bled copiously; her tortures appeared to increase, and it was evident that she was dying. The aroused family thronged around her with cries and lamentations; she did not seem to heed them, she got worse and worse, and her piercing yells fell awfully on the ears of the bystanders. At length she expired, and her corpse exhibited a most appalling spectacle, even before the spirit had well departed.

Bryan and his friend returned home. The old hag had been previously aware of the fate of Rachel Higgins, but it was not known by what means she acquired her supernatural knowledge. She was delighted at the issue of her mysterious operations. Bryan pressed her much to accept of some remuneration for her services, but she utterly rejected such proposals. She remained a few days at his house, and at length took her leave and departed, no one knew whither.

Old Rachel's remains were interred that night in the neighboring churchyard. Her fate soon became generally known, and her family, ashamed to remain in their native village, disposed of their property, and quitted the country forever. The story, however, is still fresh in the memory of the surrounding villagers; and often, it is said, amid the gray haze of a summer twilight, may the ghost of Rachel Higgins, in the form of a hare, be seen scudding over her favorite and well-remembered haunts.

Wicked Captain Walshawe
Joseph Sheridan Le Fanu

A VERY ODD thing happened to my uncle, Mr. Watson, of Haddlestone; and to enable you to understand it, I must begin at the beginning.

In the year 1822, Mr. James Walshawe, more commonly known as Captain Walshawe, died at the age of eighty-one years. The Captain in his early days, and so long as health and strength permitted, was a scamp of the active, intriguing sort; and spent his days and nights in sowing wild oats, of which he seemed to have an inexhaustible stock.

Captain Walshawe was very well known in the neighborhood of Wauling, and very generally avoided there. He had quitted the service in 1766, at the age of twenty-five, immediately previous to which period his debts had grown so troublesome that he was induced to extricate himself by running away with and marrying an heiress. He was quartered in Ireland, at Clonmel, where was a nunnery, in which, as pensioner, resided Miss O'Neill, or as she was called in the country, Peg O'Neill, the heiress.

Her situation was the only ingredient of romance in the affair, for the young lady was decidedly plain, though good-humored looking, with that style of features which is termed potato; and in figure she was a little too plump, and rather short. But she was impressible; and the handsome young English lieutenant was too much for her monastic tendencies, and she eloped. They took up their abode at Wauling, in Lancashire.

Here the Captain amused himself after his fashion, sometimes running up, of course, on business to London. He spent her income, frightened her out of her wits, with oath and threats, and broke her heart.

Latterly she shut herself up pretty nearly altogether in her room. She had an old, rather grim, Irish servant-woman in attendance, Molly Doyle. This domestic was lean and religious, and the Captain knew instinctively she hated him; and he hated her in return, and often threatened to put her out of the house, and sometimes even to kick her out of the window.

Years passed away, and old Molly Doyle remained still in her original position. Perhaps he thought that there must be somebody there, and that she was not, after all, very likely to change for the better.

He tolerated another intrusion, too and thought himself a paragon of patience and easy good-nature for so doing. A Roman Catholic clergyman, in long black frock, with a low standing collar, and a little white muslin fillet round his neck––tall, sallow, with blue chin, and dark steady eyes—used to glide up and down the stairs, and through the passages; and the Captain sometimes met him in one place and sometimes in another. But by a caprice incident to such tempers he treated this cleric exceptionally, and even with a surly sort of courtesy, though he grumbled about his visits behind his back.

Well, the time came at last, when poor Peg O'Neill—in an evil hour Mrs. James Walshawe—must cry, and quake, and pray her last. The doctor came from Penlynden, and was just as vague as usual, but more gloomy, and for about a week came and went oftener. The cleric in the long black frock was also daily there. And at last came that last sacrament in the gates of death, when the sinner is traversing those dread steps and never can be retraced.

The Captain drank a great deal of brandy and water that night, and called in Farmer Dobbs, for want of better company, to drink with him; and told him all his grievances, and how happy he and the poor lady upstairs might have been had it not been for liars, and pick-thanks, and tale-bearers. and the like, who came between them—meaning Molly Doyle—whom, as he waxed eloquent over his liquor, he came to curse and rail at by name, with more than his accustomed freedom. And he described his own natural character and amiability in such moving terms that he wept maudlin tears of sensibility over his theme; and when Dobbs was gone, drank some more grog, and took to railing and cursing again by himself; and then mounted the stairs unsteadily to see "what the devil Doyle and the other old witches were about in poor Peg's room."

When he pushed open the door, he found some half-dozen crones, chiefly Irish, from the neighboring town of Hackleton, sitting over tea and snuff, etc., with candles lighted round the corpse, which was arrayed in a strangely cut robe of brown serge. She had secretly belonged to some order—I think the Carmelite, but 1 am not certain—and wore the habit in her coffin.

"What the d _____ are you doing with my wife?" cried the Captain, rather thickly. "How dare you dress her up in this—trumpery, you—you cheating old witch; and what's that candle doing in her hand?"

I think he was a little startled, for the spectacle was grisly enough. The dead lady was arrayed in this strange brown robe, and in her rigid fingers, as in a socket, with the large wooden beads and cross wound round it, burned a wax candle, shedding its white light over the sharp features of the corpse. Molly Doyle was not to be put down by the Captain, whom she hated, and accordingly, in her phrase, "he got as good as he gave." And the Captain's wrath waxed fiercer, and he plucked the wax taper from the dead hand, and was on the point of flinging it at the old serving-woman's head.

"The holy candle, you sinner!" cried she.

"I've a mind to make you eat it, you beast," cried the Captain.

But I think he had not known before what it was, for he subsided, a little sulkily, and he stuffed his hand with the candle (quite extinct by this time) into his pocket, and said he:

"You know devilish well you had no business going on with y-y-your d—— witchcraft about my poor wife, without my leave—you do—and you'll please to take off that d—— brown pinafore, and get her decently into her coffin, and I'll pitch your devil's waxlight into the sink."

And the Captain stalked out of the room.

"An' now her poor sowl's in prison, you wretch, be the mains o' ye; an' may your own be shut into the wick o' that same candle, till it's burned out, ye savage."

"I'd have you ducked for a witch, for twopence," roared the Captain up the staircase, with his hand on the banisters, standing on the lobby. But the door of the chamber of death clapped angrily, and he went down to the parlor, where he examined the holy candle for a while with a tipsy gravity, and then with something of that reverential feeling for the symbolic, which is not uncommon in rakes and scamps, he thoughtfully locked it up in a press, where were accumulated all sorts of obsolete rubbish—soiled packs of cards, disused tobacco-pipes, broken powder-flasks, his military sword, and a dusty bundle of the *Flash Songster* and other questionable literature.

Captain Walshawe reigned alone for many years at Wauling. He was too shrewd and too experienced by this time to run violently down the steep hill that leads to ruin. Forty years acted forcibly upon the gay Captain Walshawe. Gout supervened, and was no more conducive to temper than to enjoyment, and made his elegant hands lumpy at all the small joints, and turned them slowly into crippled claws. He grew stout when his exercise was interfered with, and ultimately almost corpulent. He suffered from what Mr. Holloway calls "bad legs," and was wheeled about in a great leathernback chair, and his infirmities went on accumulating with his years.

I am sorry to say, I never heard that he repented, or turned his thoughts seriously to the future. On the contrary, his talk grew fouler, and his fun ran upon his favorite sins, and his temper waxed more truculent. But he did not sink into dotage. Considering his bodily infirmities, his energies and his malignities, which were many and active, were marvelously little abated by time.

It was a peculiarity of Captain Walshawe, that he, by this time, hated nearly everybody. My uncle, Mr. Watson, of Haddlestone, was cousin to the Captain, and his heir at law. But my uncle had lent him money on mortgage of his estates and there had been a treaty to sell, and terms and a price were agreed upon, in "articles" which the lawyers said were still in force.

I think the ill-conditioned Captain bore him a grudge for being richer that he, and would have liked to do him an ill turn. But it did not lie in his way; at least while he was living.

My Uncle Watson was a Methodist, and what they call a "class leader," and, on the whole, a very good man. He was now near fifty—grave, as beseemed his profession—somewhat dry and a little severe, perhaps—but a just man.

A letter from the Penlynden doctor reached him at Haddlestone, announcing the death of the wicked old Captain; and suggesting his attendance at the funeral and the expediency of his being on the spot to look after things at Wauling. The reasonableness of this striking my good uncle, he made his journey to the old house in Lancashire incontinently, and reached it in time for the funeral.

The day turning out awfully rainy and tempestuous, my uncle persuaded the doctor and the attorney to remain for the night at Wauling.

There was no will—the attorney was sure of that—for the Captain's enmities were perpetually shifting, and he could never quite make up his mind as to how best to give effect to a malignity whose direction was being constantly modified.

Search being made, no will was found. The papers, indeed, were all right, with one important exception: the leases were nowhere to be seen. My uncle searched strenuously. The attorney was at his elbow, and the doctor helped with a suggestion now and then. The old serving man seemed an honest, deaf creature, and really knew nothing.

My uncle Watson was very much perturbed. He fancied—but this possibly was only fancy—that he had detected for a moment a queer look in the attorney's face, and from that instant it became fixed in his mind that he knew all about the leases. Mr. Watson expounded that evening in the parlor to the doctor, the attorney and the deaf servant.

Ananias and Sapphira figured in the foreground, and the awful nature of fraud and theft, or tampering in any wise with the plain rule of honesty in matters pertaining to estates, etc., were pointedly dwelt upon; and then came a long and strenuous prayer, in which he entreated with fervor and aplomb that the hard heart of the sinner who had abstracted the leases might be softened or broken in such a way as to lead to their restitution; or that if he continued reserved and contumacious, it might at least be the will of Heaven to bring him to public justice and the documents to light. The fact is, that he was praying all this time at the attorney.

When these religious exercises were over, the visitors retired to their rooms, and my Uncle Watson wrote two or three pressing letters by the fire. When his task was done, it had grown late; the candles were flaring in their sockets, and all in bed, and I suppose, asleep, but he.

The fire was nearly out, he chilly, and the flame of the candles throbbing strangely in their sockets shed alternate glare and shadow round the old wainscoted room and its quaint furniture. Outside were the wild thunder and piping of the storm, and the rattling of distant windows sounded through the passages, and down the stairs, like angry people astir in the house.

My Uncle Watson belonged to a sect who by no means reject the supernatural, and whose founder, on the contrary, has sanctioned ghosts in the most emphatic way. He was glad, therefore, to remember, that in prosecuting his search that day, he had seen some six inches of wax candle in the press in the parlor; for he had no fancy to be overtaken by darkness in his present situation.

He had no time to lose; and taking the bunch of keys of which he was now master—he soon fitted the lock and secured the candle—a treasure in his circumstances; and lighting it, he stuffed it into the socket of one of the expiring candles, and extinguishing the other, he looked round the room in the steady light, reassured. At the same moment an unusually violent gust of the storm blew a handful of gravel against the parlor window with a sharp rattle that startled him in the midst of the roar and hubbub; and the fiame of the candle itself was agitated by the air.

My uncle walked up to bed, guarding his candle with his hand, for the lobby windows were rattling furiously and he disliked the idea of being left in the dark more than ever.

His bedroom was comfortable, though old-fashioned. He shut and bolted the door. There was a tall looking-glass opposite the foot of his four-poster on the dressing-table between the windows. He tried to make the curtains meet, but they would not draw.

He turned the face of the mirror away, therefore, so that its back was presented to the bed, pulled the curtains together, and placed a chair against them to prevent their falling open again. There was a good fire, and a reinforcement of round coal and wood inside the fender. So he piled it up to ensure a cheerful blaze through the night, and placing a little black mahogany table, with the legs of a Satyr, beside the bed, and his candle upon it, he got between the sheets, and laid his red nightcapped head upon the pillow, and disposed himself to sleep.

The first thing that made him uncomfortable was a sound at the foot of his bed, quite distinct in a momentary lull of the storm. It was only the gentle rustle and rush of the curtains which fell open again; and as his eyes opened, he saw them resuming their prependicular dependence, and sat up in his bed almost expecting to see something uncanny in the aperture.

There was nothing, however, but the dressing-table and other dark furniture, and the window-curtains faintly undulating in the violence of the storm. He did not care to get up, therefore—the fire being bright and cheery—to replace the curtains by a chair, in the position in which he had left them, anticipating possibly a new recurrence of the relapse which had startled him from his incipient doze.

So he got to sleep in a little while again, but he was disturbed by a sound, as he fancied, at the table on which stood the candle. He could not say what it was, only that he wakened with a start, and lying so in some amaze, he did distinctly hear a sound which startled him a good deal, though there was nothing necessarily supernatural in it.

He described it as resembling what would occur if you fancied a thinnish table-leaf, with a convex warp in it, depressed the reverse way, and suddenly with a string recovering its natural convexity. It was a loud, sudden thump, which made the heavy candlestick jump, and there was an end except that my uncle did not get again into a doze for ten minutes at least.

The next time he awoke it was in that odd, serene way that sometimes occurs. We open our eyes, we know not why, quite placidly, and are on the instant wide awake. He had had a nap of some duration this time, for his candle-flame was fluttering and flaring *in articulo*, in the silver socket. But the fire was still bright and cheery, so he popped the extinguisher on the socket, and almost at the same time there came a tap at his door, and a sort of crescendo "hush-sh-sh!" Once more my uncle was sitting up, scared and perturbed in his bed.

He recollected, however, that he had bolted his door; and such inveterate materialists are we in the midst of our spiritualism, that this reassured him, and he breathed a deep sigh, and began to grow tranquil. But after a rest of a minute of two, there came a louder and sharper knock at his door; so that instinctively he called out: "Who's there?" in a loud, stern key. There was no sort of response, however.

The nervous effect of the start subsided; and after a while he lay down with his back turned towards that side of the bed at which was the door, and his face towards the table on which stood the massive old candlestick, capped with its extinguisher, and in that position he closed his eyes. But sleep would not revisit them. All blinds of queer fancies began to trouble him— some of them I remember.

He felt the point of a finger, he averred, pressed most distinctly on the tip of his great toe, as if a living hand were between his sheets, and making a sort of signal of attention or silence. Then again he felt something as large as a rat make a sudden bounce in thc middle of his bolster, just under his head.

Then a voice said: "Oh!" very gently, close at the back of his head. All these things he felt certain of, and yet investigation led to nothing. He felt odd little cramps stealing now and then about him, and then, on a sudden, the middle finger of his right hand was plucked backwards, with a light playful jerk that frightened him awfully.

Meanwhile the storm kept singing and howling and ha-ha-hooing hoarsely among the limbs of the old trees and the chimney-pots; and my Uncle Watson, although he prayed and meditated as was his wont when he lay awake, felt his heart throb steadly, and sometimes thought he was beset with evil spirits, and at others that he was in the early stages of a fever.

He resolutely slept with his eyes closed however, and, like St. Paul's shipwrecked companions, wished for the day. At last another little doze seems to have stolen upon his senses, for he awoke quietly and completely as before—opening his eyes all at once, and seeing everything as if he had not slept for a moment.

The fire was still blazing redly—nothing uncertain in the

light—the massive silver candlestick, topped with its tall extinguisher, stood on the center of the black mahogany table as before; and, looking by what seemed a sort of accident to the apex of this, he beheld something which made him quite misdoubt the evidence of his eyes.

He saw the extinguisher lifted by a tiny hand from beneath, and a small human face, no bigger than a thumb-nail, with nicely proportioned features, peep from beneath it. In this Lilliputian countenance was such a ghastly consternation as horrified my uncle unspeakably.

Out came a little foot then and there, and a pair of wee legs, in short silk stockings and buckled shoes, then the rest of the figure; and, with the arms holding about the socket, the little legs stretched and stretched, hanging about the stem of the candlestick till the feet reached the base, and so down the Satyr-like leg of the table, till they reached the floor, extending elastically, and strangely enlarging in all proportions as they approached the ground, where the feet and buckles were those of a well-shaped, full-grown man, and the figure tapering upwards until it dwindled to its original fairy dimensions at the top, like an object seen in some strangely curved mirror.

Standing upon the floor he expanded, my amazed uncle could not tell how, into his proper proportions; and stood pretty nearly in profile at the bedside, a handsome and elegantly shaped young man, in a bygone military costume, with a small laced, three-cocked hat and plume on his head, but looking like a man going to be hanged—in unspeakable despair.

He stepped lightly to the hearth, and turned for a few seconds very dejectedly with his back towards the bed and the mantlepiece, and he saw the hilt of his rapier glittering in the firelight; and then walking across the room, he placed himself at the dressing table visible through the divided curtains at the foot of the bed. The fire was still blazing so brightly that my uncle saw him as distinctly as if half a dozen candles were burning.

The looking-glass was an old-fashioned piece of furniture, and had a drawer beneath it. My uncle had searched it carefully for the papers in the daytime; but the silent figure pulled the drawer quite out, pressed a spring at the side, disclosing a false receptacle behind it, and from this he drew a parcel of papers tied together with pink tape.

All this time my uncle was staring at him in a horrified state, neither winking or breathing and the apparition had not once given the smallest intimation of consciousness that a living person was in the same room. But now, for the first time, it turned its livid stare full upn my uncle with a hateful smile of significance, lifting up the little parcel of papers between his slender finger and thumb.

Then he made a long, cunning wink at him and seemed to blow out one of his checks in a burlesque grimace, which, but for the horrific circumstances, would have been ludicrous. My uncle could not tell whether this was really an intentional distortion or only one of those horrid ripples and deflections which were constantly disturbing the proportions of the figure, as if it were seen through some unequal and perverting medium.

The figure now approached the bed, seeming to grow exhausted and malignant as it did so. My uncle's terror nearly culminated at this point for he believed it was drawing near him with an evil purpose. But it was not so; for the soldier, over whom twenty years seemed to have passed in his brief transit to the dressing-table and back again, threw himself into a great high-backed armchair of stuffed leather at the far side of the fire, and placed his heels on the fender.

His feet and legs seemed indistinctly to swell, and swathings showed themselves round them, and they grew into something enormous, and the upper figure swayed and shaped itself into corresponding proportions, a great mass of corpulence, with a cadaverous and malignant face, and the furrows of a great old age, and colorless glassy eyes; and with these changes, which came indefinitely but rapidly as those of a sunset cloud, the fine regimentals faded away, and a loose, grey, woolen drapery, somehow, was there in its stead; and all seemed to be stained and rotten, for swarms of worms seemed creeping in and out, while the figure grew paler and paler, till my uncle, who liked his pipe, and employed the simile naturally, said the whole effigy grew to the color of tobacco ashes, and the clusters of worms into little wriggling knots of sparks such as we see running over the residium of a burnt sheet of paper.

And so with the strong draft caused by the fire, and the current of air from the window, which was rattling in the storm, the feet seemed to be drawn into the fireplace, and the whole figure, light as ashes, floated away with them and disappeared with a whisk up the capacious old chimney.

It seemed to my uncle that the fire suddenly darkened and the air grew icy cold, and there came an awful roar and riot of tempest, which shook the old house from top to base, and sounded like the yelling of a blood-thirsty mob on receiving a new and long-expected victim.

Good Uncle Watson used to say: "I have been in many situations of fear and danger in the course of my life, but never did I pray with so much agony before or since; for then, as now, it was clear beyond a cavil that I had actually beheld the phantom of an evil spirit."

Now there are two curious circumstances to be observed on this relation of my uncle's, who was, as I have said, a perfectly veracious man.

First: The wax candle which he took from the press in the

parlor and burnt at his bedside on that horrible night was unquestionably, according to the testimony of the old deaf servant, who had been fifty years at Wauling, that identical piece of "holy candle" which had stood in the fingers of the poor lady's corpse, and concerning which the old Irish crone, long since dead, had delivered the curious curse I have mentioned against the Captain.

Secondly: Behind the drawer under the looking-glass, he did actually discover a second but secret drawer, in which were concealed the identical papers which he had suspected the attomey of having made away with. There were circumstances too, afterward disclosed, which convinced my uncle that the old man had deposited them there preparatory to burning them, which he had nearly made up his mind to do.

Now, a very remarkable ingredient in this tale of my Uncle Watson was this, that so far as my father, who had never seen Captain Walshawe in the course of his life, could gather, the phantom had exhibited a horrible and grotesque, but unmistakable, resemblance to that defunct scamp in the various stages of his long life.

Wauling was sold in the year 1837, and the old house shortly after pulled down, and a new one built nearer to the river. I often wondered whether it was rumored to be haunted, and, if so, what stories were current about it. It was a commodious and staunch old house, and withall rather handsome; and its demolition was certainly suspicious.

Taming the Pooka
D.R. McAnally, Jr.

THE WEST AND northwest coast of Ireland shows many
remarkable geological formations, but, excepting the Giant's
Causeway, no more striking spectacle is presented than that to
the south of Galway Bay. From the sea, the mountains rise in
terraces like gigantic stairs, the layers of stone being apparently
harder and denser on the upper surfaces than beneath, so the
lower portion of each layer, disintegrating first, is washed away
by the rains and a clearly defined step is formed. These terraces
are generally about twenty feet high, and of a breadth, varying
with the situation and exposure, of from ten to fifty feet.

The highway from Ennis to Ballyvaughn, a fishing village
opposite Galway, winds, by a circuitous course, through these
freaks of nature, and, on the long descent from the high land to
the sea level, passes the most conspicuous of the neighboring
mountains, the Corkscrew Hill. The general shape of the

mountain is conical, the terraces composing it are of wonderful regularity from the base to the peak, and the strata being sharply upturned from the horizontal, the impression given is that of a broad road carved out of the sides of the mountain and winding by an easy ascent to the summit.

"'T is the Pooka's Path they call it," said the car-man. "Phat 's the Pooka? Well, that 's not aisy to say. It 's an avil sper't that does be always in mischief, but sure it niver does sarious harrum axceptin' to thim that desarves it, or thim that shpakes av it disrespictful. I never seen it, Glory be to God, but there 's thim that has, and be the same token, they do say that it looks like the finest black horse that iver wore shoes. But it is n't a horse at all at all, for no horse 'ud have eyes av fire, or be breathin' flames av blue wid a shmell o' sulfur, savin' yer presince, or a shnort like thunder, and no mortial horse 'ud take the lapes it does, or go as fur widout gettin' tired. Sure when it give Tim O'Bryan the ride it give him, it wint from Gort to Athlone wid wan jump, an' the next it tuk he was in Mullingyar, and the next was in Dublin, and back agin be way av Kilkenny an' Limerick, an' niver turned a hair. How far is that? Faith I dunno, but it 's a power av distance, an' clane acrost Ireland an' back. He knew it was the Pooka bekase it shpake to him like a Christian mortial, only it is n't agrayable in its language an' 'ull niver give ye a dacint word afther ye 're on its back, an' sometimes not before aither.

"Sure Dennis O'Rourke was afther comin' home wan night, it was only a boy I was, but I mind him tellin' the shtory, an' it was at a fair in Galway he 'd been. He 'd been havin' a sup, some says more, but whin he come to the rath, and jist beyant where the fairies dance and ferninst the wall where the polisman was shot last winther, he fell in the ditch, quite spint and tired complately. It was n't the length as much as the wideness av the road was in it, fur he was goin' from wan side to the other an' it was too much fur him entirely. So he laid shtill fur a bit and thin thried fur to get up, but his legs wor light and his head was heavy, an' whin he attimpted to get his feet an the road 't was his head that was an it, bekase his legs cud n't balance it. Well, he laid there and was bet entirely, an' while he was studyin' how he 'd raise, he heard the throttin' av a horse on the road. ''T is meself 'ull get the lift now,' says he, and laid waitin', and up comes the Pooka. Whin Dennis seen him, begob, he kivered his face wid his hands and turned on the breast av him, and roared wid fright like a bull.

"'Arrah thin, ye snakin' blaggârd,' says the Pooka, mighty short, 'lave aff yer bawlin' or I 'll kick ye to the ind av next

week,' says he to him.

"But Dennis was scairt, an' bellered louder than afore, so the Pooka, wid his hoof, give him crack on the back that knocked the wind out av him.

"'Will ye lave aff,' says the Pooka, 'or will I give ye another, ye roarin' dough-face?'

"Dennis left aff blubberin' so the Pooka got his timper back.

"'Shtand up, ye guzzlin' sarpint,' says the Pooka, 'I 'll give ye a ride.'

"'Plaze yer Honor,' says Dennis, 'I can't. Sure I 've not been afther drinkin' at all, but shmokin' too much an' atin', an' it 's sick I am, and not ontoxicated.'

"'Och, ye dhrunken buzzard,' says the Pooka, 'Don't offer fur to desave me,' liftin' up his hoof agin, an' givin' his tail a swish that sounded like the noise av a catheract, 'Did n't I thrack ye for two miles be yer breath,' says he, 'An' you shmellin' like a potheen fact'ry,' says he, 'an' the nose on yer face as red as a turkey-cock's. Get up, or I 'll lift ye,' says he, jumpin' up an' cracking his hind fut like he was doin' a jig.

"Dennis did his best, an' the Pooka helped him wid a grip o' the teeth on his collar.

"'Pick up yer caubeen,' says the Pooka, 'an' climb up. I 'll give ye such a ride as ye niver dhramed av.'

"'Ef it 's plazin' to yer Honor,' says Dennis, 'I 'd laver walk. Ridin' makes me dizzy,' says he.

"''T is not plazin',' says the Pooka, 'will ye get up or will I kick the shtuffin' out av yer cowardly carkidge,' says he, turnin' round an' flourishin' his heels in Dennis' face.

"Poor Dennis thried, but he cud n't, so the Pooka tuk him to the wall an' give him a lift an it, an' whin Dennis was mounted, an' had a tight howld on the mane, the first lep he give was down the rock there, a thousand feet into the field ye see, thin up agin, an' over the mountain, an' into the say, an' out agin, from the top av the waves to the top av the mountain, an' afther the poor soggarth av a ditcher was nigh onto dead, the Pooka come back here wid him an' dhropped him in the ditch where he found him, an' blowed in his face to put him to slape, so lavin' him. An' they found Dennis in the mornin' an' carried him home, no more cud he walk for a fortnight be razon av the wakeness av his bones fur the ride he 'd had.

"But sure, the Pooka 's a different baste entirely to phat he was afore King Bryan Boru tamed him. Niver heard av him?

Well, he was the king av Munster an' all Ireland an' tamed the
Pooka wanst fur all on the Corkschrew Hill ferninst ye.

"Ye see, in the owld days, the counthry was full av avil
sper'ts, an' fairies an' witches, an' divils entirely, and the harrum
they done was onsaycin', for they wore always comin' an' goin',
like Mulligan's blanket, an' widout so much as sayin', by yer
lave. The fairies 'ud be dancin' on the grass every night be the
light av the moon, an' stalin' away the childhre, an' many 's the
wan they tuk that niver come back. The owld rath on the hill
beyant was full av the dead, an' afther nightfall they 'd come
from their graves an' walk in a long line wan afther another to
the owld church in the valley where they 'd go in an' stay till
cock-crow, thin they 'd come out agin an' back to the rath. Sorra
a parish widout a witch, an' some nights they 'd have a great
enthertainmint on the Corkschrew Hill, an' you 'd see thim, wid
shnakes on their arrums an' necks an' ears, be way av jewels, an'
the eyes av dead men in their hair, comin' for miles an' miles,
some ridin' through the air on shticks an' bats an' owls, an' some
walkin', an' more on Pookas an' horses wid wings that 'ud come
up in line to the top av the hill, like the cabs at the dure o' the
theayter, an' lave thim there an' hurry aff to bring more.

"Sometimes the Owld Inimy, Satan himself, 'ud be there at
the enthertainmint, comin' an a monsthrous dhraggin, wid grane
shcales an' eyes like the lightnin' in the heavens, an' a roarin'
fiery mouth like a lime-kiln. It was the great day thin, for they
do say all the witches brought their rayports at thim saysons fur
to show him phat they done.

"Some 'ud tell how they shtopped the wather in a spring, an'
inconvanienced the nabers, more 'ud show how they dhried the
cow's milk, an' made her kick the pail, an' they 'd all laugh like
to shplit. Some had blighted the corn, more had brought the
rains on the harvest. Some towld how their enchantmints made
the childhre fall ill, some said how they set the thatch on fire,
more towld how they shtole the eggs, or spiled the crame in the

churn, or bewitched the butther so it 'ud n't come, or led the shape into the bog. But that was n't all.

"Wan 'ud have the head av a man murthered be her manes, an' wid it the hand av him hung fur the murther; wan 'ud bring the knife she 'd scuttled a boat wid an' pint in the say to where the corpses laid av the fishermen she 'd dhrownded; wan 'ud carry on her breast the child she 'd shtolen an' meant to bring up in avil, an' another wan 'ud show the little white body av a babby she 'd smothered in its slape. And the corpse-candles 'ud tell how they desaved the thraveller, bringin' him to the river, an' the avil sper'ts 'ud say how they dhrew him in an' down to the bottom in his sins an' thin to the pit wid him. An' owld Belzebub 'ud listen to all av thim, wid a rayporther, like thim that 's afther takin' down the spaches at a Lague meetin', be his side, a-writing phat they said, so as whin they come to be paid, it 'ud n't be forgotten.

"Thim wor the times fur the Pookas too, fur they had power over thim that wint forth afther night, axceptin' it was on an arriant av marcy they were. But sorra a sinner that had n't been to his juty reglar 'ud iver see the light av day agin afther meetin' a Pooka thin, for the baste 'ud aither kick him to shmithereens where he stud, or lift him on his back wid his teeth an' jump into the say wid him, thin dive, lavin' him to dhrownd, or shpring over a clift wid him an' tumble him to the bottom a bleedin' corpse. But was n't there the howls av joy whin a Pooka 'ud catch a sinner unbeknownst, an' fetch him on the Corkschrew wan o' the nights Satan was there. Och, God defind us, phat a sight it was. They made a ring wid the corpse-candles, while the witches tore him limb from limb, an' the fiends drunk his blood in red-hot iron noggins wid shrieks o' laughter to smother his schreams, an' the Pookas jumped on his body an' thrampled it into the ground, an' the timpest 'ud whishle a chune, an' the mountains about 'ud kape time, an' the Pookas, an' witches, an' sper'ts av avil, an' corpse-candles, an' bodies o' the dead, an' divils, 'ud all jig together round the rock where owld Belzebub 'ud set shmilin', as fur to say he 'd ax no betther divarshun. God's presince be wid us, it makes me crape to think av it.

"Well, as I was afther sayin', in the time av King Bryan, the Pookas done a dale o' harrum, but as thim that they murthered wor dhrunken bastes that wor in the shebeens in the day an' in the ditch be night, an' was n't missed whin the Pookas tuk them, the King paid no attintion, an' small blame to him that 's.

"But wan night, the queen's babby fell ill, an' the king says to his man, says he, 'Here, Riley, get you up an' on the white mare an' go fur the docther.'

"'Musha thin,' says Riley, an' the king's counthry house was in the break o' the hills, so Riley 'ud pass the rath an' the Corkschrew on the way afther the docther; 'Musha thin,' says he, aisey and on the quiet, 'it 's mesilf that does n't want that same job.'

"So he says to the king, 'Won't it do in the mornin'?'

"'It will not,' says the king to him. 'Up, ye lazy beggar, atin' me bread, an' the life lavin' me child.'

"So he wint, wid great shlowness, tuk the white mare, an' aff, an' that was the last seen o' him or the mare aither, fur the Pooka tuk 'em. Sorra a taste av a lie 's in it, for thim that said they seen him in Cork two days afther, thrading aff the white mare, was desaved be the sper'ts, that made it seem to be him whin it was n't that they 've a thrick o 'doin'.

"Well, the babby got well agin, bekase the docther did n't get there, so the king left botherin' afther it and begun to wondher about Riley an' the white mare, and sarched fur thim but did n't find thim. An' thin he knewn that they was gone entirely, bekase, ye see, the Pooka did n't lave as much as a hair o' the mare's tail.

"'Wurra thin,' says he, 'is it horses that the Pooka 'ull be stalin'? Bad cess to its impidince! This 'ull niver do. Sure we 'll be ruinated entirely,' says he.

"Mind ye now, it 's my consate from phat he said, that the king was n't consarned much about Riley, fur he knewn that he cud get more Irishmen whin he wanted thim, but phat he meant to say was that if the Pooka tuk to horse-stalin', he 'd be ruinated entirely, so he would, for where 'ud he get another white mare? So it was a mighty sarious question an' he retired widin himself in the coort wid a big book that he had that towld saycrets. He 'd a sight av larnin', had the king, aquel to a school-masther, an' a head that 'ud sarcumvint a fox.

"So he read an' read as fast as he cud, an' afther readin' widout shtoppin', barrin' fur the bit av' sup, fur siven days an' nights, he come out, an' whin they axed him cud he bate the Pooka now, he said niver a word, axceptin' a wink wid his eye, as fur to say he had him.

"So that day he was in the fields an' along be the hedges an' ditches from sunrise to sunset, collectin' the matarials av a dose dur the Pooka, but phat he got, faith, I dunno, no more does any wan, fur he never said, but kep the saycret to himself an' did n't say it aven to the quane, fur he knewn that saycrets run through a woman like wather in a ditch. But there was wan thing about it that he cud n't help tellin', fur he wanted it but cud n't get it widout help, an' that was three hairs from the Pooka's tail, axceptin' which the charm 'ud n't work. So he towld a man he had, he 'd give him no end av goold if he 'd get thim fur him, but the felly pulled aff his caubeen an' scrotched his head an' says, 'Faix, yer Honor, I dunno phat 'll be the good to me av the goold if the Pooka gets a crack at me carkidge wid his hind heels,' an' he wud n't undhertake the job on no wages, so the king begun to be afeared that his loaf was dough.

"But it happen'd av the Friday, this bein' av a Chewsday, that the Pooka caught a sailor that had n't been on land only long enough to get bilin' dhrunk, an' got him on his back, so jumped over the clift wid him lavin' him dead enough, I go bail. Whin they come to sarch the sailor to see phat he had in his pockets, they found three long hairs round the third button av his top-coat. So they tuk thim to the king tellin' him where they got thim, an' he was greatly rejiced, bekase now he belaved he had the Pooka sure enough, so he ended his inchantmint.

"But as the avenin' come, he riz a doubt in the mind av him thish-a-way. Ev the three hairs wor out av the Pooka's tail, the charm 'ud be good enough, but if they was n't, an' was from his mane inshtead, or from a horse inshtead av a Pooka, the charm 'ud n't work an' the Pooka 'ud get atop av him wid all the feet he had at wanst an' be the death av him immejitly. So this nate and outprobrious argymint shtruck the king wid great force an' fur a bit, he was onaisey. But wid a little sarcumvintion, he got round it, for he confist an' had absolution so as he 'd be ready, thin he towld wan av the sarvints to come in an' tell him afther supper, that there was a poor widdy in the boreen beyant the Corkschrew that wanted help that night, that it 'ud be an arriant av marcy he 'd be on, an' so safe agin the Pooka if the charm did n't howld.

"'Sure, phat 'll be the good o' that?' says the man, 'It 'ull be a lie, an' won't work.'

"'Do you be aisey in yer mind,' says the king to him agin, 'do as yer towld an' don't argy, for that 's a pint av mettyfisics,' says he, faix it was a dale av deep larnin' he had, 'that 's a pint av mettyfisics an' the more ye argy on thim subjics, the less ye know,' says he, an' it 's thrue fur him. 'Besides, aven if it 's a lie, it 'll desave the Pooka, that 's no mettyfishian, an' it 's my belafe that the end is good enough for the manes,' says he, a-thinking av the white mare.

"So, afther supper, as the king was settin' afore the fire, an' had the charm in his pocket, the sarvint come in and towld him about the widdy.

"'Begob,' says the king, like he was surprised, so as to desave the Pooka complately, 'Ev that 's thrue, I must go relave her at wanst.' So he riz an' put on sojer boots, wid shpurs on 'em a fut acrost, an' tuk a long whip in his hand, for fear, he said, the widdy 'ud have dogs, thin wint to his chist an' tuk his owld stockin' an' got a suv'rin out av it,—Och, 't was the shly wan he was, to do everything so well,—an' wint out wid his right fut first, an' the shpurs a-rattlin' as he walked.

"He come acrost the yard, an' up the hill beyant you an' round the corner, but seen nothin' at all. Thin up the fut path round the Corkscrew n' met niver a sowl but a dog that he cast a shtone at. But he did 't go out av the road to the widdy's, for he was afeared that if he met the Pooka an' he caught him in a lie, not bein' in the road to where he said he was goin', it 'ud be all over wid him. So he walked up an' down bechuxt the owld church below there an' the rath on the hill, an' jist as the clock was shtrikin' fur twelve, he heard a horse in front av him, as he was walkin' down, so he turned an' wint the other way, gettin' his charm ready, an' the Pooka come up afther him.

"'The top o' the mornin' to yer Honor,' says the Pooka, as perlite as a Frinchman, for he seen be his close that the king was n't a common blaggârd like us, but was wan o' the rale quolity.

"'Me sarvice to ye,' says the king to him agin, as bowld as a ram, an' whin the Pooka heard him shpake, he got perliter than iver, an' made a low bow an shcrape wid his fut, thin they wint on together an' fell into discoorse.

"''T is a black night for thravelin',' says the Pooka.

"'Indade it is,' says the king, 'it 's not me that 'ud be out in it, if it was n't a case o' needcessity. I 'm on an arriant av charity,' says he.

"'That 's rale good o' ye,' says the Pooka to him, 'and if I may make bowld to ax, phat 's the needcessity?'

"''T is to relave a widdy-woman,' says the king.

"'Oho,' says the Pooka, a-throwin' back his head laughin' wid great plazin' ness an' nudgin' the king wid his leg on the arrum, beways that it was a joke it was bekase the king said it was to relave a widdy he was goin'. 'Oho,' says the Pooka, ''t is mesilf that 's glad to be in the comp'ny av an iligint jintleman that 's on so plazin' an arriant av marcy,' says he. 'An' how owld is the widdy-woman?' says he, bustin' wid the horrid laugh he had.

"'Musha thin,' says the king, gettin' red in the face an' not likin' the joke the laste bit, for jist betune us, they do say that afore he married the quane, he was the laddy-buck wid the wimmin, an' the quane's maid towld the cook, that towld the footman, that said to the gârdener, that towld the nabers that many 's the night the poor king was as wide awake as a hare from sun to sun wid the quane a-gostherin' at him about that same. More betoken, there was a widdy in it, that was as sharp as a rat-thrap an' surrounded him whin he was young an' had n't as much sinse as a goose, an' was like to marry him at wanst in shpite av all his relations, as widdys unhershtand how to do. So it 's my consate that it was n't dacint for the Pooka to be afther laughin' that-a-way, an' shows that avil sper'ts is dirthy blaggârds that can't talk wid jintlemin. 'Musha,' thin, says the king, bekase the Pooka's laughin' was n't agrayable to listen to, 'I don't know that same, fur I niver seen her, but, be jagers, I belave she 's a hundherd, an' as ugly as Belzebub, an' whin her owld man was alive, they tell me she had a timper like a gandher, an' was as aisey to manage as an armful o' cats,' says he. 'But she 's in want, an' I 'm afther bringin' her a suv'rin,' says he.

"Well, the Pooka sayced his laughin', fur he seen the king was very vexed, an' says to him, 'And if it 's plazin', where does she live?'

"'At the ind o' the boreen beyant the Corkschrew,' says the king, very short.

"'Begob, that 's a good bit,' says the Pooka.

"'Faix, it 's thrue for ye,' says the king, 'more betoken, it 's up hill ivery fut o' the way, an' me back is bruk entirely wid the stapeness,' says he, be way av a hint he 'd like a ride.

"'Will yer Honor get upon me back,' says the Pooka. 'Sure I 'm afther goin' that-a-way, an' yu don't mind gettin' a lift?' says he, a-fallin' like the stupid baste he was, into the thrap the king had made fur him.

"'Thanks,' says the king, 'I b'lave not. I 've no bridle nor saddle,' says he, 'besides, it 's the shpring o' the year, an' I 'm afeared ye 're sheddin', an' yer hair 'ull come aff an' spile me new britches,' says he, lettin' on to make axcuse.

"'Have no fear,' says the Pooka. 'Sure I niver drop me hair. It 's no ordinary garron av a horse I am, but a most oncommon baste that 's used to the quolity,' says he.

"'Yer spache shows that,' says the king, the clever man that he was, to be perlit that-a-way to a Pooka, that 's known to be a divil out-en-out, 'but ye must exqueeze me this avenin', bekase, d'ye mind, the road 's full o' shtones an' monsthrous stape, an' ye look so young, I 'm afeared ye 'll shtumble an' give me a fall,' says he.

"'Arrah thin,' says the Pooka, 'it 's thrue fur yer Honor, I do look young,' an' he begun to prance on the road givin' himself airs like an owld widdy man afther wantin' a young woman, 'but me age is owlder than ye 'd suppoge. How owld 'ud ye say I was,' says he, shmilin'.

"'Begorra, divil a bit know I,' says the king, 'but if it 's agrayble to ye, I 'll look in yer mouth an' give ye an answer,' says he.

"So the Pooka come up to him fair an' soft an' stratched his mouth like as he thought the king was wantin' fur to climb in, an' the king put his hand on his jaw like as he was goin' to see the teeth he had: and thin, that minnit he shlipped the three hairs round the Pooka's jaw, an' whin he done that, he dhrew thim tight, an' said the charm crossin' himself the while, an' immejitly the hairs wor cords av stale, an' held the Pooka tight, be way av a bridle.

"'Arra-a-a-h, how, ye bloody baste av a murtherin' divil ye,' says the king, pullin' out his big whip that he had consaled in this top-coat, an' giving the Pooka a crack wid it undher his stummick, 'I 'll give ye a ride ye won't forgit in a hurry,' says he, 'ye black Turk av a four-legged nagur an' you shtaling me white mare,' says he, hittin' him agin.

"'Oh my,' says the Pooka, as he felt the grip av the iron on his jaw an' knewn he was undher an inchantmint, 'Oh my, phat 's this at all,' rubbin' his breast wid his hind heel, where the whip had hit him, an' thin jumpin' wid his fore feet out to cotch the air an' thryin' fur to break away. 'Sure I 'm ruined, I am, so I am,' says he.

"'It 's thrue fur ye,' says the king, 'begoo it 's the wan thrue thing ye iver said,' says he, a-jumpin' on his back, an' givin' him the whip an' the two shpurs wid all his might.

"Now I forgot to tell ye that whin the king made his inchantmint, it was good fur siven miles round, and the Pooka knewn that same as well as the king an' so he shtarted like a cunshtable was afther him, but the king was afeared to let him go far, thinkin' he 'd do the siven miles in a jiffy an' the inchantmint 'ud be broken like a rotten shtring, so he turned him up the Corkschrew.

"'I 'll give ye all the axercise ye want,' says he, 'in thravellin' round this hill,' an' round an' round they wint, the king shtickin' the big shpurs in him every jump an' crakin' him wid the whip till his sides run blood in shtrames like a mill race, an' his schreams av pain wor heard all over the worruld so that the king av France opened his windy and axed the polisman why he did n't shtop the fightin' in the shtrate. Round an' round an' about the Corkschrew wint the king, a-lashin' the Pooka, till his feet made the path ye see on the hill bekase he wint so often.

"And whin mornin' come, the Pooka axed the king phat he 'd let him go fur, an' the king was gettin' tired an' towld him that he must niver shtale another horse, an' never kill another man, barrin' furrin blaggârds that was n't Irish, an' whin he give a man a ride, he must bring him back to the shpot where he got him an' lave him there. So the Pooka consinted, Glory be to God, an' got aff, an' that 's the way he was tamed, an' axplains how it was that Dennis O'Rourke was left be the Pooka in the ditch jist where he found him."

"More betoken, the Pooka 's an althered baste every way, fur now he dhrops his hair like a common horse, and it 's often found shtrickin' to the hedges where he jumped over, an' they do say he does n't shmell half as shtrong o' sulfur as he used, nor the fire out o' his nose is n't so bright. But all the king did fur him 'ud n't taiche him to be civil in his spache, an' whin he meets ye in the way, he spakes just as much like a blaggârd as ever. An' it 's out av divilment entirely he does it, bekase he can be perlite as ye know be phat I towld ye av him sayin' to the king, an' that proves phat I said to ye that avil sper'ts can't larn rale good manners, no matther how hard they thry.

"But the fright he got never left him, an' so he kapes out av the highways an' thravels be the futpaths, an' so is n't often seen. An' it 's my belafe that he can do no harrum at all to thim that fears God, an' there 's thim that says he niver shows himself nor meddles wid man nor mortial barrin' they're in dhrink, an' mebbe there 's something in that too, fur it does n't take much dhrink to make a man see a good dale."

The Gollan
A. E. Coppard

THERE WAS ONCE a peasant named Goose who had worked his back crooked with never a Thank-ye from Providence or Man, and he had a son, Gosling, whom the neighbors called The Gollan for short. The Gollan was an obedient child and strong, though not by nature very willing. He was so obedient that he would do without question whatever anybody told him to do. One day he was bringing his mother three eggs in a basket and he met a rude boy.

"Hoi," called the rude boy, "are those eggs the bouncing eggs?"

"Are they?" enquired The Gollan.

"Try one and see," the rude boy said.

The Gollan took one of the eggs from the basket and dropped it to the ground, and it broke.

"Haw!" complained the rude one, "you did not do it properly. How could an egg bounce if you dropped it so? You must throw it hard and it will fly back into your hand like a bird."

So The Gollan took another and dashed it to the ground and waited. But the egg only lay spilled at his feet.

"No, no, no! Stupid fellow!" the rude boy cried. "Look. Throw the other one up in the air high as you can and all three will bounce back into your basket."

So The Gollan threw the last egg up on high, but it only dropped beside the others and all lay in a slop of ruins.

"Oh dear! What will my mother say? Oh dear!" wept The Gollan.

The rude boy merely put his thumb to his nose and ran off upon his proper business, laughing.

The Gollan grew up a great powerful fellow, and whatever anyone told him to do, it might be simple, it might be hard, he did it without repining, which shows that he had a kind heart anyway, though he had little enough inclination to work; indeed he had no wish to at all.

One day his father said to him: "My son, you are full of strength and vigor, you are the prop of my old age and the apple of my two eyes. Take now these five and twenty pigs and go you to market and dispose of them. Beware of false dealing, and you may hear wonders."

"What wonders should I hear?"

"Mum," said his father, "is the word. Say nothing and scare nobody."

He gave him two noggins of ale and off went The Gollan. And it was a queer half and half day, however, but full of color. There were poppies in the green corn, charlock in the swedes, and weak sunlight in the opaline sky. He tried to drive the pigs but they had their minds set upon some other matters and would not go where they should because of distractions and interruptions. There was the green corn, there were the swedes, and there were heifers in the lane, lambs afield, and hens in every hedge, so before he had gone a mile the pigs were all astray.

"I don't care where those pigs go," then said The Gollan to himself. "I don't trouble about those pigs as long as I have my strength and vigor." So he lay down under a nut hazel-bush and was soon sleeping.

In the course of time—long or short makes no odds—he heard someone whistling shrilly, and waking up he looked about him to the right hand and to the left and soon saw a person caught hard and fast in a catchpole, a little plump man with a red beard and bright buckled shoes.

"Well met, friend!" the little man called out. "Pray release me from this trap and I will make your fortune." So The Gollan went and put out all his strength and vigor, with a heave and a hawk and a crash, until he had drawn the little plump man out of the trap and set him free.

"Thanks, friend," said the leprechaun—for he was that and no less, not like any man you ever read about. "You have done me a kind service. Ask any reward you will and I will give it."

"Sir," said the Gollan, "there is no matter about that. I am the prop of my father's age and the apple of his two eyes. I have strength and vigor with which I work for what I need."

"Unhappy is that man," the leprechaun answered, "who serves his need and not his choice. You have strength and vigor, but how do you use it?"

The Gollan drew himself up proudly: "I can crack rocks and hew trees."

"Well, then," replied the other, "crack on, and hew."

"Alas," The Gollan explained, "I have four fingers and a

thumb on one hand, four fingers and a thumb on the other, all of them able—but not one of them willing." And he confided to the leprechaun that it was his doom and distress to be at the beck and call of everyone because of his strength and vigor, and he with no heart to refuse to do a deed required of him.

"That cannot be endured. I can easily remedy it," said the leprechaun. "I will make you invisible to mankind, except only when you are asleep. Nobody will be able to see you when you are awake and walking, therefore they will not be able to give you a task of any kind."

So he made The Gollan invisible there and then, and no one saw The Gollan any more, save his parents when he was sleeping, and his life became a bed or roses and a bower of bliss. Where is The Gollan?—people would say. But though they knew he was thereabout they could not set eyes on him and they could not find him. If The Gollan were only with us—they would say—he would do this tiresome labor, he would do it well. But as he was no longer visible to them they could not catch him and they could not ask him. The Gollan would be about in the sunlight day after day doing nothing at all, and got so blown up with pride that he thought:

"I am invisible, no one can task me in my strength and vigor. I am king of all the unseen world, and that is as good as twenty of these other kings. I live as I choose, and I take my need as I want it."

But though it was all very grand to be invisible The Gollan soon found out that there was small blessing in it. He could be seen by none save when he slept, but the truth is neither could he see anybody—man, woman, or child. No one could hear him, but then he himself could hear no one—man, woman, or child. It was the same way with smelling, touching and tasting. Animals and birds he could see, and he could talk to them, but they were so hard of understanding that he might as well have conversed with a monument or a door. Sure, he had kept his wits but he had lost his five senses, and that is cruel fortune.

After a while his heart grew weary for the sight of his friends and the talk and sounds of people, he was tired of seeing animals and birds only, so he went to a hawk he knew that had the most piercing gaze, and said:

"Friend, lend me your two eyes for a while and I will pawn you my own for their safe return."

"Will I? Will I?" mused the hawk.

"You will!" The Gollan sternly said.

So they exchanged, but The Gollan was greatly deceived by these hawk eyes. He went about wearing them far and near, and he saw thousands of mice and birds and moles, but those eyes never set their gaze on a single human creature, good, bad, or medium. What was worse, rascally things, they never seemed to want to! The farther he wandered the more sure it became that those eyes were merely looking out for moles and voles and such like. He saw nothing else except a jackass with fine upstanding ears straying in a bethistled waste whom he accosted:

"Friend, lend me your two ears for a while. I will pawn you my own for their safe return."

"Will you? Won't you?" mused the ass.

"I will," declared The Gollan, for he longed to hear human speech again, or a song to cheer him.

So they exchanged. But The Gollan was more deceived and bewildered than ever, for he never caught the sound of any pleasant human talk. What he heard was only an ass's bald portion, vile oaths, denunciations, and abuse. And although it all rushed into one ear and quickly fell out of the other, it was not good hearing at all; it was not satisfactory. When he heard a pig grunting not far off he hastened to the pig, saying:

"Friend, lend me your nose. I will pawn you mine for its safe return."

"Ask me no more," said the pig, surveying him with a rueful smile as he suffered The Gollan to make the exchange.

But something kept The Gollan from smelling anything save what a pig may smell. Instead of flowers, the odor of fruit, or the cook's oven, the swinish nostrils delighted only in the vapors of swill and offal and ordure. Surely—thought The Gollan—it is better to be invisible and senseless than to live thus. So he tried no further, but gave back the eyes, the ears, and the nose and received his pledges again.

Now at that time the king of the land was much put about by the reason of a little pond that lay in front of his palace. It was a meager patch of water and no ways good.

"If only this were a lake," sighed the king, "a great lake of blue water with neat waves and my ships upon it and my swans roving and my snipe calling and my fish going to and fro, my realm would be a great realm and the envy of the whole world."

And one day, as he was wandering and wondering what he could do about this, he came upon The Gollan lying on a green bank drowsing and dreaming. Of course when the king set eyes on him, he saw him and knew him.

"Hoi, Gollan!" the king roared at him. "Stretch out that water for me!" Just like that. The Gollan woke up and at once became invisible again, but he was so startled at being roared at that without thinking, just absent-mindedly, he stretched out the water of the king's pond and there and then it became a fine large lake with neat waves and ships and swans and such like, beautiful—though when he learned the right of it The Gollan was crabby and vexed, "I am the king of the unseen world, and that's as good as any twenty of these other kings." Still, he could not alter it back again. Whatever he did had to stay as it was once done: it could neither be changed nor improved.

However, by the reason of his fine new lake and ships the king's realm became the envy of all other nations, who began to strive after it and attack it. The king was not much of a one for martial dispositions and so the whole of his country was soon beleaguered and the people put to miserable extravagances.

Now although The Gollan could not directly see or hear anything of this, yet one way and another he came to know something of the misfortune, and then he was worn to a tatter with rage and fury by the reason he was such a great one for the patriotism. And he was powerless to help now his five senses were gone from him.

"O, what sort of a game is this," he thought, "now the world is in ruins and I have no more senses than a ghost or a stone! I had the heart of an ass when I took that red-haired villain out of his trap and had his reward. Reward! Take it back! Take it back, you palavering old crow of a catchpole! You have cramped me tight and hauled me to a grave. Take it back, you!"

"Well met, friend," a voice replied, and there was the old leprechaun bowing before him. "Your wish is granted."

True it was. They were standing beside a field of corn ripe and ready, waving and sighing it was. The Gollan could hear once more, he could touch, taste, and smell again, and he could see his own royal king as clear as print on a page of history hurrying down the road towards them.

"What else can I do for you?" asked the little red-haired man.

"I fancy," said The Gollan, jerking his thumb towards the king, "he is running to ask me for a large great army."

"You shall have that," said the leprechaun, vanishing away at the king's approach.

"Gollan," the king says, "I want a large great army."

"Yes, Sir," says The Gollan. "Will you have the grenadiers, the bombardiers, or men of the broad-sword?"

He said he would have the bombardiers.

Well, The Gollan made a pass of his hand over that field of corn, and the standing stalks at once began to whistle and sway sideways. Before you could blink a lash there they were, 50,000 men and noblemen, all marking time, all dressed to glory with great helmets and eager for battle.

"Gollan," says the king, "will you undertake the command of this my noble army?"

"I will that, Sir."

"Lead on, then," says the king, and "may the blood of calamity never splash upon one single rib of the whole lot of you."

Which, it is good to say, it never did. The Gollan then marched them straightway to battle by the shore of the lake.

"Get ready now," cried General Gollan, "here comes the artillery with their big guns!"

The bombardiers began to prepare themselves and first gave a blast on their trumpets, but the enemy got ready sooner and fired off a blast on all their culverins, mortars, and whatnot. Ah, what a roar they let out of that huge and fatal cannonade! It would have frightened the trunk of a tree out of its own bark, and at the mere sound of it every man of General Gollan's army toppled to the earth like corn that is cut, never to rise again.

"What is it and all!" cried the distracted Gollan. "Is this another joke of that palavering old crow of a catchpole? By the soul of my aunty!" he exclaimed, as he surveyed his exposed position amid all those fallen bombardiers, so neat, so gallant, so untimely dead, "By the soul of my aunty I think I'd rather be invisible now!"

In a twink he was invisible once more, and his five senses

gone again; but none of his friends ever had time to enquire what became of him because the conquering general painfully exterminated them all.

Unseen, unknown, the good Gollan lived on for many years in great privation, and when he at last came to die (though nobody knew even about that) he had grown mercifully wise and wrote his own epitaph—though nobody ever saw it:

To choose was my need, but need brooks no choosing.

A Play-House in the Waste

George Moore

"IT'S A CLOSED MOUTH that can hold a good story," as the saying goes, and very soon it got about that Father MacTurnan had written to Rome saying he was willing to take a wife to his bosom for patriotic reasons, if the Pope would relieve him of his vow of celibacy. And many phrases and words from his letter (translated by whom—by the Bishop or Father Meehan?— nobody ever knew) were related over the Dublin firesides, till at last out of the talk a tall gaunt man emerged, in an old overcoat, green from weather and wear, the tails of it flapping as he rode his bicycle through the great waste bog that lies between Belmullet and Crossmolina. His name! We liked it. It appealed to our imagination. MacTurnan! It conveyed something from afar like Hamlet or Don Quixote. He seemed as near and as far from us as they, till Pat Comer, one of the organizers of the

IAOS, came in and said, after listening to the talk that was going round:

"Is it of the priest that rides in the great Mayo bog you are speaking? If it is, you haven't got the story rightly." As he told us the story, so it is printed in this book. And we sat wondering greatly, for we seemed to see a soul on its way to heaven. But round a fire there is always one who cannot get off the subject of women and blasphemy—a papist generally he is; and it was Quinn that evening who kept plaguing us with jokes, whether it would be a fat girl or a thin that the priest would choose if the Pope gave him leave to marry, until at last, losing all patience with him, I bade him be silent, and asked Pat Comer to tell us if the priest was meditating a new plan for Ireland's salvation. "For a mind like his," I said, "would not stand still and problems such as ours waiting to be solved."

"You're wrong there! He thinks no more of Ireland, and neither reads nor plans, but knits stockings ever since the wind took his play-house away."

"Took his play-house away!" said several.

"And why would he be building a play-house," somebody asked, "and he living in a waste?"

"A queer idea, surely!" said another. "A play-house in the waste!"

"Yes, a queer idea," said Pat, "but a true one all the same, for I have seen it with my own eyes—or the ruins of it—and not later back than three weeks ago, when I was staying with the priest himself. You know the road, all of you—how it straggles from Foxford through the bog alongside of bogholes deep enough to drown one, and into which the jarvey and myself seemed in great likelihood of pitching, for the car went down into great ruts, and the horse was shying from one side of the road to the other, and at nothing so far as we could see."

"There's nothing to be afeared of, yer honor; only once was he near leaving the road, the day before Christmas, and I driving the doctor. It was here he saw it—a white thing gliding—and the wheel of the car must have gone within an inch of the boghole."

"And the doctor. Did he see it?" I said.

"He saw it too, and so scared was he that the hair rose up and went through his cap."

"Did the jarvey laugh when he said that?" we asked Pat Comer; and Pat answered: "Not he! Them fellows just speak as the words come to them without thinking. Let me get on with my story. We drove on for about a mile, and it was to stop him from clicking his tongue at the horse that I asked him if the bog was Father MacTurnan's parish." "Every mile of it, sir," he said, "every mile of it, and we do be seeing him buttoned up in his old coat riding along the roads on his bicycle going to sick calls."

"Do you often be coming this road?" says I.

"Not very often, sir. No one lives here except the poor people, and the priest and the doctor. Faith! there isn't a poorer parish in Ireland, and every one of them would have been dead long ago if it had not been for Father James."

"And how does he help them?"

"Isn't he always writing letters to the Government asking for relief works? Do you see those bits of roads?"

"Where do those roads lead to?"

"Nowhere. Them roads stops in the middle of the bog when the money is out."

"But," I said, "surely it would be better if the money were spent upon permanent improvements—on drainage, for instance."

The jarvey didn't answer; he called to his horse, and not being able to stand the clicking of his tongue, I kept on about the drainage.

"There's no fall, sir."

"And the bog is too big," I added, in hope of encouraging conversation.

"Faith it is, sir."

"But we aren't very far from the sea, are we?"

"About a couple of miles."

"Well then," I said, "couldn't a harbor be made?"

"They were thinking about that, but there's no depth of water, and everyone's against emigration now."

"Ah! the harbor would encourage emigration."

"So it would, your honor."

"But is there no talk about home industries, weaving, lacemaking?"

"I won't say that."

"But has it been tried?"

"The candle do be burning in the priest's window till one in the morning, and he sitting up thinking of plans to keep the people at home. Now, do ye see that house, sir, fornint my whip at the top of the hill? Well, that's the play-house he built."

"A play-house?"

"Yes, yer honor. Father James hoped the people might come from Dublin to see it, for no play like it had ever been acted in Ireland before, sir!"

"And was the play performed?"

"No, yer honor. The priest had been learning them all the summer, but the autumn was on them before they had got it by rote, and a wind came and blew down one of the walls."

"And couldn't Father MacTurnan get the money to build it up?"

"Sure, he might have got the money, but where'd be the use

when there was no luck in it?"

"And who were to act the play?"

"The girls and the boys in the parish, and the prettiest girl in all the parish was to play Good Deeds."

"So it was a miracle play," I said.

"Do you see that man? It's the priest coming out of Tom Burke's cabin, and I warrant he do be bringing him the Sacrament, and he having the holy oils with him, for Tom won't pass the day; we had the worst news of him last night."

"And I can tell you," said Pat Comer, dropping his story for a moment and looking round the circle, "it was a sad story the jarvey told me. He told it well, for I can see the one-roomed hovel full of peatsmoke, the black iron pot with traces of the yellow stirabout in it on the hearth, and the sick man on the pallet bed, and the priest by his side mumbling prayers together. Faith! these jarveys can tell a story—none better."

"As well as yourself, Pat," one of us said. And Pat began to tell of the miles of bog on either side of the straggling road, of the hill-top to the left, with the play-house showing against the dark and changing clouds; of a woman in a red petticoat, a handkerchief tied round her head, who had flung down her spade the moment she caught sight of the car, of the man who appeared on the brow and blew a horn. "For she mistook us for bailiffs," said Pat, "and two little sheep hardly bigger than geese were driven away."

"A play-house in the waste for these people," I was saying to myself all the time, till my meditations were interrupted by the jarvey telling that the rocky river we crossed was called the Greyhound—a not inappropriate name, for it ran swiftly . . . Away down the long road a white cottage appeared, and the jarvey said to me, "That is the priest's house." It stood on the hillside some little way from the road, and all the way to the door I wondered how his days passed in the great loneliness of the bog.

"His reverence isn't at home, yer honor—he's gone to attend a sick call."

"Yes, I know—Tom Burke."

"And is Tom better, Mike?"

"The devil a bether he'll be this side of Jordan," the jarvey answered, and the housekeeper showed me into the priest's parlor. It was lined with books, and I looked forward to a pleasant chat when we had finished our business. At that time I was on a relief committee, and the people were starving in the poor parts of the country.

"I think he'll be back in about an hour's time, yer honor." But the priest seemed to be detained longer than his housekeeper expected, and the moaning of the wind round the cottage reminded me of the small white thing the horse and the doctor had seen gliding along the road. "The priest knows the story— he will tell me," I said, and piled more turf on the fire—fine sods of hard black turf they were, and well do I remember seeing them melting away. But all of a sudden my eyes closed. I couldn't have been asleep more than a few minutes when it seemed to me a great crowd of men and women had gathered about the house, and a moment after the door was flung open, and a tall, gaunt man faced me.

"I've just come," he said, "from a deathbed, and they that have followed me aren't far from death if we don't succeed in getting help." I don't know how I can tell you of the crowd I saw round the house that day. We are accustomed to see poor people in towns cowering under arches, but it is more pitiful to see people starving in the fields on the mountain side. I don't know why it should be so, but it is. But I call to mind two men in ragged trousers and shirts as ragged, with brown beards on faces yellow with famine; and the words of one of them are not easily forgotten: "The white sun of Heaven doesn't shine upon two poorer men than upon this man and myself." I can tell you I didn't envy the priest his job, living all his life in the waste listening to tales of starvation, looking into famished faces. There were some women among them, kept back by the men, who wanted to get their word in first. They seemed to like to talk about their misery . . . and I said:

"They are tired of seeing each other. I am a spectacle, a show, an amusement for them. I don't know if you can catch my meaning?"

"I think I do," Father James answered. And I asked him to come for a walk up the hill and show me the play-house.

Again he hesitated, and I said: "You must come, Father MacTurnan, for a walk. You must forget the misfortunes of those people for a while." He yielded, and we spoke of the excellence of the road under our feet, and he told me that when he conceived the idea of a play-house, he had already succeeded in persuading the inspector to agree that the road they were making should go to the top of the hill. "The policy of the Government," he said, "from the first was that relief works should benefit nobody except the workers, and it is sometimes very difflcult to think out a project for work that will be perfectly useless. Arches have been built on the top of hills, and roads that lead nowhere. A strange sight to the stranger a road must be that stops suddenly in the middle of a bog. One wonders at first how a Government could be so foolish, but when one thinks of it, it is easy to understand that the Government doesn't wish to spend money on works that will benefit a class. But the road that leads nowhere is difficult to make, even though starving men are employed upon it; for a man to work well there must be an end in view, and I can tell you it is difficult to bring even starving men to engage on a road that leads nowhere. If I'd told everything I am telling you to the inspector, he wouldn't have agreed to let the road run to the top of the hill; but I said to him: "The road leads nowhere; as well let it end at the top of the hill as down in the valley." So I got the money for my road and some money for my play-house, for of course the play-house was as useless as the road; a play-house in the waste can neither interest or benefit anybody! But there was an idea at the back of my mind all the time that when the road and the play-house were finished, I might be able to induce the Government to build a harbor?"

"But the harbor would be of use."

"Of very little," he answered. "For the harbor to be of use a great deal of dredging would have to be done."

"And the Government needn't undertake the dredging. How very ingenious! I suppose you often come here to read your breviary?"

"During the building of the play-house I often used to be up here, and during the rehearsals I was here every day."

"If there was a rehearsal," I said to myself, "there must have been a play." And I affected interest in the grey shallow sea and the erosion of the low-lying land—a salt marsh filled with pools.

"I thought once," said the priest, "that if the play were a great success, a line of flat-bottomed steamers might be built."

"Sitting here in the quiet evenings," I said to myself, "reading his breviary, dreaming of a line of steamships crowded with visitors! He has been reading about the Oberammergau performances." So that was his game—the road, the playhouse, the harbor—and I agreed with him that no one would have dared to predict that visitors would have come from all sides of Europe to see a few peasants performing a miracle play in the

Tyrol.

"Come," I said, "into the play-house and let me see how you built it."

Half a wall and some of the roof had fallen, and the rubble had not been cleared away, and I said:

"It will cost many pounds to repair the damage, but having gone so far you should give the play a chance."

"I don't think it would be advisable," he muttered, half to himself, half to me.

As you may well imagine, I was anxious to hear if he had discovered any aptitude for acting among the girls and the boys who lived in the cabins.

"I think," he answered me, "that the play would have been fairly acted; I think that, with a little practice, we might have done as well as they did at Oberammergau."

An odd man, more willing to discuss the play that he had chosen than the talents of those who were going to perform it, and he told me that it had been written in the fourteenth century in Latin, and that he had translated it into Irish.

I asked him if it would have been possible to organize an excursion from Dublin—"Oberammergau in the West."

"I used to think so. But it is eight miles from Rathowen, and the road is a bad one, and when they got here there would be no place for them to stay; they would have to go all the way back again, and that would be sixteen miles."

"Yet you did well, Father James, to build the play-house, for the people could work better while they thought they were accomplishing something. Let me start a subscription for you in Dublin."

"I don't think that it would be possible—"

"Not for me to get fifty pounds?"

"You might get the money, but I don't think we could ever get a performance of the play."

"And why not?" I said.

"You see, the wind came and blew down the wall. The people are very pious; I think they felt that the time they spent rehearsing might have been better spent. The play-house disturbed them in their ideas. They hear Mass on Sundays, and there are the Sacraments, and they remember they have to die. It used to seem to me a very sad thing to see all the people going to America; the poor Celt disappearing in America, leaving his own country, leaving his language, and very often his religion."

"And does it no longer seem to you sad that such a thing should happen?"

"No, not if it is the will of God. God has specially chosen the Irish race to convert the world. No race has provided so many missionaries, no race has preached the Gospel more frequently to the heathen; and once we realize that we have to die, and very soon, and that the Catholic Church is the only true Church, our ideas about race and nationality fade from us. We are here, not to make life successful and triumphant, but to gain heaven. That is the truth, and it is to the honor of the Irish people that they have been selected by God to preach the truth, even though they lose their nationality in preaching it. I do not expect you to accept these opinions. I know that you think very differently, but living here I have learned to acquiesce in the will of God."

He stopped speaking suddenly, like one ashamed of having expressed himself too openly, and soon after we were met by a number of peasants, and the priest's attention was engaged; the inspector of the relief works had to speak to him; and I didn't see him again until dinner-time.

"You have given them hope," he said.

This was gratifying to hear, and the priest sat listening while I told him of the looms already established in different parts of the country. We talked about half an hour, and then, like one who suddenly remembers, the priest got up and fetched his knitting.

"Do you knit every evening?"

"I have got into the way of knitting lately—it passes the time."

"But do you never read?" I asked, and my eyes went towards the bookshelves.

"I used to read a great deal. But there wasn't a woman in the parish that could turn a heel properly, so I had to learn to knit."

"Do you like knitting better than reading?" I asked, feeling ashamed of my curiosity.

"I have constantly to attend sick calls, and if one is absorbed in a book one doesn't like to put it aside."

"I see you have two volumes of miracle plays!"

"Yes, and that's another danger: a book begets all kinds of ideas and notions into one's head. The idea of that play-house came out of those books."

"But," I said, "you don't think that God sent the storm because He didn't wish a play to be performed?"

"One cannot judge God's designs. Whether God sent the storm or whether it was accident must remain a matter for conjecture; but it is not a matter of conjecture that one is doing certain good by devoting oneself to one's daily task, getting the Government to start new relief works, establishing schools for weaving. The people are entirely dependent upon me, and when I'm attending to their wants I know I'm doing right."

The play-house interested me more than the priest's ideas of right and wrong, and I tried to get him back to it; but the subject seemed a painful one, and I said to myself: "The jarvey will tell me all about it tomorrow. I can rely on him to find out the whole story from the housekeeper in the kitchen." And sure enough, we hadn't got to the Greyhound River before he was leaning across the well of the car talking to me and asking if the priest was thinking of putting up the wall of the play-house.

"The wall of the play-house?" I said.

"Yes, yer honor. Didn't I see both of you going up the hill in the evening time?"

"I don't think we shall ever see a play in the play-house."

"Why would we, since it was God that sent the wind that blew it down?"

"How do you know it was God that sent the wind? It might have been the devil himself, or somebody's curse."

"Sure it is of Mrs. Sheridan you do be thinking, yer honor, and of her daughter—she that was to be playing Good Deeds in the play, yer honor; and wasn't she wake coming home from the learning of the play? And when the signs of her wakeness began to show, the widow Sheridan took a halter off the cow and tied Margaret to the wall, and she was in the stable till the child was born. Then didn't her mother take a bit of string and tie it round the child's throat, and bury it near the play-house; and it was three nights after that the storm rose, and the child pulled the thatch out of the roof."

"But did she murder the child?"

"Sorra wan of me knows. She sent for the priest when she was dying, and told him what she had done."

"But the priest wouldn't tell what he heard in the confessional," I said.

"Mrs. Sheridan didn't die that night; not till the end of the week, and the neighbors heard her talking of the child she had buried, and then they all knew what the white thing was they had seen by the roadside. The night the priest left her he saw the white thing standing in front of him, and if he hadn't been a priest he'd have dropped down dead; so he took some water from the boghole and dashed it over it, saying, 'I baptise thee in the name of the Father, and of the Son, and of the Holy Ghost!'"

The driver told his story like one saying his prayers, and he seemed to have forgotten that he had a listener.

"It must have been a great shock to the priest."

"Faith it was, sir, to meet an unbaptised child on the roadside, and that child the only bastard that was ever born in the parish—so Tom Mulhare says, and he's the oldest man in the county."

"It was altogether a very queer idea—this play-house."

"It was indeed, sir, a quare idea, but you see he's a quare man. He has been always thinking of something to do good, and it is said that he thinks too much. Father James is a very quare man, your honor."

The Legend of Knockgrafton

Thomas Crofton Crocker

THERE WAS ONCE a poor man who lived in the fertile glen of Aherlow, at the foot of the gloomy Galtee mountains, and he had a great hump on his back: he looked just as if his body had been rolled up and placed upon his shoulders; and his head was pressed down with the weight so much that his chin, when he was sitting, used to rest upon his knees for support. The country people were rather shy of meeting him in any lonesome place, for though, poor creature, he was as harmless and as inoffensive as a new-born infant, yet his deformity was so great that he scarcely appeared to be a human creature, and some ill-minded persons had set strange stories about him afloat. He was said to have a great knowledge of herbs and charms; but certain it was that he had a mighty skilful hand in plaiting straws and rushes into hats and baskets, which was the way he made his livelihood.

Lusmore, for that was the nickname put upon him by reason of his always wearing a sprig of the fairy cap, or lusmore (the foxglove), in his little straw hat, would ever get a higher penny for his plaited work than anyone else, and perhaps that was the reason why someone, out of envy, had circulated the strange stories about him. Be that as it may, it happened that he was returning one evening from the pretty town of Cahir toward Cappagh, and as little Lusmore walked very slowly, on account of the great hump upon his back, it was quite dark when he came to the old moat of Knockgrafton, which stood on the right-hand side of his road.

Tired and weary was he, and noways comfortable in his own mind at thinking how much farther he had to travel, and that he should be walking all the night; so he sat down under the moat to rest himself, and began looking mournfully enough upon the moon, which

"Rising in clouded majesty, at length
Apparent Queen, unveil'd her peerless light,
And o'er the dark her silver mantle threw."

Presently there rose a wild strain of unearthly melody upon the ear of little Lusmore; he listened, and he thought that he had never heard such ravishing music before. It was like the sound of many voices, each mingling and blending with the other so strangely that they seemed to be one, though all singing different strains, and the words of the song were these:

Da Luan, Da Mort, Da Luan, Da Mort, Da Luan, Da Mort;

There would be a moment's pause, and then the round of melody went on again.

Lusmore listened attentively, scarcely drawing his breath lest he might lose the slightest note. He now plainly perceived that the singing was within the moat; and though at first it had charmed him so much, he began to get tired of hearing the same round sung over and over so often without any change; so availing himself of the pause when *Da Luan, Da Mort,* had been sung three times, he took up the tune, and raised it with the words *agus Da Dardeen,* and then went on singing with the voices inside of the moat, *Da Luan, Da Mort,* finishing the melody, when the pause again came, with *agus Da Dardeen.**

The fairies within Knockgrafton, for the song was a fairy melody, when they heard this addition to the tune, were so much delighted that, with instant resolve, it was determined to bring the mortal among them, whose musical skill so far exceeded theirs, and little Lusmore was conveyed into their company with the eddying speed of a whirlwind.

Glorious to behold was the sight that burst upon him as he came down through the moat, twirling round and round, with the lightness of a straw, to the sweetest music that kept time to his motion. The greatest honor was then paid him, for he was put above all the musicians, and he had servants tending upon him, and everything to his heart's content, and a hearty welcome to all; and, in short, he was made as much of as if he had been the first man in the land.

Presently Lusmore saw a great consultation going forward among the fairies, and, notwithstanding all their civility, he felt very much frightened, until one stepping out from the rest came up to him and said:

"Lusmore! Lusmore!

* The words *La Luan, Da Mort agus Da Dardeen* are Irish for "Monday, Tuesday, and Wednesday too."

Doubt not, nor deplore,
For the hump which you bore
On your back is no more;
Look down on the floor,
And view it, Lusmore! Lusmore!"

When these words were said poor little Lusmore felt himself so light, and so happy, that he thought he could have bounded at one jump over the moon, like the cow in the history of the cat and the fiddle; and he saw, with inexpressible pleasure, his hump tumble down upon the ground from his shoulders. He then tried to lift up his head, and he did so with becoming caution, fearing that he might knock it against the ceiling of the grand hall, where he was; he looked round and round again with the greatest wonder and delight upon everything, which appeared more and more beautiful; and, overpowered at beholding such a resplendent scene, his head grew dizzy, and his eyesight became dim. At last he fell into a sound sleep, and when he awoke he found that it was broad daylight, the sun shining brightly, and the birds singing sweetly; and that he was lying just at the foot of the moat of Knockgrafton, with the cows and sheep grazing peacefully round about him. The first thing Lusmore did, after saying his prayers, was to put his hand behind to feel for his hump, but no sign of one was there on his back, and he looked at himself with great pride, for he had now become a well-shaped, dapper little fellow, and more than that, found himself in a full suit of new clothes, which he concluded the fairies had made for him.

Toward Cappagh he went, stepping out as lightly, and springing up at every step as if he had been all his life dancing-master. Not a creature who met Lusmore knew him without his hump, and he had a great work to persuade everyone that he was the same man—in truth he was not, so far as the outward appearances went.

Of course it was not long before the story of Lusmore's hump got about, and a great wonder was made of it. Through the country, for miles round, it was the talk of everyone, high and low.

One morning, as Lusmore was sitting contented enough at his cabin door, up came an old woman to him and asked him if he could direct her to Cappagh.

"I need give you no directions, my good woman," said Lusmore, "for this is Cappagh; and whom may you want here?"

"I have come," said the woman, "out of Decie's country, in the county of Waterford, looking after one Lusmore, who, I have heard tell, had his hump taken off by the fairies; for there is a son of a gossip of mine who has got a hump on him that will be his death; and maybe, if he could use the same charm as Lusmore the hump may be taken off him. And now I have told you the reason of my coming so far: 'tis to find out about this charm, if I can."

Lusmore, who was ever a good-natured little fellow, told the woman all the particulars, how he had raised the tune for the fairies at Knockgrafton, how his hump had been removed from his shoulders, and how he had got a new suit of clothes into the bargain.

The woman thanked him very much, and then went away quite happy and easy in her own mind. When she came back to her gossip's house, in the county of Waterford, she told her everything that Lusmore had said and they put the little hump-backed man, who was a peevish and cunning creature from his birth, upon a car, and took him all the way across the county. It was a long journey, but they did not care for that, so the hump was taken from off him; and they brought him, just at nightfall, and left him under the old moat of Knockgrafton.

Jack Madden, for that was the humpy man's name, had not been sitting there long when he heard the tune going on within the moat much sweeter than before; for the fairies were singing it the way Lusmore had settled their music for them, and the song was going on: *Da Luan, Da Mort, Da Luan, Da Mort, Da Luan, Da Mort, agus Da Dardeen,* without ever stopping. Jack Madden, who was in a great hurry to get quit of his hump, never thought of waiting until the fairies had done, or watching for a fit opportunity to raise the tune higher again than Lusmore had; so having heard them sing it over seven times without stopping, out he bawls, never minding the time or the humor of the tune, or how he could bring his words in properly, *agus Da Dardeen, agus Da Hena,* thinking that if one day was good, two were better; and that if Lusmore had one new suit of clothes given him, he should have two.*

No sooner had the words passed his lips than he was taken up and whisked into the moat with prodigious force; and the fairies came crowding round about him with great anger, screeching and screaming, and roaring out:

"Who spoiled our tune? Who spoiled our tune?" and one stepped up to him above all the rest, and said:

"Jack Madden, Jack Madden
Your words come so bad in
The tune we felt glad in;—
This castle you're had in,
That your life we may sadden;
Here's two humps for Jack Madden!"

And twenty of the strongest fairies brought Lusmore's hump, and put it down upon poor Jack's back, over his own, where it became fixed as firmly as if it was nailed on with twelve-penny

---

* *Da Hena* is Thursday.

nails, by the best carpenter that ever drove one. Out of their castle they then kicked him; and in the morning, when Jack Madden's mother and her gossip came to look after their little man, they found him half dead, lying at the foot of the moat, with the other hump upon his back. Well to be sure, how they did look at each other! but they were afraid to say anything, lest a hump might be put upon their own shoulders. Home they brought the unlucky Jack Madden with them, as downcast in their hearts and their looks as ever two gossips were; and what through the weight of his other hump, and the long journey, he died soon after, leaving, they say, his heavy curse to anyone who would go to listen to fairy tunes again.

The Three Wishes
William Carleton

IN ANCIENT TIMES there lived a man called Billy Dawson, and he was known to be a great rogue. They say he was descended from the family of the Dawsons, which was the reason, I suppose, of his carrying their name upon him.

Billy, in his youthful days, was the best hand at doing nothing in all Europe; devil a mortal could come next or near him at idleness; and, in consequence of his great practice that way, you may be sure that if any man could make a fortune by it he would have done it.

Billy was the only son of his father, barring two daughters, but they have nothing to do with the story I'm telling you. Indeed it was kind father and grandfather for Billy to be handy at the knavery as well as at the idleness, for it was well known that not one of their blood ever did an honest act, except with a roguish intention. In short, they were altogether a *dacent* connection and a credit to the name. As for Billy, all the villainy of the family, both plain and ornamental, came down to him by way of legacy, for it so happened that the father, in spite of all his cleverness, had nothing but his roguery to *lave* him.

Billy, to do him justice, improved the fortune he got. Every day advanced him farther into dishonesty and poverty, until, at the long run, he was acknowledged on all hands to be the completest swindler and the poorest vagabond in the whole parish.

Billy's father, in his young days, had often been forced to acknowledge the inconvenience of not having a trade, in consequence of some nice point in law, called the "Vagrant Act," that sometimes troubled him. On this account he made up his mind to give Bill an occupation, and he accordingly bound him to a blacksmith; but whether Bill was to *live* or *die* by *forgery* was a puzzle to his father—though the neighbors said that *both* was most likely. At all events, he was put apprentice to a smith for seven years, and a hard card his master had to play in managing him. He took the proper method, however, for Bill was so lazy and roguish that it would vex a saint to keep him in order.

"Bill," says his master to him one day that he had been sunning himself about the ditches, instead of minding his business, "Bill, my boy, I'm vexed to the heart to see you in such a bad state of health. You're very ill with that complaint called an *all-overness*; however," says he, "I think I can cure you. Nothing will bring you about but three or four sound doses every day of a medicine called 'the oil o' the hazel.' Take the first dose now," says he, and he immediately banged him with a hazel cudgel until Bill's bones ached for a week afterward.

"If you were my son," said his master, "I tell you that, as long as I could get a piece of advice growing convenient in the hedges, I'd have you a different youth from what you are. If working was a sin, Bill, not an innocenter boy ever broke bread than you would be. Good people's scarce, you think; but however that may be, I throw it out as a hint, that you must take your medicine till you're cured, whenever you happen to get unwell in the same way."

From this out he kept Bill's nose to the grinding stone, and whenever his complaint returned he never failed to give him a hearty dose for his improvement.

In the course of time, however, Bill was his own man and his own master, but it would puzzle a saint to know whether the master or the man was the more precious youth in the eyes of the world.

He immediately married a wife, and devil a doubt of it, but if *he* kept *her* in whisky and sugar, *she* kept *him* in hot water. Bill drank and she drank; Bill fought and she fought; Bill was idle and she was idle; Bill whacked her and she whacked Bill. If Bill gave her one black eye, she gave him another, *just to keep herself in countenance*. Never was there a blessed pair so well met, and a beautiful sight it was to see them both at breakfast time, blinking at each other across the potato basket, Bill with his right eye black, and she with her left.

In short, they were the talk of the whole town; and to see Bill of a morning staggering home drunk, his shirt sleeves rolled up on his smutted arms, his breast open, and an old tattered leather apron, with one corner tucked up under his belt, singing one minute and fighting with his wife the next—she, reeling beside him with a discolored eye, as aforesaid, a dirty ragged cap on one side of her head, a pair of Bill's old slippers on her feet, a squalling child on her arm—now cuffing and dragging Bill, and again kissing and hugging him! Yes, it was a pleasant picture to see this loving pair in such a state!

This might do for a while, but it could not last. They were idle, drunken, and ill conducted; and it was not to be supposed that they would get a farthing candle on their words. They were, of course, *druv* to great straits; and faith, they soon found that their fighting and drinking and idleness made them the laughing sport of the neighbors; but neither brought food to their *childhre*, put a coat upon their backs, nor satisfied their landlord when he came to look for his own. Still, the never a one of Bill but was a funny fellow with strangers, though, as we said, the greatest rogue unhanged.

One day he was standing against his own anvil, completely in a brown study—being brought to his wit's end how to make out a breakfast for the family. The wife was scolding and cursing in the house, and the naked creatures of children squalling about her knees for food. Bill was fairly at an amplush, and knew not where or how to turn himself, when a poor, withered old beggar came into the forge, tottering on his staff. A long white beard fell from his chin, and he looked as thin and hungry that you might blow him, one would think, over the house. Bill at this moment had been brought to his senses by distress, and his heart had a touch of pity toward the old man, for, on looking at him a second time, he clearly saw starvation and sorrow in his face.

"God save you, honest man!" said Bill.

The old man gave a sigh, and raising himself with great pain on his staff, he looked at Bill in a very beseeching way.

"Musha, God save you kindly!" says he. "Maybe you could give a poor, hungry, helpless ould man a mouthful of something to ait? You see yourself I'm not able to work; if I was, I'd scorn to be beholding to anyone."

"Faith, honest man," said Bill, "if you knew who you're speaking to, you'd as soon ask a monkey for a churnstaff as me for either mate or money. There's not a blackguard in the three kingdoms so fairly on the *shaughran* as I am for both the one and the other. The wife within is sending the curses thick and heavy on me, and the *childhre's* playing the cat's melody to keep her in comfort. Take my word for it, poor man, if I had either mate or money I'd help you, for I know particularly well what it is to want them at the present speaking; an empty sack won't stand, neighbor."

So far Bill told him truth. The good thought was in his heart, because he found himself on a footing with the beggar; and nothing brings down pride, or softens the heart, like feeling what it is to want.

"Why, you are in a worse state than I am," said the old man; "you have a family to provide for, and I have only myself to support."

"You may kiss the book on that, my old worthy," replied Bill; "but come, what I can do for you I will; plant yourself up here beside the fire, and I'll give it a blast or two of my bellows that will warm the old blood in your body. It's a cold, miserable, snowy day, and a good heat will be of service."

"Thank you kindly," said the old man; "I *am* cold, and a warming at your fire will do me good, sure enough. Oh, but it *is* a bitter, bitter day; God bless it!"

He then sat down, and Bill blew a rousing blast that soon made the stranger edge back from the heat. In a short time he felt quite comfortable, and when the numbness was taken out of his joints, he buttoned himself up and prepared to depart.

"Now," says he to Bill, "you hadn't the food to give me, but *what you could you did*. Ask any three wishes you choose, and be they what they may, take my word for it, they shall be granted."

Now, the truth is, that Bill, though he believed himself a great man in point of 'cuteness, wanted, after all, a full quarter of being square, for there is always a great difference between a wise man and a knave. Bill was so much of a rogue that he could not, for the blood of him, ask an honest wish, but stood scratching his head in a puzzle.

"Three wishes!" said he. "Why, let me see—did you say *three*?"

"Ay," replied the stranger, "three wishes—that was what I said."

"Well," said Bill, "here goes—aha!—let me alone, my old worthy!—faith I'll overreach the parish, if what you say is true. I'll cheat them in dozens, rich and poor, old and young; let me alone, man—I have it here," and he tapped his forehead with great glee. "Faith, you're the sort to meet of a frosty morning, when a man wants his breakfast; and I'm sorry that I have neither money nor credit to get a bottle of whisky, that we might take our morning together."

"Well, but let us hear the wishes," said the old man; "my time is short, and I cannot stay much longer."

"Do you see this sledge hammer?" said Bill. "I wish, in the first place, that whoever takes it up in their hands may never be able to lay it down till I give them lave; and that whoever begins to sledge with it may never stop sledging till it's my pleasure to release him.

"Secondly—I have an armchair, and I wish that whoever sits down in it may never rise out of it till they have my consent.

"And, thirdly—that whatever money I put into my purse, nobody may have power to take it out of it but myself!"

"You Devil's rip!" says the old man in a passion, shaking his staff across Bill's nose. "Why did you not ask something that would sarve you both here and hereafter? Sure it's as common as the market cross, that there's not a vagabone in His Majesty's dominions stands more in need of both."

"Oh! By the elevens," said Bill, "I forgot that altogether! Maybe you'd be civil enough to let me change one of them? The sorra purtier wish ever was made than I'll make, if only you'll give me another chance at it."

"Get out, you reprobate," said the old fellow, still in a passion. "Your day of grace is past. Little you knew who was speaking to you all this time. I'm St. Moroky, you blackguard, and I gave you an opportunity of doing something for yourself and your family; but you neglected it, and now your fate is cast, you dirty, bog-trotting profligate. Sure, it's well known what you are! Aren't you a byword in everybody's mouth, you and your scold of a wife? By this and by that, if ever you happen to come across me again, I'll send you to where you won't freeze, you villain!"

He then gave Bill a rap of his cudgel over the head and laid him at his length beside the bellows, kicked a broken coal scuttle out of his way, and left the forge in a fury.

When Billy recovered himself from the effects of the blow and began to think on what had happened, he could have quartered himself with vexation for not asking great wealth as one of the wishes at least; but now the die was cast on him, and he could only make the most of the three he pitched upon.

He now bethought him how he might turn them to the best account, and here his cunning came to his aid. He began by sending for his wealthiest neighbors on pretence of business, and when he got them under his roof he offered them the armchair to sit down in. He now had them safe, nor could all the art of man relieve them except worthy Bill was willing. Bill's plan was to make the best bargain he could before he released his prisoners; and let him alone for knowing how to make their purses bleed. There wasn't a wealthy man in the country he did not fleece. The parson of the parish bled heavily; so did the lawyer; and a rich attorney, who had retired from practice, swore that the Court of Chancery itself was paradise compared to Bill's chair.

This was all very good for a time. The fame of his chair, however, soon spread; so did that of his sledge. In a short time neither man, woman, nor child would darken his door; all avoided him and his fixtures as they would a spring gun or mantrap. Bill, so long as he fleeced his neighbors, never wrought a hand's turn; so that when his money was out he found himself as badly off as ever. In addition to all this, his character was fifty times worse than before, for it was the general belief that he had dealings with the old boy. Nothing now could exceed his misery, distress, and ill temper. The wife and he and their children all fought among one another. Everybody hated them, cursed them, and avoided them. The people thought they were acquainted with more than Christian people ought to know. This, of course, came to Bill's ears, and it vexed him very much.

One day he was walking about the fields, thinking of how he could raise the wind once more; the day was dark, and he found himself, before he stopped, in the bottom of a lonely glen covered by great bushes that grew on each side. "Well," thought he, when every other means of raising money failed him, "it's reported that I'm in league with the old boy, and as it's a folly to have the name of the connection without the profit, I'm ready to make a bargain with him any day—so," said he, raising his voice, "Nick, you sinner, if you be convanient and willing why stand out here; show your best leg—here's your man."

The words were hardly out of his mouth when a dark, sober-looking old gentleman, not unlike a lawyer, walked up to him. Bill looked at the foot and saw the hoof. "Morrow, Nick," says

Bill.

"Morrow, Bill," says Nick. "Well, Bill, what's the news?"

"Devil a much myself hears of late," says Bill; "is there anything *fresh* below?"

"I can't exactly say, Bill; I spend little of my time down now; the Tories are in office, and my hands are consequently too full of business here to pay much attention to anything else."

"A fine place this, sir," says Bill, "to take a constitutional walk in; when I want an appetite I often come this way myself—hem! *High* feeding is very bad without exercise."

"High feeding! Come, come, Bill, you know you didn't taste a morsel these four-and-twenty hours."

"You know that's a bounce, Nick. I ate a breakfast this morning that would put a stone of flesh on you, if you only smelt at it."

"No matter; this is not to the purpose. What's that you were muttering to yourself a while ago? If you want to come to the brunt, here I'm for you."

"Nick," said Bill, "you're complate; you want nothing barring a pair of Brian O'Lynn's breeches."

Bill, in fact, was bent on making his companion open the bargain, because he had often heard that, in that case, with proper care on his own part, he might defeat him in the long run. The other, however, was his match.

"What was the nature of Brian's garment?" inquired Nick.

"Why, you know the song," said Bill:

Brian O'Lynn had no breeches to wear,
So he got a sheep's skin for to make him a pair;
With the fleshy side out and the wooly side in,
'They'll be pleasant and cool,' says Brian O'Lynn.

"A cool pare would sarve you, Nick."

"You're mighty waggish today, Misther Dawson."

"And good right I have," said Bill; "I'm a man snug and well to do in the world; have lots of money, plenty of good eating and drinking, and what more need a man wish for?"

"True," said the other; "in the meantime it's rather odd that so respectable a man should not have six inches of unbroken cloth in his apparel. You're as naked a tatterdemalion as I ever laid my eyes on; in full dress for a party of scarecrows, William?"

"That's my own fancy, Nick; I don't work at my trade like a gentleman. This is my forge dress, you know."

"Well, but what did you summon me here for?" said the other; "you may as well speak out, I tell you, for, my good friend, unless you do, I shan't. Smell that."

"I smell more than that," said Bill; "and by the way, I'll thank you to give me the windy side of you—curse all sulphur, I say. There, that's what I call an improvement in my condition. But as you *are* so stiff," says Bill, "why, the short and long of it is—that—ahem—you see I'm—tut—sure you know I have a thriving trade of my own, and that if I like I needn't be at a loss; but in the meantime I'm rather in a kind of a so—so—don't you *take*?"

And Bill winked knowingly, hoping to trick him into the first proposal.

"You must speak aboveboard, my friend," says the other. "I'm a man of few words, blunt and honest. If you have anything to say, be plain. Don't think I can be losing my time with such a pitiful rascal as you are."

"Well," says Bill. "I want money, then, and am ready to come into terms. What have you to say to that, Nick?"

"Let me see—let me look at you," says his companion, turning him about. "Now, Bill, in the first place, are you not as finished a scarecrow as ever stood upon two legs?"

"I play second fiddle to you there again," says Bill.

"There you stand, with the blackguards' coat of arms quartered under your eye, and—"

"Don't make little of *black*guards," said Bill, "nor spake disparagingly of your *own* crest."

"Why, what would you bring, you brazen rascal, if you were fairly put up at auction?"

"Faith, I'd bring more bidders than you would," said Bill, "if you were to go off at auction tomorrow. I tell you they should bid *downward* to come to your value, Nicholas. We have no coin *small* enough to purchase you."

"Well, no matter," said Nick. "If you are willing to be mine at the expiration of seven years, I will give you more money than ever the rascally breed of you was worth."

"Done!" said Bill. "But no disparagement to my family, in the meantime; so down with the hard cash, and don't be a *neger*."

The money was accordingly paid down; but as nobody was present, except the giver and receiver, the amount of what Bill got was never known.

"Won't you give me a luck penny?" said the old gentleman.

"Tut," said Billy, "so prosperous an old fellow as you cannot want it; however, bad luck to you, with all my heart! and it's rubbing grease to a fat pig to say so. Be off now, or I'll commit suicide on you. Your absence is a cordial to most people, you infernal old profligate. You have injured my morals even for the short time you have been with me, for I don't find myself so virtuous as I was."

"Is that your gratitude, Billy?"

"Is it gratitude *you* speak of, man? I wonder you don't blush when you name it. However, when you come again, if you bring a third eye in your head you will see what I mane, Nicholas, *ahagur*."

The old gentleman, as Bill spoke, hopped across the ditch on his way to *Downing* Street, where of late 'tis thought he possesses much influence.

Bill now began by degrees to show off, but still wrought a little at his trade to blindfold the neighbors. In a very short time, however, he became a great man. So long indeed as he was a poor rascal, no decent person would speak to him; even the proud servingmen at the "Big House" would turn up their noses at him. And he well deserved to be made little of by others, because he was mean enough to make little of himself. But when it was seen and known that he had oceans of money, it was wonderful to think, although he was *now* a greater blackguard than ever, how those who despised him before began to come round him and court his company. Bill, however, had neither sense nor spirit to make those sunshiny friends know their distance; not he—instead of that he was proud to be seen in decent company, and so long as the money lasted, it was "hail fellow well met" between himself and every fair-faced *spunger* who had a horse under him, a decent coat to his back, and a good appetite to eat his dinners. With riches and all, Bill was the same man still; but, somehow or other, there is a great difference between a rich profligate and a poor one, and Bill found it so to his cost in *both* cases.

Before half the seven years was passed, Bill had his carriage and his equipages; was hand and glove with my Lord This, and my Lord That; kept hounds and hunters; was the first sportsman at the Curragh; patronized every boxing ruffian he could pick up; and betted night and day on cards, dice, and horses. Bill, in short, *should* be a blood, and except he did all this, he could not presume to mingle with the fashionable bloods of his time.

It's an old proverb, however, that "what is got over the Devil's back is sure to go off under it," and in Bill's case this proved true. In short, the old boy himself could not supply him with money so fast as he made it fly; it was "come easy, go easy," with Bill, and so sign was on it, before he came within two years of his time he found his purse empty.

And now came the value of his summer friends to be known. When it was discovered that the cash was no longer flush with him—that stud, and carriage, and hounds were going to the hammer—whish! off they went, friends, relations, pot companions, dinner eaters, black-legs, and all, like a flock of crows that had smelled gunpowder. Down Bill soon went, week after week and day after day, until at last he was obliged to put on the leather apron and take to the hammer again; and not only that, for as no experience could make him wise, he once more began his taproom brawls, his quarrels with Judy, and took to his "high feeding" at the dry potatoes and salt. Now, too, came the cutting tongues of all who knew him, like razors upon him. Those that he scorned because they were poor and himself rich now paid him back his own with interest; and those that he had measured himself with, because they were rich, and who only countenanced him in consequence of his wealth, gave him the hardest word in their cheeks. The Devil mend him! He deserved it all, and more if he had got it.

Bill, however, who was a hardened sinner, never fretted himself down an ounce of flesh by what was said to him or of him. Not he; he cursed, and fought, and swore, and schemed away as usual, taking in everyone he could; and surely none could match him at villainy of all sorts and sizes.

At last the seven years became expired, and Bill was one morning sitting in his forge, sober and hungry, the wife cursing him, and the children squalling as before; he was thinking how he might defraud some honest neighbor out of a breakfast to stop their mouths and his own, too, when who walks in to him but old Nick to demand his bargain.

"Morrow, Bill!" says he with a sneer.

"The Devil welcome you!" says Bill. "But you have a fresh memory."

"A bargain's a bargain between two *honest* men, any day," says Satan; "when I speak of honest men, I mean yourself and *me*, Bill"; and he put his tongue in his cheek to make game of the unfortunate rogue he had come for.

"Nick, my worthy fellow," said Bill, "have bowels; you wouldn't do a shabby thing; you wouldn't disgrace your own character by putting more weight upon a falling man. You know what it is to get a *comedown* yourself, my worthy; so just keep your toe in your pump, and walk off with yourself somewhere else. A *cool* walk will sarve you better than my company, Nicholas."

"Bill, it's no use in shirking," said his friend; "your swindling tricks may enable you to cheat others, but you won't cheat *me*, I guess. You want nothing to make you perfect in your way but to travel; and travel you shall under my guidance, Billy. No, no— I'm not to be swindled, my good fellow. I have rather a—a— better opinion of myself, Mr. D., than to think that you could outwit one Nicholas Clutie, Esq.—ahem!"

"You may sneer, you sinner," replied Bill, "but I tell you that I have outwitted men who could buy and sell you to your face. Despair, you villain, when I tell you that *no attorney* could stand before me."

Satan's countenance got blank when he heard this; he wriggled and fidgeted about and appeared to be not quite comfortable.

"In that case, then," says he, "the sooner I *deceive* you the better; so turn out for the *Low Countries*."

"Is it come to that in earnest?" said Bill. "And are you going to act the rascal at the long run?"

"'Pon honor, Bill."

"Have patience, then, you sinner, till I finish this horseshoe— it's the last of a set I'm finishing for one of your friend the attorney's horses. And here, Nick, I hate idleness; you know it's the mother of mischief; take this sledge hammer and give a dozen strokes or so, till I get it out of hands, and then here's with you, since it must be so."

He then gave the bellows a puff that blew half a peck of dust in Clubfoot's face, whipped out the red-hot iron, and set Satan sledging away for bare life.

"Faith," says Bill to him, when the shoe was finished, "it's a thousand pities ever the sledge should be out of your hand; the great *Parra Gow* was a child to you at sledging, you're such an able tyke. Now just exercise yourself till I bid the wife and *childhre* good-by, and then I'm off."

Out went Bill, of course, without the slightest notion of coming back; no more than Nick had that he could not give up the sledging, and indeed neither could he, but was forced to work away as if he was sledging for a wager. This was just what Bill wanted. He was now compelled to sledge on until it was Bill's pleasure to release him; and so we leave him very industriously employed, while we look after the worthy who outwitted him.

In the meantime Bill broke cover and took to the country at large; wrought a little journey work wherever he could get it, and in this way went from one place to another, till, in the course of a month, he walked back very coolly into his own forge to see how things went on in his absence. There he found Satan in a rage, the perspiration pouring from him in torrents, hammering with might and main upon the naked anvil. Bill calmly leaned back against the wall, placed his hat upon the side of his head, put his hands into his breeches pockets, and began to whistle *Shaun Gow's* hornpipe. At length he says, in a very quiet and good-humored way:

"Morrow, Nick!"

"Oh!" says Nick, still hammering away. "Oh! you double-distilled villain (hech!), may the most refined ornamental (hech!) collection of curses that ever was gathered (hech!) into a single nosegay of ill fortune (hech!) shine in the buttonhole of your conscience (hech!) while your name is Bill Dawson! I denounce you (hech!) as a doublemilled villain, a finished, hot-pressed knave (hech!), in comparison of whom all the other knaves I ever knew (hech!), attorneys included, are honest men. I brand you (hech!) as the pearl of cheats, a tiptop take-in (hech!). I denounce you, I say again, for the villainous treatment (hech!) I have received at your hands in this most untoward (hech!) and unfortunate transaction between us; for (hech!) unfortunate, in every sense, is he that has anything to do with (hech!) such a prime and finished impostor."

"You're very warm, Nicky," says Bill; "what puts you into a passion, you old sinner? Sure if it's your own will and pleasure to take exercise at my anvil, *I'm* not to be abused for it. Upon my credit, Nicky, you ought to blush for using such blackguard language, so unbecoming your grave character. You cannot say that it was I set you a-hammering at the empty anvil, you profligate.

"However, as you are so very industrious, I simply say it would be a thousand pities to take you from it. Nick, I love industry in my heart, and I always encourage it, so work away; it's not often you spend your time so creditably. I'm afraid if you weren't at that you'd be worse employed."

"Bill, have bowels," said the operative; "you wouldn't go to lay more weight on a falling man, you know; you wouldn't disgrace your character by such a piece of iniquity as keeping an inoffensive gentleman advanced in years, at such an unbecoming and rascally job as this. Generosity's your top virtue, Bill; not but that you have many other excellent ones, as well as that, among which, as you say yourself, I reckon industry; but still it is in generosity you shine. Come, Bill, honor bright, and release me."

"Name the terms, you profligate."

"You're above terms, William; a generous fellow like you never thinks of terms."

"Good-by, old gentleman!" said Bill very coolly. "I'll drop in to see you once a month."

"No, no, Bill, you infern—a—a—. You excellent, worthy, delightful fellow, not so fast; not so fast. Come, name your terms, you sland—My dear Bill, name your terms."

"Seven years more."

"I agree; but—"

"And the same supply of cash as before, down on the nail here."

"Very good; very good. You're rather simple, Bill; rather soft, I must confess. Well, no matter. I shall yet turn the tab—a—hem! You are an exceedingly simple fellow, Bill; still there will come a day, my *dear* Bill—there will come—'

"Do you grumble, you vagrant? Another word, and I double the terms."

"Mum, William—mum; *tace* is Latin for a candle."

"Seven years more of grace, and the same measure of the needful that I got before. Ay or no?"

"Of grace, Bill! Ay! Ay! Ay! There's the cash. I accept the terms. Oh, blood! The rascal—of grace! Bill!"

"Well, now drop the hammer and vanish," says Billy; "but what would you think to take this sledge, while you stay, and give me a—Eh! Why in such a hurry?" he added, seeing that

Satan withdrew in double-quick time.

"Hello! Nicholas!" he shouted. "Come back; you forgot something!" And when the old gentleman looked behind him, Billy shook the hammer at him, on which he vanished altogether.

Billy now got into his old courses; and what shows the kind of people the world is made of, he also took up with his old company. When they saw that he had the money once more and was sowing it about him in all directions, they immediately began to find excuses for his former extravagance.

"Say what you will," said one, "Bill Dawson's a spirited fellow that bleeds like a prince."

"He's a hospitable man in his own house, or out of it, as ever lived," said another.

"His only fault is," observed a third, "that he is, if anything, too generous and doesn't know the value of money; his fault's on the right side, however."

"He has the spunk in him," said a fourth; "keeps a capital table, prime wines, and a standing welcome for his friends."

"Why," said a fifth, "if he doesn't enjoy his money while he lives, he won't when he's dead; so more power to him, and a wider throat to his purse."

Indeed, the very persons who were cramming themselves at his expense despised him at heart. They knew very well, however, how to take him on the weak side. Praise his generosity, and he would do anything; call him a man of spirit, and you might fleece him to his face. Sometimes he would toss a purse of guineas to this knave, another to that flatterer, a third to a bully, and a fourth to some broken-down rake—and all to convince them that he was a sterling friend—a man of mettle and liberality. But never was he known to help a virtuous and struggling family—to assist the widow or the fatherless, or to do any other act that was truly useful. It is to be supposed the reason of this was that as he spent it, as most of the world do, in the service of the Devil, by whose aid he got it, he was prevented from turning it to a good account. Between you and me, dear reader, there are more persons acting after Bill's fashion in the same world than you dream about.

When his money was out again, his friends played him the same rascally game once more. No sooner did his poverty become plain than the knaves began to be troubled with small fits of modesty, such as an unwillingness to come to his place when there was no longer anything to be got there. A kind of virgin bashfulness prevented them from speaking to him when they saw him getting out on the wrong side of his clothes. Many of them would turn away from him in the prettiest and most delicate manner when they thought he wanted to borrow money from them—all for fear of putting him to the blush for asking it. Others again, when they saw him coming toward their houses about dinner hour, would become so confused, from mere gratitude, as to think themselves in another place; and their servants, seized, as it were, with the same feeling, would tell Bill that their masters were "not at home."

At length, after traveling the same villainous round as before, Bill was compelled to betake himself, as the last remedy, to the forge; in other words, he found that there is, after all, nothing in this world that a man can rely on so firmly and surely as his own industry. Bill, however, wanted the organ of common sense, for his experience—and it was sharp enough to leave an impression—ran off him like water off a duck.

He took to his employment sorely against his grain, but he had now no choice. He must either work or starve, and starvation is like a great doctor—nobody tries it till every other remedy fails them. Bill had been twice rich; twice a gentleman among blackguards, but always a blackguard among gentlemen, for no wealth or acquaintance with decent society could rub the rust of his native vulgarity off him. He was now a common blinking sot in his forge; a drunken bully in the taproom, cursing and browbeating everyone as well as his wife; boasting of how much money he had spent in his day; swaggering about the high doings he carried on; telling stories about himself and Lord This at the Curragh; the dinners he gave—how much they cost him—and attempting to extort credit upon the strength of his former wealth. He was too ignorant, however, to know that he was publishing his own disgrace and that it was a mean-spirited thing to be proud of what ought to make him blush through a deal board nine inches thick.

He was one morning industriously engaged in a quarrel with his wife, who, with a three-legged stool in her hand, appeared to mistake his head for his own anvil; he, in the meantime, paid his addresses to her with his leather apron, when who steps in to jog his memory about the little agreement that was between them but old Nick. The wife, it seems, in spite of all her exertions to the contrary, was getting the worst of it; and Sir Nicholas, willing to appear a gentleman of great gallantry, thought he could not do less than take up the lady's quarrel, particularly as Bill had laid her in a sleeping posture. Now Satan thought this too bad, and as he felt himself under many obligations to the sex, he determined to defend one of them on the present occasion; so as Judy rose, he turned upon her husband and floored him by a clever facer.

"You unmanly villain," said he, "is this the way you treat your wife? 'Pon honor Bill, I'll chastise you on the spot. I could not stand by, a spectator of such ungentlemanly conduct, without giving you all claim to gallant—" Whack! The word was divided in his mouth by the blow of a churnstaff from Judy, who no sooner saw Bill struck than she nailed Satan, who "fell" once more.

"What, you villain! That's for striking my husband like a murderer behind his back," said Judy, and she suited the action to the word. "That's for interfering between man and wife. Would you murder the poor man before my face, eh? If he bates me, you shabby dog you, who has a better right? I'm sure it's nothing out of your pocket. Must you have your finger in every pie?"

This was anything but *idle* talk, for at every word she gave him a remembrance, hot and heavy. Nicholas backed, danced, and hopped; she advanced, still drubbing him with great perseverance, till at length he fell into the redoubtable armchair, which stood exactly behind him. Bill, who had been putting in two blows for Judy's one, seeing that his enemy was safe, now got between the Devil and his wife, *a situation that few will be disposed to envy him.*

"Tenderness, Judy," said the husband; "I hate cruelty. Go put the tongs in the fire, and make them red-hot. Nicholas, you have a nose," said he.

Satan began to rise but was rather surprised to find that he could not budge.

"Nicholas," says Bill, "how is your pulse? You don't look well; that is to say, you look worse than usual."

The other attempted to rise but found it a mistake.

"I'll thank you to come along," said Bill. "I have a fancy to travel under your guidance, and we'll take the *Low Countries* in our way, won't we? Get to your legs, you sinner; you know a bargain's a bargain between two *honest* men, Nicholas, meaning *yourself* and *me*. Judy, are the tongs hot?"

Satan's face was worth looking at as he turned his eyes from the husband to the wife and then fastened them on the tongs, now nearly at a furnace heat in the fire, conscious at the same time that he could not move out of the chair.

"Billy," said he, "you won't forget that I rewarded you generously the last time I saw you, in the way of business."

"Faith, Nicholas, it fails me to remember any generosity I ever showed you. Don't be womanish. I simply want to see what kind of stuff your nose is made of and whether it will stretch like a rogue's conscience. If it does we will flatter it up the chimly with red-hot tongs, and when this old hat is fixed on the top of it, let us alone for a weathercock."

"Have a *fellow feeling*, Mr. Dawson; you know we ought not to dispute. Drop the matter, and I give you the next seven years."

"We know all that," says Billy, opening the red-hot tongs very coolly.

"Mr. Dawson," said Satan, "if you cannot remember my friendship to yourself, don't forget how often I stood your father's friend, your grandfather's friend, and the friend of all your relations up to the tenth generation. I intended, also, to stand by your children after you, so long as the name of Dawson—and a respectable one it is—might last."

"Don't be blushing, Nick," says Bill; "you are too modest; that was ever your failing; hold up your head, there's money bid for you. I'll give you such a nose, my good friend, that you will have to keep an outrider before you, to carry the end of it on his shoulder."

"Mr. Dawson, I pledge my honor to raise your children in the world as high as they can go, no matter whether they desire it or not."

"That's very kind of you," says the other, "and I'll do as much for your nose."

He gripped it as he spoke, and the old boy immediately sung

out; Bill pulled, and the nose went with him like a piece of warm wax. He then transferred the tongs to Judy, got a ladder, resumed the tongs, ascended the chimney, and tugged stoutly at the nose until he got it five feet above the roof. He then fixed the hat upon the top of it and came down.

"There's a weathercock," said Billy; "I defy Ireland to show such a beauty. Faith, Nick, it would make the purtiest steeple for a church in all Europe, and the old hat fits it to a shaving."

In this state, with his nose twisted up the chimney, Satan sat for some time, experiencing the novelty of what might be termed a peculiar sensation. At last the worthy husband and wife began to relent.

"I think," said Bill, "that we have made the most of the nose, as well as the joke; I believe, Judy, it's long enough."

"What is?" says Judy.

"Why, the joke," said the husband.

"Faith, and I think so is the nose," said Judy.

"What do you say yourself, Satan?" said Bill.

"Nothing at all, William," said the other; "but that—ha! ha!—it's a good joke—an excellent joke, and a goodly nose, too, as it *stands*. You were always a gentlemanly man, Bill, and did things with a grace; still, if I might give an opinion on such a trifle—"

"It's no trifle at all," says Bill, "if you spake of the nose."

"Very well, it is not," says the other; "still, I am decidedly of opinion that if you could shorten both the joke and the nose without further violence, you would lay me under very heavy obligations, which I shall be ready to acknowledge and *repay* as I ought."

"Come," said Bill, "shell out once more, and be off for seven years. As much as you came down with the last time, and vanish."

The words were scarcely spoken, when the money was at his feet and Satan invisible. Nothing could surpass the mirth of Bill and his wife at the result of this adventure. They laughed till they fell down on the floor.

It is useless to go over the same ground again. Bill was still incorrigible. The money went as the Devil's money always goes. Bill caroused and squandered but could never turn a penny of it to a good purpose. In this way year after year went, till the seventh was closed and Bill's hour come. He was now, and had been for some time past, as miserable a knave as ever. Not a shilling had he, nor a shilling's worth, with the exception of his forge, his cabin, and a few articles of crazy furniture. In this state he was standing in his forge as before, straining his ingenuity how to make out a breakfast, when Satan came to look after him. The old gentleman was sorely puzzled how to get at him. He kept skulking and sneaking about the forge for some time, till he saw that Bill hadn't a cross to bless himself with. He immediately changed himself into a guinea and lay in an open place where he knew Bill would see him. "If," said he, "I once get into his possession, I can manage him." The honest smith took the bait, for it was well gilded; he clutched the guinea, put it into his purse, and closed it up. "Ho! Ho!" shouted the Devil out of the purse. "You're caught, Bill; I've secured you at last, you knave you. Why don't you despair you villain, when you think of what's before you?"

"Why, you unlucky ould dog," said Bill, "is it there you are? Will you always drive your head into every loophole that's set for you? Faith, Nick *achora,* I never had you bagged till now."

Satan then began to tug and struggle with a view of getting out of the purse, but in vain.

"Mr. Dawson," said he, "we understand each other. I'll give the seven years additional and the cash on the nail."

"Be aisey, Nicholas. You know the weight of the hammer, that's enough. It's not a whipping with feathers you're going to get, anyhow. Just be aisey."

"Mr. Dawson, I grant I'm not your match. Release me, and I double the case. I was merely trying your temper when I took the shape of a guinea."

"Faith and I'll try yours before I lave it, I've a notion." He immediately commenced with the sledge, and Satan sang out with a considerable want of firmness. "Am I heavy enough?" said Bill.

"Lighter, lighter, William, if you love me. I haven't been well latterly, Mr. Dawson—I have been delicate—my health, in short, is in a very precarious state, Mr. Dawson."

"I can believe *that*,' said Bill, "and it will be more so before I have done with you. Am I doing it right?"

"Bill," said Nick, "is this gentlemanly treatment in your own respectable shop? Do you think, if you dropped into my little place, that I'd act this rascally part toward you? Have you no compunction?"

"I know," replied Bill, sledging away with vehemence, "that you're notorious for giving your friends a *warm* welcome. Divil an ould youth more so; but you must be daling in bad coin, must you? However, good or bad, you're in for a sweat now, you sinner. Am I doin' it purty?"

"Lovely, William—but, if possible, a little more delicate."

"Oh, how delicate you are! Maybe a cup o' tay would sarve you, or a little small gruel to compose your stomach?"

"Mr. Dawson," said the gentleman in the purse, "hold your hand and let us understand one another. I have a proposal to make."

"Hear the sinner anyhow," said the wife.

"Name your own sum," said Satan, "only set me free."

"No, the sorra may take the toe you'll budge till you let Bill off," said the wife; "hould him hard, Bill, barrin' he sets you clear of your engagement."

"There it is, my posy," said Bill; "that's the condition. If you don't give *me up*, here's at you once more—and you must double the cash you gave the last time, too. So, if you're of that opinion, say *ay*—leave the cash and be off."

The money appeared in a glittering heap before Bill, upon which he exclaimed, "The *ay* has it, you dog. Take to your pumps now, and fair weather after you, you vagrant; but, Nicholas—Nick—here, here—" The other looked back and saw Bill, with a broad grin upon him, shaking the purse at him. "Nicholas, come back," said he. "I'm short a guinea." Nick shook his fist and disappeared.

It would be useless to stop now, merely to inform our readers that Bill was beyond improvement. In short, he once more took to his old habits and lived on exactly in the same manner as before. He had two sons—one as great a blackguard as himself, and who was also named after him; the other was a well-conducted, virtuous young man called James, who left his father and, having relied upon his own industry and honest perseverance in life, arrived afterward to great wealth and built the town called Castle Dawson, which is so called from its founder until this day.

Bill, at length, in spite of all his wealth, was obliged, as he himself said, "to travel"—in other words, he fell asleep one day and forgot to awaken; or, in still plainer terms, he died.

Now, it is usual, when a man dies, to close the history of his life and adventures at once; but with our hero this cannot be the case. The moment Bill departed he very naturally bent his steps toward the residence of St. Moroky, as being, in his opinion, likely to lead him toward the snuggest berth he could readily make out. On arriving, he gave a very humble kind of knock, and St. Moroky appeared.

"God save your Reverence!" said Bill, very submissively.

"Be off; there's no admittance here for so poor a youth as you are," said St. Moroky.

He was now so cold and fatigued that he cared like where he went, provided only, as he said himself, "he could rest his bones and get an air of the fire." Accordingly, after arriving at a large black gate, he knocked, as before, and was told he would get *instant* admittance the moment he gave his name.

"Billy Dawson," he replied.

"Off, instantly," said the porter to his companions, "and let His Majesty know that the rascal he dreads so much is here at the gate."

Such a racket and tumult were never heard as the very mention of Billy Dawson created.

In the meantime, his old acquaintance came running toward the gate with such haste and consternation that his tail was several times nearly tripping up his heels.

"Don't admit that rascal," he shouted; "bar the gate—make every chain and lock and bolt fast—I won't be safe—and I won't stay here, nor none of us need stay here, if he gets in—my bones are sore yet after him. No, no—begone, you villain— you'll get no entrance here—I know you too well."

Bill could not help giving a broad, malicious grin at Satan, and, putting his nose through the bars, he exclaimed, "Ha! You ould dog, I have you afraid of me at last, have I?"

He had scarcely uttered the words, when his foe, who stood inside, instantly tweaked him by the nose, and Bill felt as if he had been gripped by the same red-hot tongs with which he himself had formerly tweaked the nose of Nicholas.

Bill then departed but soon found that in consequence of the inflammable materials which strong drink had thrown into his nose, that organ immediately took fire, and, indeed, to tell the truth, kept burning night and day, winter and summer, without ever once going out from that hour to this.

Such was the sad fate of Billy Dawson, who has been walking without stop or stay, from place to place, ever since; and in consequence of the flame on his nose, and his beard being tangled like a wisp of hay, he has been christened by the country folk Will-O'-the-Wisp, while, as it were, to show the mischief of his disposition, the circulating knave, knowing that he must seek the coldest bogs and quagmires in order to cool his nose, seizes upon that opportunity of misleading the unthinking and tipsy night travelers from their way, just that he may have the satisfaction of still taking in as many as possible.

The Sexton of Cashel
D.R. McAnally, Jr.

ALL OVER IRELAND, from Cork to Belfast, from Dublin to Galway, are scattered the ruins of churches, abbeys, and ecclesiastical buildings, the relics of a country once rich, prosperous and populous. These ruins raise their castellated walls and towers, noble even in decay, sometimes in the midst of a village, crowded with the miserably poor; sometimes on a mountain, in every direction commanding magnificent prospects; sometimes on an island in one of the lakes, which, like emeralds in a setting of deeper green, gem the surface of the rural landscape and contribute to increase the beauty of scenery not surpassed in the world.

Ages ago the voice of prayer and the song of praise ceased to ascend from these sacred edifices, and they are now visited only by strangers, guides, and parties of humble peasants, the foremost bearing on their shoulders the remains of a companion to be laid within the hallowed enclosure, for although the church is in ruins, the ground in and about it is still holy and in service when pious hands lay away in the bosom of earth the bodies of those who have borne the last burden, shed the last tear, and succumbed to the last enemy. But among all the pitiable spectacles presented in this unhappy country, none is better calculated to inspire sad reflections than a rural graveyard. The walls of the ruined church tower on high, with massive cornice and pointed window; within stand monuments and tombs of the Irish great; kings, princes, and archbishops lie together, while about the hallowed edifice are huddled the graves of the poor; here, sinking so as to be indistinguishable from the sod; there, rising in new-made proportions; yonder marked with a wooden cross, or a round stick, the branch of a tree rudely trimmed, but significant as the only token bitter poverty could furnish of undying love; while over all the graves, alike of the high born and of the lowly, the weeds and nettles grow.

"Sure there 's no saxton, Sorr," said car-man Jerry Magwire, in answer to a question, "We dig the graves ourselves whin we put them away, an' sometimes there 's a fight in the place whin two berryin's meet. Why is that? Faith, it 's not for us to be talkin' o' them deep subjects widout respict, but it 's the belafe that the last wan berrid must be carryin' wather all the time to the sowls in Purgathory till the next wan comes to take the place av him. So, ye mind, when two berryin's happen to meet, aitch party is shtrivin' to be done foorst, an' wan thries to make the other lave aff, an' thin they have it. Troth, Irishmen are too handy wid their fishts entirely, it 's a weak pint wid 'em. But it 's a sad sight, so it is, to see the graves wid the nettles on thim an' the walls all tumblin'. It is n't every owld church that has a caretaker like him of Cashel. Bedad, he was betther nor a flock av goats to banish the weeds.

"Who was he? Faith, I niver saw him but the wan time, an' thin I had only a shot at him as he was turnin' a corner, for it was as I was lavin' Cormac's chapel the time I wint to Cashel on a pinance, bekase av a little throuble on me mind along av a pig that was n't mine, but got mixed wid mine whin I was afther killin' it. But, as I obsarved, it was only a shot at him I had, for it was n't aften that he was seen in the daytime, but done all his work in the night, an' it is n't me that 'ud be climbin' the Rock av Cashel afther the sun 'ud go to slape. Not that there 's avil sper'ts there, for none that 's bad can set fut on that holy ground day or night, but I 'm not afther wantin' to meet a sper't av any kind, even if it 's good, for how can ye tell about thim. Sure aven the blessed saints have been desaved, an' it 's not for a sinner like me to be settin' up for to know more than thimselves. But it was the long, bent body that he had, like he 'd a burdhen on his back, as they say, God be good to him, he had on his sowl, an' the great, blue eyes lookin' out as if he was gazin' on the other worruld. No, I did n't run down the rock, but I did n't walk aither, but jist bechuxt the two, wid a sharp eye round the corners that I passed. No more do I belave there was harrum in him, but, God's prisence be about us, ye can't tell.

"He was a man o' Clare be the name av Paddy O'Sullivan, an' lived on the highway betune Crusheen an' Ennis, an' they do say that whin he was a lad, there was n't a finer to be seen in the County; a tall, shtrappin' young felly wid an eye like a bay'net, an' a fisht like a shmith, an' the fut an' leg av him 'ud turn the hearts o' half the wimmin in the parish. An' they was all afther him, like they always do be whin a man is good lookin', sure I 've had a little o' that same exparience mesilf. Ye need n't shmile. I know me head has no more hair on it than an egg, an' I think me last tooth 'ull come out tomorrer, bad cess to the day, but they do say that forty years ago, I cud have me pick av the gurruls, an' mebbe they 're mishtaken an' mebbe not. But I was sayin', the gurruls were afther Paddy like rats afther chaze, an' sorra wan o' thim but whin she spied him on the road, 'ud shlip behind the hedge to shmooth her locks a bit an' set the shawl shtraight on her head. An' whin there was a bit av a dance, niver a boy 'ud get a chance till Paddy made his chice to dance wid, an' sorra a good word the rest o' the gurruls 'ud give that same. Och, the tongues that wimmin have! Sure they 're sharper nor a draggin's tooth. Faith, I know that well too, for I married two o' them an' larned a deal too afther doin' it, an' axin' yer pardon, it 's my belafe that if min knewn as much before marryin' as afther, bedad, the owld maid population 'ud be greatly incrased.

"Howandiver, afther a bit, Paddy left carin' for thim all, that, in my consate, is a moighty safe way, and begun to look afther wan. Her name was Nora O'Moore, an' she was as clever a gurrul as 'ud be found bechuxt Limerick an' Galway. She was kind o' resarved like, wid a face as pale as a shroud, an' hair as black as a crow, an' eyes that looked at ye an' never seen ye. No more did she talk much, an' whin Paddy 'ud be sayin' his fine spaches, she 'd listen wid her eyes cast down, an' whin she 'd had enough av his palaver, she 'd jist look at him an' somehow Paddy felt that his p'liteness was n't the thing to work wid. He cud n't undhershtand her, an' bedad, many 's the man that 's caught be not undhershtandin' thim. There 's rivers that 's quiet on top bekase they 're deep, an' more that 's quiet bekase they 're not deep enough to make a ripple, but phat 's the differ if ye can't sound thim, an' whin a woman 's quiet, begorra, it 's not aisy to say if she 's deep or shallow. But Nora was a deep wan, an' as good as iver drew a breath. She thought a dale av Paddy, only she 'd be torn limb from limb afore she 'd let him know it till he confist first. Well, my dear, paddy wint on, at firsht it was only purtindin' he was, an' whin he found she cud n't be tuk wid his chaff, he got in airnest, an' afore he knewn it, he was dead in love wid Nora, an' had as much show for gettin' out agin as a shape in a bog, an' sorra a bit did he know at all at all, whether she cared a traneen for him. It 's funny entirely that whin a man thinks a woman is afther him, he 's aff like a hare, but if she does n't car a rap, begob, he 'll give the nose aff his face to get her. So it was wid paddy an' Nora, axceptin' that Paddy did n't know that Nora wanted him as much as he wanted her.

"So, wan night, whin he was bringin' her from a dance that they 'd been at, he said to her that he loved her betther than life an' towld her would she marry him, an' she axed was it jokin' or in airnest he was, an' he said cud she doubt it whin he loved her wid all the veins av his heart, an' she trimbled, turnin' paler than iver, an' thin blushin' rosy red for joy an' towld him yes, an' he kissed her, an' they both thought the throuble was all over foreiver. It 's a way thim lovers has,, an' they must be axcused, bekase it 's the same wid thim all.

"But it wan n't at all, fur Nora had an owld squireen av a father, that was as full av maneness as eggs is av mate. Sure he was the divil entirely at home, an' niver left off wid the crassness that was in im. The timper av him was spiled be rason o' losing his bit o' money wid cards an' racin', an' like some min, he tuk it out wid his wife an' dawther. There was only the three o' thim in it, an' they do say that whin he was crazy wid dhrink, he 'd bate thim right an' lift, an' turn thim out o' the cabin into the night, niver heeding, the baste, phat 'ud come to thim. But they niver said a word thimselves, an' the nabers only larned av it be seein' thim.

"Well. Whin O'Moore was towld that Paddy was kapin' comp'ny wid Nora, an' the latther an' her mother towld him she wanted fur to marry Paddy, thw owld felly got tarin' mad, fur he was as proud as a paycock, an' though he 'd nothin' himself, he riz agin the match, an' all the poor mother an' Nora cud say 'ud n't sthir him.

"'Sure I 've nothin' agin him,' he 'd say, 'barrin' he 's as poor as a fiddler, an' I want Nora to make a good match.'

"Now the owld felly had a match in his mind fur Nora, a lad from Tipperary, whose father was a farmer there, an' had a shmart bit av land wid no end av shape grazin' on it, an' the Tipperary boy was n't bad at all, only as shtupid as a donkey, an' whin he 'd come to see Nora, bad cess to the word he 'd to say, only look at her a bit an' thin fall aslape an' knock his head agin the wall. But he wanted her, an' his father an' O'Moore put their heads together over a glass an' aggrade that the young wans 'ud be married.

"'Sure I don't love him a bit, father,' Nora 'ud say.

"'Be aff wid yer nonsinse,' he 'd say to her. 'Phat does it matther about love, whin he 's got more nor a hunderd shape. Sure I wud n't give the wool av thim fur all the love in Clare,' says he, an' wid that the argymint 'ud end.

"So Nora towld paddy an' Paddy said he 'd not give her up for all the men in Tipperary or all the shape in Ireland, an' it was aggrade that in wan way or another, they 'd be married in spite av owld O'Moore, though Nora hated to do it, bekase, as I was afther tellin' ye, she was a good gurrul, an' wint to mass an' to her duty reg'lar. But like the angel that she was, she towld her mother an' the owld lady was agrayble, an' so Nora consinted.

"But O'Moore was shrewder than a fox whin he was sober, an' that was whin he 'd no money to shpend in dhrink, an' this being' wan o' thim times, he watched Nora an' begun to suspicion somethin'. So he made belave that everything was right an' the next time that Murphy, that bein' the name o' the Tipperary farmer, came, the two owld fellys settled it that O'Moore an' Nora 'ud come to Tipperary av the Winsday afther, that bein' the day o' the fair in Ennis that they knew Paddy 'ud be at, an' whin they got to Tipperary, they 'd marry Nora an' young Murphy at wanst. So owld Murphy was to sind the câr afther thim an' everything was made sure. So, av the Winsday, towards noon, says owld O'Moore to Nora,—-

"'Be in a hurry now, me child, an' make yersel' as fine as ye can, an' Murphy's câr 'ull be here to take us to the fair.'

"Nora did n't want to go, for Paddy was comin' out in the afthernoon, misthrustin' that owld O'Moore 'ud be at the fair. But O'Moore only towld her to make hast wid hersilf or they 'd be late, an' she did. So the câr came, wid a boy dhriving, an' owld O'Moore axed the boy if he wanted to go to the fair, so that Nora cud n't hear him, an' the boy said yes, an' O'Moore towld him to go an' he 'd dhrive an' bring him back tomorrer. So the boy wint away, an' O'Moore an' Nora got up an' shtrarted. Whin they came to the crass-road, O'Moore tuk the road to Tipperary.

"'Sure father, ye 're wrong,' says Nora, 'that 's not the way.'

"'No more is it,' said the owld desayver, 'but I 'm afther wantin' to see a frind o' mine over here a bit an' we 'll come round to the Ennis road on the other side,' says he.

"So Nora thought no more av it, but whin they wint on an' on, widout shtoppin' at all, she begun to be disquisitive agin.

"'Father, is it to Ennis or not ye 're takin' me,' says she.

"Now, be this time, they 'd got on a good bit, an' the owld villin seen it was no use thryin' to desave her any longer.

"'I 'm not,' says he, 'but it 's to Tipperary ye 're goin', where ye 're to be married to Misther Murphy this blessed day, so ye are, an' make no throuble about it aither, or it 'll be the worse for ye,' says he, lookin' moighty black.

"Well, at first Nora thought her heart 'ud shtand still. 'Sure, Father dear, ye don't mane it, ye cud n't be so cruel. It 's like a blighted tree I 'd be, wid that man,' an' she thried to jump aff the câr, but her father held her wid a grip av stale.

"'Kape still,' says he wid his teeth closed like a vise. 'If ye crass me, I 'm like to murdher ye. It 's me only escape from prison, for I 'm in debt an' Murphy 'ull help me,' says he. 'Sure,' says he, saftenin' a bit as he seen the white face an' great pleadin' eyes, 'Sure ye 'll be happy enough wid Murphy. He loves ye, an' ye can love him, an' besides, think o' the shape.'

"But Nora sat there, a poor dumb thing, wid her eyes lookin' deeper than iver wid the misery that was in thim. An' from that minit, she did n't spake a word, but all her sowl was determined that she 'd die afore she 'd marry Murphy, but how she 'd get out av it she did n't know at all, but watched her chance to run.

"Now it happened that owld O'Moore, bein' disturbed in his mind, mistuk the way, an' whin he come to the crass-roads, wan to Tipperary an' wan to Cashel, he tuk the wan for the other, an' whin the horse thried to go home to Tipperary, he wud n't let him, but pulled him into the Cashel road. Faix, he might have knewn that if he 'd let the baste alone, he 'd take him right, fur horses knows a deal more than ye 'd think. That horse o' mine is only a common garron av a baste, but he tuk me from Ballyvaughn to Lisdoon Varna wan night whin it was so dark that ye cud n't find yer nose, an' wint be the rath in a gallop, like he 'd seen the good people. But niver mind, I 'll tell ye the shtory some time, only I was thinkin' O'Moore might have knewn betther.

"But they tuk the Cashel road an' wint on as fast as they cud, for it was afthernoon an' gettin' late. An' O'Moore kept lookin' about an' wonderin' that he did n't know the counthry, though he 'd niver been to Tipperary but wanst, an' afther a while, he gev up that he was lost entirely. No more wud he ax the people on the road, but gev thim 'God save ye' very short, for he was afeared Nora might make throuble. An' by an' by, it come on to rain, an' whin they turned the corner av a hill, he seen the Rock o' Cashel wid the churches onit, an' thin he stopped.

"'Phat 's this at all,' says he. 'Faix, if that is n't Cashel I 'll ate it, an' we 've come out o' the way altogether.'

"Nora answered him niver a word, an' he shtarted to turn round, but whin he looked at the horse, the poor baste was knocked up entirely.

"'We 'll go on to Cashel,' says he, 'an' find a shebeen, an' go back in the mornin'. It 's hard luck we 're afther havin',' says he.

"So they wint on, an' jist afore they got to the Rock, they seen a nate lodgin' house be the road an' wint in. He left Nora to sit be the fire, while he wint to feed the horse, an' whin he come back in a minit, he looked for her, but faith, she 'd given him the shlip an' was gone complately.

"'Where is me dawther?' says he.

"'Faith, I dunno,' says the maid. 'She walked out av the dure on the minit,' says she.

"Owld O'Moore run, an' Satan an' none but himself turned him in the way she was afther takin.' God be good to thim, no wan iver knewn phat tuk place, but whin they wint wid a lanthern to sarch fur thim whin they did n't raturn, they found the marks o' their feet on the road to the strame. Half way down the path they picked up Nora's shawl that was torn an' flung on the ground an' fut marks in plenty they found, as if he had caught her an' thried to howld her an' cud n't, an' on the marks wint to the high bank av the strame, that was a torrent be razon av the rain. An' there they ended wid a big slice o' the bank fallen in, an' the sarchers crassed thimselves wid fright an wint back an' prayed for the repose av their sowls.

"The next day they found thim, a good Irish mile down the strame, owld O'Moore wid wan hand howlding her gown an' the other wan grippin' her collar an' the clothes half torn aff her poor cowld corpse, her hands stratched out afore her, wid the desperation in her heart to get away, an' her white face wid the great eyes an' the light gone out av thim, the poor craythur, God give her rest, an' so to us all.

"They laid thim dacintly, wid candles an' all, an' the wake that they had was shuparb, fur the shtory was towld in all the counthry, wid the vartues av Nora; an' the O'Brian's come from Ennis, an' the O'Moore's from Crusheen, an' the Murphy's an' their frinds from Tipperary, an' more from Clonmel. There was a power av atin' an' slathers av dhrink fur thim that wanted it, fur, d' ye mind, thim of Cashel thried fur to show the rale Irish hoshpitality bekase O'Moore an' Nora were sint there to die an' they thought it was their juty to thrate thim well. An' all the County Clare an' Tipperary was at the berryin', an' they had three keeners, the best that iver was, wan from Ennis, wan from Tipperary, an' wan from Limerick, so that the praises av Nora wint on day an' night till the berryin' was done. An' they made Nora's grave in Cormac's Chapel just front o' the Archbishop's tomb in the wall an' berried her first, an' tuk O'Moore as far from her as they cud get him, an' put his grave as clost be the wall as they cud go fur the shtones an' jist ferninst the big gate on the left hand side, an' berried him last, an' sorra the good word they had fur him aither.

"Poor Paddy wint nayther to the wake nor to the berryin', fur afther they towld him the news, he sat as wan in a dhrame, no more cud they rouse him. He 'd go to his work very quite, an' niver shpake a word. An' so it was, about a fortnight afther, he says to his mother, says he, 'Mother I seen Nora last night an' she stood be me side an' laid her hand on me brow, an' says "Come to Cashel, Paddy dear, an' be wid me."' An' his mother was frighted entirely, for she parsaved he was wrong in his head. She thried to aise his mind, but the next night he disappared. They folly 'd him to Cashel, but he dodged an' kept from thim complately whin they come an' so they left him. In the day he 'd hide an' slape, an' afther night, Nora's sper't 'ud mate him an' walk wid him up an' down the shtones av the Chapel an' undher the arches av the Cathaydral, an' he cared fur her grave, an' bekase she was berried there, fur the gravs av all thim that shlept on the Rock. No more had he any frinds, but thim o' Cashel 'ud lave pitaties an' bread where he 'd see it an' so he lived. Fur sixty wan years was he on the Rock an' never left it, but he 'd sometimes show himself in the day whin there was a berryin', an' say, 'Ye 've brought me another frind,' an' help in the work, an' never was there a graveyard kept like that o' Cashel.

"When he got owld, an' where he cud look into the other worruld, Nora came ivery night an' brought more wid her, sper'ts av kings an' bishops that rest on Cashel, an' there 's thim that 's seen the owld man walkin' in Cormac's Chapel, Nora holdin' him up an' him discoorsin' wid the mighty dead. They found him wan day, cowld an' shtill, on Nora's grave, an' laid him be her side, God rest his sowl, an' there he slapes to-day, God be good to him.

"They said he was only a poor owld innocent, but all is aqualized, an' thim that 's despised sometimes have betther comp'ny among the angels than that of mortials."

Daniel O'Rourke

Thomas Crofton Croker

PEOPLE may have heard of the renowned adventures of Daniel O'Rourke, but how few are there who know that the cause of all his perils, above and below, was neither more nor less than his having slept under the walls of the Pooka's tower. I knew the man well. He lived at the bottom of Hungry Hill, just at the right-hand side of the road as you go toward Bantry. An old man was he, at the time he told me the story, with gray hair and red nose; and it was on the 25th of June, 1813, that I heard it from his own lips, as he sat smoking his pipe under the old poplar tree, on as fine an evening as ever shone from the sky. I was going to visit the caves in Dursey Island, having spent the morning at Glengariff.

"I am often *axed* to tell it, sir," said he, "so that this is not the first time. The master's son, you see, had come from beyond foreign parts in France and Spain, as young gentlemen used to go before Buonaparte or any such was heard of; and sure enough there was a dinner given to all the people on the ground, gentle and simple, high and low, rich and poor. The *ould* gentlemen were the gentlemen after all, saving your honor's presence. They'd swear at a body a little, to be sure, and, maybe, give one a cut of a whip now and then, but we were no losers by it in the end; and they were so easy and civil, and kept such rattling houses, and thousands of welcomes; and there was no grinding for rent, and there was hardly a tenant on the estate that did not taste of his landlord's bounty often and often in a year; but now it's another thing. No matter for that, sir, for I'd better be telling you my story.

"Well, we had everything of the best, and plenty of it; and we ate, and we drank and we danced, and the young master by the same token danced with Peggy Barry, from the *Bohereen*—a lovely young couple they were, though they are both low enough now. To make a long story short, I got, as a body may say, the same thing as tipsy almost, for I can't remember ever at all, no ways, how it was I left the place; only I did leave it, that's certain. Well, I thought for all that, in myself, I'd just step to Molly Cronohan's, the fairy woman, to speak a word about the bracket heifer that was bewitched; and so as I was crossing the stepping-stones of the ford of Ballyashenogh, and as looking up at the stars and blessing myself—for why? it was Lady-day—I missed my foot, and souse I fell into the water. 'Death alive!' thought I, 'I'll be drowned now!' However, I began swimming, swimming, swimming away for the dear life, till at last I got ashore, somehow or other, but never the one of me can tell how, upon a *dissolute* island.

"I wandered and wandered about there, without knowing where I wandered, until at last I got into a big bog. The moon was shining as bright as day, or your fair lady's eyes, sir (with the pardon for mentioning her), and I looked east and west, and north and south, and every way, and nothing did I see but bog, bog, bog—I could never find out how I got into it; and my heart grew cold with fear, for sure and certain I was that it would be my *berrin* place. So I sat down upon a stone which, as good luck would have it, was close by me, and I began to scratch my head, and sing the *Ullagone*—when all of a sudden the moon grew black, and I looked up, and saw something for all the world as if it was moving down between me and it, and I could not tell what it was. Down it came with a pounce, and looked at me full in the face; and what was it but an eagle? as fine a one as ever flew from the kingdom of Kerry. So he looked at me in the face, and says he to me, 'Daniel O'Rourke,' says he, 'how do you do?' 'Very well, I thank you, sir,' says I; 'I hope you're well'; wondering out of my senses all the time how an eagle came to speak like a Christian. 'What brings you here, Dan?' says he. 'Nothing at all, sir,' says I; 'only I wish I was safe home again.' 'Is it out of the island you want to go, Dan?' says he. ''Tis, sir,' says I: so I up and told him how I had taken a drop too much, and fell into the water; how I swam to the island; and how I got into the bog and did not know my way out of it. 'Dan,' says he, after a minute's thought, 'though it is very improper for you to get drunk on Lady-day, yet as you are a decent, sober man, who 'tends mass well and never flings stones at me or mine, nor cries out after us in the fields—my life for yours,' says he; 'so get up on my back, and grip me well for fear you'd fall off, and I'll fly you out of the bog.' 'I am afraid,' says I, 'your honor's making game of me; for who ever heard of riding horseback on an eagle before?' ''Pon the honor of a gentleman,' says he, putting his right foot on his breast, 'I am quite in earnest: and so now either take my offer or starve in the bog—besides, I see that your weight is sinking the stone.'

"It was true enough as he said, for I found the stone every minute going from under me. I had no choice; so thinks I to myself, faint heart never won fair lady, and this is fair persuadance. 'I thank your honor,' says I, 'for the loan of your civility; and I'll take your kind offer.'

"I therefore mounted upon the back of the eagle, and held him tight enough by the throat, and up he flew in the air like a lark. Little I knew the trick he was going to serve me. Up—up—up, God knows how far up he flew. 'Why then,' said I to him—thinking he did not know the right road home—very civilly, because why? I was in his power entirely; 'sir,' says I, 'please your honor's glory, and with humble submission to your better judgment, if you'd fly down a bit, you're now just over my cabin, and I could be put down there, and many thanks to your worship.'

"'*Arrah*, Dan,' said he, 'do you think me a fool? Look down the next field, and don't you see two men and a gun? By my word it would be no joke to be shot this way, to oblige a drunken blackguard that I picked up off of a *could* stone in a bog.' 'Bother you,' said I to myself, but I did not speak out, for where was the use? Well, sir, up he kept flying, flying, and I asking him every minute to fly down, and all to no use. 'Where in the world are you going, sir?' says I to him. 'Hold your tongue, Dan,' says he: 'mind your own business, and don't be interfering with the business of other people.' 'Faith, this is my business, I think,' says I. 'Be quiet, Dan,' says he: so I said no more.

"At last where should we come to, but to the moon itself. Now you can't see it from this, but there is, or there was in my time, a reaping-hook sticking out of the side of the moon, this way (drawing the figure thus, Ω, on the ground with the end of his stick).

"'Dan,' said the eagle, 'I'm tired with this long fly; I had no notion 'twas so far.' 'And my lord, sir,' said I, 'who in the world *axed* you to fly so far—was it I? Did not I beg and pray and beseech you to stop half an hour ago?' 'There's no use talking, Dan,' said he; 'I'm tired bad enough, so you must get off, and sit down on the moon until I rest myself.' 'Is it sit down on the moon?' said I, 'is it upon that little round thing, then? why, then, sure I'd fall off in a minute, and be *kilt* and spilt and smashed all to bits; you are a vile deceiver—so you are.' 'Not at all, Dan, said he; 'you can catch fast hold of the reaping-hook that's sticking out of the side of the moon, and 'twill keep you up.' 'I won't then,' said I. 'Maybe not,' said he, quite quiet. 'If you don't, my man, I shall just give you a shake, and one slap of my wing, and send you down to the ground, where every bone in your body will be smashed as small as a drop of dew on a cabbage-leaf in the morning.' 'Why, then, I'm in a fine way,' said I to myself, 'ever to have come along with the likes of you;' and so giving him a hearty curse in Irish, for fear he'd know what I said, I got off his back with a heavy heart, took hold of the reaping hook, and sat down upon the moon, and a mighty cold seat it was, I can tell you that.

"When he had me there fairly landed, he turned about on me, and said: 'Good morning to you, Daniel O'Rourke,' said he; "I think I've nicked you fairly now. You robbed my nest last year' ('twas true enough for him, but how he found it out is hard to say), 'and in return you are freely welcome to cool your heels dangling upon the moon like a cockthrow.'

"'Is that all, and is this the way you leave me, you brute, you,' says I. 'You ugly, unnatural *baste*, and is this the way you serve me at last? Bad luck to yourself, with your hook'd nose, and to all your breed, you blackguard.' 'Twas all to no manner of use;

he spread out his great big wings, burst out a-laughing, and flew away like lightning. I bawled after him to stop; but I might have called and bawled for ever, without his minding me. Away he went, and I never saw him from that day to this sorrow fly away with him! You may be sure I was in a disconsolate condition, and kept roaring out for the bare grief, when all at once a door opened right in the middle of the moon, creaking on its hinges as if it had not been opened for a month before, I suppose they never thought of greasing 'em, and out there walks—who do you think, but the man in the moon himself? I knew him by his bush.

"'Good-morrow to you, Daniel O'Rourke,' said he; 'how do you do?' 'Very well, thank your honor,' said I. 'I hope your honor's well.' 'What brought you here, Dan?' said he. So I told him how I was a little overtaken in liquor at the master's, and how I was cast on a dissolute island, and how I lost my way in the bog, and how the thief of an eagle promised to fly me out of it and how, instead of that, he had fled me up to the moon.

"'Dan,' said the man in the moon, taking a pinch of snuff when I was done, 'you must not stay here.' 'Indeed, sir,' says I, ''tis much against my will I'm here at all; but how am I to go back?' 'That's your business,' said he; 'Dan, mine is to tell you that here you must not stay; so be off in less than no time.' 'I'm doing no harm,' says I, 'only holding on hard by the reaping-hook, lest I fall off.' 'That's what you must not do, Dan,' says he. 'Pray, sir,' say I, 'may I ask how many you are in family, that you would not give a poor traveler lodging: I'm sure 'tis not so often you're troubled with strangers coming to see you, for 'tis a long way.' 'I'm by myself, Dan,' says he; 'but you'd better let go the reaping-hook.' 'Faith, and with your leave,' says I, 'I'll not let go the grip, and the more you bid me, the more I won't let go;—so I will.' 'You had better, Dan,' says he again.

'why, then, my little fellow,' says I, taking the whole weight of
him with my eye from head to foot, 'there are two words to that
bargain; and I'll not budge, but you may if you like.' 'We'll see
how that is to be,' says he; and back he went, giving the door
such a great bang after him (for it was plain he was huffed) that
I thought the moon and all would fall down with it.

"Well, I was preparing myself to try strength with him, when
back again he comes, with the kitchen cleaver in his hand, and,
without saying a word, he gives two bangs to the handle of the
reaping-hook that was keeping me up, and *whap*! it came in
two. 'Good-morning to you, Dan,' says the spiteful little old
blackguard, when he saw me cleanly falling down with a bit of
the handle in my hand; I thank you for your visit and fair
weather after you, Daniel.' I had not time to make answer to
him, for I was tumbling over and over and rolling and rolling, at
the rate of a fox-hunt. 'God help me!' says I, 'but this is a pretty
pickle for a decent man to be seen in at this time of night: I am
now sold fairly.' The word was not out of my mouth when,
whiz! what should fly by close to my ear but a flock of wild
geese, all the way from my own bog of Ballyasheenogh, else
how should they know *me*? The *ould* gander, who was their
general, turning about his head, cried out to me, 'Is that you,
Dan?' 'The same,' said I, not a bit daunted now at what he said,
for I was by this time used to all kinds of *bedevilment*, and,
besides, I knew him of ould. 'Good-morrow to you,' says he,
'Daniel O'Rourke; how are you in health this morning?' 'Very
well, sir,' says I, 'I thank you kindly,' drawing my breath, for I
was mightily in want of some. 'I hope your honor's the same.'
'I think 'tis falling you are, Daniel,' says he. 'You may say that,
sir,' says I. 'And where are you going all the way so fast?' said
the gander. So I told him how I had taken the drop, and how I
came on the island, and how I lost my way in the bog, and how

the thief of an eagle flew me up to the moon, and how the man in the moon turned me out. 'Dan,' said he, 'I'll save you: put out your hand and catch me by the leg, and I'll fly you home.' 'Sweet is your hand in a pitcher of honey, my jewel,' says I, though all the time I thought within myself that I don't much trust you; but there was no help, so I caught the gander by the leg, and away I and the other geese flew after him fast as hops.

"We flew, and we flew, and we flew, until we came right over the wide ocean. I knew it well, for I saw Cape Clear to my right hand, sticking up out of the water. 'Ah, my lord,' said I to the goose, for I thought it best to keep a civil tongue in my head anyway, 'fly to land if you please.' 'It is impossible, you see, Dan'; said he, 'for a while, because you see we are going to Arabia.' 'To Arabia!' said I; 'that's surely some place in foreign parts, far away. Oh! Mr. Goose: why then, to be sure, I'm a man to be pitied among you.' 'Whist, whist, you fool,' said he, 'hold your tongue; I tell you Arabia is a very decent sort of place, as like West Carbery as one egg is like another, only there is a little more sand there.'

"Just as we were talking, a ship hove in sight, scudding so beautiful before the wind. 'Ah! then, sir,' said I, 'will you drop me on the ship, if you please?' 'We are not fair over it,' said he; 'if I dropped you now you would go splash into the sea.' 'I would not,' says I; 'I know better than that, for it is just clean under us, so let me drop now at once.'

"'If you must, you must,' said he; 'there, take your way'; and he opened his claw, and faith he was right—sure enough I came down plump into the very bottom of the salt sea! Down to the very bottom I went, and I gave myself up then forever, when a whale walked up to me, scratching himself after his night's sleep, and looked me full in the face, and never the word did he say, but lifting up his tail, he splashed me all over again with the cold salt water till there wasn't a dry stitch upon my whole carcass! and I heard somebody saying—'twas a voice I knew, too—'Get up, you drunken brute, off o' that,' and with that I woke up and there was Judy with a tub full of water, which she was splashing all over me for, rest her soul! though she was a good wife, she never could bear to see me in drink, and had a bitter hand of her own.

"'Get up,' said she again: 'and of all places in the parish would no place *sarve* your turn to lie down upon but under the *ould* walls of Carrigapooka? an *uneasy* resting I am sure you had of it.' And sure enough I had: for I was fairly bothered out of my senses with eagles, and men of the moons, and flying ganders, and whales, driving me through bogs, and up to the moon, and down to the bottom of the green ocean. If I was in drink ten times over, long would it be before I'd lie down in the same spot again, I know that."

The Field of Boliauns
Joseph Jacobs

ONE FINE DAY in harvest—it was indeed Ladyday in harvest, that everybody knows to be one of the greatest holidays in the year—Tom Fitzpatrick was taking a ramble through the ground, and went along the sunny side of a hedge; when all of a sudden he heard a clacking sort of noise a little before him in the hedge. "Dear me," said Tom, "but isn't it surprising to hear the stonechatters singing so late in the season?" So Tom stole on, going on the tops of his toes to try if he could get a sight of what was making the noise, to see if he was right in his guess. The noise stopped; but as Tom looked sharply through the bushes, what should he see in a nook of the hedge but a brown pitcher, that might hold about a gallon and a half of liquor; and by-and-by a little wee teeny tiny bit of an old man, with a little *motty* of a cocked hat stuck upon the top of his head, a deeshy daushy leather apron hanging before him, pulled out a little wooden stool, and stood up upon it, and dipped a little piggin into the pitcher, and took out the full of it, and put it beside the stool, and then sat down under the pitcher, and began to work at putting a heel-piece on a bit of a brogue just fit for himself. "Well, by the powers," said Tom to himself, "I often heard tell of the Lepracauns, and, to tell God's truth, I never rightly believed in them—but here's one of them in real earnest. If I go knowingly to work, I'm a made man. They say a body must never take their eyes off them, or they'll escape."

Tom now stole on a little further, with his eye fixed on the little man just as a cat does with a mouse. So when he got up quite close to him, "God bless your work, neighbor," said Tom.

The little man raised up his head, and "Thank you kindly," said he.

"I wonder you'd be working on the holiday!" said Tom.

"That's my own business, not yours," was the reply.

"Well, maybe you'd be civil enough to tell us what you've got in the pitcher there?" said Tom.

"That I will with pleasure," said he; "it's good beer."

"Beer!" said Tom. "Thunder and fire! where did you get it?"

"Where did I get it, is it? Why, I made it. And what do you think I made it of?"

"Devil a one of me knows," said Tom; "but of malt, I suppose, what else?"

"There you're out. I made it of heath."

"Of heath!" said Tom, bursting out laughing; "sure you don't think me to be such a fool as to believe that?"

"Do as you please," said he, "but what I tell you is the truth. Did you never hear tell of the Danes?"

"Well, what about them?" said Tom.

"Why, when they were here they taught us to make beer out

of the heath, and the secret's in my family ever since."

"Will you give a body a taste of your beer?" said Tom.

"I'll tell you what it is, young man, it would be fitter for you to be looking after your father's property than to be bothering decent quiet people with your foolish questions. There now, while you're idling away your time here, there's the cows have broke into the oats, and are knocking the corn all about."

Tom was taken so by surprise with this that he was just on the very point of turning round when he recollected himself; so, afraid that the like might happen again, he made a grab at the Lepracaun, and caught him up in his hand; but in his hurry he overset the pitcher, and spilled all the beer, so that he could not get a taste of it to tell what sort it was. He then swore that he would kill him if he did not show him where his money was. Tom looked so wicked and so bloody-minded that the little man was quite frightened; so says he, "Come along with me a couple of fields off, and I'll show you a crock of gold."

So they went, and Tom held the Lepracaun fast in his hand, and never took his eyes from off him, though they had to cross hedges and ditches, and a crooked bit of bog, till at last they came to a great field all full of boliauns, and the Lepracaun pointed to a big boliaun, and says he, "Dig under that boliaun, and you'll get the great crock all full of guineas."

Tom in his hurry had never thought of bringing a spade with him, so he made up his mind to run home and fetch one; and that he might know the place again he took off one of his red garters, and tied it round the boliaun.

Then he said to the Lepracaun, "Swear ye'll not take that garter away from that boliaun." And the Lepracaun swore right away not to touch it.

"I suppose," said the Lepracaun, very civilly, "you have no further occasion for me?"

"No," says Tom; "you may go away now, if you please, and God speed you, and may good luck attend you wherever you go."

"Well, good-bye to you, Tom Fitzpatrick," said the Lepracaun; "and much good might it do you when you get it."

So Tom ran for dear life, till he came home and got a spade, and then away with him, as hard as he could go, back to the field of boliauns; but when he got there, lo and behold! not a boliaun in the field but had a red garter, the very model of his own, tied about it; and as to digging up the whole field, that was all nonsense, for there were more than forty good Irish acres in it. So Tom came home again with his spade on his shoulder, a little cooler than he went, and many's the hearty curse he gave the Lepracaun every time he thought of the neat turn he had served him.